'Anglo-Catholic
in Religion'

Other books by Barry Spurr

The Word in the Desert

Lytton Strachey

Studying Poetry

See the Virgin Blest: The Virgin Mary in English Poetry

'Anglo-Catholic in Religion'

T.S. Eliot and Christianity

Barry Spurr

The Lutterworth Press

The Lutterworth Press
P.O. Box 60
Cambridge
CB1 2NT

www.lutterworth.com
publishing@lutterworth.com

ISBN: 978 0 7188 3073 1

British Library Cataloguing in Publication Data
A catalogue record is available from the British Library

First published in 2010

Contents

Preface

T.S. Eliot's declaration of his Anglo-Catholicism was made in the 'Preface' to *For Lancelot Andrewes* (1928):

> To make my present position clear.... I have made bold to unite these occasional essays.... The general point of view may be described as classicist in literature, royalist in politics, and anglo-catholic in religion. I am quite aware that the first term is completely vague, and easily lends itself to clap-trap; I am aware that the second term is at present without definition, and easily lends itself to what is almost worse than clap-trap, I mean temperate conservatism; the third term does not rest with me to define.[1]

His formulation was based on the description, fifteen years earlier, of Charles Maurras' counterrevolutionary convictions – '*classique, catholique, monarchique*' – in the *Nouvelle Revue Française* (March, 1913), to which Eliot was then a subscriber,[2] and may also have been inspired by a similar triplicity of convictions uttered by the philosopher, T.E. Hulme (whose thought exercised considerable influence on Eliot), who, in 1912, intended to explain 'why I believe in original sin, why I can't stand romanticism, and why I am a certain kind of Tory'.[3]

The announcement had been born of genial provocation, as Eliot explained, many years after he had made it, in 'To Criticize the Critic' (1961). His 'old teacher and master' from Harvard, the Humanist, Irving Babbitt, had passed through London in the year (1927) of Eliot's baptism and confirmation. Eliot 'knew that it would come as a shock to him to learn that any disciple of his had so turned his coat' by defecting from Humanism to Christianity,

> but all Babbitt said was: 'I think you should come out into the open'. I may have been a little nettled by this remark;

the quotable sentence turned up in the preface to the book of
essays I had in preparation, swung into orbit, and has been
circling my little world ever since.[4]

By the 1960s, Eliot found himself

constantly irritated by having my words, perhaps written
thirty or forty years ago, quoted as if I had uttered them yes-
terday.[5]

Nonetheless, he points out that the description of his religious beliefs, in the quotable sentence of 1928, remained accurate. Virginia
Woolf's acerbic speculation that Eliot would 'drop Christianity with
his wife, as one might empty the fishbones after the herring', was
premature.[6] Those beliefs and, hence, that allegiance persisted 'unchanged'.[7] In his essay of 1955, 'Goethe as the Sage', Eliot (in
another self-portrait) varied the tripartite formula, but retained the
Catholicism, noting that he possessed

a Catholic cast of mind, a Calvinistic heritage, and a Pur-
itanical temperament.[8]

Although she had been a friend and generous supporter, Woolf remained cynical about Eliot's declared allegiance. Such critics of
his conversion, he wrote (in 1929) to Paul Elmer More (a fellow-
American whose religious journey was similar to Eliot's and who
described Eliot as his 'intimate acquaintance'[9]), interpreted it as 'an
escape or an evasion, certainly a defeat'.[10] Even More was guarded
in his support. He had written to his sister, late in 1928:

Eliot himself, in the preface of a new book of essays which
he has sent me, comes out clearly on his new platform:
classicism, royalism, and Anglo-Catholicism. This is the
sort of thing that is going on in England. There is some
claptrap mixed up in it, but they mean something serious
too – at least there are elements of a wholesome reaction
from the maelstrom of follies that has almost engulfed the
world. With their classicism they contrive to mix the freest
of free verse, with their royalism an ultra democracy, and
with their Anglo-Catholicism a good dose of skepticism
plus bravado; but they may come to terms with themselves
later on.[11]

A year later, in a letter to Austin Warren, the New England critic,
More focuses explicitly on the implications of Eliot's conversion for

his poetry – a matter of much concern to those who saw Eliot as the leader of the new movement in verse and who feared that his religious commitment would stifle that creativity:

> I remember that last summer after reading his *Andrewes* with its prefatial program of classicism, royalism (the divine right of kings!) and Anglo-Catholicism, I asked him whether, when he returned to verse, he would write the same sort of stuff that he once called poetry, or whether he had seen a new light. His answer was: 'I am absolutely unconverted'.... He is avowedly and, no doubt, sincerely religious; but just what his religion means to him, I do not know.[12]

Eliot's fidelity not only to Christianity but to a particular variety of it, over a period of nearly forty years until his death in 1965, is the dominant element in his life and work, through those several decades. It

> ultimately affected his imagination, his writing, and all the other categories that his life comprised. It gave Eliot the great relation, and the grand poetic, he had always sought.[13]

Yet, a third of a century ago, when I first undertook research, at Oxford, into Eliot's Christianity and proposed the title which this book bears for the subject of my thesis, my supervisor, Helen Gardner, *doyenne* of Eliot scholars, immediately objected to my use of Eliot's phrase. She complained that it conveyed an impression of his Christianity that was too narrow. Accordingly, I accepted her broader but blander proposal: 'Christian Faith and Practice in the later Life and Work of T.S. Eliot'. By the time we had finished working on my dissertation, however, Dame Helen conceded that Eliot was more of an Anglo-Catholic than she had supposed and that his own early description of his faith was accurate.

Over the period since I completed my initial, unpublished study there have been numerous biographical and literary-critical accounts of Eliot and his poetry and prose. All of them, in one way or another, have inevitably mentioned his Christianity. None of them has revealed an informed understanding of Anglo-Catholicism in general; of its character in the first half of the twentieth century when Eliot was drawn to it and became one of its best-known lay representatives; of the details of Eliot's adaptation of its beliefs and practices to his own circumstances; of how his formal adoption of it was the culmination of his intellectual, cultural, artistic, spiritual and personal development to that point, and how it continued to shape his life and work until his death; or of its special influence on his poetry – for example, in detailed analysis of his appropriation of liturgical language and of his incorporation into his poetry of what he regarded as crucial doctrinal principles. As Edwin Muir has written, 'the first condition of any genuine criticism of Mr. Eliot's religion is that it should be understood'.[14]

Moreover, such information that has been supplied about his Anglo-Catholicism has been usually ill-informed and cursory, and, often, simply erroneous. Observing that 'Eliot's considerable influence in Anglo-Catholic thinking has been underestimated by his biographers', Michael Yelton further remarked that they 'do not appear fully to understand the various groupings in the Church of England'.[15] Indeed, they do not always understand the 'various groupings' in Christianity at large and they can be all at sea in commentary on particular articles of belief which were vital for Eliot. In an essay on 'religion' in Eliot, 'the intercession of the Virgin' is called one of the 'articles of the Anglican creed'[16] when it is nothing of the kind, but, rather, an Anglo-Catholic (and, of course, Roman Catholic) belief, to which Eliot gives expression in *Ash-Wednesday* and in 'The Dry Salvages', IV.

Then, commentators on Eliot's faith confuse Anglo-Catholicism with Roman Catholicism (or, just, 'Catholicism'); present it as if it were another term for High Church Anglicanism, and, generally, shy away from coming to grips with what precisely it was.[17] Even otherwise reliable commentators can be misleading when they turn to Eliot's religion. One of them states, for example, that the dominant linguistic forms in *Ash-Wednesday* (Eliot's most liturgical poem) derive 'from the Catholic liturgy'.[18] In a general sense, this is true, to the extent that Anglo-Catholic liturgy derives from the liturgical usages of Latin Christianity. But most readers would assume, from this phrase, that Eliot's direct sources were the Roman Catholic liturgy (such as his contemporary, David Jones, uses in his richly liturgical poems), in its pre-conciliar Latin form. And this is wide of the mark, as they come, precisely, from the Anglo-Catholic liturgy (in English), from Anglo-Catholic prayer manuals and from such quintessentially English sources as the Authorized Version of the Bible, as in the use of the phrase 'the cool of the day' (Genesis 3:8; *Ash-Wednesday*, II).[19] David Moody states – as an example of Eliot's alleged biblical orientation – that the poet was drawn to the 'classic statement of the Incarnation, at the beginning of the Gospel according to John'. But, again, while this is based in truth, it is misleading with regard to Eliot's Christianity. It was the liturgical presentation of this biblical material, in the 'Last Gospel' at the end of Mass, to which Eliot was 'drawn' and which (very importantly, for Anglo-Catholics) presented the doctrine of the Incarnation in the context of the offering of the sacrament of the altar. Moody is puzzled by the capitalisation of 'Word', in reference to that gospel, in *Ash-Wednesday*, V. 'Is the capital a typographical convention, or theological?' he wonders.[20] Had he consulted The English Missal, used in the Anglo-Catholic liturgy at Eliot's parish church, he would have found the answer to this mystery, where the capitalisation is plainly there: 'In the beginning was the Word...', as indeed it is in the Authorized Version from which the Missal translation is directly taken. And when Moody tells the uninformed reader that Eliot used the prayer 'to the Virgin after the Catholic Mass'[21] in the phrase, 'And after this our exile', that reader may then be led to assume that Eliot, as an Anglican, drew from prayers from another communion, not his own, when the source, precisely, is the prayer to the Virgin, *Salve Regina*, as he would have regularly encountered it in public and private Anglo-Catholic devotions (and not necessarily, or even usually 'after... Mass'). Such are the errors into which ignorance of Anglo-Catholicism can lead even an otherwise meticulous scholar of Eliot's work.

This imprecision is especially ironic in the cases both of Anglo-Catholicism and T.S. Eliot himself. For what distinguishes that system of belief and practice, within Anglicanism (*just* within it), and what characterises Eliot, temperamentally (and especially when it came to matters of doctrine and spiritual observance), was precision. Indeed, this is one of the main reasons why Eliot was drawn to, and announced his allegiance to (precisely) Anglo-Catholicism, when the declaration that his position was that of an 'Anglican in religion' (or even a 'Christian in religion', for that matter) might otherwise have been considered sufficiently descriptive and provocative in the circumstances. And we note that he did not say 'Catholic in religion', which would have been true (doctrinally-speaking, from his perspective), but, again, not sufficiently precise. The Anglo-Catholicism to which he adhered was nothing if not dogmatic in its keenness to affirm its Catholic credentials in the non-ecumenical, absolutist climate of international, pre-conciliar Roman Catholicism – but also, as the coinage suggests, it was conscious of its Englishness. The characteristics of a crusade – with rallies and battle-cries, heroic exemplars and victories for the faith – mark the optimistic Anglo-Catholicism of the period *'entre deux guerres'*, and differentiate it sharply from the doctrinally evasive, morally defensive (some would say, chaotic) and numerically declining Anglo-Catholicism of today. It was comparably stringent in matters of moral behaviour and religious observance and, even, in nurturing and insisting upon seemingly trivial pious customs and mannerisms. Eliot was scrupulous with regard to the observance of all of these requirements and expectations of his religion (which responded to deep-seated characteristics of his personality) and we should at least pay him the compliment of being similarly precise in our presentation of it and in commentary on its role in his life and work.[22]

He also regarded the correct understanding of a writer's religious position as being an essential component in the process of the appreciation of his art. Obviously this is especially the case when the writer focuses on religious matters in his work. Summarising the biography of David Jones, his friend and fellow-poet, Eliot wrote

> he is a Londoner of Welsh and English descent. He is decidedly a Briton. He is also a Roman Catholic, and he is a painter who has painted some beautiful pictures and designed some beautiful lettering. All these facts about him are important.[23]

The fact of Eliot's Anglo-Catholicism is similarly important, for the same reasons of interpretation and appreciation. Russell Kirk (who knew Eliot well over many years, and has written one of the best books about him and his achievement) has argued that leaving Christianity out of the discussion of Eliot's poetry and prose 'would be very like omitting any mention of Stoic philosophy from a criticism of Seneca … or taking the gods away from the classical authors':

> Life and letters cannot endure in little coffin-like compartments. How could one criticize Pascal or Coleridge, say, without taking into account their religion? How, then, Eliot?[24]

And in taking it into account, as we must, we also need to get it right.

It is the purpose of this book to explore and explain the genesis, development and character of Eliot's Christianity – the faith which, for forty years, was central to his life and a seminal influence in his work throughout that period. His widow, Mrs Valerie Eliot, has told me that her 'husband's religious side has been neglected by most writers, and a major book is badly needed'.[25] It is time that Eliot's challenge for the term 'Anglo-Catholic' to be defined, in relation to his own life and work, was met.

*

I am grateful for advice about Eliot's faith and its practice to the late Dame Helen Gardner, who initially challenged me to probe and prove the Anglo-Catholic character of Eliot's Christianity, and to several other friends and associates of Eliot, clerical and lay, who are also now deceased. My indebtedness to them is revealed at the various points in the book where they are mentioned and their information is recorded. My particular gratitude to the late Mary Trevelyan, Eliot's fellow-worshipper at St Stephen's Gloucester Road in the 1940s and 50s and the late George Every (one-time Brother of the Society of the Sacred Mission, Kelham, which Eliot visited) is explained in the first two appendices. I also record my thanks to the late Professor Nigel Yates, who, a few months before his death in January, 2009, sent me his unpublished article, 'Walsingham and Inter-War Anglo-Catholicism'.

I am indebted to the Revd Dr Nicholas Cranfield, who sent me a copy of the anniversary issue (devoted to Eliot) of *The Southern Review* (Autumn, 1985); to my former student, Dr Stephen McInerney, who alerted me to some important references during my research and writing, and the Revd Richard Waddell, OGS, who carefully perused the typescript, with particular attention to matters of liturgy and theology, and made several valuable suggestions. Mr David Anderson, AO, assisted with proof-reading, with particular attention to quotations in French. At the Lutterworth Press, my publisher, Mr Adrian Brink has been encouraging throughout, and brought his own considerable knowledge of English religious history to an informed commentary on drafts of my chapters. I want also to thank Mr Ian Bignall, at Lutterworth, for his editorial work and suggestions. Mr Michael Yelton and Dr John Salmon (who took the photograph for the cover) provided invaluable assistance with illustrations. I am indebted to Professors Denis Donoghue, Manju Jain, and Ronald Schuchard, and Dr Jason Harding for their generous comments. Any imperfections that remain are entirely my responsibility.

List of Abbreviations

The following abbreviations of titles of works by T.S. Eliot are used in endnote references:

ASG	After Strange Gods
CPP	The Collected Poems and Plays
FLA	For Lancelot Andrewes
GH	George Herbert
ICS	The Idea of a Christian Society
NTDC	Notes towards the Definition of Culture
OPP	On Poetry and Poets
RD	Reunion by Destruction
SE	Selected Essays
SW	The Sacred Wood
TCTC	To Criticize the Critic
TR	The Rock
UPUC	The Use of Poetry and the Use of Criticism

Chapter One

The Sources of Faith:
Familial and Philosophical
(1888-1917)

> I found no discipline in humanism; only a little intellectual
> discipline from a little study of philosophy. But the difficult
> discipline is the discipline and training of emotion; this the
> world has great need of, so great need that it hardly under-
> stands what the word means; and this I have found is only
> attainable through dogmatic religion.... Only those have the
> right to talk of discipline who have looked into the Abyss.
> (Eliot, 'Religion without Humanism', 1930[1])

A favourite pilgrimage destination for Eliot's devotees is the small
church of St Michael in the Somerset village of East Coker (which
gives the title to the second of Eliot's *Four Quartets*). Eliot had visited East Coker in August, 1937 and in 1940 he completed and sent
the poem, 'East Coker', to press.[2] The poet's ashes are interred in
the church, with the inscription (from the first line of 'East Coker'),
'In my beginning is my end ...', a reversal of Mary Stuart's motto,
'En ma fin est mon commencement'. This is inscribed on an appropriately oval-shaped stone which represents the circularity of the idea
and could remind us of the circular imagery in the poem, where its
speaker communes with his rural ancestors and a literary predecessor
of the sixteenth century, Sir Thomas Elyot. Eliot's language modul-
ates briefly to that of Elyot's *Boke Named the Governour*:

> In daunsinge, signifying matrimonie –
> A dignified and commodious sacrament....
>   Round and round the fire
> Leaping through the flames, or joined in circles....[3]

Among these folk, in this mystic communion with the dead, may
be Andrew Eliot, a cordwainer (or shoemaker), who set out from
East Coker in 1668, after the Restoration of the monarchy and episcopacy, for the Massachusetts Bay Colony in New England. This was

a Puritan theocracy where his Calvinistic Christianity would be free
from persecution. (Similarly, on Eliot's mother's side, the Stearns,
one of her ancestors had been amongst the original settlers of the
Bay Colony.) To the extent that Eliot recalls his seventeenth-century
East Coker family here, he sets them, ironically (through the words of
Sir Thomas Elyot's courtesy book) in a sacramental context which,
regarding matrimony, such strict Protestants would have firmly repudiated – only two sacraments being acknowledged at the Reformation
as being of divine institution (Baptism and the Lord's Supper), while
Catholic theology affirms seven (including, of course, marriage), and
so, therefore, does Anglo-Catholicism.

The original Calvinism of those religious emigrants was theologically diluted by their descendants over the centuries into Unitarianism,
while elements of the original Puritan spirit, in matters of moral principle and temperament, were retained. As the Anglo-Catholic novelist,
Rose Macaulay put it, succinctly: 'the weaker they got on religion the
stronger they got on morals'.[4] Eliot was highly critical of a religious
system which had jettisoned theology and prioritised morality, which
could not survive (he believed) in a vacuum. He came to see this as
the antithesis of the Anglo-Catholic understanding of moral issues
and conduct:

> there is no such thing as just Morality … for any man who
> thinks clearly, as his Faith is so will his Morals be.… I am
> sure in my own mind that I have not adopted my faith in
> order to defend my views of conduct, but have modified my
> views of conduct to conform with what seem to me the im-
> plications of my beliefs. The real conflict is not between one
> set of moral prejudices and another, but between the theistic
> and the atheistic faith; and it is all for the best that the div-
> ision should be sharply drawn.[5]

To the liberal Christian and the Humanist, such dogmatism in moral
theology is one of the least digestible of the precepts of orthodoxy,
and simply anathema to Unitarianism:

> The Unitarian knows that the story of his faith in modern
> times is an unbroken record of the removal from religion
> of all those creeds and dogmas which are based on fear and
> which bring gloom to the human heart.[6]

But, as Eliot commented,

> the question of the repugnance of a doctrine is not the same
> as that of its truth[7]

and he contended that, without a dogmatic framework, morality cannot survive, because it then becomes merely personalised (in the subjective, Romantic way):

> when morals cease to be a matter of tradition and orthodoxy
> – that is, the habits of the community formulated, corrected,
> and elevated by the continuous thought and direction of the
> Church – and when each man is to elaborate his own, then
> *personality* becomes a thing of alarming importance.[8]

The philosopher T.E. Hulme (praised by Eliot for his theological perception[9]) put the matter even more forcefully, identifying the 'fundamental error … of placing Perfection in *humanity*',

> thus giving rise to that bastard thing Personality, and all the
> bunkum that follows from it.[10]

1

By the later nineteenth century, in the earliest period of Eliot's life, which he was later to recall as a 'struggle', 'over many years so blindly and errantly',[11] he was dominated by his family's well-established Unitarian heritage. This is the most significant of the formative influences comprising what Eric Sigg has called his 'deep American past, extending far back in time before his birth',[12] in opposition to which Eliot's Anglo-Catholicism was, much later, to emerge. Yet the degree to which Eliot negated and disposed of the legacy of New England Puritanism (to the extent that it was preserved in his family's Unitarianism) is questionable. Reflecting late in his life, he wrote

> no man wholly escapes from the kind, or wholly surpasses
> the degree of culture which he acquired from his early en-
> vironment[13]

– and by 'culture', Eliot means deep-seated formative convictions, including religious ideas. Austin Warren, for example, argues that the source of the poet's abiding asceticism (which could be accommodated to aspects of Anglo-Catholicism, such as its emphasis on the monastic life, to which Eliot was strongly drawn, and to such disciplines as fasting, which he rigorously observed) derived from that heritage.[14] And, indeed, some aspects of Calvinist theology that are central, too, to Catholic teaching – such as the doctrine of Original Sin (utterly repudiated by Unitarianism) – were at the very heart of his Anglo-Catholic faith. The first sin in the New England Primer is, appropriately enough, Original Sin.[15]

Formidable amongst Eliot's Unitarian progenitors was the poet's grandfather, William Greenleaf Eliot, notable for his 'energy, cheer, light, and liberalism' and for a character 'as virtuous as his achievements were legion'.[16] He was 'all New England conscience'.[17] The first sermon he delivered in his Cambridge Divinity School course was on 'Philanthropy', and it was as a Unitarian philanthropist that he dominated 'the religious life of St Louis until his death in 1887'.[18] Eliot's mother wrote a biography of her father-in-law subtitled *Minister, Educator, Philanthropist* (1904) and Eliot remembered that the family's idea of 'the Great Man' was his grandfather whose eminence he could not hope to attain.[19]

The faith and practice of Unitarianism, epitomised by William as 'a joy-giving, health-bestowing and saving religion'[20] – and characterised by his grandson, in his mockery of it to Ezra Pound, as a matter of 'social helpfulness and sermons'[21] – was satirically summarised by Henry Adams ('a cousin of ours', Eliot had reminded his mother[22]):

> Nothing quieted doubt so completely as the mental calm of the Unitarian clergy. In uniform excellence of life and character, moral and intellectual, the score of Unitarian clergymen about Boston, who controlled society and Harvard College, were never excelled. They proclaimed as their merit that they insisted on no doctrine, but taught, or tried to teach, the means of leading a virtuous, useful, unselfish life, which they held to be sufficient for salvation. For them, difficulties might be ignored; doubts were waste of thought; nothing exacted solution. Boston had solved the universe; or had offered and realized the best solution yet tried. The problem was worked out.[23]

Unitarianism, it was quipped, had its own trinitarianism (having rejected the orthodox belief in Father, Son and Spirit as consubstantial, coeternal): affirming the fatherhood of God, the brotherhood of man, and the neighbourhood of Boston.

Eliot was to travel as far from these religious principles (which he mocked, in his own mischievous triplet, as 'the religion of the blue sky, the grass and flowers'[24]) as the Unitarians had removed themselves, doctrinally, from their Calvinist forbears: for them, 'the men who wrote the Bible and the early Christians were liberals'; it was a 'creedless rational faith'.[25] Eliot's dissociation from this happy heterodoxy, which he termed the 'Boston Doubt', a belief in 'nothing',[26] may have been initiated by his father who eschewed the Unitarian ministry, reflecting that 'too much pudding choked the dog',[27] although his older brother, Thomas Lamb Eliot, Eliot's uncle, became, like their revered father, a distinguished pastor.

Every article of the Unitarian creed – wherein (as Sigg notes) 'rational opposition to Original Sin amounted to Unitarian dogma': it was 'one of the most pernicious tenets of the Calvinism that Unitarianism intended to overthrow'[28] – was contradicted by Eliot's later Anglo-Catholicism. Charles William Eliot, a distant relative who became President of Harvard, had proposed the 'religion of the future', the tenets of which amounted to an antithesis of orthodox Christianity in general and Catholic doctrine in particular:

(1) 'the religion of the future will not be based on authority, either spiritual or temporal'...
(2) 'no personifications of the primitive forces of nature';
(3) 'no worship, express or implied, of dead ancestors, teachers, or rulers';
(4) 'the primary object will not be the personal welfare or safety of the individual in this world or the other... but... service to others, and... contributions to the common good';
(5) It 'will not be propitiatory, sacrificial, or expiatory';
(6) It 'will not perpetuate the Hebrew anthropomorphic representations of God';
(7) It 'will not be gloomy, ascetic, or maledictory'.[29]

These liberating principles had their contemporary transatlantic counterpart in Francis Abbot's 'fifty pungent propositions' for 'the extinction of faith in the Christian Confession' and the development of a humanistic 'Free Religion', promulgated on behalf of the Free Religion Association which had sprung from British Unitarianism and spurned 'deference to the authority of the Bible, the Church, or the Christ'.[30]

Not surprisingly, President Eliot was an undiscriminating ecumenist, promoting a 'new ideal of God' which would comprehend

the Jewish Jehovah, the Christian Universal father, the modern physicist's omnipresent and exhaustless Energy, and the biological conception of a Vital Force.[31]

The Unitarian commentator, L.A. Garrard, argued that 'the ideal religion is an eclecticism, combining the best out of all the historical religions and omitting whatever seems false or outmoded'.[32] That T.S. Eliot was later to describe even the reunification of Anglicans and Methodists as a 'mass movement of licentious oecumenicity'[33] shows how far he had removed himself from his Unitarian background. He scorned 'universalists'

> who maintain that the ultimate and esoteric truth is one...
> that it is a matter of indifference to which one of the great
> religions we adhere.[34]

Ecumenism meant 'substituting a vague Christianity which the modern mind despises, for a precise Christianity which it may hate but must respect'.[35] As David Edwards writes, with authority and finality, Eliot 'was no ecumenist'.[36]

2

That President Eliot's 'optimistic faith in the natural goodness of the human will' – rejecting the outmoded teaching of Original Sin – was, in turn, rejected by the poet[37] was due to various potent influences, including the philosophy of Hulme (who was killed in Flanders in 1917) who had indicted Romantics as 'all those who do not believe in the Fall of Man'.[38] Evelyn Waugh (perhaps, indeed, deriving his Hulmean philosophy from Eliot, whose outspoken opposition to Humanism he admired) put the anti-Romantic position, with regard to this doctrine, bluntly:

> The children of Adam are not a race of noble savages who
> need only a divine spark to perfect them. They are aborig-
> inally corrupt.[39]

As Ronald Schuchard has noted, Hulme's writings 'showed Eliot that Original Sin was the basic element in the classical compound'.[40] Crucial, too, for Eliot, was the influence of the French poet, Charles Baudelaire, whom he had read while at Harvard and in Paris (in 1910). Jacques Rivière contended that Baudelaire was, for Eliot, *'le merveilleux introducteur au christianisme'*.[41] The Frenchman had argued, in his *Journaux Intimes*, regarding the *'théorie de la vraie civilisation'*,

> *elle n'est pas dans le gaz, ni dans la vapeur, ni dans les*
> *tables tournantes, elle est dans la diminution des traces du*
> *péché originel.*[42]

Compellingly, for Eliot, these ideas were given expression in Baudelaire's revolutionary poetry, in *Les Fleurs du Mal*:

> I think that from Baudelaire I learned first, a precedent for
> the poetical possibilities, never developed by any poet writ-
> ing in my own language, of the more sordid aspects of the
> modern metropolis, of the possibility of fusion between the
> sordidly realistic and the phantasmagoric.[43]

For Eliot, such convictions (and their artistic realisation), combined
with his intense suffering during the period of his first marriage from
1915, in the midst (what is more) of the harrowing circumstances of
life in London during the First World War, would have been sufficient
to put paid forever to President Eliot's cheery optimism based on the
Unitarian conviction that the world was 'essentially friendly' under
an 'infinitely loving' God, who

> looks on the universe in the same spirit as Jesus beheld the
> lilies of Galilee. Life is good.[44]

Alfred Hall concludes his 'Introduction' to *Aspects of Modern Unitarianism* with a telling quotation from Browning's 'Fra Lippo Lippi':

> This world's no blot for us,
> Nor blank; it means intensely, and means good.[45]

No one was less likely than Eliot, once he had attained years
of discernment about the human condition, to be susceptible to the
Positivist and Unitarian 'Religion of Humanity' to which so many
disaffected Evangelicals of the later nineteenth century subscribed
(Unitarianism was, in Charles Darwin's grandfather, Erasmus's provocative phrase, 'a feather bed to catch a falling Christian'[46]) and
which Eliot's mother encapsulated in her ecumenical poem, 'Saint
Barnabas: A Missionary Hymn':

> No longer shall the law thy tribes divide,
> Through faith and love all shall be justified.
> Let me go forth, O Lord![47]

'What faith in life may be I know not', Eliot was to write in the
Criterion in 1933. 'For the Christian, faith in death is what matters'.[48]
Paul Elmer More, Eliot's friend and fellow-convert, dismissed the
poet's family's faith as 'about the poorest sham in the whole field of
pseudo-religion'.[49]

The critique of 'faith in life' which is the doctrine of Original Sin
was, for Eliot, not only a Calvinist and Catholic teaching. He argued
that 'the classicist point of view', the antithesis of the 'vague emotion-
ality' of Romantic individualism, is 'essentially a belief in Original

Sin', implying 'the necessity for austere discipline'.[50] The appeal of orthodox Christianity was that it proposed the only plausible remedy to the 'aboriginal' problem:

> It is after these moments, alone with God and awareness of our worthiness, but for Grace, of nothing but damnation, that we turn with most thankfulness and appreciation to our awareness of our membership [of the Body of Christ].[51]

He recognised 'the evil which is present in human nature at all times and in all circumstances'[52] – including the time and circumstance of birth. The 'perception of Good and Evil,' he declared, ' – whatever choice we may make – is the first requisite of the spiritual life'.[53] Reflecting on Eliot's poetry, Kathleen Raine observed:

> Mr Eliot gave hell back to us…. The shallow progressive philosophies both religious and secular of our parents' generation sought to eliminate evil from the world. Mr Eliot's visions of hell restored a necessary dimension to our universe.[54]

Eliot's interest, too, in the writings of Blaise Pascal, the seventeenth-century French theologian drawn to the Jansenism of Port-Royal des Champs (where his sister had become a nun), reflects his profound sense of the corrupt character of human nature and the concomitant necessity for God's grace. This, for Pascal, was combined with a deep-seated scepticism in the faith, adding to his appeal for Eliot. Pascal, he wrote, was

> the type of one kind of religious believer, which is highly passionate and ardent, but passionate only through a powerful and regulated intellect… facing unflinchingly the demon of doubt which is inseparable from the spirit of belief.[55]

In affirming the teachings of such advocates of the doctrine of Original Sin, Eliot never underestimated the difficulty of acceding to these principles, especially as 'every man who thinks and lives by thought must have his own scepticism, that which stops at the question, that which ends in denial, or that which leads to faith and which is somehow integrated into the faith which transcends it'.[56]

Certainly, in the way of scepticism leading to denial, Eliot's doubt about Unitarian theology was complete. 'All that concerned my family', he told an American friend, 'was "right and wrong", what was "done and not done"'.[57] The Eliots' religion, George Every has written, was 'morality, not belief'.[58] Two years before his baptism and confirmation, admonishing the Humanist, John Middleton Murry, Eliot pointed out that

> I happened to be brought up in the most 'liberal' of 'Christian' creeds – Unitarianism.... If one discards dogma, it should be for a more celestial garment, not for nakedness.[59]

He wrote to Herbert Read that 'one ought to have as precise and clear a creed as possible, when one thinks at all'. So, far from discarding articles of faith, 'we need more dogma'.[60]

The dogma that was to become central to Eliot's Anglo-Catholic faith, that of the Incarnation (of God becoming man in Jesus), may have been less repugnant to Unitarians than Original Sin, but they had rejected it, too, as contradicting their teaching about man becoming more God-like, rather than the reverse. For the Unitarian, Jesus was only an historical personage – ' "the first-born among many brethren" rather than the "only-begotten" Son of God'[61] – who had 'realized his own moral nature perfectly and completely'. And, so, the Atonement was 'purposeless or repulsive', the Resurrection a 'legend'[62] and predestination an illusion. Essentially, 'a person's task lay in cultivating the conscience'[63] and fostering community:

> discipleship, not assent to dogmas, is the hallmark of the Christian.... The relationship of human beings to one another is of paramount importance for any religion.[64]

3

In addition to the formidable heritage on his father's side, Eliot encountered the same principles, at least as strenuously held and advocated by his mother, Charlotte Champe Stearns, who addressed religious concerns in accomplished, if undistinguished verse. She had progressed, doctrinally, from orthodox Calvinist origins, through associations with Quakerism to Unitarianism. Her story resembles that of her near contemporary, George Eliot, who similarly evolved from an adolescent Evangelicalism to the radicalism of English Unitarianism. T.S. Eliot remembered that

> I was brought up in an environment of that intellectual and puritanical rationalism which is found in the novels of George Eliot – an author greatly admired in my family.[65]

Both George Eliot and Eliot's mother were attracted to Savonarola, the fifteenth-century Dominican reformer. He is the hero of Charlotte Eliot's eponymous dramatic poem (dedicated 'To My Children') and she and her family had encountered him in George Eliot's *Romola* (1862-3). Savonarola expressed their residual Puritanism combined with a passion for social reform. For 'the Yankees', Van Wyck Brooks has written, Savonarola was a 'culture hero...the Italian Cromwellian Puritan...who tried to restore the liberty of the Florentine people'.[66]

Yet Charlotte (like George, who attended Anglo-Catholic services and delighted in the artistic heritage of Spanish Catholicism) was not bigoted towards the Catholic faith, allowing the young Eliot to be taken to Mass by his devout Irish nurse, Annie Dunne. When it is remembered that this was in an era when advertisements for such positions in Protestant households regularly carried the warning: 'Catholics [or 'Irish', implying the same thing] should not apply', this appointment and Annie's religious freedom with the child was a definite sign of that liberalism on which Unitarians prided themselves and, in this case at least, it proved spiritually advantageous. Eliot described Annie as 'the earliest personal influence' on him,[67] and in a witty review of Bertrand Russell's 'Why I Am Not a Christian', in 1927, Eliot recalled that Russell's 'argument of the First Cause (as put to J. Stuart Mill by James Mill) was put to me, at the age of six, by a devoutly Catholic Irish nursemaid'.[68] What Annie introduced him to, in Catholicism, was by no means confined to philosophy:

> My nanny (when I was at an age when a nanny, especially to the much-the-youngest child of a large family, is more important than anybody else) was an Irish girl from County Cork, and I was devoted to her – she sometimes took me into the local Catholic Church when she went to say her prayers, and I liked it very much: the lights, the coloured statues and paper flowers, the lived-in atmosphere, and the fact that the pews had little gates that I could swing on.[69]

Peter Ackroyd imagines the sensual impact of the experience on the infant Eliot:

> He was always susceptible to smells and noises, with an intensity which suggests hypersensitivity, and the entrance into a Roman church no doubt inspired a passage which he once wrote in an essay on Arthur Symons – how the sens- itive child may be entranced by the effigies, the candles and the incense.[70]

Eliot repeatedly emphasises, both in poetry and prose, the importance of the influence of our earliest experiences. A writer's art, he argues, 'must be based on the accumulated sensations of the first twenty-one years'.[71] He placed particular stress on an author's 'sensitive life since early childhood ... the faded poor souvenirs of passionate moments',[72] while also remarking that 'I am quite well aware how unpleasant early youth can be or how few sensitive men were happy in it'.[73] What was true of the influence of childhood and youth on artistry could well have been true with regard to later religious beliefs too, especially if they were recalled with delight (as Eliot's Irish-Catholic nanny was) in the midst of more general unhappiness. That would add to their appeal.

There is whimsy in this recollection of early church-going too, as the grown man remembers his childhood self swinging on the pew-doors. As we shall see, one of the elements of the Anglo-Catholicism which Eliot was much later to embrace was – amidst all the solemnity and disciplined mortification – a robust and leavening enjoyment of the humorous, even ridiculous aspects of religion and of life itself.

This initiation, in his childhood, into the sensual appeal of the Catholic tradition in Christianity may be the most important early explanation of Eliot's eventual attraction to Anglo-Catholicism. What he experienced in St Louis with Annie Dunne was replicated, many years later, on his entrance into the Anglo-Catholic City churches, such as St Magnus the Martyr, London Bridge – the fishermen's church – of which John Betjeman writes:

> the whole district smells of fish, but inside the church there
> is the abrupt change to a smell of incense....[74]

There was its visual beauty, too, which Eliot commemorated in the midst of the squalor of Jazz-Age London: 'where the walls of Magnus Martyr hold / Inexplicable splendour of Ionian white and gold' (in the third section of *The Waste Land*, 1922).[75] Such beauty of holiness was deliberately cultivated in specifically Anglo-Catholic churches as the appropriate setting for the 'Real Presence' of the Lord as confected in the Mass and 'reserved' in the tabernacle.

Indeed, Mrs Eliot's Savonarola enunciates an interpretation of the Eucharistic Presence true to the teachings her son was later to embrace:

> For though the heaven itself cannot contain
> Its own Creator, He doth humbly deign
> In bread and wine to manifest again
> His presence to our senses.[76]

She hung an engraving of the Immaculate Conception by Murillo in her own bedroom, as well as a portrayal of St Ambrose, an upholder of orthodoxy in the Latin Church,[77] as Unitarianism, scorning dogmatic religion, was ecumenical a century before the concept became fashionable. Although at the disadvantage of distance from Europe, Charlotte Eliot revealed a breadth of outlook, poetically expressed, that cannot have failed to have made an impression on her literary son, introducing him to aspects of Catholic cult and culture, although he was destined to criticise sharply the theological imprecision that had made such an introduction possible. Eliot's publication of *Savonarola* in 1926, at a time when his formal adherence to Anglicanism was imminent, was not only an act of filial piety, but the expression of a broader indebtedness, reflected two years later in his dedication of *For Lancelot Andrewes* (with its essays on such as Niccolo Machiavelli and Richard Crashaw) 'For My Mother'.

In the Portland home of Eliot's uncle (his father's elder brother who had entered the Unitarian ministry), moreover, the feasts of the Church's year were regularly observed, being associated with some quaint customs and a form of ceremony. Herbert Howarth has likened the rule of life in Thomas Lamb Eliot's home to the devoutly, quasi-conventual familial arrangement of the Ferrars at Little Gidding,[78] which, through the centuries, has held such strong appeal for Catholic-minded Anglicans and which is the subject of Eliot's last great poem. George Herbert, who was a friend of the community at Little Gidding and bequeathed his poems to Nicholas Ferrar, is the subject of Eliot's last prose work, his essay on the poet of 1962.

4

Eliot became completely hostile to liberal Christianity's watered-down doctrine, but in the Unitarian dedication to social action and education we can see an abiding influence in his later educational theory and in his works of social criticism, such as *The Idea of a Christian Society* and *Notes towards the Definition of Culture*. Eliot's grandfather was a powerful influence for social consciousness, across the generations. Writing from St Louis in 1852, Emerson noted that

> Mr Eliot, the Unitarian minister, is the Saint of the West, and has a sumptuous church, and crowds to hear his really good sermons.[79]

Perhaps because he had heard so many of them, sermons and sermonising were not to Eliot's taste. He is on record as having preached only one himself, in the rarefied context of the chapel of the Cambridge college, Magdalene, where he was Honorary Fellow, and there is just one in his creative work, in *Murder in the Cathedral*, preached by the archbishop. 'Yes, the sermon in *Murder* is a good one', he told Mary Trevelyan, but added: 'I shall never write another'.[80]

His qualified commendation of the Coleridgean theory of the 'clerisy' – 'instruments in the great and indispensable work of per-petuating, promoting, and increasing the civilization of the nation'[81] – in the course of his presentation of his theory of the 'Community of Christians',[82] approximates to the Unitarians' role as arbiters of social morality (in which pulpit oratory would have played its part) and their significant contributions to education. The Unitarian 'public service' of his family, Eliot recalled, was expressed in three domains: 'the Church, the City, and the University':

> The Church meant, for us, the Unitarian Church of the Mes-siah, then situated in Locust Street, a few blocks west of my father's house … the City was St. Louis … the University was Washington University.… These were the symbols of Religion, the Community and Education.

Speaking at that university in 1953, Eliot affirmed that 'reverence' for such institutions is 'a very good beginning for any child', for it taught

> that personal and selfish aims should be subordinated to the general good which they represent.[83]

In a private and confidential letter to Mary Trevelyan, in 1942, Eliot identified in himself an hereditary taint which expressed itself in an irresistible tendency to serve on committees. All members of the family suffer from this, he notes, with the exception of his sister who prefers to stay indoors and write letters to the newspapers. In his own case, the inheritance explained his involvement in several public-ations and organisations at this time, such as the *Christian News-Letter*, the Christian Frontier Council, as well as through various 'good works' such as a dinner with an old Cheshire acquaintance in financial decline after a career as a portrait-painter of horses; a request from Storm Jameson for a poem for her *Red Cross Book*; the winding-up of an estate; a summons to testify in a divorce case – and many more things besides.[84]

Eliot could admire the Unitarians' 'emotional reserve and intel-lectual integrity' too.[85] He bore witness, in his own temperament, to their Puritanism, identifying a 'native Calvinism' in himself which he could not suppress,[86] while in a lecture in 1953 (glancing at contem-porary McCarthyism), he claimed that Nathaniel Hawthorne – whom

he describes as the 'greatest' of nineteenth-century New England
authors – contained 'something' in his works

> that can best be appreciated by the reader with Calvinism
> in his bones and witch-hanging (not witch-hunting) on his
> conscience.[87]

But he had much earlier criticised 'the family Fear and Conscience'
which was stifling his sister Marian – the 'family temperament' will
'always put the little things in front of the big'.[88] And he had held
up the drawing-room provinciality of Unitarian *mores* to scorn in a
letter to Eleanor Hinkley, from Oxford in 1915, in a 'scene' he had
composed on the occasion of the announcement of the engagement
of his cousin, the Revd Frederick May Eliot, a future President of
the American Unitarian Association, to Elizabeth Berkeley Lee.

> F: (on one knee) My Elizabeth!
> (Sensation among the old ladies in the front row)
> He rises, his boots creaking as he does so. 'There, that's
> settled'. Looks at his watch. 'Now I must be off to address
> a meeting of the Church Lads Brigade in Arlington'. Starts
> to put on his rubbers. 'Oh, I forgot'. Advances f.c. 'Permit
> me'. Kisses her decorously in exact centre of left cheek.
> CURTAIN[89]

Valerie Eliot calls this a *'jeu d'esprit'*, in her footnote to the letter, but
its comedy is contemptuous. The tone is similar to Eliot's mockery,
a few months before, of a Thanksgiving Day sermon: '"And what
are we, the young men of America, doing to help build the city of
God?..." (Silence, followed by breathing)'.[90]

Eliot's dissociation from the liberal theology and parochialism,
if not vestiges of the social responsibility and something of the
temperamental character of his Unitarian forebears, was complete
by the time he had finally left Harvard for Europe in 1914.[91] Once
he had become an Anglo-Catholic, he could be savage in his repudiation of

> that isolated, cantankerous, often narrow, bigoted and heret-
> ical society.[92]

5

The young Eliot inevitably knew Episcopalians – the American version of Anglicans. They lived within the same social class. Yet the
influence on him of Episcopalianism (which we might have supposed

would have drawn him towards Anglicanism) is almost imperceptible, although many Unitarians – as Eric Sigg has pointed out – 'headed for Canterbury' by this route,[93] acquiring the high theology and liturgy of the Episcopalian Church after the all-but-non-existent doctrine and spirituality of a Unitarianism dedicated to their negation. Culturally, in New England, the adjustment from Unitarianism to Episcopalianism would have been painless, whereas conversion to the other Western Catholic alternative, Romanism (which, particularly in Boston, had predominantly Irish, working-class origins) would have been social suicide.

Eliot attended Milton Academy and Harvard with Harrison Bird Child (1889-1944) who became an Episcopalian priest. Jean Verdenal called him Eliot's '*grand ami Child*', indicating that Eliot had talked warmly of him to his French friend and Eliot had written to Eleanor Hinkley in 1914 asking her 'if you have seen Harry [Child] let me know how he is' (8th September), envisaging Child at the centre of a circle of 'very attractive' friends (again to Hinkley; 21st March, 1915).[94] In November, 1914, writing from Oxford, he had referred specifically to Child's vocation, indicating his detachment from such a commitment, but his 'particular sympathy' for the motivation behind it. The language of this long passage is unusually convoluted – so much so that Eliot has written 'What syntax' in the margin. The syntactic awkwardness could be expressive of the perplexities of Eliot's own religious convictions (or lack of them) in the face of Child's certitude. We notice the slipperiness of his thinking in the course of it: 'poor' Harry's enterprise is 'strained and forced', yet principled; he is 'appealing', yet 'pathetic'. And very noticeable is Eliot's reluctance to name the 'thing', the 'programme', 'something', 'anything' to which Child has committed himself. Eliot could have vaguely 'drifted' into a similar state, he surmises, but that – decisively – would have been to 'err', wittily varying the usual connotation of that verb as a movement from faith to doubt. But now he is too wise to possess 'strong convictions in any theory'. One should have theories, he notes, with a Wildean flippancy, but 'one need not believe in them'. And for all his compliments to Harry on his unnamed undertaking, he entertains the notion that these will only be 'two or three merely wasted years', spent in testing his priestly vocation, although such wastage may be the cause of subsequent embittered regret. With its contradictions and evasions, this important passage is one of those moments in his letters where Eliot appears to be talking less to his correspondent and about his ostensible subject, than to himself and about himself.

Later, in 1916, Eliot asked Eleanor Hinkley to 'give my affection to Harry Child, if you see him',[95] and at just this period when Eliot's progress towards his classmate's religious position was beginning to be clarified, Child and, with him, Episcopalianism, disappear from Eliot's life for many years. Child died in 1944. Later in the 1940s, Eliot's first sustained association with the Episcopalian clergy began in the form of his twenty-year-long friendship with the American priest, William Turner Levy.[96] Had Eliot remained in America (which he was still contemplating, as late as 1915 – 'whether I want to get married, and have a family, and live in America all my life[97]) and been drawn to Catholic faith and practice there, it is unlikely that he would have found his spiritual home in Episcopalianism. For whereas the Church of England was for him 'the English Catholic Church'[98] (being, then, the faith of the majority of the Christian people in Britain and inextricably bound up with the history and culture of the populace in general) no-one could claim the same for Episcopalianism in the United States, with its very small membership in terms of the total population, in spite of exercising an influence well beyond its size due to the membership of socially prominent families.

6

More important over the course of Eliot's early years than the influences – encouraging or otherwise – of the many various forms of Christianity in the process of his dissociation from Unitarianism and movement towards Anglo-Catholicism, was his exploration of contending contemporary philosophical theories during his graduate study at Harvard from 1909 to 1914 – in spite of the fact that the University, as he described it in retrospect, in 1926, was still, in those days, a 'stronghold of Unitarianism'.[99]

Philosophy at Harvard, during the period of Eliot's studies, was dominated by the 'science versus religion controversy', the debate between 'idealism and scientific materialism', and the attempt (as Manju Jain encapsulates it) to defend 'religious truths and spiritual values against the challenge of Darwinism'.[100] The school was led by William James, Josiah Royce and George Santayana, the last of whom, a Spanish-Catholic aesthete, was not as attractive to Eliot as we might have expected. He disapproved of Santayana's 'essentially feminine' attitude, Jain argues, and so his influence on Eliot is 'difficult to estimate'.[101] In Royce's seminars, however, Eliot grappled with philosophical problems which 'were to be his major preoccupations over a prolonged period of time':

> Eliot's serious concern [was] with the whole question of the
> foundation of religious belief and its place in a scientific,
> secular society.[102]

Royce's theory of the 'organic nature' of the Christian community
(in *The Problem of Christianity*), based on tradition, may have influenced Eliot's social thinking, but his 'paradigmatic community
was the scientific one', seeking 'to establish the kingdom of God on
earth'.[103]

Irving Babbitt, who taught Eliot in 1909-10 and whose defence of
classicism was opposed to the liberal, forward-looking inclination of
Harvard philosophy in these years, was another compelling influence.
Eliot described him, along with Paul Elmer More, as 'the two wisest
men that I have known',[104] and was still arguing, as late as 1955, with
regard again to Babbitt and More, that it was necessary that the

> views of such writers become more widely diffused and trans-
> lated, modified, adapted, even adulterated, into action.[105]

The 'views' of Babbitt that Eliot had explicitly in mind were his social,
rather than his theological theories. The authoritarianism of Babbitt's
Democracy and Leadership originated in his desire for that order in
society which had also informed Eliot's appreciation of the *camelots
du roi* of the *Action Française* and of Machiavelli.

But Eliot did not accept Babbitt's theory that Humanism, however orderly, might serve as a substitute for religion. It sounded
'alarmingly like very liberal Protestant theology of the nineteenth
century ... Protestant theology in its last agonies', Eliot was to write in
For Lancelot Andrewes[106] – like Unitarianism, in other words. In the
Criterion, Eliot accused Babbitt of possessing no 'coherent system',
no 'philosophical technique',[107] while at the Malvern Conference in
1941, he described the Humanism of 'Babbitt and his disciples' as

> an attempt to devise a philosophy of life without a
> metaphysic ... humanism of its nature stops short of a
> philosophy.[108]

He had already said that

> Professor Babbitt knows too much ... he knows too many
> religions and philosophies, has assimilated their spirit too
> thoroughly ... to be able to give himself to any.[109]

All this religious knowledge had led to a disabling intellectual pride,
preventing a personal commitment. Paul Elmer More made an assessment which could as easily have been Eliot's:

A certain final lack of humility I must find in Babbitt's attempt to cut out for himself an individual path in religion, rather than submit to the great institutional experience of the race.[110]

Yet, as we have seen, Eliot began 'as a disciple of Mr. Babbitt'[111] and retained his respect for him as a magus, but within the restricted dimension of his learned speculation on the theory of society and of particular ideas about the articulate man's place in it. To this extent, Babbitt's organic conception of the social order influenced the later development of Eliot's idea of a Christian state. And, most importantly, for all Babbitt's theological shortcomings – just becoming apparent to the young graduate student emerging from Unitarianism – he had developed a classical response to what Eliot regarded as the chaotic individuality of Romanticism. His mistake was to imagine that Humanism would be a sufficiently stringent and authoritative corrective of such excesses. Babbitt had denounced Rousseau, in his *Masters of Modern French Criticism* – as Eliot did some years later, in his London lecture course – and expressed qualified approval for Charles Maurras' classicism, which Eliot was to encounter in Paris in 1910-11. But the crucial difference between Babbitt and Maurras was that the Frenchman, although an unbeliever, recognised (as Eliot was to put it in his essay on Babbitt) that the Catholic Church 'may perhaps be the only institution left in the Occident that can be counted upon to uphold civilised standards'.[112]

Also, in Paris, Eliot attended the weekly lectures of Henri Bergson at the Collège de France, to the point of 'conversion'. Bergson was concerned to restate the problems of metaphysics in terms of the non-mathematical sciences. In 'Rhapsody on a Windy Night' (written in Paris in March, 1911), Eliot poeticises the Bergsonian idea of time in perpetual flux and a disciple of Bergson appears in Eliot's 'Dialogue on Dramatic Poetry' (1928). Bergson taught that it was possible to transcend sense data and fragmented memories through immediate intuition or an act of pure perception. But, as Jain argues, 'Rhapsody' ultimately denies this – 'perception remains fragmented in the poem' – suggesting the ephemeral character of Eliot's appropriation of Bergsonism.[113] 'My only conversion', Eliot reflected, in 1948, 'by the deliberate influence of any individual, was a temporary conversion to Bergsonism'.[114]

It would seem, indeed, from the 'Dialogue', that a more lasting Parisian impression was made on Eliot by another kind of transcendental experience – High Mass at the Madeleine. For 'B' addresses 'E', there, telling him of a man who 'was not a believer, but a Bergsonian' who nonetheless

> went to High Mass every Sunday.... I can testify that
> the Mass gave him extreme, I may even say immoderate
> satisfaction.... His dramatic desires were satisfied by the
> Mass.[115]

And this is in response to the views of 'E' himself (whom we may
assume to be Eliot at thirty-nine, baptised and confirmed, while 'B' is
the aesthetic Eliot of his much earlier Bergsonian phase):[116]

> I say that the consummation of the drama, the perfect and
> ideal drama, is to be found in the ceremony of the Mass....
> The only dramatic satisfaction that I find now is in a High
> Mass well performed.[117]

Earlier, in 1925, Eliot remembered the Roman rite during his Paris
sojourn, with a similar vocabulary of aesthetic appreciation of its
performance:

> Is not the High Mass – as performed, for instance, at the
> Madeleine in Paris – one of the highest developments of
> dancing?[118]

Also in Paris, at that time, his friend, Jean Verdenal, to whom Eliot
was to dedicate *Prufruck and Other Observations* in 1917 (Verdenal
having died in the Dardanelles two years before), was alerting him to
a contemporary tendency in Parisian thought towards a recovery of
'*croyance catholique et littérale du dogme*'.[119] By 1917, reviewing
Peter Coffey's Thomistic work, *Epistemology*, Eliot was writing that
the Catholic Church was 'the only Church which can even pretend to
maintain a philosophy of its own'.[120]

George Every, whom Eliot knew for many years as a professed
brother in the Anglican Society of the Sacred Mission, told me that
Eliot frequented the High Mass at the City church of St Magnus the
Martyr after the First World War, and Every commented that 'the
influence of the liturgy on the drama was indeed apparent to him
before he was a believer. Images out of *Murder in the Cathedral* and
The Family Reunion belong to this time'.[121]

A decade later, Eliot had found a church in London, St Stephen's,
Gloucester Road in South Kensington which was to satisfy his worshipping requirements for the rest of his life. He had the singular
good fortune there to encounter Father Eric Cheetham, its vicar,
who, in addition to profound spiritual qualities (to which we shall
refer later and which made a deep impression on Eliot) had also, in
a way familiar in Anglo-Catholicism, a remarkable theatrical flair

which he applied to the liturgy. One of Cheetham's altar servers during Eliot's time as a parishioner was the screen actor, Christopher Lee. He remembered the priest 'drawing parallels between [the Church's] deep need for ritual and the ritual framework of the theatre'.[122]

What Eliot had experienced as a child, with Annie Dunne in St Louis, recaptured at the Madeleine in 1910 and at Magnus Martyr in Lower Thames Street in 1922 proved to be of more profound and enduring influence than Bergsonism or Babbitt's Humanism.

7

Eliot's study of Eastern languages and religions at Harvard also needs consideration in surveying the process of elimination (as it turned out) that brought him eventually to orthodox Christianity. Returning from Paris to Harvard in later 1911, taking a room in Ash Street, in which (Conrad Aiken recalled) he hung 'a Gauguin Crucifixion, brought from Paris',[123] Eliot took the course in Sanskrit and read the *Bhagavad Gita*. The next year, he studied the sacred books of Buddhism and was given, by his instructor, Charles Rockwell Lanman, the 'Fable of the Thunder', containing the 'da da da' passage which he was to use in the final section of *The Waste Land*, 'What the Thunder Said'. Some traces of these studies are to be found as late as *Four Quartets* ('Eliot's fusion of ideas from Hinduism and Buddhism, with a nod to the fortuitous parallels in Heraclitus, has an almost ironic use' in 'The Dry Salvages', the third Quartet, according to Grover Smith[124]), but for Marja Palmer to claim that 'Buddhist beliefs' are 'consistently worked out' in *Four Quartets*[125] overstates the case. Insofar as any 'beliefs' are explored there, they are Christian ones. Eliot wrote the poem as a well-known Anglo-Catholic of more than a decade's standing. He was never a Buddhist. Manju Jain puts the matter succinctly when, in referring to Eliot's study of eastern religions at Harvard, she observes that it 'gave him an alternative world view but it did not provide him with a mainstay in his search for a defining belief'. He found that in Christian theology, which revealed to him the 'inferiority' of oriental philosophy and religion.[126] 'Wisdom that is not Christian', Eliot reflected in 1940 (when he was in the midst of writing *Four Quartets*), 'turns to folly'.[127]

While studying Eastern thought, Eliot continued the pursuit of theories in the Western tradition. In an essay, 'The Relationship between Politics and Metaphysics' (written some time in 1913-14), he rejected pragmatism because of its 'anthropocentrism', articulating instead the search for an absolute point outside 'the flux of history', the epiphanic moment to be symbolised, in his later poetry, by the 'still point of the turning world'.[128] Eliot also eschewed scientific materialism and was even more hostile to idealism: in a paper on ethics of 1912 or 1913, he opined that 'chance…a gigantic hand organ of atoms, grinding out predictable variations on the same tune, would fill the vast silences which idealism leaves empty'.[129] This impatience with the unspecified Hegelian 'Absolute Mind', even before he had immersed himself in F.H. Bradley's theories, is also revealed in his poem, 'Afternoon' (1914), in which the speaker equates 'the unconscious, the ineffable, the absolute'.[130] Eliot marked in his copy of Walter Pater's *Renaissance* Blaise Pascal's fearful comment about the eternal silence of immense spaces.[131]

Contrariwise, what he was seeking, whether from the East or the West, was a system of belief in which the juxtaposition of the temporal and the eternal was concentrated in their connection, and ultimately resolved. Although decades from articulating it affirmatively, what Eliot was searching for was the philosophy embodied in the theology of the Incarnation (the Word of God being made flesh, in the birth of Christ), which is at the very heart of Anglo-Catholic doctrine and spirituality and the sacraments which are derived from it, Catholic teaching affirming that the entire sacramental system, central to the faith, is an extension of the Incarnation.

Eliot's exposure to the sheer proliferation of choices and the flux of possibilities in Harvard and Parisian philosophy became itself a negative influence. In a seminar paper which he read on 9th December, 1913, 'on the methodology of the social sciences', Eliot doubted the adequacy of 'philosophical systems and theories to explain reality', having asserted, in an essay of April, 1913, that 'ultimate truth remains inaccessible'.[132] He aspired to a permanent conviction, transcending intellectual fashions and which was authoritative, not only in terms of its contemporary proponents but by virtue of the weight of history – in particular, European culture and civilisation – upon it.

The final stage of his protracted philosophical investigations produced Eliot's doctoral thesis on Bradley, completed in Oxford and London and eventually published as 'a tormented book' (in Jain's assessment)

> haunted by the author's need to find meaning and order in a universe that appears to be discordant, inchoate, indefinable, and swarming with contradictions.

She wisely warns against attempting to deduce Eliot's own philosophy from his account of Bradley's:

> there is a danger of mistaking his analysis of Bradley's theories for an expression of Eliot's opinion.[133]

In particular, the 'Absolute' of Bradley's idealism presented Eliot not with a solution to the 'riddling speculations of metaphysics' in which he had been engaged for several years, but with 'the void' of which, like Pascal, he was 'terrified'.[134] So far from being the culmination of Eliot's philosophical searchings, Bradley's theories convinced Eliot of the shortcomings of all metaphysical systems, as he suggests, in a dismissive simile, in the later book of the thesis:

> From the critic's standpoint the metaphysician's world may be real only as the child's bogey is real.... Metaphysical systems are condemned to go up like a rocket and come down like a stick.[135]

Eliot wanted the ultimate vision of truth to be defined and placed, not ineffable, as it appeared in the void of Bradley's eternity where the soul is absorbed into 'an undifferentiated, abstract, impersonal Absolute'. In the domain of morality, moreover, Eliot's sense of the limitations of human nature also contradicted 'any idealist notion of perfectibility'.[136]

8

Eliot's dissatisfaction with the theoretical explanations of reality and religion which his studies had proposed, even before the Bradleyan denouement of his philosophical career, had prompted his somewhat fitful investigation of irrational phenomena in this period. In a manuscript, probably of 1914, Eliot wrote that 'I agree thoroughly with Mr Russell when he speaks of cause as a superstition: I only question whether we could live without superstition'. And, again, in a seminar of 17th March, 1914, he asked: 'Can we do without superstition?'[137]

Eliot's interest in mystical and hallucinatory states of consciousness received little encouragement at Harvard. Psychology there, under William James, had become 'increasingly experimental and positivist'.[138] On that reckoning, 'a mystic event was simply an event that had not yet found its proper explanation'.[139] Eliot took copious notes from E. Murisier's *Les Maladies du sentiment religieux* (1901) where it was explained how depressive states were derived from pathological forms of mysticism. The 'low physical vitality' of mystics, as revealed in several French studies, particularly interested him.[140]

Eliot's early engagement with the 'occult' has received 'scant critical acknowledgement', Thomas Gibbons notes, exploring the poet's association with 'a thriving tradition of "Esoteric Christianity"' within Edwardian mysticism. This attracted individuals such as Charles Williams, 'to whom Eliot acknowledged his indebtedness', and who was a prominent member of the Hermetic Order of the Golden Dawn, which also included W.B. Yeats. Interest in the occult is occasionally encountered in the biographies of otherwise ultra-orthodox Anglo-Catholics, too – such as Father Hope Patten of Wal-singham – especially those from the Edwardian period. Patten was remembered 'passing from time to time into a form of delirium and imagining the presence of various historical figures'.[141] When Eliot, in an obituary of 1935, referred to A.R. Orage's 'life-long Theosophical and occultist interests', he confessed that he did so with 'the reformed drunkard's abhorrence of intemperance', confirming his earlier intoxication. There are allusions to psychic experience in the manuscripts of *The Waste Land*, according to Gibbons, and in 'The Love Song of J. Alfred Prufrock':

> Eliot regarded himself as a voyant, capable of piercing the
> veil of the material world and perceiving occult realities.[142]

In this exploration, however, Eliot was concerned not only with the spiritual facets of mysticism but the processes whereby the mystical state is attained – in particular, its authoritative rules and disciplines. By 1916, writing of Paul Elmer More in the *New Statesman*, Eliot said that 'man requires an askesis, a formula to be imposed upon him from above'.[143]

His note-cards from his Harvard years make it clear that Eliot was less interested in the occult than in expressions of orthodox Christian mysticism, referring to a reading of Dean Inge's *Studies of English Mystics*, of Walter Hilton's steps to perfection, paraphrases of Julian of Norwich (who was to be remembered thirty years later in 'Little Gidding', the fourth Quartet) and in a brief allusion to 'St John of the Cross, The Dark Night of the Soul'[144] (the model for the *via negativa* meditated upon in 'East Coker', the second Quartet). Also making a special impression on the student Eliot were the writings of the contemporary English exponent of the mystical life, Evelyn Underhill, who had published her well-known study, *Mysticism*, in 1911. Eliot copied out her definition of mysticism as

the expression of the innate tendency of the human
spirit towards complete harmony with the transcendental
order...

and also her assertion that

the dogmas of Christianity are necessary to an adequate description of mystical experience.

Here was an Anglo-Catholic teacher of spirituality who, having had
mystical experiences herself which brought her from agnosticism to
Christianity, synthesised the intellectual and emotional components
of the faith and the material and transcendental dimensions of life,
finding the focus of her beliefs (as Eliot was to do) in the doctrine of
the Incarnation. Eliot met her, many years later in 1930, at a lunch
with her cousin, Francis, who was Eliot's confessor until he left
London to become Dean of Rochester in 1932.[145] Eliot paraphrased
her teaching:

The Incarnation, which is for popular Christianity synonymous with the historical birth and earthly life of Christ, is
for the mystic not only this but also a perpetual cosmic and
personal process.[146]

To attain such profound and elusive knowledge, Eliot came to believe
that the extreme asceticism of the anchoretic life, with its detailed
rules, was necessary. Writing, in 1928, to the priest (William Force
Stead) who had recently baptised him, Eliot expressed 'a desire for
the most severe, the most Latin kind of discipline, Ignatian or other',
since he felt 'that nothing could be too ascetic, too violent' for his
own needs.[147]

Eliot decisively dissociated himself from the heterodox manifestations of spiritualism. A 'spiritualist' he had encountered in his
'workingmen's class in English Literature' (on 'mostly social and
religious topics'),[148] who 'wanted to give me mental treatment for a
cold in the head', and who 'writes articles on the New Mysticism', is
dismissed as 'mad', although 'not much madder than most people';
while Yeats' obsession with 'psychical research' bored him: it was
'the only thing he ever talks about, except Dublin gossip'.[149] Eliot
sharply differentiated Christian mysticism from what he regarded as
the charlatanism of the occult,

which seeks contact with the sources of supernatural power,
divorced from religion and theology,

spawning 'cults whose aims are not far removed from those of magic'.[150] In a well-known passage in the third Quartet, 'The Dry Salvages' ('To communicate with Mars...'),[151] he catalogues and dismisses the various processes of forecast and divination of psychics and psychologists, even as he acknowledges the appeal of such consolations in times of acute distress (as in the years of the Second World War when he was completing *Four Quartets*), 'whether on the shores of Asia or in the Edgware Road'.

Many years previously, Eliot had satirised the self-proclaimed possessors of such supernatural powers, and the therapies they purveyed, in the person of Madame Sosostris, 'famous clairvoyante', in the opening section of *The Waste Land*. There is 'much chatter about mysticism', he noted, 'in the modern world'. There, 'the word means some spattering indulgence of emotion, instead of the most terrible concentration and askesis'. This was true mysticism, which found its culmination in the Catholic tradition:

> it takes perhaps a lifetime merely to realise that men like the forest sages, and the desert sages, and finally the Victorines and John of the Cross and (in his fashion) Ignatius *really mean what they say*.[152]

Yet Eliot's early dabbling in this more orthodox tradition did not provide a substantial alternative to his contemporary philosophical investigations, which only diminished gradually as his Christian faith developed. In the years after he had finally put Harvard behind him, had completed his doctoral dissertation on F.H. Bradley and had settled in England to pursue his poetic and literary-critical careers, Eliot contributed extensively to philosophical debate, largely in the form of review essays, on subjects relating to ethics, metaphysics and religion.[153]

Reflecting on his years of study in philosophy, Eliot could justly observe (in Prufrockian phrase and imagery):

> I have searched the world through dialectic ways;
> I have questioned restless nights and torpid days,
> And followed every by-way where it led;
> And always find the same unvaried
> Intolerable interminable maze.[154]

This had not been a futile activity, however, as he noted in 1952, recalling 'the time when I myself was a student of philosophy – I speak of a period of some thirty-five to forty years ago':

even if some of its avenues turn out to be blind alleys, it
is, after all, worth while exploring a blind alley, if only to
discover that it is blind.[155]

'The conversion to Christianity', he reflected in 1937, 'is apt to be
due, I think, to a latent dissatisfaction with all secular philosophy'.[156]
Eliot took what he needed, philosophically and poetically, from these
texts, his teachers and their seminars. His was to be a long journey to
his ideological and spiritual home (he asserted that he had come to a
full acceptance of Christianity 'perhaps insensibly over a long period
of time')[157] and, once he was in sight of his destination, it turned out
to offer only a continuing quest. He wrote, soon after his baptism and
confirmation,

it is rather trying to be supposed to have settled oneself in
an easy chair when one has just begun a long journey on
foot.[158]

Clement of Alexandria had put the matter succinctly in similarly ped-
estrian metaphor: 'we may not be taken up and transported to our
journey's end, but must travel thither on foot, traversing the whole
distance of the narrow way'.[159] The idea is given memorable expression at the end of Eliot's first 'Christian' poem, 'Journey of the Magi'
(published in August, 1927), where the solitary Magus, in the midst
of his now-alien people and having already undertaken an arduous
journey (backwards, through time) to the Christ-child, realises that a
further (and, it is implied, ongoing) dying to this world is required of
him. In tune with this, some five years into his commitment, at Easter
1932, Eliot was expressing the difficulty of the Christian's vocation:

the Christian ... must try to follow his religion out to the bitter
end.... I think ... of the words of Pascal, to be recalled even,
and perhaps especially on the day of the Resurrection: 'The
Christ will be in agony even to the end of the world'.[160]

'We must find our own faith', he had written in the *Criterion* in January, 1926, 'and having found it, fight for it against all comers'.[161]
Christianity itself, Eliot believed, was not static, but ever-changing,
in various aspects of theological emphasis and practice, and this, too,
posed a challenge to its adherents, as he observed at the beginning of
the very year in which he was to be baptised:

Christianity will probably continue to modify itself, as in the
past, into something that can be believed in (I do not mean
conscious modifications like modernism, etc., which always

have the opposite effect). The majority of people live below
the level of belief or doubt. It takes application, and a kind
of genius, to believe anything, and to believe *anything* (I do
not mean merely to believe in some 'religion') will probably
become more and more difficult as time goes on.[162]

The faith, he observed, was 'frightening, frightful and scandalous' to
the 'secular mind', but that mind, he continued, was one 'which we
are all compelled to some extent to share'.[163] It was important, therefore, to remain hopeful and to recall the saints:

> when we consider the quality of the integration required for
> the full cultivation of the spiritual life, we must keep in mind
> the possibility of grace and the exemplars of sanctity in order
> not to sink into despair.[164]

9

It can certainly be argued that 'what is remarkable is the extent to
which many of [Eliot's] later, post-*Waste Land* concerns are already
incipient in the early work',[165] especially with reference to the idea of
questing and searching and the difficulties of that enterprise, aesthetically and spiritually. But the disadvantage of hindsight is that we
can too easily perceive intimations of Eliot's mature development
and systematic ideological convictions in the disparate intellectual
investigations and allegiances of his formative years – finding him,
that is to say, an Anglo-Catholic *in embryo* at Harvard. Assuredly, he
was not himself susceptible to such pious retrospectives:

> I am surprised to think that any indications of Christian trad-
> ition were present in Prufrock [the poem]. I was certainly
> quite ignorant and unconscious of them myself, and at the
> time, or at least before the poem was finished, was entirely
> a Bergsonian.[166]

When Eliot went up to Oxford in October, 1914, to the very home
and heartland of Anglo-Catholicism, he did not choose to go to such
a college as Keble (founded to commemorate one of the great heroes
of the Oxford Movement, and in those days a centre of the burgeoning Catholic Revival), but to Merton, where he was working under
Harold Joachim, Fellow and Tutor in Philosophy, although it was
not required that a postgraduate student reside in the college of his
supervisor. Nor is there any indication (in his letters through the several

months he was at Oxford) of his attendance at any of the great Oxford shrines of the movement – such as St Barnabas, in suburban Jericho – or of interest, indeed, in the diocese's religious life, or in religion at all. This is the period during which Eliot wrote his dismissive letter about Harry Child's Episcopalian priestly vocation, to which we have already referred. Indeed, while at Oxford, Eliot noted his 'fatal disposition toward scepticism'.[167] Although appreciating aspects of university life and some people there, he generally did not enjoy his brief stay, disliking provincial cities in general and university towns in particular, and yearning for London: 'the food and climate are execrable, I suffer indigestion, constipation, and colds constantly; and the university atmosphere'.[168]

Aware of the temptation to rewrite the poet's past, Jain rightly repudiates Lyndall Gordon's suggestion that 'the turning-point' in Eliot's life came 'not at the time of his baptism in 1927, but in 1914'[169] – that is, in his last year at Harvard when Eliot's interest was developing in the lives of mystics and saints. But the 'saints' that Gordon has in mind are Saint Sebastian and Saint Narcissus, about whom Eliot wrote what Gordon describes as 'intense religious poems' but the former of which Louis Menand reads, more persuasively, as a 'spooky and sadistic erotic' work.[170] These Swinburnian poems are definitely 'intense' – there was a widespread fascination in the *fin de siècle* with Sebastian.[171] But they are certainly not 'religious', in any orthodox sense. Gordon, unsympathetic towards her subject's Anglo-Catholicism and, in particular, the sacramentalism central to its teaching, diminishes the importance of Eliot's later baptism and confirmation, finding evidence, much too early, of a Christian conversion in poems which are more perceptively described by Jain as

> the morbid and self-indulgent preoccupations ... [of] a somewhat belated adolescent rebellion on Eliot's part against the austere and ascetic Unitarian background of his childhood.[172]

His lyrics on Sebastian and Narcissus, in other words, indicate that Mrs Eliot's apprehension about her son – 'I cannot bear to think of your being alone in Paris.... My dear boy, the very words give me a chill'[173] – was well-founded, at least in terms of his imaginative exploits. Eliot's decadent poeticising of Sebastian and Narcissus was the antithesis of his mother's Puritan enthusiasm for Savonarola and his bonfire of the vanities.

Gordon, however, finds a philosophical bond, rather than a separation, between mother and son. Determined to dissociate Eliot's spirituality from the onset of his Anglo-Catholicism, she reads his poem of 1910, 'Silence', as proof that 'through his mother, in particular, Eliot was steeped in Emersonian thinking which gave final authority to the individual's private light (there is nothing else beside, Eliot wrote in "Silence")'.[174] But as Jain comments:

> There is in fact no connection between Eliot's assertion and Emersonian thought in the poem. Eliot is here describing a moment of peace when the seas of experience are suddenly still, and his state of being terrified at such peace. And when he concludes that there is nothing else beside, the tone of voice far from being affirmative, suggests that fear of the void which recurs so frequently in his poetry.[175]

It would have been uncharacteristic, indeed, for Eliot to have celebrated the Romantic conception of the 'individual's private light', considering his strident repudiation of such idiosyncratic revelation – the antithesis of Classicism and Catholicism, as he appreciated them – in his introduction to his mother's *Savonarola* and, elsewhere, in his ridiculing of the Protestant 'inner voice'.[176] The 'Individual Conscience', he reflected, 'is no reliable guide'.[177] The 'Inner Light', as he judged it, was 'the most untrustworthy and deceitful guide that ever offered itself to wandering humanity'.[178] Charlotte Eliot, having come under Quaker as well as Unitarian influence, was bound to have been an exponent of it (as her son observed):

> Whatever documentary value pertains to the following series of scenes of the life of Savonarola is due to its rendering of a state of mind contemporary with the author [that is, in the early 1890s].... The same is true of Mr Bernard Shaw's St Joan. This Savonarola is a disciple of Schleiermacher, Emerson, Channing and Herbert Spencer, this St Joan is a disciple of Nietzsche, Butler and every chaotic and immature intellectual enthusiasm of the later nineteenth century.[179]

Gordon, affirmative of individuality and, concomitantly – in dealing with Eliot's later Anglo-Catholicism – suspicious about external authorities and Christian orthodoxy 'imposed ... from above' (in Eliot's phrase), insists upon the poet's commitment to the 'private light' of Emerson which he explicitly repudiated.

Eliot equated the 'Inner Voice' with 'Whiggery',[180] and quoting from Middleton Murry, the Humanist he loved to hate, turned on Lloyd George:

'The English writer, the English divine, the English statesman,
inherit no rules from their forebears; they inherit only this: a
sense that in the last resort they must depend upon the inner
voice'. This statement does, I admit, appear to cover certain
cases; it throws a flood of light upon Mr. Lloyd George.[181]

Lloyd George's religious background in the Church of the Disciples
of Christ, which had hived off from the Baptist denominations, was
of dissenters from a Dissenting sect. Donald McCormick, who gives
an account of the extraordinary religious atmosphere of the future
prime minister's youth, including terpsichorean orgies, opines that
the excessive emotionalism engendered in the chapel to which the
Lloyds belonged explained Lloyd George's 'character and career' in
later life, which Eliot found so unpalatable.[182] Such was the malignant
influence of the doctrine of the Inner Voice.

So far from this, 'I am convinced', Eliot told Bertrand Russell
(also accused by Eliot of 'Whiggery'[183]) in 1917,

that there is something beneath Authority in its historical
forms which needs to be asserted clearly without reasserting
impossible forms of political and religious organisation
which have become impossible.[184]

The insistent if stylistically clumsy repetition of 'impossible' is a sign
of Eliot's consciousness of his correspondent's philosophical position,
but the capitalisation of 'Authority' here – and earlier in the letter, coupled with 'Reverence' – is a signal of the persuasion of Eliot's thoughts
at this time. Certainly, the emphasis on authority and the need for the
individual to assent to it was a *leitmotif* of the contemporary Anglo-
Catholic polemic. In the straightforwardly entitled and forthrightly
written, *Anglo-Catholicism*, of 1913, A.E. Manning Foster writes:

If we accept the Christian religion at all we must accept it
upon some sort of authority…. When we come down to bedrock, we must believe in *something outside ourselves*…. A
man has got to accept some authority.[185]

But Eliot's assent to such authority, in its Christian, Anglo-Catholic
form, should not be construed simplistically. Jain's declarations that
Eliot 'abandoned the speculations of metaphysics for the dogmas of
theology' and that 'his later acceptance of the dogmas of Christianity'
was 'an acceptance which answered a need for a stable resting point
beyond the flux of history',[186] while not being untrue, are too simple.
Certainly, Eliot came to be a severe critic of the 'great deal of ingen-

uity' which is 'expended on half-baked philosophies'.[187] He became convinced of the 'incredibility of every alternative to Christianity that offers itself' and of the 'futility of non-Christian lives'.[188] In acknowledging his submission to 'dogmas', it is important to note the rarity, subsequently, with which signs of a die-hard ideological position of the kind traditionally espoused by the dogmatist (and convert) in religion appear in Eliot's poetry and prose. And we remember the persistent value that he set upon scepticism as a part of faith. In these matters, the comparison is striking with the writings of his contemporary, newly-minted Roman Catholics, the Welsh poet and painter, David Jones and the novelist Evelyn Waugh. Eliot mocked zealotry, such as characteristically encountered in the zeal of the convert: 'the "true old enthusiastic breed" of dulness'.[189]

Its most serious drawback, from his viewpoint, was undoubtedly its tendency to emphasise personal experience – the 'conversion experience', indeed – with its suggestion of Protestant revivalism rather than the incremental process by which Catholic orthodoxy is assimilated, culminating in submission. The individuality (or, as Eliot might have put it, personality) of Protestantism is contradicted by Catholicism, the 'essence' of which 'is the subordination of the individual to the whole'.[190] Moreover, the witnessing and testimony which customarily ensue from the Protestant conversion experience contrast with the principle of 'reserve' in communicating religious knowledge which was the subject of one of the most famous of the Oxford Tracts for the Times (which were the genesis of the Anglo-Catholic Revival) and which, predictably, particularly angered Evangelicals.[191]

To pluck Eliot from the 'flux of history', as Jain does, too easily, diminishes the abiding tension between the diurnal and eternal worlds, which (it is not too much to say) is the life of his later poetry. Beyond this world, the resolution of this tension in their separation was what he indubitably aspired to. But most of his writing – and, we can imagine, his spiritual life – is about the difficulty of attaining to worthiness for the beatific vision and, more positively, about the celebration of the rare intersections of the spiritual and the temporal, here and now, in an incarnational interpretation of creation and of human life in its midst. It is in the poetic presentation of the striving for that perception and the expression of the experience of such epiphanies that we find the power of his writing, where

The hint half guessed, the gift half understood, is Incarnation.[192]

'I take for granted,' Eliot wrote in 1937, 'that Christian revelation is the only full revelation; and that the fullness of Christian revelation resides in the essential fact of the Incarnation'.[193]

In 1952, Eliot commented that the philosophy he favoured 'accepts explicitly a dogmatic theology', but that very theology presupposed the incapacity of the ordinary believer always and everywhere to attain to the perfection of belief and moral character it proposed. Eliot differentiated his 'occupation' from that of the saint:

> to apprehend
> The point of intersection of the timeless
> With time, is an occupation for the saint....
>
> For most of us, there is only the unattended
> Moment, the moment in and out of time,
> The distraction fit, lost in a shaft of sunlight....
>
> ('The Dry Salvages', V[194])

He addressed *The Idea of a Christian Society* (1939) not to 'a society of saints, but of ordinary men'.[195]

Jain's judgement that 'Eliot's sense of the limitations of pragmatism, with its relativistic and nihilistic implications, led him to accept the dogmas of Christian theology'[196] is also too narrow, excluding the host of other influences that encouraged that acceptance. It was not only as a disappointed philosopher that Eliot submitted to Anglo-Catholicism. And we should remember that he was not a professional theologian and never claimed even to be an amateur one. Because of his intellectual training and acuteness, he was naturally keen to be persuaded, by theological argument, of the validity of Catholic doctrine and its veracity (so far as that could be determined, by an individual), and he occasionally went into battle in theological and ecclesiastical disputes. But his faith was inspired – at least as significantly – by historical, temperamental, aesthetic and literary considerations. Further, 'the dogmas of Christian theology' is too broad a term to account for the specific focus of Eliot's faith and poetry on certain doctrines – especially Original Sin and the Incarnation.

As Jewel Spears Brooker neatly summarises it:

> He had tried Bergsonism, Eros, Aestheticism, Humanism, Idealism and had seriously considered Buddhism.... Christianity was the only scheme which satisfied both his intellectual and his emotional needs, the only scheme which permitted him to unify his life and his art ... the Christian scheme was the only one which worked.[197]

And within that scheme, only Catholicism was truly persuasive and authoritative. The Anglican version of it (which also satisfied his requirements regarding the important connection between a Church and the culture of its people) that Eliot came to profess and practise offered to him the orderliness, wholeness and stability of the understanding of life and its purpose, including the mental satisfaction

> which neither the intellectual training of philosophy or science, nor the wisdom of humanism, nor the negative instruction of psychology can give.[198]

Chapter Two
Towards Anglo-Catholicism
(1917-1927)

1

The initial appearance of Eliot's interest in identifiably Anglo-Catholic matters is to be found in a letter of 1911, when (with the enthusiasm of a young man after his first visit to London) he lists the sights he has seen for a friend at home – his cousin, Eleanor Hinkley. Written on Eliot's return to Paris, he delights in recording that he avoided the conventional sightseer's destinations:

> I have just discussed my trip with the prim but nice English lady at the pension. She said 'And did you go through the Tower? No! Madame Tussaud's? No! Westminster Abbey? No! ...'

What is striking is his account – emphatically, copiously listed – of what he did see:

> I then said – do you know
>
> St. Helens
> St. Stephens
> St. Bartholomew the Great
> St. Sepulchre
> St. Ethelreda [sic].[1]

All but the last (St Etheldreda, the Roman Catholic church in Ely Place, Holborn, now a centre for the celebration of the traditional Latin Mass) are Anglican City churches, scattered about that famous one square mile.[2] Eliot was being mischievous, both to the 'English lady' and his cousin, for he later points out that he did indeed visit such predictable sights as the National Gallery and the British Museum, although, again, we notice that this later, less eccentric list includes the most important of City churches, St Paul's Cathedral.

While there may be something here, *in embryo*, of the Anglo-Catholic delight in church inspections, Eliot would have been even less religiously prepared, we can only assume, for what St Helen's, Bishopsgate, and the rest, had to offer than the worldly visitor he envisaged at the tiny church at Little Gidding, more than thirty years later: 'if you came by day not knowing what you came for ...' ('Little Gidding', I).[3] What is striking is that he visited the churches, and so many of them, at all.

Eliot's first encounter with several of these historic sacred places in the midst of the commercial heart of the capital was destined to develop, in the years of his work in the City at Lloyds Bank (from 1917 to 1925), into a deep appreciation, expressed in both prose and poetry – as in the choruses to *The Rock* of 1934 (see Chapter 7). Their unobtrusive but potentially redemptive presence amongst men and women who, like Phlebas the Phoenician in *The Waste Land*, were bound to 'turn the wheel' of commerce,[4] stirred him to question whether (as he was to put it later)

> our society, which had always been so assured of its superiority and rectitude, so confident of its unexamined premises, [was] assembled round anything more permanent than a congeries of banks, insurance companies and industries, and had it any beliefs more essential than a belief in compound interest and the maintenance of dividends?[5]

The churches' architect, Sir Christopher Wren, in his rebuilding of fifty-one of them after the fire of 1666, had himself represented and articulated the triplicity of affiliations which Eliot had admired in Charles Maurras and by which he was to define his own convictions. In 'the time of Wren', Sheila Kaye-Smith has written, 'the Church of England stood closer to Anglo-Catholic ideals than at almost any other time between the Reformation and the Oxford Movement'.[6] Wren was a royalist, appointed by his friend Charles II to undertake this extraordinary task, the crowning achievement of which was St Paul's. He designed, furthermore, in the classical style, as the exteriors and interiors of dozens of his churches testify, the tall fluted Ionic columns supporting the barrel-vaulted nave of St Magnus the Martyr, London Bridge, being the feature that particularly caught Eliot's classical eye. And Wren was a high churchman: all of his designs give prominence to the font and altar, emphasising (as John Betjeman has noted in his book on *The City of London Churches*)

> the two sacraments essential to salvation in the Catholic Church, baptism and Holy Communion.[7]

A decade after Eliot's initial encounter with the City churches – but six years before his own baptism and confirmation, admitting him to that communion – he had strongly criticised a proposal to demolish nineteen of them:

> They give to the business quarter of London a beauty which its hideous banks and commercial houses have not quite defaced.... the least precious redeems some vulgar street.... As the prosperity of London has increased, the City Churches have fallen into desuetude.... The loss of these towers, to meet the eye down a grimy lane, and of these empty naves, to receive the solitary visitor at noon from the dust and tumult of Lombard Street, will be irreparable and unforgotten.[8]

Eliot's crucial words (and we should note the sequence) are 'beauty', 'redeems' and 'receive'. He speaks of the churches' aesthetic value amidst the hideousness of the profane world; then of the way each 'redeems' the 'vulgar street'. But, climactically and personally, he records that they 'receive' the 'visitor' – itself another significant word, for a visitor is not yet a member. Obviously, in this sense, *he* had been such a visitor. But in another meaning of the term there is the idea of churches being open to receive committed Christians who would visit them – indeed, seek them out – for private prayer (apart from public worship), reflecting the Catholic understanding of churches as consecrated buildings, places of special holiness. Particularly, if the Blessed Sacrament is 'reserved' in them, the devout experience not only the desire to make a visit, but are encouraged to do so, in Catholic and Anglo-Catholic spirituality. This is in order that the Real Presence of the Lord, thus reserved, might be acknowledged and its special inspiration for concentrating the mind on private prayer be drawn on, in addition to the formal occasions of public worship in the liturgy itself. As well, in Anglo-Catholic churches (unlike other Anglican churches), there are usually shrines to such as the Virgin Mary, before which the visitor will light a votive candle and make a brief prayer for her intercession in the course of a private visit of this kind. Eliot's concentration in his later poetry on the importance of particular times and places where a spiritual experience has occurred – 'you are here to kneel / where prayer has been valid' ('Little Gidding', I)[9] – indicates that he placed a particular value on the availability of such places and opportunities, in churches and elsewhere.

The experience of witnessing visitors in church engaged in private prayer may have been of crucial importance. George Every recalled that he could remember only one occasion when Eliot 'gave something like a testimony to the motives of his conversion':

St Mary Woolnoth

What sticks in my mind is his description of the impression made on him by people praying, I think in a church, or it would not have been so obvious, but certainly outside a time of service. He suddenly realised that prayer still went on and could be made. It wasn't simply of historic and cultural interest. People did pray and he might.[10]

Eliot's reference to 'the solitary visitor at noon from the dust and tumult of Lombard Street' identifies the City church that was most familiar to him, St Mary Woolnoth, on the corner of Lombard Street and King William Street, 'where Saint Mary Woolnoth kept the hours' (*The Waste Land*, I).[11] Pre-dating the Norman Conquest, rebuilt by William the Conqueror, patched up after the Great Fire, St Mary Woolnoth was reconstructed from 1716 by Wren's pupil, Nicholas Hawksmoor, who, over ten years, built 'the most original church in the City',[12] with an interior of baroque elegance, marked by four rows of three slender Corinthian pillars forming a square. It has – Betjeman observed – a sumptuousness 'markedly different from the curves and lightness of Wren'.[13] In his 'Notes on the Waste Land', Eliot points out that the 'dead sound' of the chime from St Mary Woolnoth, on the 'final stroke of nine', was 'a phenomenon which I have often noticed'.[14] The dedication of the church to the Blessed Virgin Mary chimes also with Eliot's devotion to her veneration – yet another mark of his Anglo-Catholicism to which we will refer later – revealed in his own life of prayer and observance, and in his poetry.

Similarly, the other City church which Eliot was to single out for poetic treatment, St Magnus the Martyr, by Wren himself (1671-6), has an interior that is 'rich', Betjeman notes, by the standards of his other churches. Eliot was bound to celebrate it in the midst of the desiccated urban wasteland. 'The interior of St. Magnus Martyr', Eliot wrote five years before his baptism, 'is to my mind one of the finest among Wren's interiors'.[15] To make this observation and, further, to go into print with it, indicates that Eliot had been studying these interiors. Moreover, this was one of the leading shrines of the Anglo-Catholic movement and it is very notable that Eliot should not only refer to it, but, in the midst of a poem of almost unrelieved negativity, present it so positively (if somewhat uncomprehendingly) in terms of the exquisite beauty of its interior: its 'Inexplicable splendour of Ionian white and gold' (the liturgical colours, we should note, of Eastertide and resurrection, a concept otherwise denied repeatedly throughout *The Waste Land*).[16] Its famous twentieth-century vicar, the Revd Henry Joy Fynes-Clinton (1876-1959), took on the living there in 1921 and remained at St Magnus until his death. From the beginning of his incumbency, the parish was the centre of the activities of the Catholic League (the principal Anglo-Papalist organisation in the Church of England, the most extreme form of Anglo-Catholicism[17]) and in 1922, the year of the publication of *The Waste Land* in which his church gained a literary fame he could scarcely have envisaged, Fynes-Clinton instituted the Fraternity of Our Lady de Salve Regina which held devotions there every day at midday.[18] Daily Mass would have been celebrated, too, for the weekday City worker and visitor.

Interior of St Magnus the Martyr

Eliot's initial attraction to (and commemoration of) St Mary Woolnoth and St Magnus the Martyr was at least partly an aesthetic response to their high degree of decoration. 'Yes, I should love to write a book on Wren', he wrote to Richard Aldington in 1921 (at the time when Eliot was suffering extreme depression and was being treated by an eminent nerve specialist) 'or at least on the *églises assassinées* [murdered churches] of London',[19] quoting Marcel Proust who coined the phrase in *En mémoire des églises assassinées* to describe the French cathedrals wrecked by the Germans during the First World War. In 1926, before Eliot had officially become a member of the Church of England,

he and Bonamy Dobrée had led a hymn-chanting procession
through the streets, in protest against schemes to pull down
'redundant' City churches, and they had succeeded in preventing that atrocity.[20]

Eliot's aesthetic delight was a compelling ingredient in the genesis
of his Anglo-Catholicism. Writing (in 1936) to Paul Elmer More that
More's pilgrimage from Calvinism, through Harvard Humanism, to
Anglicanism was a 'spiritual biography. . . oddly, even grotesquely,
more like my own, so far as I can see, than that of any human being I
have known', Eliot noted that his friend had journeyed from 'a form
of worship from which the office of the imagination and the aesthetic
emotions had... been so ruthlessly evicted' to one where they were
satisfied.[21] This, too, was Eliot's journey.

But for Eric Sigg to comment that his 'Christianity was that of an
aesthete', meeting 'the needs his aestheticism had once addressed',
is inadequate.[22] The original aesthetic stimulus was combined, in
the case of the City churches, for example, with an appreciation of
their historical significance (as representative of the Restoration of
the seventeenth-century Church of England) and, ultimately, with
Eliot's response to the moral and spiritual importance of their abiding presence and, no doubt, his growing understanding that, within
some of them, at least – the explicitly Anglo-Catholic ones – there
was reserved the sacramental presence of the Lord before which he
had seen people praying.[23] Once this multi-layered degree of com-
prehension (aesthetic, historical, moral, theological and spiritual)
had been attained, he would have recognised that the churches'
beauty was not merely artistically satisfying. More importantly, it
was expressive of Anglo-Catholic teaching about the extension of the
Incarnation in the sacraments (especially the sacrament of the altar,
the Mass) and the appropriate beauty of the architectural and richly
liturgical setting of their celebration, in consecrated buildings with
solemn worship, as outward and visible signs expressing the inward
and spiritual grace of God:

> We thank Thee for the lights that we have kindled,
> The light of altar and of sanctuary....
> O Light Invisible, we give thanks to Thee for Thy great
>   glory![24]

The 'light... of sanctuary' to which Eliot refers is the white or red
sanctuary light indicating the reservation of the sacrament, acknowledged by the visitor, on entering the church, by his or her bending of

the right knee in genuflection – another practice, in Anglicanism, that is distinctively Anglo-Catholic. This is done in the direction of the reservation (either on the high altar or on the altar of a side-chapel). A bowing of the head to the altar cross is conventional when there is no reservation of the sacrament in tabernacle or aumbry. In a Roman Catholic church, of course, reservation (requiring genuflection) is usual. Eliot's explicit addition – referring to the light 'of sanctuary' – implies the Anglo-Catholic custom of reservation and, more generally, singles out the sacredness of that most holy part of the church where the altar is placed, the sacrifice of the Mass is offered and the tabernacle is centrally located.

2

Eliot's early appreciation of the distinctive aestheticism of Anglo-Catholicism also needs to be placed in the context of his response to the artistic heritage of Western Christendom at large, even to its anthropological and sociological origins. More than ten years before his *soi-disant* conversion (still sometimes misrepresented as if it suddenly happened in 1927),[25] he had reviewed Emile Durkheim's *The Elementary Forms of the Religious Life: A Study in Religious Sociology* for the *Westminster Gazette*, focusing on 'ritual as organising and strengthening man'.[26] Derivations of 'ritual' – 'ritualism' and 'ritualists' – were terms (as he was probably aware) which had been used, usually derisively, of Anglo-Catholicism and Anglo-Catholics since the later nineteenth century (when ceremonial became a pronounced element in the previously doctrinally-preoccupied Catholic Revival). But Eliot, in the decade prior to his formal association with that tradition, was already placing importance upon ancient religious ceremony as a source of classical order in what he perceived to be the chaotic, post-Romantic world.

He had become a 'ritualist' long before he officially became an Anglo-Catholic. His study of Aristophanes, in F.N. Cornford's 1914 account, *The Origin of Attic Comedy*, prompted Eliot to be 'the first to reintroduce this ritual element into the theatre'[27] in his initial experimentation with poetic drama in *Sweeney Agonistes*, the origins of which are also to be dated from before his 'conversion', and in the later, fuller expression of the ritual dimension of the theatre in *The Rock* and *Murder in the Cathedral* where the ceremonial component is more precisely Christian and liturgical.

Eliot's journey towards what he regarded as the true home of English Catholic Christianity drew its early aesthetic inspiration from the larger Western Christian heritage. Writing to Conrad Aiken, in 1914, he effusively conveyed his enthusiasm for that European tradition:

> O a wonderful Crucifixion of Antonello of Messina. There are three great St. Sebastians (so far as I know):
>
> 1) Mantegna (ca d'Oro) [Venice]
> 2) Antonello of Messina (Bergamo)
> 3) Memling (Brussels).

These prompted the poem 'The Love Song of St. Sebastian', sent to Aiken later that month, in draft form, with the comment:

> The S. Sebastian title I feel almost sure of; I have studied S. Sebastians.[28]

The use of 'S.' for 'St' is one of the customs of Anglo-Catholicism, indicating its bond with Latin Christianity. At this stage, Eliot was probably unaware of the particular significance of the usage, common in Anglo-Catholic circles until recent times (and signaling, again, an ethos separate from ordinary Anglicanism). His use of the Latin abbreviation here is a small sign of his attention to the traditions of Catholic culture – at this point, mediated only artistically – appealing to the meticulous personality, destined to be drawn to a movement scrupulous in the observance of ritual minutiae as well as the more substantial disciplines of the faith.

In Eliot's Baedeker, *London and Its Environs* (in his possession from 1910), he had marked Leonardo da Vinci's *Madonna and Child with John the Baptist* and also Antonio Pollaiulo's *Martyrdom of St. Sebastian* (both in the National Gallery).[29]

He had also studied 'many a notable Descent from the Cross' (the most famous of which are by Rubens) in these years, toying with the idea of calling *Inventions of the March Hare*, '*Descent from the Cross*', a title which Christopher Ricks argues would 'more pertain to certain of the poems, than to the collection'.[30] One of its undatable poems, 'The Little Passion', speaks of 'one inevitable cross'; and another, 'He said: This universe is very clever', of March, 1910, has

> He said: 'this crucifixion was dramatic'.[31]

Sending a postcard to Ezra Pound from France in 1920, Eliot remarks of its depiction of the porch of the Collegiate Church of Saint-Ours at Loches, that

> this is the best thing I have found.... Amboise has some of the best Renaissance Gothic I have ever seen.[32]

And, in poetry, he wrote warmly, in July, 1917, of the basilica of Sant'Apollinare at Ravenna:

> Et Saint Apollinaire, raide et ascétique,
> Vieille usine désaffectée de Dieu, tient encore
> Dans ses pierres écroulantes la forme précise de
>   Byzance.[33]

On a later visit to Italy, arriving at the Vatican in the summer of 1926, just months before his baptism and confirmation, Eliot fell to his knees at the entrance:

> his sister-in-law remembered being with him and his first wife, Vivien, when they all together entered St. Peter's, Rome. Vivien, who wasn't easily impressed, said something like 'It's very fine', and then they suddenly saw that Tom was on his knees praying…. It was the first hint that his brother and sister-in-law had that his conversion was imminent, and they naturally misunderstood it. They thought he was going to Rome, and perhaps he thought so himself…. at this point his Christianity was becoming more than an interest, [rather] an experience which had to be practised.[34]

3

It was to the English Catholic Church, however, that Eliot pledged his allegiance. As his enthusiasm for the Anglican City churches indicates, they embodied both the ancient Catholic faith of the land and the centuries-old bond with the history and traditions of English life which those churches, constructed in the heart of London, plainly affirm. We know that he regarded the two steps of becoming an English citizen and a member of the English Church as essentially one.[35]

The problem with this familiar idea of the unity of Eliot's dual contemporary acts of joining the Church of England and becoming a British subject – expressive of his convictions about the necessary interdependency of a culture and religion of a people – is that it has led uninformed commentators into another misinterpretation of Eliot's Christianity. Alan Marshall, for example, speaks of the poet's membership of the 'national Church'.[36] In fact, Eliot (typically, for an Anglo-Catholic) was highly critical of this conception. He believed that the only way the 'national Church' could 'safeguard…the purity or the catholicity of its doctrine' would be by recognising that

'theology has no frontiers'.[37] In other words, the extent to which a
Church was nationalistic impaired its validity, doctrinally. He rejected
Middleton Murry's concept of a 'National Church' which 'degraded'
Christianity to nationalism, rather than raising the nationalism to
Christianity,[38] and repudiated the identification of the Church with
an 'oligarchy or class', which was one of the dangers, he argued,
of 'an established Church'.[39] Eliot criticised the conception of the
'Community of Christians' as

> merely the nicest, most intelligent and public-spirited of the
> upper-middle-class[40]

– as in his own family's Unitarian tradition with its air of social and
moral superiority. Yet J.C.C. Mays accuses Eliot of mimicking 'upper-
class English patterns of belief' by joining the Church of England,[41]
implying (one gathers) that Anglo-Catholicism was a species of high
and dry Anglicanism, tending to the royalism and nationalism which
Eliot favoured, socio-culturally. But, as a general rule, the higher
one moves socially in England (up to the Royal Family), the lower
the Anglicanism.[42] Anglo-Catholicism, in its most admirable manifestations, was conspicuous in socially-deprived areas – on Tyneside,
for example, and, in London: in Pimlico, Shoreditch, Holborn, Ken-
nington and Paddington where many heroic Anglo-Catholic priests
exercised their ministries and, indeed, were persecuted, even imprisoned, for their ritualism. A strong strain of Christian socialism, far removed from 'upper-class English patterns of belief' –
religious or political – was a characteristic of Anglo-Catholicism for
generations. Those aristocrats who publicly aligned themselves with
the movement – such as, most notably, Viscount Halifax – did not
confirm their position in high society, but sacrificed it. Any idea that
Eliot joined the Church of England's Anglo-Catholic wing in order
to secure a degree of 'upper-class' standing in the society at large
cannot be sustained.

To the extent that he regarded the Church of England as the 'national Church', he did so very ambiguously:

> I prefer to think of the Church [of England] as what I believe
> it is more and more coming to be, not the 'English Church',
> but national as 'the Catholic Church in England'.[43]

Only insofar as Anglicanism could be regarded as Catholic, as a part
of European Christendom, was it acceptable to Eliot, while he deeply
appreciated its roots in English culture. W.H.S. Pickering's account
of Anglo-Catholicism is subtitled 'a study in religious ambiguity'[44]

and one element of that ambiguity was its combination of definite Englishness along with its identification with the international Catholic faith. This particular paradox was essential to its appeal to Eliot and he would have argued, no doubt, that it was typical of Catholic cultures worldwide. How similar are Dutch and Spanish Roman Catholicism? The various expressions of Catholic belief were united by the common doctrinal foundation and the 'inheritance from Greece and from Israel'. Catholicism 'is still,' Eliot wrote in 1933, 'as it always has been, the great repository of wisdom'.[45]

4

Intimations of Eliot's theological development are apparent in the same period as the evolution of his aesthetic attraction to ritual, his artistic appreciation of the Western Church, and of the bonds between the English Church and English history and culture. Bracingly confronting his recognition of the 'immense panorama of futility and anarchy which is contemporary history'[46] were Anglo-Catholicism's systematic theology, its strict order of liturgical observance and its moral demands.

In 1916, in his Oxford lectures on French literature, Eliot criticised Rousseau for his opposition to 'Authority in matters of religion':

> His great faults were
>   1) Intense egotism
>   2) Insincerity.

Anticipating, in the third person, his tripartite formula about himself of 1928, Eliot observed that

> a classicist in art and literature will therefore be likely to adhere to a monarchical form of government, and to the Catholic Church.[47]

In the poems and reviews he was writing in these years, moreover, Eliot engages familiarly with Christian texts and teachings, at the same time that he is promoting his doctrine of impersonality in art. The tone of Christian reference he adopts is usually wry and satirical, but the engagement is securely there. The epigraph to 'Burbank with a Baedeker', of 1918, for example, translates as

> nothing stays if not divine; all else is smoke....[48]

'The Hippopotamus', David Moody points out, contains echoes from the hymnals of Unitarianism, Methodism and Anglicanism.[49]

Its epigraph addresses it to the Laodiceans, rebuked by God 'because thou art lukewarm, and neither cold nor hot' (Revelation 3:16). 'Mr Eliot's Sunday Morning Service' (1917) savages the Church for failing to preserve the knowledge of salvation in the incarnate Word. But that very negativity may be read as the expression of a regret at the failure of the preservation as much as a rejection of institutional Christianity. Similarly, in 1916, Eliot had criticised the Revd Hastings Rashdall, in a review of his *Conscience and Christ*, for attempting to make Christianity easier by focusing on ethical matters:

> For Canon Rashdall the following of Christ is 'made easier' by thinking of him 'as the being in whom that union of God and man after which all ethical religion aspires is the most fully accomplished'.

Pondering this, Eliot observes that 'certain saints found the following of Christ very hard', but, he concludes sarcastically, 'modern methods have facilitated everything'.[50] The reader might have supposed that Canon Rashdall had Unitarian leanings and that Eliot was already ripe for Catholic orthodoxy.

In these years of the various intimations of his Anglo-Catholicism, however, Eliot was sensitive, in the literary *demi-monde*, about allegations of such propensities, as in this witty riposte of 1919 to Lytton Strachey:

> You are very – ingenuous – if you can conceive me conversing with rural deans in the cathedral close. I do not go to cathedral towns but to centres of industry. My thoughts are absorbed in questions more important than ever enter the heads of deans – as why it is cheaper to buy steel bars from America than from Middlesbrough.[51]

He protests too much, mindful of the recipient of the letter, that militant atheist, with his satire of all religious personages and principles, and who had recently enjoyed a great success on the publication of *Eminent Victorians* (1918) with its scathing denunciation of theological controversy and superstition in the biography of Cardinal Manning. Strachey, after all, was named by Eliot as a leading figure in the irreligious 'generation of Mr. Shaw, and Mr. Wells, and Mr. Strachey, and Mr. Ernest Hemingway'.[52] Yet only a year later, Eliot (so dismissive of cathedral towns) advises his mother, regarding her forthcoming visit from America, that 'we have made all sorts of plans for you when you come in the spring – both for London and visiting other cathedral towns' [53] and a few months on, he is more specific:

I should like to take you to some cathedral town like Exeter.[54]

These places are singled out, as are no others (such as Stratford, for example, for the literary Mrs Eliot) as possible and agreeable destinations. This was a regime at least as suited to the son's developing interests as to the mother's tolerant Unitarian ecumenism.

Chapter Three

The Struggle for Existence
(1915-1933)

Of all the influences on Eliot in these pre-conversion years, the most urgent in the development of his yearning, psychologically and spiritually, for what he eventually embraced as the Christian solution to personal and social despair was the profound unhappiness of his marriage, from 1915, to Vivienne Haigh-Wood.[1] It was a source of his Anglo-Catholic commitment at least as profound as the persuasion of his intellectual and aesthetic development and the progress of his sense of English culture and history and his intimations of spiritual and theological truth in this period. Brand Blanshard (a fellow-American who had formed a friendship with Eliot when they were together at Merton College, Oxford) identified this aspect of the story of the genesis of Eliot's Christianity when he observed that his friend

> had reached the edge of a nervous collapse, and he reached
> out in desperation for something stable to hold to.[2]

Yet the long-standing idea of Eliot as the unfortunate victim of Vivien's physical and mental illness was replaced, in Michael Hastings' play, *Tom and Viv* (1984) – and the later film – with the image of the poet as callously impotent in the presence of his wife's pain, conspiring with her family to have her permanently institutionalised until her death in 1947.

The publication of the first volume of Eliot's letters, in 1988, covering the early years of their marriage and its disintegration, revealed the inadequacy of both conceptions. In this matter, as in our account of the development of Eliot's faith in general, it is vital to get as close as we can to the truth, for all the elements (including psychological and personal trauma) which led to Eliot's Christian commitment have a decisive bearing on the kind of commitment that it was.

The inclusion in the volume, also, of letters by Vivien, by Eliot's older brother Henry and various friends and professional associates of the poet, enriches our interpretation of Eliot's personal situation. We learn of it not only from his own perspective, but from theirs. What emerges – most significantly, in Vivien's letters – is Eliot's sympathy for his wife. Rather than providing evidence of the poet's idea of himself as the undeserving victim of her suffering or as wilfully dissociated from it, the correspondence indicates that the couple's hypersensitivity to and concern for each other was one of the causes of their accumulating misery. Even within the formality of the conventions of correspondence, the letters have the immediacy and ring of truth. Vivien's, in particular, become more emphatically personal as her anxieties deepen. They are a *cri de coeur*.

The evidence of the letters, also, demands that we place the Eliots' situation in contexts larger than the pressing, intimate problems of their own personalities and relationship. The stress of life in London during the First World War – a recurring topic – intensified their anxiety: 'You cannot realise what it is to live in the midst of alarms of war!' Eliot exclaimed to his mother in 1917.[3] Their flat at Crawford Mansions was cramped and noisy, adding to his frustration of having to undertake such writing as he could manage after his daily labour in Lloyds Bank. Life in London was 'like being in a wilderness', Vivien wrote to her mother-in-law:

> Living where we do ... in a little noisy corner, with slums and low streets and poor shops close around us ... we are just 2 waifs who live perched up in our little flat – no-one around us knows us, or sees us, or bothers to care how we live or what we do, and whether we live or not.[4]

Theirs was, in Eliot's phrase in 'Four Elizabethan Dramatists' (1924), a 'moment-to-moment struggle for existence'.[5]

The combination of these privations and the Eliots' physical and psychological illnesses led to their nervous collapses in 1921, which found expression in *The Waste Land* of the following year. It provided striking evidence of the poet's own theories (based, no doubt, on these experiences, already expressed, and recalled a few years later) of the link between 'the man who suffers and the mind which creates'[6] and that 'poetry not only must be found through suffering but can find its material only in suffering'.[7] The grace and comfort of faith, as countless Christians have witnessed, may provide, in the midst of life's trials, the only sufficient 'cure of woe' and the sinner's refuge.[8]

1

Writing in 1916 to his brother Henry after some fifteen months of marriage, Eliot reflects that

> the present year has been, in some respects, the most awful
> nightmare of anxiety that the mind of man could conceive.[9]

The principal reason for this distress was Vivien's persistent illness.
Accordingly, Eliot urges his brother to write to her, 'for she is very
fond of you', although Vivien and Henry had not yet met. A month
later, Vivien wrote to her brother-in-law, beginning the recital of her
medical afflictions (including bad teeth and eyes, stomach troubles,
neuralgia, severe migraine, sinusitis, rheumatism, laryngitis, neuritis,
colitis, and glandular problems, combined with Eliot's hernia and
tachycardia) which persists, both in her letters and Eliot's, for a
decade.

The combination of physical pain and psychological distress becomes familiar in both Vivien's and Eliot's letters, and a sense of
the singularity and intensity of their suffering – often indicated by
underlining (rendered as italics) – is a motif, recurring in various
guises. No drug alleviates Vivien's migraine; while in one of Eliot's
letters to his brother, he indicates that it would be a great help for
him to know that there was someone who would look after Vivien
in case he died. Aged twenty-eight, he adds two anxious postscripts
to this appeal for assistance in extremis, dwelling on the matter, with
special emphases:

> I should like you to be the person to make yourself respon-
> sible for her in my stead. *Will you do that?*
> I want *all* of my family to take the sort of interest in her
> which would persist after my death; but I depend *especially*
> on you.[10]

Although Eliot's premonitions of disaster and demise are unjustified,
rationally speaking, these febrile appeals indicate a genuine concern
for his wife's welfare in the midst of his agitation, as well as his acute
sense of his own physical fragility.

For this, he proffered a psychological explanation, pointing out that
he brought to his marriage what he described to Richard Aldington as
an 'emotional derangement which has been a lifelong affliction'. He
called it *'aboulie'*.[11] This delibilitating disorder was the antithesis of
the Bergsonian *élan vital*, not to mention the Unitarian *joie de vivre*.
Either it was aggravated by his various physical ailments in these years,

or – psychosomatically – the source of them, and was intensified by the even more numerous and extreme maladies of Vivien, to which (again) it probably contributed. Yet, like the *mélancolie élégante* of Baudelaire (his capacity for suffering, even his celebration of suffering, which struck a responsive chord in Eliot), this deeply troubling negative experience could lead to an appreciation of the need to transcend suffering, as Eliot suggests of Baudelaire:

> he had to discover Christianity for himself. In this pursuit he was alone in the solitude which is only known to saints. To him the notion of Original Sin came spontaneously, and the need for prayer.[12]

Another persistent theme in the letters is the preoccupation with ageing – 'I grow old … I grow old', as Prufrock lamented[13] (written when Eliot was just twenty-two). It was given further poetic treatment in 'A Cooking Egg', composed in the spring of 1919, where both Pipit and the speaker (like that kind of egg) are past their prime. The epigraph to the poem,[14] written by Eliot at thirty, is from *Le Grand Testament* of François Villon –

> In the thirtieth year of my life
> When I have drunk up all my shame …

– wherein the poet confesses his sins in preparation for eternity.

In these trying circumstances, they both yearned for a break away from London. Eliot wrote to his mother, in May, 1917 of Vivien's urgent need of a holiday, noting also his wife's sensitivity to thunderstorms. There was the prospect of a fortnight in her family's house in Hampstead, on the edge of London, with its better air.[15] The change, however, was not restorative. Vivien notes of Eliot that

> he was so desperately tired – he wanted badly to write a longer letter – but he was too tired. …

The aptly wearisome repetition speaks of her identification with his condition which she explains:

> I worry very much about his health – it seems he has not average strength – and added to that he lives as no average man does. The incessant, never ending grind, day and evening – and always *too* much to do, so that he is always behind hand, never up to date – therefore always tormented – and if *forced* to rest or stop a minute it only torments him the more to feel that inexorable pile of work piling up against him.

The repeated references to torment are not substantially ameliorated by Vivien's subsequent observation that, at Hampstead,

> Tom enjoys and revels in the *large* and airy rooms in this house, the peace and quiet of the neighbourhood…

for such ephemeral relief should be set within her larger perspective of their married life through 'these 2 years of noisy struggle'.[16] The problems, we see, are multifarious and multiplying.

The impact of mundane domestic circumstances on their physical and mental health, repeatedly stressed, is reminiscent of the connections in Eliot's poetry between aspects of urban existence and psychological depression, such as the 'damp souls of housemaids / Sprouting despondently at area gates'[17] or where

> Weeping, weeping multitudes
> Droop in a hundred A.B.C.'s[18]

and in the agitated marital exchange in the second section of *The Waste Land*. The woman's voice, there: 'what shall we do tomorrow? / What shall we ever do?'[19] has the same febrile and emphatic cadence of Vivien's reflections on their intensifying, accumulating problems.

2

Initially relieving the tensions of the Eliots' relationship, but later adding to them, was Vivien's sexual affair with Bertrand Russell early in her marriage. Eliot had known Russell since 1914 when the philosopher was a visiting professor at Harvard and had described his pupil as 'extraordinarily silent'.[20] Russell, by his own account, became 'great friends with him, and subsequently with his wife':

> As they were desperately poor, I lent them one of the two bedrooms in my flat [34 Russell Chambers, Bury Street, W.C.], with the result that I saw a great deal of them. I was fond of them both, and endeavoured to help them in their troubles until I discovered that their troubles were what they enjoyed.[21]

This waspish comment obviously relates to more than the Eliots' financial woes and is not inconsistent with the evidence in the letters of both Eliot's and Vivien's tendency to dwell on their problems (and, in the case of minor medical complaints, magnify them). The 'bedroom' which Russell says that he allocated to the Eliots was 'in fact', Peter Ackroyd points out, only 'a tiny closet room – Eliot himself slept in the hall or in the sittingroom, which suggests a certain lack of married intimacy'.[22]

This gave Russell the opportunity for close observation of the couple, and, as a result, he provides what remains the most convincing explanation for the marriage of this ill-sorted pair, with a forecast of difficulties ahead:

> She is light, a little vulgar, adventurous, full of life.... He is exquisite and listless; she says she married him to stimulate him, but she finds she cannot do it. Obviously he married her in order to be stimulated. I think she will soon be tired of him.... He is ashamed of his marriage, and very grateful if one is kind to her.[23]

If Russell became sexually attracted to Vivien, it was of Eliot that he spoke more warmly:

> I have come to love him, as if he were my son. He is becoming much more of a man.

And he endorses the impression, conveyed by the letters, of Eliot's unremitting concern for Vivien:

> He has a profound and quite unselfish devotion to his wife, and she is really very fond of him.

But Russell had also observed, only a few months after the marriage's beginning, that Vivien

> has impulses of cruelty to him from time to time. It is a Dostojevsky type of cruelty, not a straightforward every-day kind.

Russell, whose own marital difficulties might have given him pause, reports his attempts to rectify the Eliots' already unsteady relationship:

> I am every day getting things more right between them, but I can't let them alone at present, and of course I myself get very much interested.

What the 'things' are, and in what, precisely, he is getting 'very much interested', we can only speculate about, but a sexual explanation would seem plausible. He might 'love' Eliot, but Vivien captivated him:

> She is a person who lives on a knife-edge, and will end as a criminal or a saint – I don't know which yet. She has a perfect capacity for both.[24]

An extraordinary opportunity for the further stimulation of Russell's interest was the holiday Eliot allowed him to take with Vivien in Devon at the beginning of 1916. After five days, Eliot came down, having thanked Russell for what had occurred during his absence. This expression of gratitude is effusive beyond anything that would be required in appreciation of an excursion for rest and relaxation (for what Valerie Eliot ingenuously describes in her note to the letter as 'a change of air'):

> Dear Bertie
> This is wonderfully kind of you – really the last straw (so to speak) of generosity.... Vivien says you have been an angel to her.... I am sure you have done *everything* possible and handled her in the very best way – better than I – I often wonder how things would have turned out but for you – I believe we shall owe her life to you even....
> Aff[ectionately].
Tom[25]

The proliferation of superlatives, uncharacteristic of Eliot's personality or epistolary style – except when he is talking of negative experiences – indicates that Russell's services were themselves extraordinary, beyond mere companionship for a few days in the bracing air at Torquay. The focus of the effusion is the underlined 'everything' (we remember that this is one philosopher writing to another – '*everything*' implies 'absolutely everything'), but we particularly notice that the commendation is expressed in physical terms – Russell had 'handled her in the very best way' – and the unfavourable comparison with Eliot's own handling: 'better than I'. What Russell had done, in Eliot's reckoning, was nothing less than to save Vivien's life. Eliot was not one to use language carelessly, and certainly not to a correspondent whom he regarded as one of the few great prose-stylists in English of the twentieth century. It is difficult to imagine what explanation, other than a physical, indeed sexual one, can be persuasively advanced for this profound gratitude by Eliot for Russell's intervention.

And if that is not the explanation, one wonders why Russell (in a letter, several months later in September, 1916, to Ottoline Morrell) reflects that

> I shall soon have come to the end of the readjustment with Mrs E. I think it will all be all right, on a better basis. As soon as it is settled, I will come to Garsington.[26]

Ottoline knew the Eliots – she had met Vivien in March, 1916.[27] Why would Russell obscure Vivien's identity (which he gives in a note in his *Autobiography*) as 'Mrs E.', in a letter to his current lover and write so coyly of 'it' being 'all right' and 'settled', if the matter in question was not extremely delicate (even by Bloomsbury's frank standards) and if he was not concerned that his letter to the indiscreet Ottoline might be seen by others' eyes? If he had been merely escorting or even counselling Vivien in Devon and had become infatuated with her in the process, there would have been no impropriety in mentioning any of this explicitly, particularly in the free-thinking circumstances of his relationship with Ottoline and in her circle. A sexual liaison is the only explanation. In the same month, Eliot wrote 'Mr. Apollinax', a caricature of the notoriously lustful Russell as 'Priapus in the shrubbery'.[28]

That a 'better basis' for the relationship between the Eliots and Russell had been established over the next twelve months is indicated by Vivien's report to Eliot's mother that the philosopher had 'promised to go shares with us'[29] in a country cottage in Marlow, Buckinghamshire. They took a lease on the place for five years. But further evidence of a relationship that had been, however briefly, more than platonic and from which some embers of the passion inevitably remained is indicated in a letter by Vivien to Ottoline, eighteen months later:

> I am amused by your description of Bertie's weekend at Garsington. He came straight from there to this flat [at 18 Crawford Mansions, W.1], in the early hours of a Monday morning, to fetch away another instalment of possessions I had fetched from Marlow. He seemed dreadfully out of temper. Unfortunately I was not dressed, so had to shout to him from the bathroom, as cheerfully as I could. But the response was painful. I was sorry, really. I had asked him to come to tea when he fetched them, and I had come up from Marlow specially. I thought we might have talked a little and come to, at any rate, amicable relations. But it is no good. I will make no more attempts at all. But it is strange how one does miss him! Isn't it hard to put him *quite* out of one's mind?[30]

Vivien appreciated that her correspondent would understand her response, as Ottoline, too, had now joined the ranks of Russell's former lovers. Again, if Vivien's relationship with the philosopher had been merely platonic, why would there have been a necessity to establish 'amicable relations', and why, in spite of that, would Vivien still 'miss

him' so fervently: 'Isn't it hard to put him *quite* out of one's mind?'
Vivien directs the rhetorical question to another married woman who
had had a similar experience with Russell and could appreciate her
situation.

The matter of the dating of the supposed affair, indeed, is problem-
atic. Ackroyd argues that it was not until autumn, 1917 that the sexual
liaison occurred, as revealed by Russell in a letter to his mistress, Lady
Constance Malleson, in which he described the experience as 'hellish
and loathsome'.[31] From this evidence, originally adduced by Robert
Bell, Ronald Schuchard has explained a perceived transformation
in Eliot's poetry at this time from that of 'bawdy balladeer' into a
'savage comedian':

> to cope with the humiliation, to protect himself from the
> moral ugliness and stupidity, Eliot turned savagely to the
> sexual caricature of Sweeney and his friends. In so doing,
> he gradually created a personal myth of sexual betrayal,
> psychological retribution, and moral degeneration.[32]

But Eliot's specific satire of Russell, 'Mr. Apollinax' is (as Grover
Smith argues) 'good-humoured … not hostile … humorous rather than
perturbing',[33] and Sweeney, Eliot's common common man, bears no
resemblance to the aristocratic philosopher. Certainly, in July, 1917,
Eliot had written *'Lune de Miel'*, in which he juxtaposes unhappy
newlyweds and the church of 'Saint Apollinaire' at Ravenna:

> on one hand, the squalor, pettiness and impermanence of the
> honeymooners are underlined; on the other, the permanence
> of the classical basilica and the spiritual and aesthetic values
> it represents are emphasized.[34]

There is no evidence, in Eliot's letters of these months, of his specific disenchantment with Russell. The transformation, in the subject
matter of his poetry, may have had the larger explanation of the
general deterioration of Eliot's marriage, to which Russell's contribution was an early, ambiguous and ephemeral aspect. During
the marriage's 'honeymoon' period, in fact, Eliot was grateful for
Russell's intervention, even if that did not prove, ultimately, to be
efficacious.

By 1918, the Eliots' problems had further intensified. Writing again
to his mother that 'we are feeling the strain of this trying time very
much' ('the combined effect of sudden hot weather and the strain of
a long winter', as he put it in his previous letter to her – 22nd May
1918[35]), Eliot concludes,

One can hardly think or talk – only wait.[36]

We hear an echo of these phrases in the parched incantation of the last section of *The Waste Land*, 'What the Thunder Said':

Amongst the rock one cannot stop or think....

But the incantatory pulse of Eliot's poetry is exemplified more specifically in Vivien's prose – as in this haunting declaration, to Henry:

life is so feverish and yet so dreary at the same time, and one is always waiting, waiting for something. Generally waiting for some particular strain to be over.[37]

We notice that her pointed vocabulary of suffering ('strain') is the same as Eliot's in the previous letters and that she uses the formally detached construction – 'one is always waiting' – as he so often does in both his letters and his poetry ('one thinks of all the hands...', for example, in 'Preludes').[38] The effect of this depersonalising technique is to distance and generalise, and thereby validate, the experience that is being recounted. In this instance, it could be read as Vivien's attempt to resist succumbing to the anxieties which are threatening to engulf her.

3

In spite of Eliot's acute frustrations and disappointments during the early years of his marriage, he had been establishing himself as a man of letters – as a leader writer for *The Times Literary Supplement*, for example – and as a public lecturer. His poetry, both the well-known published works (*Prufrock and Other Observations* had come out in 1917) and those revealed recently in Christopher Ricks' *Inventions of the March Hare*, was proliferating. But as he became more productive and successful, and less apprehensive about his professional future, Vivien became increasingly unbalanced, and dissatisfied, as in her complaint to an old friend, the author Mary Hutchinson, where 'Tom' is denounced for not being

A French artist, or a Flirt, or Amusing or even Rather Fun.

The facetious capitalisation, takes some of the sting out of the indictment and Vivien concludes calling Mary 'little cat', hoping that she will be seeing her 'at Edith's party':

you will know me by my paisley shawl. Goodnight my dear. When may I come and spend the night? I embrace you.[39]

In February, 1920, Eliot's Sweeney poems, written from 1918, were published by The Ovid Press, under the title *Ara Vus* [*sic*] *Prec*. James Longbeach has described the collection as

> a book about pain, pain in all its guises, psychological and physical, the pain of belonging and the pain of standing apart. Most of all, it is a book about the pain of sexuality, the pain of Arnaut Daniel, whose sin was lust.[40]

The voice of Daniel is heard in Dante's *Purgatorio*: 'Ara vos prec ...' ('And so I pray you ...'). A cancelled epigraph to 'Prufrock' referring to Daniel shows that Eliot had been reflecting upon his process of purgation for several years and from well before his marriage.[41] The unhappiness of his life with Vivien would undoubtedly have intensified it, while assisting in stirring his search for the amelioration of his pain in a religious commitment.

Ironically, while Eliot's literary productivity was burgeoning, his poetry expressed unremitting despair. His own accounts of his writing are invested with a sense of futility. He told Ottoline that

> I have just finished an article on Dante ['Dante as a "Spiritual Leader"', for *The Athenaeum*] – under difficulties, as you may imagine: and I feel that anything I can say about such a subject is trivial. I feel so completely inferior in his presence – there seems really nothing to do but to point to him and be silent. Vivien says to tell you she will write as soon as she can.[42]

Eliot's sense of the extremity of Vivien's condition is confirmed by the doctors – who 'have never seen so bad a case' – and the inadequacy of such treatment of the problem as was available is registered in his observation that they 'hold out no definite hope, and have so far done her no good':

> meanwhile she is in screaming agony, and I fear the exhaustion might just snuff her out.[43]

Eliot had diagnosed himself as a 'neurasthenic', feeling, once more, 'tired and depressed'.[44] He revealed symptoms of 'nerves' to John Quinn, his American patron, noting the combination, again, of physical and psychological distress.[45] Yet Marja Palmer argues that 'concealment had become a habit with Eliot in his private life'.[46] On the contrary – as the letters reveal – he was remarkably frank about his problems, not only to his family and friends but (as in this letter to Quinn) even to professional acquaintances. After several years' association, Eliot still addresses his letter to 'My dear Mr Quinn'.

It was the public image that he cultivated that was to conceal Eliot's private reality – as he confessed in some self-mockery of the 1930s:

> How unpleasant to meet Mr. Eliot!
> With his features of clerical cut,
> And his brow so grim
> And his mouth so prim
> And his conversation, so nicely
> Restricted to What Precisely
> And If and Perhaps and But.[47]

Conrad Aiken, his Harvard friend, referred to Eliot's gradual acquisition of a 'liturgical appearance', expressive of his 'extremely controlled, precise, disciplined' personality.[48] But 'only those,' as Eliot observed in 'Tradition and the Individual Talent' in 1919, 'who have personality and emotions know what it means to want to escape from these things'.[49]

Vivien, who was even more outspoken in her letters, had become suicidal by 1921. Writing to Scofield Thayer, she registered her condition with a clear-sightedness which, in the circumstances, is startling – that her mind had left her and she was becoming insane.[50]

Thayer, editor of *The Dial* from 1919 to 1925, was an appropriate recipient of these disturbing confidences. A psychotic who became Freud's patient, he was certified in 1930, and spent the remaining fifty-two years of his life in confinement.[51]

A month later, Vivien writes to her brother-in-law – 'a bloody angel', as she calls him, with grimly humorous gratitude for his financial generosity to them – apologising for her erratic behaviour ('just like a wild animal') when they farewelled Henry after his English visit. Her record of the mutual accusations over trivialities to which their marriage had lately descended gives a sad insight into the degree of unhappiness of their life together by this stage (reminiscent of the middle section of 'A Game of Chess' in the contemporaneous *Waste Land*). Vivien assesses the result of the years of their marriage with a characteristic emphasis:

> if ever two people made *such* a fearful mess of their obvious possibilities.

The irony of her observation is that in spite of the 'mess', even because of it, Eliot was on the verge of demonstrating to the world the fulfilment of his promise as a poet:

> to her the marriage brought no happiness ... to me, it brought
> the state of mind out of which came *The Waste Land*.[52]

Vivien's letter to Henry closes with a devastating finality, punctuated
with an urgent, underlined imperative explicitly contradicting the
doctrine of 'impersonality' which Eliot had been elaborating in his
contemporary criticism, practising in his poetry, discerning in the
Catholic faith and – perhaps, for his sanity's sake – cultivating in his
personal life:

> Good-bye Henry. And *be personal*, you must be personal,
> or else its [*sic*] no good. Nothing's any good.
>
> Vivien[53]

4

The letters from which quotations have been taken, with their sustained account of physical and psychological suffering, by both Eliot
and Vivien, cover a period of six years. They present a record of
illness and unhappiness which would have broken the spirits, not
to say the marriages, of much hardier people than the Eliots. Their
persistence in their life together – to this point and, indeed, for
another decade, increasingly unhappily – indicates a remarkable determination to endure the trials of their problems. The final failure of
such a commitment would have been concomitantly devastating.

Members of their circle naturally noted the decline. At a dinner at
the Sitwells', Lytton Strachey observed

> Eliot – very sad and seedy – it made one weep.[54]

On 15th October, 1923, Eliot told Bertrand Russell that

> Vivien has had a frightful illness, and nearly died, in the
> spring.[55]

After ten years of marriage, Eliot acknowledged that Russell's early
predictions of disaster had come true; and as he had turned to the
philosopher, before, for sexual help for Vivien, he now asks for psychological counsel for himself:

> I want words from you which only you can give. But if you
> have now ceased to care at all about either of us ... I will
> understand. In case of that, I will tell you now that every-
> thing has turned out as you predicted 10 years ago. You are
> a great psychologist.[56]

A fortnight later, Eliot told Russell that the situation had reached a crisis for which the only solution was separation, for the sanity of both of them:

> her health is a thousand times worse. Her only alternative would be to live alone – if she could. And the fact that living with me has done her so much damage does not help me to come to any decision. I need the help of someone who understands her – I find her still perpetually baffling and deceptive. She seems to me like a child of 6 with an immensely clever and precocious mind.... I can never escape from the spell of her persuasive (even coercive) gift of argument.... I feel quite desperate.[57]

Russell is silent about whether or not he acceded, on this occasion, to Eliot's urgent request for assistance.

What is noteworthy about a marriage in such circumstances is not that its failure had to be eventually admitted, but that it survived for as long as it did. It may not have had even its genesis in passionate love, but the jaded assessments of it that have come to prevail obscure the admirable aspects of the Eliots' achievement of a degree of mutuality. It was only when their psychological and physical suffering had long passed a bearable intensity – by any ordinary standards of cohabitation – that Eliot arranged their separation, through his solicitors, in consultation with Vivien's family and various friends, and after consulting his spiritual counsellors:[58] 'What other way can I find', he wrote in exasperation to Maurice Haigh-Wood, her brother,[59] whose persisting friendship with Eliot, beyond Vivien's death and into Eliot's second marriage, is further evidence against the charges of Eliot's cruelty to Maurice's sister.[60]

We would not acquit Eliot from responsibility for the breakdown of the marriage – in the letters, he registers in considerable detail his own physical and psychological debility, with its negative consequences, not only for himself but for Vivien. But neither should we indict him as the source of their problems. The Eliots' marriage – perhaps like all unhappy marriages – failed because of faults and shortcomings, beyond contemporary medical and psychiatric treatment,[61] which they brought to their marriage and which, instead of being ameliorated by the relationship, were both aggravated by it and mutually aggravating. Writing to Conrad Aiken in 1914, Eliot observed that 'I think now that all my good stuff [in poetry] was done before I had begun to worry – three years ago'. This 'worrying' had begun, in other words, in 1911, four years before he married Vivien.[62]

In a review of Stendhal and Flaubert for *The Athenaeum* in 1919, Eliot could write with appreciation, from his own experience, that:

> they suggest unmistakably the awful separation between pot-
> ential passion, and any actualisation possible in life. They
> indicate also the indestructible barriers between one human
> being and another.[63]

His *via dolorosa* through the wasteland of both his personal life and the social and civilisational anarchy at the period of the 'breaking of nations' and its aftermath was among the most significant of the motivations of his religious commitment. And (if a positive theme can be discerned in this sad story) his solicitude, indeed, for Vivien, over all these years, was an indication of his natural possession of something of that charitable spirit which the Christian faith is supposed to stir in its adherents and which his later care for the invalid, John Hayward, also exemplified. When Vivien died, in January, 1947, Eliot wrote a week later to Mary Trevelyan (in a letter dated for Charles King and Martyr – 30th January) expressing his annoyance that his name was not included in the death notice in the press, and remarks that Vivien's death was a surprise as she had been enjoying good health, in spite of a weak heart. He adds that this accentuated his sense of shock, and he found himself more disintegrated than he could have expected.

5

Slowly emerging, through the 1920s, was Eliot's conviction – born of reactions to his early familial experience and philosophical study, his aesthetic responses and the theorising of them, and a developing historical and theological understanding, in combination with intense personal suffering in the decline of his marriage – that only Catholic Christianity provided the redemptive answer to the overwhelming questions of human existence. This conviction, I have been arguing, should be understood and evaluated (as Eliot said of the 'spiritual pilgrimage' to Anglicanism of his friend, Paul Elmer More) with 'reference to the process by which he arrived at it'.[64]

What Eliot called 'the hatred of life' – which he experienced in these years and which his poetry of the time forcefully expresses (as in 'Gerontion', 1920, for example: 'I that was near your heart was removed therefrom / To lose beauty in terror, terror in inquisition')[65] – became, for him, a kind of 'mystical experience'.[66] Human exis-tence was a painful process which could only be understood in terms of Christian revelation:

we desire and fear both sleep and waking; the day brings relief from the night, and the night brings relief from the day; we go to sleep as to death, and we wake as to damnation. We move, outside of the Christian faith, between the terror of the purely irrational and the horror of the purely rational.[67]

As Denis Donoghue has argued, Christianity appealed to Eliot because it gave meaning and purpose to suffering.[68]

*

It was precisely in Anglo-Catholic contexts that experiences of third parties testify to what the final stages of the Eliots' life together in the early 1930s had been reduced. In 1933, the centenary of the Oxford Movement which initiated the Catholic revival in the Church of England, a great Anglo-Catholic congress was held in London, including meetings at the filled-to-capacity Royal Albert Hall. The literary critic, Grover Smith, was given (in 1954) 'a horrifying *viva voce* description', by Elizabeth Bowen, of her attendance, in Vivien's company, at one of these meetings where Eliot was expected to appear:

Miss Bowen told me of Vivienne's jealousies and harpy-like tenacity, of her pinched, ravaged features and the stupefying fumes of ether which often enveloped her. She also recalled the day on which, having left his wife, Eliot was due back in London from America [where he had delivered the Page-Barbour Lectures at the University of Virginia]. Vivienne insisted on Elizabeth's accompanying her to the Albert Hall, where Eliot was expected to attend some great Church of England 'rally'. There, in the gallery, the two women sat while bishops and other clergy filed in, far below; and Elizabeth, seeing Vivienne begin to tense herself and draw in her breath, realized that her hysterical threat on their taxi journey, to 'let out a piercing scream' the moment Eliot walked onto the platform, was about to be carried out. Happily for the peace of that convocation, he failed to appear.[69]

In 1930, Robert Sencourt had stayed with the Eliots at their home, 68 Clarence Gate Gardens. He writes of Vivien, at the time, that she

seems to have been positively hostile to his new-found church affiliations, deriding them as 'monastic'.... She was developing a tendency to find fault with everything, both in herself and in those around her. She did not join in his worship.[70]

And she had not attended either his baptism or confirmation.[71]

Chapter Four

Anglo-Catholicism
'entre deux guerres'
(1918-1939)

> The Church of England has always regarded itself, as have
> the Eastern Churches, as a living member of one visible
> Church: it does not concede that it was founded (in the
> sense in which a local church has had a human founder) by
> Henry VIII, or by the Regents of Edward VI, or by Queen
> Elizabeth, but holds itself to derive from Augustine.
>
> (Eliot, *Reunion by Destruction*, 1943)[1]

Eliot's Anglo-Catholicism, formed and fashioned in 'the years of
l'entre deux guerres',[2] was focused on a trinity of values: aesthetic,
historical and spiritual. The movement, at large, attempted to recall the
modern English Church to its ancient, pre-Reformation origins and its
persisting Catholic character and heritage, through the Reformation
period to the present. Anglo-Catholics concede that Protestants within
the Church of England, vehemently opposed to Catholic doctrines,
ceremonial and spiritual practices and the nomenclature that goes
with them, and under the influence of European Reformed theology,
took advantage of the sixteenth-century political rupture between
England and Rome. They attempted to modify or even eradicate the
entire Catholic character of the English Church:

> Calvin, from his pontifical throne in Geneva, directed this
> mostly motley crew of foreigners, bullied Cranmer, and
> sought to impose their views on the English nation.[3]

But Anglo-Catholics insist that in spite of serious incursions into its
official documents and customs, the essential Catholic character of
Anglicanism remained unimpaired and (especially they argue, in this
regard) The Book of Common Prayer (although produced in the heat
of so-called Reformation in England, by Cranmer himself) stands as
testimony to the Church's determination to preserve the necessary
elements of Catholic faith and practice rather than dispose of them:

> The Prayer-book is absolutely Catholic. Not only is it mainly
> a translation from the old pre-Reformation service books but
> it does not contain a prayer or a service in which a Catholic
> from any part of Christendom could not take part ... it is int-
> rinsically and essentially Catholic. It teaches the great central
> truths which mark out Catholicism from sectarianism – the
> sacramental system, Baptismal Regeneration, Confession
> and Absolution, the Real Presence, Apostolical Succession.[4]

In the earlier days of the Catholic Revival, in the nineteenth century,
The Book of Common Prayer (later to be repudiated by 'advanced'
Anglo-Catholics) was seen as a resource of Catholic teaching and pra-
ctice that had been insufficiently appreciated, containing ordinances
and liturgical requirements (the Daily Offices of Morning and Evening
Prayer, for example, and frequent celebration of the Eucharist),[5] of
Catholic provenance, which had fallen into desuetude.

As Sheila Kaye-Smith affirmed, in 1925, two years before Eliot's
embrace of these principles,

> Anglo-Catholics believe that whatever the abuses, difficulties
> and failures of the Church of England, she is nevertheless the
> Catholic Church in this country, and to her alone [in England]
> belong the keys of heaven and the divine commission to feed
> and teach Christ's flock.[6]

And this was a view that was held by many who would not have
explicitly identified themselves with Anglo-Catholicism. Cyril Foster
Garbett, Archbishop of York in the mid-twentieth century and who
had earlier brought Anglo-Catholics in Southwark to heel, taught
that

> The Church of England is the historic Catholic Church of
> this land, and its religion is that of the 'holy Catholic Church'
> in which its members proclaim their belief whenever they
> say the Creeds.[7]

In opposition to the popular notion within Anglicanism (and the
official Roman Catholic teaching, to this day) that the Church of
England was 'established' at the Reformation, Anglo-Catholics have
always decisively denied the creation of a new English Church at
that time and, indeed, are bound to do so, if their claims are to have
any validity:

> People seem to think that Henry VIII, or Edward VI, or
> Elizabeth, having perhaps 'disestablished' an older Church,

went on next, of set purpose, to 'establish' a new one....
But as a matter of history and as a matter of law, nothing
of the kind ever happened; it is certain no ruler, no English
Parliament, thought of setting up a new Church, but simply
of reforming the existing English Church. Nothing was
further from the mind of Henry VIII or of Elizabeth than
the thought that either of them was doing anything new....
Henry and Elizabeth had no more thought of establishing a
new Church than they had of founding a new nation.[8]

This had been a core teaching from the beginning of the Catholic
Revival:

The facts of history compel us to assume, the absolute identity of the Church of England after the Reformation with the
Church of England before the Reformation.... No act was
done by which legal and historical continuity was broken....
There was no one particular moment called the Reformation
at which the State of England determined to take property
from one Church or set of people and to give it to another.[9]

In the nineteenth century, the leading Tractarian, Edward Pusey,
saw Anglican bishops as part of the succession that, so far from being
initiated in the sixteenth century, was like 'a golden chain' which, 'link
by link', could be traced back to the Apostles, 'with whom and with
their successors Christ promised to be always'.[10] It is 'impossible to
insist too strongly upon the matter of Apostolical Succession', writes
Manning-Foster in *Anglo-Catholicism,*

since the whole theory of the Catholic Church rests upon it,
and no sacrament can be valid unless it is administered by a
validly ordained ministry.[11]

Tractarianism, Geoffrey Rowell has observed, along with the contemporary Ultramontane movement in Roman Catholicism, 'both sought
to re-affirm apostolic authority within their respective churches'.[12]

The doctrine of Apostolic Succession and its preservation in Anglicanism led to the 'Branch Theory' of the nature of the global
Catholic Church – that in the English 'branch', a valid succession
of episcopal ordination had been maintained. This, too, had been
formulated by the theologians of the Oxford Movement who, while
refusing allegiance to Rome,

maintained that the Catholic Church consisted of three great
bodies separated from one another: the Eastern Church,

the Roman Church, and the Anglican Church. The Church
of England was simply the Catholic Church in England.
Roman Catholics were schismatics in England.[13]

Keble and Newman both regarded the Church of England as 'the
Catholic Church in England'.[14]

These deeply regrettable separations had occurred at the great
schism between East and West in 1054 and within Western Christianity at the time of the Reformation in the sixteenth century. But
the three branches sprang from the common root of apostolic
Christianity. Its belonging to Catholicism at large, Anglo-Catholics
taught, was

> the one valid claim on our allegiance that the Church of
> England possesses.... that it is part of the One Holy Catholic
> and Apostolic Church. If it is not that it is nothing.[15]

The Church of England acknowledges the three great creeds and the
four general (or ecumenical) councils of the early Church, as Jeremy
Taylor affirmed:

> The Church of England receives the four first Generals [that
> is, General Councils] as of highest regard not that they are
> infallible, but that they have determined wisely and holily.[16]

The revival of these confronting principles in the Church of England
in the nineteenth century was linked to earlier manifestations of
scholarly Catholic thought and spirituality in the English Church
(principally, in the seventeenth century and especially that devoted
to patristic learning) by the extensive scholarly project, *The Library
of Anglo-Catholic Theology*, the several volumes of which began to
appear in the 1840s (the first volume containing ninety-six sermons
by Lancelot Andrewes). This gave wide currency (from the later
nineteenth century onwards) to the phrase, 'Anglo-Catholic'.

Ollard's study, *The Anglo-Catholic Revival* (also published, like
Kaye-Smith's account, in 1925), gives abundant evidence of the
traditions of Anglo-Catholicism, dating from the early seventeenth
century: Archbishop Laud (1573-1645), Ollard writes, was a 'life-long
Anglo-Catholic'[17] and, in the eighteenth century, less convincingly,
he claims Dr Johnson for the movement.[18] Nonetheless, the term itself
and much of the character of the Catholic revival in the Church of
England were the products of developments in the nineteenth century
when Anglo-Catholic thought and practice, following its limited and
unsustained impact in earlier periods of the post-Reformation Church

of England, began to exercise a much more extensive and enduring influence on the parish clergy and laity.[19] Ollard sees the recovery of the religious life in England (one of the most important contributions of the Anglo-Catholic movement) beginning at the Huntingdonshire hamlet of Little Gidding under the Ferrars in the 1620s,[20] but the quasi-monastic devotional worship there, mixed with the domestic regime of the families involved, bears little resemblance to the institutional communities of celibate 'religious', under vows, established in the later nineteenth century which took their inspiration, rather, from the orders of the wider Western Church.[21]

Yet many Anglicans, and certainly most Englishmen and women, regarded Anglo-Catholicism with the age-old (indeed, even pre-Reformation) suspicion they brought to papal Roman Catholicism, towards which Anglo-Catholicism was seen, understandably, to be leading the Established Church. This prejudice was aggravated in the middle of the nineteenth century, at the very time of the movement getting into its stride, by the Pope's restoration of the Roman Catholic hierarchy in England in 1850, under Cardinal Wiseman. This was widely regarded as an example of papal aggression. Protestants and even less partisan Anglicans sensed that their nation was being engulfed by various varieties of popery, and, if anything, Anglo-Catholicism was more insidious, being the enemy within. The founding of various Catholic societies in the Church of England in the second half of the nineteenth century seemed to indicate a determined campaign to Romanise Anglicanism. To those ready to have their fears and prejudices stirred up and reinforced, it mattered little that the societies' inspiration was the mediaeval English Church rather than the contemporary Roman one. Their very titles smacked of people's ideas of Rome: the Confraternity of the Blessed Sacrament (1862), the Guild of All Souls (1873) – to pray and offer Masses for the faithful departed – and several Marian societies: the Confraternity of the Children of Mary (1880), the Union of the Holy Rosary (1886) and the League of Our Lady (1904).

When the parliamentary Public Worship Regulation Act of 1874 conspicuously failed to stem the Catholic tide in the Church of England (and unintentionally turned Anglo-Catholic parish priests into martyrs when they were imprisoned for flouting it), direct action groups entered the battle. These included John Kensit's Protestant Truth Society (parodying the Catholic Truth Society) and Lady Wimbourne's League for the Defence of the Reformed Faith of the Church of England. Walter Walsh's *Secret History of the Oxford Movement* (recounting the devious activities of 'men who work in the dark to destroy the Protestantism of the Church and Nation'[22]) went through five editions between 1897 and 1899.

Parliament had tried, again, to resolve the disputes over ritual by establishing, in 1904, a Royal Commission on Ecclesiastical Discipline, but its conclusion, in 1906, was that 'the law of public worship in the Church of England is too narrow for the religious life of the present generation'. In other words, the provisions of The Book of Common Prayer (or, at least, the way in which they were customarily used) were inadequate for the modern age. Effectively, this gave a mandate to the ongoing Anglo-Catholicising of the Church of England.[23]

Moreover, Anglo-Catholicism was not only regarded as 'un-english' but 'unmanly', as David Hilliard has argued, pointing out the correlation in the popular imagination, which remains to this day (not without justification), between 'male homosexuality and Anglo-Catholic religion'.[24] The idea of an unmarried parish-priesthood was unfamiliar in Anglicanism, prior to nineteenth-century Anglo-Catholicism, and although being unmarried did not necessarily imply that a priest was homosexual, it certainly did nothing to dispel suspicions that he might be. Such considerations were significant in the aftermath of Oscar Wilde's scandalous trial which 'did untold damage', stirring up speculation of homosexual leanings with regard to any mature, single man (especially if his professional domain, such as the Anglo-Catholic sanctuary, was sensitive to beauty).[25] Cartoons (in periodicals such as *Punch*) caricatured Anglo-Catholic priests in the mode of 1890s aesthetes, with flowing hair parted down the middle, *à la* Oscar, gesturing extravagantly, in ornate sanctuaries, attended by effeminate-looking servers, while John Bull stood apart in an attitude of outraged macho disdain. Not all Anglo-Catholic priests were unmarried, but an Anglo-Catholic priest who had 'committed matrimony', as the satirical phrase went, was an increasingly remarkable phenomenon. Certainly, nearly all of those with whom Eliot came to have close associations were unmarried and, of course, priests whom he knew in religious life were all single. Anglo-Catholic clergy-houses, such as that at St Stephen's, Gloucester Road, where Eliot lived for several years, were celibate establishments bearing strong similarities to male religious communities. Many Anglo-Catholic laymen, like most of their priests, were also unmarried. 'Beware of the Anglo-Catholics', Charles Ryder's monitory cousin, Jasper, tells him in his early days at Oxford, in Waugh's *Brideshead Revisited* (set in the very period of Eliot's conversion), 'they're all sodomites with unpleasant accents'.[26]

An 'Anglican clergyman' visiting Aelred Carlyle's Anglo-Catholic monastic foundation on Caldey Island felt it was necessary to point out that the monks were not 'weak and degenerate beings, but strong, fine, healthy, manly specimens'.[27]

It has long been assumed that Anglo-Catholicism is 'attractive to those of homosexual inclinations':[28]

> The ritual and ceremony in Anglo-Catholicism gives them opportunities which are emotionally attractive. Something of the female dress, or certainly male dress of an exotic kind, is to be seen in eucharistic vestments, lace cottas, cassocks, especially those which fit tightly to the body, buckled shoes, the wearing of medals and crosses, birettas, to name but a few. All of these can have a 'sexual' thing for both priests and servers.... It is not only dressing up but acting itself which appeals to a large number of homosexuals.... The acting out of religion in ritual has its obvious attractions.... Moving around the sanctuary, standing at the high altar, using a censer, carrying candles, taking part in processions of the Blessed Sacrament, all give the impression of being on the stage, of being in a play, of performing before an audience. It applies to servers and priests alike.[29]

Powerful in this appeal to scarcely-repressed homoeroticism was the fact that the sanctuary, where the ritual was mainly enacted, was an exclusively male domain. It was not only that homosexuals who were so inclined could satisfy their aesthetic and theatrical bents in the rich liturgical celebrations, but – unlike the theatre – it was an all-male affair, whether in the clergy-house, or in church itself. More profoundly, in a society such as Britain's, prior to the sexual revolution and the decriminalising of homosexual acts, the Anglo-Catholic sanctuary, as well as the affiliated societies and organisations which the movement inspired, could provide an entire social life (and, no doubt for some, opportunities for sexual satisfaction) amongst like-minded men, while being engaged in what could hardly be a reproved activity – the worship of Almighty God – from being a pre-pubescent boat-boy with the incense-boat to being a master of ceremonies, directing the entire ceremonial regime, in authoritative maturity. No one would suggest that all Anglo-Catholic priests and servers were homosexual or, even if that was their inclination, that they were acting upon it, or, worse still, that their reason for devotion to the Church and its liturgy was simply the opportunity Anglo-Catholicism seemed to afford for homosexual contact. But it is undeniable that elements of these matters are much more likely to be found in Anglo-Catholicism (and Roman Catholicism) than in any other branch of the Christian Church. One of the sub-themes of Rose Macaulay's Anglo-Catholic novel, *The Towers of Trebizond*, is the troubled relationship (which, as the details are hinted at but not spelt out, makes it more obviously *verboten*) between the artistic characters Charles and David who, while not Anglo-Catholics themselves, contribute that expected ingredient to the generally Anglo-Catholic atmosphere.

The 'camp' aspects of Anglo-Catholicism are also closely associated with another of its features which those for whom it is unsympathetic find puzzling or (if they are earnest Christians themselves) a focus of criticism. This is the value which Anglo-Catholics, often very devout and serious in their practice and study of their faith, place on humour and the sense of the ridiculous in religion and religious persons. Certainly, Eliot was spiritually ascetic and customarily dour of temperament, but, equally, as has been well-attested, he had a keen sense of humour, including the bawdy, and, especially as his fame blossomed and brought its material rewards, he learnt to enjoy the pleasant indulgences of life. As Alec Guinness recalled, Eliot had a finely developed 'love of the good things of this world' – such as 'enormous dry martinis' – for all the 'austerity' of his faith.[30] Such apparently contradictory traits would have been effortlessly accommodated in Anglo-Catholic circles as, perhaps, in no other religious environment.

The aptly-entitled *Merrily on High* is one of the best-known accounts of mid-twentieth-century Anglo-Catholicism in the form of the autobiography of its priest-author, Colin Stephenson, who succeeded Hope Patten as vicar of Walsingham and administrator of the shrine of Our Lady.[31] The phrase, from the jolly Christmas carol, 'Ding-dong merrily on high', captures both Stephenson's own buoyant personality and love of a good story, and the *joie de vivre* of confident Anglo-Catholicism in its heyday. Such light-heartedness could be indulged without impinging upon the serious matters of faith and devotion, part of the explanation of the role of humour in Catholic life, at large, being the very serious matter of the recognition that human existence on earth is a kind of nonsense. For Evelyn Waugh, Baron Alder writes,

> Humans were exiles on earth for whom life would always seem absurd. There was nothing for them to do but laugh.[32]

It was said of Bishop Frank Weston (an Anglo-Catholic hero, of whom more, below) that there was, on his face, 'a smile on the point of breaking with laughter that I find in all who really understand and practise that essentially happy creed, the Catholic Faith'.[33]

1

The Catholic Revival, which had stirred such interest and controversy well beyond ecclesiastical circles, had taken its immediate source and inspiration from the generation succeeding the scholarly Oxford Movement of the earlier decades of the nineteenth century. Its beginning is usually dated from John Keble's assize sermon on 'national apostasy', preached before the University of Oxford on 14th July, 1833, and which was a protest against the suppression of ten Irish bishoprics. At that embryonic stage of the revival, its proponents were known as the 'Apostolics'[34] because of their attention to the early ('apostolic') period of the Church and their devotion to the doctrine of the Apostolic Succession, the unbroken continuation, through the centuries, of Jesus' original commissioning of the apostles to lead his Church.

Keble cooperated with his friend, John Henry Newman (who, like him, was a Fellow of Oriel College), and many others, in the composition and dissemination of the numerous *Tracts for the Times*, recalling Anglican clergy to the Catholic character of their Church. In the next generation, priests coming under the influence of these teachings took the theological principles of the Tractarians (as they had, by then, become known) regarding, preeminently, the doctrine of the Incarnation – of the Word being made flesh and dwelling amongst humanity – to where humanity, at large, was to be found: in the parishes of the great industrial cities which were burgeoning in the Victorian age and which presented a host of challenges, evangelical, spiritual and socio-political, for a Church which, all agreed, was woefully ill-equipped to meet them.

The doctrinal foundations having been firmly laid, their ritual elaboration could follow (not as an incidental, arbitrary adornment, but as their necessary, outward and visible expression). Catholic theology about the character of the Church, its clergy and its sacraments was made manifest not only in preaching and writing about these matters, but in attention to the fabric and decoration of churches and cathedrals and, most strikingly, to slowly but surely returning the celebration of the Eucharist, which had been marginalised and neglected for centuries, to where it rightly belonged, at the centre of liturgical life. Church building, in the Gothic style, expressed both the nineteenth-century Romantic fascination with the original 'Romance' period of the later Middle Ages, but also – very pertinently, for Anglo-Catholics – the inspiration deriving from the mediaeval (pre-Reformation) period of Church history, the great 'Age of Faith', expressed in all its glory in the splendid cathedrals of England and Europe.

The neglect of the Mass in English Church life was notorious: in 1810, there were only three communicants on Easter Day in St Paul's Cathedral itself.[35] But even seventy years on, when, in the 1880s, the priest Peter Tindall was appointed vicar of the parish church of Ashford in Kent – which was regarded as an 'important living' and certainly not an obscure backwater – both church and parish were still 'sunk in the depths of protestantism':

> its only altar was an uncovered wooden table; beneath it, a dust-covered wine-bottle into which was poured back after evening communion what was left in the chalice.

Tindall set about transforming the place, in a process that was occurring across the country and, indeed, the Anglican world. He acquired brass candlesticks and a large brass altar-cross. In time,

> the chief Sunday service was a Sung Eucharist, with a large congregation and a devout and well-trained choir. The Eucharist was said daily.

He was reputed to 'hear more confessions than any other priest in East Kent'. It was not until his successor, however, that eucharistic vestments were introduced.[36]

The advances Anglo-Catholicism made during the later nineteenth and early twentieth centuries are astonishing, particularly when we remember the state of impoverishment of the Church's worship and witness which the movement encountered and the febrile resistance to its proposals:

> In 1854 a daily service was held in only 650 churches in England, whereas in 1919 Matins and Evensong were read daily in 5,427 churches. In 1854 there was a weekly Mass only in 128 churches, the others contenting themselves with one a month or even one a quarter; in 1919 the Mass was offered weekly in 11,842 churches, while the offering of the daily Mass has risen from three churches in 1854 to 1,215 in 1919.[37]

Membership of the Church Union, which represented organised Anglo-Catholic interests, grew from 23,000 in 1865 to 40,000 by the turn of the century.[38] Colin Buchanan, from the Evangelical tradition, notes that the Anglo-Catholic movement 'had a revolutionary effect' on and was an 'astonishing force within the Church of England'.[39] Kaye-Smith observes (in 1925) that

> if one of the early Tractarians … could return and see the
> English Church to-day, it would appear to him almost as if
> a miracle had happened…. the leaven has penetrated to the
> outermost edge of the lump.[40]

Indeed, the statistic that they would have found most striking and
important is the increase in the frequency of the celebration of Mass.
This testifies to the influence of the Anglo-Catholic emphasis on the
sacramental system at large, deriving ultimately from the movement's
concentration on the doctrine of the Incarnation.

Pontifical High Mass was celebrated at the White City Stadium
in 1933 to commemorate the centenary of the Oxford Movement.
There was a congregation of fifty thousand people.[41] Colin Buchanan
notes that

> hundreds, if not thousands of parishes, went over to candles
> and wafers [for Holy Communion, as in the Roman Church]
> and eastward position [at the altar, also in Roman Catholic
> style, for the celebration of Mass] between 1900 and 1940.[42]

Anglo-Catholics regarded the Protestant preoccupation with the Atonement (Christ's saving work on the Cross) as a failure to appreciate the
entirety of the redemptive mystery initiated by the Incarnation. From
this followed the Protestant neglect of the eucharist, the sacramental
expression and extension of the truth of the doctrine of the Word made
flesh. For the Tractarians, indeed, the Incarnation was 'the central and
all-important doctrine, from which the Atonement drew its value and
significance'.[43] 'Until God Himself was made manifest in the flesh',
John Keble reflected in Tract 89, revelation had been the preserve
of poetry.[44] The reciprocity of Incarnation (the eternal moment in
time) and Atonement ('the Passion and Sacrifice') is expressed by
Eliot in the pageant play, *The Rock* (1934), in a repetitive, incantatory
language reminiscent of Lancelot Andrewes' sermons:

> Then came, at a predetermined moment, a moment in
>   time and of time,
> A moment not out of time, but in time, in what we call
>   history:
> transecting, bisecting the world of time, a moment in
>   time but not like a moment of time,
> A moment in time but time was made through that
>   moment:
>   for without the meaning there is no time, and that
>   moment of time gave the meaning.

*Anglo-Catholic rally in honour of the
centenary of the Oxford Movement, 1933*

> Then it seemed as if men must proceed from light to
>   light,
>   in the light of the Word,
> Through the Passion and Sacrifice saved in spite of
>   their negative being.[45]

Elizabeth Drew points out that the 'bedded axle-tree' in Eliot's 'Burnt Norton' similarly draws together the Incarnation and the Atonement by reminding us, in one phrase, of Bethlehem's crib and Calvary's 'wrath-bearing tree' (as Eliot calls it in 'Gerontion').[46]

The Incarnation, celebrating God's visitation of the earth, also presented a rebuttal of the Puritan-Protestant spurning of the created order, of the works of fallen men's hands and of the beauty of the physical and sensual world. The Anglo-Catholic adornment of churches, the nurturing of solemn ceremony, gorgeous vestments for the sacred ministers and glorious music – stirring the sense of the numinous in liturgy and in the lives that were to be inspired by it – were revelations of the doctrine of the Incarnate Word, of God with us. Rose Macaulay's Anglo-Catholic narrator writes, rhapsodically, that

> I would go to High Mass in some church or other, and
> the Christian Church would build itself up before me and
> round me, with its structure of liturgical words and music,

which was like fine architecture being reared up into the
sky, while the priests moved to and fro before the altar in
their glittering coloured robes and crosses, and the rows of
tall candles lifted their flames like yellow tulips, and the
incense flowed about us. Here was the structure, I would
think, in which the kingdom was enshrined, or whose doors
opened on the kingdom.[47]

Central to this recovery of a 'high' idea of the liturgical and sacramental life of the Church of England was the Catholic conception
of the priesthood, priests being ordained (as The Ordinal in The
Book of Common Prayer declared) to administer and celebrate the
sacraments, as well as to preach the Word. They were also ordained
to absolve sinners. The connection between a zeal for the recovery of
the Mass and the encouragement of auricular (or private, sacramental)
confession amongst their people were dual hallmarks of an Anglo-
Catholic priest and parish. The Tractarian idea, Geoffrey Rowell
has written, was that 'valid sacraments and apostolic ministry went
together … were of the *esse* of the church'.[48]

Virtually every parish church throughout the Anglican Communion, in one way or another, reflected (and reflects) aspects of
innovations which, when they were introduced, were considered
'popish' and smacking of abhorrent Jesuitry. It is hardly surprising
that these daring innovations were so conspicuous, given that most
services in the Church of England, prior to the movement's impact,
were conducted in quasi-Protestant 'dreariness, sluttishness and irrev-
erence'.[49] Yet it is now difficult to recapture the challenging impact
of the Revival's radical proposals and to credit that the ritual and
other innovations could stir such heated and sustained controversies,
for decades. When the privately-printed manual advising Anglican
confessors about the sacrament of penance, *The Priest in Absolution*
(by John Chambers of the Society of the Holy Cross) was published
in 1877, there was 'a hurricane of scandalized protest'.[50] The
Evangelical Dean of Ripon, Hugh McNeile, urged that the hearing
of confessions should be a capital offence.[51] Yet, by the 1920s, many
English diocesan bishops required sacramental confession of their
ordination candidates.[52] Nonetheless, as David Gregg has argued, the
'confessional has remained a particularity of anglo-catholicism' and

the emergence of the practice owed much to the fashion of
imitating Rome, and its establishment among the Tractarians
must go down as yet another 'romantic' revival of a basically
medieval innovation.[53]

Eliot's recourse to the sacrament of penance, which we will consider in detail in the next chapter, is perhaps the feature of his faith which most decisively marks him as an Anglo-Catholic.

Anglo-Catholic sacramental and liturgical novelties (as they were seen to be by critics) included the priest wearing the surplice when preaching (when he was expected to remove it and to put on the black preaching gown before ascending the pulpit); frontals and flowers on altars and two candles lit thereon at service; bowing of the head at the Holy Name and in acknowledgement of the altar; eagle lecterns; the sign of the cross; mixing a little water with wine at the communion; weekday communion services; the use of the stole and eucharistic vestments, and the singing of portions of the liturgy (such as the Versicles and Responses at Morning and Evening Prayer). All of these came to be usual, increasingly, in thousands of parish churches and virtually all Anglican cathedrals (setting the standards for diocesan liturgical worship) in the course of the twentieth century, although most of the bishops and clergy who used (and use) them would not regard themselves as explicitly Anglo-Catholic in doctrine or ceremonial and many, indeed, would repudiate the label while pursuing the ritual and other advances which the movement secured. Even Evangelicals, at the furthest distance from the Revival, and very critical of it, were celebrating the Holy Communion weekly by the 1920s, and no longer resisted wearing the surplice in the pulpit, a custom which had been widely regarded in the nineteenth century as a sure badge of dreaded Rome.

2

When Eliot became an Anglo-Catholic, a third generation had passed, from the days of the founding of the movement, and of the work and witness of an inspirational company of famous priests, especially in London, who had acquired legendary status for their combination of Catholic faith and spirituality and heroic achievements amongst the most disadvantaged of the metropolis' poor, especially in the East End and in other impoverished and often very dangerous parochial areas. The famous priests of the slums, such as Lowder, Mackonochie, Stanton and Dolling, were all much-admired 'shepherds of souls',[54] their gospel of the poor being advanced in their parishes while they similarly made progress there liturgically. By 1866, at St Alban's Holborn, Alexander Mackonochie had established six points of ceremonial: the use of the eastward position at the celebration of Mass, the mixed chalice of water with wine at the Holy Communion, unleavened bread, altar lights, eucharistic vestments and incense.[55]

More surprisingly, Anglo-Catholic priests had also transformed the religious life of many villages and market towns (where there was only the one church and the people either had to accept Anglo-Catholicism, or worship, as Anglicans, in another community, or – as no doubt happened in some cases – give up religion altogether). While Anglo-Catholicism rarely impregnated suburbia successfully,[56] there is a roll-call of famous priests and parishes in towns and villages in the inter-war years: for example, Alfred Hope Patten at Walsingham (Norfolk); Bernard Walke at St Hilary (Cornwall) – where the stone high altar enclosed the relics of St Rose of Lima – and Alban Baverstock at Hinton Martel (Dorset), who, similarly, had transformed his parish church into a replica of a village church in Catholic Europe.[57] Perhaps the most famous, apart from Hope Patten's Walsingham (established in the 1920s and a later appeal for which, in 1957, included Eliot amongst its supporters)[58] was Conrad Noel's parish church at Thaxted, in the Diocese of Chelmsford, where elements of Roman Catholicism were combined with neo-mediaevalism and extreme socialism.[59] In 1918, placing an advertisement for a curate in *The Church Times* (the newspaper of the High Church and Anglo-Catholic parties), Noel asked for 'healthy active revolutionary, good singing voice'.[60] The Anglo-Catholic ideal that the clergy of the Church of England should be seen 'as professionals, rather than as part of the village squirearchy'[61] must have been much more obvious and challenging in supposedly conservative rural areas, such as these, than in the cities. So, in a sense, the gains that were made in provincial and country places were more remarkable than those in London, particularly when it is remembered that the long episcopate there (1901-39) of 'Uncle Arthur' Winnington-Ingram was indulgent of them or, at least, ineffective in the attempts to bring them to heel. In 'A Lincolnshire Church', published in 1948, but written a few years earlier, John Betjeman describes the interior of this remote bastion of Anglo-Catholicism:

> The door swung easily open
> (Unlocked, for these parts, is odd)
> And there on the south aisle altar
> Is the tabernacle of God.
> There where the white light flickers

> By the white and silver veil
> A wafer dipped in a wind-drop
> Is the presence the angels hail....
> There where the white light flickers
> Our Creator is with us yet,
> To be worshipped by you and the woman
> Of the slacks and the cigarette....
> The great door shuts, and lessens
> That roar of churchyard trees
> And the presence of God Incarnate
> Has brought me to my knees.[62]

What is distinctively Anglo-Catholic here is that even the poem's very observant church-visitor concentrates solely on the Real Presence and its representation of the Incarnation. Nothing else, in comparison, matters or is registered.

Usually outside London, also, were the religious communities for men and women living under vows and pursuing the full round of Catholic liturgical and spiritual life, less inhibited by episcopal authority and Protestant agitation by and amongst the laity in parishes. Arguably, these foundations were the most notable centres of the Catholic movement in the Church of England, reversing the Reformation's dissolution of the monasteries. A list given by Peter Anson, in his story of one of the most remarkable founders of a community for men in the Church of England, Abbot Aelred Carlyle (1874-1955), shows the extraordinary flourishing of the religious life in the latter half of the nineteenth century. Fourteen communities were established between 1842 and 1894.[63] There were, for example, by 1925, more women under religious vows in sisterhoods founded during the Revival than there were at the time of the Henrician dissolution.[64] The development of the religious life had not been foreseen by the fathers of the Oxford Movement, and John Keble wrote some lines critical of such retirement from 'the world', echoing the very vocabulary of the Puritan Milton's critique of a 'fugitive and cloistered virtue':

> We need not bid for cloistered cell
> Our neighbour and our friend farewell....[65]

As the different founders and subsequent superiors (inevitably, strong personalities) of these institutions placed their stamp on the various communities, they developed a variety of churchmanship, along broad Catholic lines. Some were more Anglo-Catholic than others. The Community of the Resurrection at Mirfield, for example, evolved (in the inter-war period) into a distinctly Roman-like organisation, a trend that was advanced further under its controversial Superior, Raymond Raynes, who led it from 1943 to 1958.[66] A community with which Eliot had much to do, the Society of the Sacred Mission at Kelham, was less interested in fidelity to Roman ways and its best-known member, Fr Gabriel Hebert, criticised the non-communicating High Mass beloved of the most extreme Anglo-Catholics.[67]

The concentration of Anglo-Catholic work and witness, however, was in London. Rose Macaulay's Fr Chantry-Pigg, requiring assurance that Dr Halide was 'a fully Catholic Anglican', is told that, when in London, she had attended 'such as'

> All Saints Margaret Street, St. Mary's Grarm Street [an old Anglo-Catholic joke: 'Graham Street' made to rhyme with 'Farm Street', Mayfair, where the Jesuits' most fashionable church was located and always referred to by its address; the address of St Mary's has been changed to Bourne Street, so the joke has been spoiled], St. Stephen's Gloucester Road, St. Augustine's Kilburn ... the Annunciation Bryanston Street.[68]

Chantry-Pigg, being Anglo-Papalist, is not re-assured: 'All Saints Margaret Street seemed to him practically Kensitite', recalling the Protestant agitator John Kensit (1853-1902), hammer of the ritualists, and his followers, who regularly attempted to break up Anglo-Catholic liturgies.[69] We note the inclusion of Eliot's church, St Stephen's, Gloucester Road, in the familiar catalogue.

The following pen portrait of Marcus Atlay, vicar of St Matthew's Westminster from 1914, describes a priest typical of the third generation of the movement and of Anglo-Catholic churchmanship of the first quarter of the twentieth century:

> the dignified and reverent manner in which he said Mass; his uncompromising devotion to the Blessed Sacrament and our Lady; his arresting and dominating figure in the pulpit ... his wise counsel on the hearing of confessions; his evangelical insistence on the duty of parish priests to visit their people; his charming way with men and children; his great kindness to the old and ailing, the sick and dying; his unfailing sense of humour.[70]

In a different part of the metropolis, but also in this tradition, was John Groser, vicar of Stepney (1929-47), who played Thomas in the 1951 film of *Murder in the Cathedral*. He was a Christian socialist and made Christ Church, Watney Street,

a centre to which many notable persons in the political, artistic, and religious life of the day resorted – Herbert Read,
Aneurin Bevan, C.S. Lewis, T.S. Eliot, R.H. Tawney, and
many future Labour leaders....

Groser's radical politics were remembered in an obituary in *The
Church Times*:

This cassocked, handsome priest, with socialist views and a
monkish appearance, was a natural people's leader for protest meetings, demonstrations against high rents, opposition
to Fascist marches, and the rest of the radical activities of
that grim era. Groser understood the spiritual value of revolt.
'Those who live among the very poor', he said, 'are glad
when they show signs of revolt, a spark of resistance. It
shows that they have not completely lost their manhood.
Atheist Russia is a criticism of ourselves. I believe that the
religion of incarnation seriously worked out in a new social
order is the only salvation'.[71]

Groser, like his clerical forebears in the East End, was the committed
member of a religious movement that had larger concerns than the
minutiae of ritual.

The London church to which Eliot belonged from the early years
of his Anglo-Catholic life, St Stephen's, Gloucester Road, was in
fashionable Kensington and remains an Anglo-Catholic shrine to this
day. It had been identified, in the years just prior to Eliot becoming a
parishioner there, as one of a nucleus of 'hard-line' Anglo-Catholic
parishes in the Diocese of London under its vicar, Lord Victor Seymour
(1859-1935), who was the incumbent from 1900 to 1929.[72] This notoriety persisted under the vicar of Eliot's time, Father Eric Cheetham
(1929-1956). The Blessed Sacrament was reserved continuously in the
church (one of the marks of a definite Anglo-Catholic parish). Bishop
Winnington-Ingram, half-heartedly attempting to impose some discipline on the liturgical chaos of his vast Diocese with regard to practices
such as this (and customs such as adoration of the Reserved Sacrament
which developed from it), wrote to the vicars of some 170 churches
in 1928, attempting to regulate reservation. A group known as 'The
Twenty One' organised themselves in opposition. Most of them were
from impoverished areas in the East End, but Lord Victor Seymour,
along with four others from the West End, also subscribed to resist
Winnington-Ingram's regulations that reservation should only occur
for the communion of the sick and in a place not behind or above the

altar.[73] Essentially, these rules were to prevent adoration of the reserved Elements and, particularly, the service of Benediction during which the Host was removed from the tabernacle, placed in a monstrance, raised up to bless the people and adored; or – worst of all – processions on the feast of Corpus Christi (specifically celebrating the eucharistic mystery), when it was taken outside, under a canopy, and triumphantly exposed in the open streets.[74] In defiance, the Twenty-One put forward the characteristic Anglo-Catholic argument that the Church of England was not autonomous but part of the wider Catholic Church (where what they were doing was the usual, taken-for-granted custom).[75] Typically, the bishop's disciplinary program achieved nothing (his statement that 'in London there was no disobedience, but that was only because there were no rules to obey',[76] indicates how committed he was to bringing his numerous Anglo-Catholic priests into line and as they called him 'Uncle Arthur' it would seem that they had taken his benign measure very well).[77] Eliot began worshipping in a church where 'full Catholic privileges', as the phrase went, were already securely in place.

As John Fenwick has pointed out, services associated with the consecrated elements, such as Benediction and processions of the Host, were as popular as they were in the inter-war period because Holy Communion was less often received, the Anglo-Catholic High Mass usually being a non-communicating celebration so far as the laity were concerned. The 'substitute cultus' around the Sacrament developed for this reason:[78]

> Anglo-Catholics in the 1920's and 1930's continued to opp-
> ose the Parish Communion, stressing the importance of the
> Sung Mass at 11.00 a.m. when the sacrifice was offered and
> none [in the congregation] should communicate.[79]

3

The achievements of this movement, of which Atlay's and Cheetham's ministries and parish churches represented examples of the full flour-ishing, had been consolidated by the time Eliot came into its orbit and became one of its leading lay exponents (in the same years of his burgeoning fame as a writer):

> By the 1920s, the Anglo-Catholics were beginning to enter
> into their inheritance, no longer a barely tolerated party, but
> the central moving force within the Church, reshaping its
> ethos and symbolism.[80]

In the period '*entre deux guerres*', Anglo-Catholicism was enjoying its protracted heyday:

> in retrospect, [this] can be seen as the most triumphant phase of Anglo-Catholicism in the Church of England.[81]

By this time, the influence of the Revival was by no means confined to England, but flourished in other parts of the Church in communion with the see of Canterbury – such as the Episcopal Church in the United States and the Church of England in Australia. In overseas provinces and in the mission field, entire dioceses had been founded along Anglo-Catholic lines. In those places, the controversies which always threatened to thwart Anglo-Catholic developments in established parishes and dioceses in Britain were unknown and Catholic teaching and custom could proceed unhindered. During the inter-war decades, Anglo-Catholicism's golden age, the heady vision of restoring the Church of England to the full expression of that Catholic character which, Anglo-Catholics maintain, it has always innately possessed, could be seriously entertained. Eliot was, as it were, getting with strength: 'almost all the energy in the Church of England,' writes Michael Yelton of these years, 'was Catholic in inspiration.... Anglo-Catholicism appeared to be an irresistible force within the Anglican Communion':

> from 1900 to at least 1940 Anglo-Catholicism was a dynamic force – indeed the most dynamic force within the Church of England at that time.[82]

'Intellectual Anglo-Catholicism', John Wain has written, 'reached the crest of its short but very real period of influence on English life' in these years.[83] In 1925, at the very time that Eliot was approaching his religious commitment, it could be affirmed that

> Anglo-Catholicism has now established itself in the Church of England. It is no longer merely on the defensive, nor is it conscious still of a great way to make in the recovery of Catholic doctrine and practice for its own adherents. Indeed it seems as if all the Catholic treasures which the Church of England has for so long renounced and set aside have at least been taken out and shown her. The full doctrine of the Catholic Church, without hesitation or qualification, has been preached in Anglican pulpits, the full discipline of the Catholic Church has been applied in Anglican confess-

ionals, the full ceremonial of the Catholic Church and all
the traditional ornaments of her ministers have beautified
Anglican Sanctuaries.[84]

In the inter-war years perhaps a quarter of English Anglicans could
be regarded as of Anglo-Catholic persuasion.[85]

We have to resist, however, the idea that Anglo-Catholicism was
more united than it was. Within the broad description, there was considerable variety of emphasis and application of Catholic doctrine
and practice. The Anglo-Catholicism of the 1930s variously drew inspiration from four different sources: the ideal of the primitive Church;
the mediaeval English Church; the English High Church tradition,
particularly as it developed from the earlier seventeenth century, and,
of course, the contemporary Western Church, as centred in Rome.[86]
Eliot, as we will see in the next chapter, drew variously on these
traditions, in his writings and in his own Anglo-Catholicism.

Because of different sources of inspiration, there was heated debate amongst Anglo-Catholics about the kind of liturgy that should
be celebrated. Various schools of liturgical thought came into existence, reflecting the ideals and authorities we have just described.
The most restrained, deriving from the earliest Tractarian period of
the Anglo-Catholic movement, was loyal to The Book of Common
Prayer (1662) and the High Church tradition of the seventeenth-
century Caroline divines (such as Lancelot Andrewes).[87] Andrewes'
chapel at Winchester House in London was the seminal design for
what became the Laudian mode.

In the spirit of what Graham Parry has called the Anglican Counter-
Reformation, Andrewes moved the altar to the east, atop three steps,
put candlesticks upon it and the sanctuary was railed off.[88] Supporters
of this tradition argued strenuously for a Catholic interpretation of the
Prayer Book, intending that such elements as its provision for auricular
confession in extraordinary circumstances should become normative.

The second group looked back further, to the First Prayer Book
of Edward VI (1549) – much closer in time and character to its
Catholic sources than the Book of 1662 – and essentially sought
to recover pre-Reformation, mediaeval ceremony, purged of super-
stitious and other dubious accretions. This so-called 'English Use'
took Percy Dearmer's *Parson's Handbook* (first published in 1899
and regularly revised afterwards) as its authority.[89] Finally, the most
advanced school – dismissive of The Book of Common Prayer (or
'Comic Prayer' as they could call it) and debunking the English Use
as 'British Museum Religion' – argued that the Church of England

should worship in the same way as the Western Church at large, as if the cataclysm of the Reformation had never happened, and be up to date with the developments in Catholic worship as determined in Rome, using the current 'Latin Use' (although most of them used it in a vernacular translation). In the most extreme parishes of this group – St Saviour's, Hoxton, in the East End, under Fr E.E. Kilburn (vicar there from 1907 until 1923), was the best-known example – the ceremonial was indistinguishable from the Roman rite and the liturgy entirely in Latin:

> On 10th June 1917, the Sunday within the Octave of Corpus Christi, Father Kilburn held what was almost certainly the first public outdoor procession of the Blessed Sacrament in the Church of England since the Reformation. In fact, the day had begun with three low masses at 7, 8, and 9, followed by High Mass at 11 with a procession inside the church using an ombrellino over the monstrance. There was then Benediction followed by Exposition from 12.30 to 6.30.[90]

The bible of the ceremonial for Western Use Anglo-Catholics was *Ritual Notes*, which, giving directions for the correct performance of the liturgy along contemporary Roman lines, went through no less than six editions in the decade following its original publication in 1894. This was used in conjunction with The English Missal (a translation, in Cranmerian language, of the *Missale Romanum*) in leading Anglo-Catholic parishes such as Eliot's.

The anonymous author of *Ritual Notes* scornfully repudiates the defenders of the English Use, lauding the Western liturgy as

> a living Rite, which is the common form of worship enjoyed by more than one hundred and fifty millions of our fellow Catholics in Western Christendom.... It seems, therefore, little less than an absurdity to prefer a dead and buried Use, the adoption of which would put us out of harmony with the rest of the Western Church.

Furthermore, the writer emphasises that the detailed descriptions of ritual which follow (which are much more intricate and exhaustive than the modest '*Notes*' would suggest) have as their goal, not only putting before the people 'a beautiful and dignified ritual', but, as clergy and acolytes submit to these intricate rules, sustaining

Exterior of Nashdom Abbey

that Objective Worship which is the leading idea involved
in all the principal Services of the Church, by the direction
of the devotion towards some recognizable Divine Presence,
especially in the Holy Eucharist, itself the special embodi-
ment of objective worship and its full realization.[91]

Nothing could be further removed from 'the simple religion of the
heart' of biblical Protestantism or of the moralistically-didactic, theo-
logically-denuded Unitarianism of Eliot's upbringing.

So, while there was some characteristically Anglican movement
and flexibility between the contrasting bodies of Anglo-Catholic opinion (and the parishes which tended to be aligned to them), even in
the more restrained places the ceremonial enrichment was such that,
although the Prayer Book language may have been used, the general
trend, across the various schools of thought and practice, was in the
decided direction of the classical Western (Roman) rite. Eliot was too
enamoured of the seventeenth-century Church to dismiss The Book
of Common Prayer – he had a profound admiration for its prose,
which is without parallel in vernacular liturgies, its genius made all
the more evident by the risible banalities of the modern, twentieth-
century attempts to write liturgical English, both in Anglicanism

High Mass at Nashdom Abbey

and Roman Catholicism (the first signs of which were beginning to appear in Eliot's last years in commissions to revise such as the Psalter, and which he savagely criticised). Yet he was also deeply devoted to the Latin language and traditions of the Catholic West. In his day, his own London parish (which we will discuss in detail in the next chapter) followed the Western ceremonies, and much of the music there, chant and polyphony, was in Latin. So, in that respect, his liturgical life was focused on principles and practices tending to the most 'advanced' of the three schools of thought. When Eliot determined to enter one of the men's religious communities permanently – an intention overturned, as it eventuated, by his late second marriage – his choice of Nashdom Abbey indicated a definite preference for the Anglo-Papalist wing of Anglo-Catholicism.[92] This was suggested much earlier in his Anglo-Catholic life in his subscription to a building fund for the establishment of the church of St Francis of Assisi, North Kensington, near his own church in South

Kensington. It was dedicated in 1936 and became another centre of 'Western Use' Anglo-Catholicism.[93]

The Anglo-Catholic Aunt Dot, in Rose Macaulay's *Towers of Trebizond*, advocating more televising by the BBC of Anglo-Catholic liturgy, neatly differentiates between more general Anglo-Catholicism and what Father Chantry-Pigg would prefer, at the ultramontane end of the Western Use party:

> We have this superb service, with everything people like, beautiful singing, clouds of incense, priests in fine vestments moving about in the most impressive way, the action of the Mass, a magnificent liturgy, and all in English but for the Kyrie and a few oddments, so it really can be followed.... Mind you, I wouldn't let [Father Hugh] take part, he'd put in far too much Latin and worry people.[94]

John Betjeman captures it, too, in his 'verse autobiography', 'Summoned by Bells':

> Those were the days when that divine baroque
> Transformed our English altars and our ways.
> Fiddle-back chasuble[95] in mid-Lent pink
> Scandalized Rome and Protestants alike.[96]

One of the features of this tradition which markedly differentiates it from ordinary (one might say, easy-going Anglicanism) is its stress on the observance of what the non-Catholic Christian would see as the minutiae of faith, of rules and regulations, going well beyond such general Christian demands on the laity as Sunday worship and private prayer and Bible study. For Anglo-Catholics, 'holy days of obligation' – great holy days, such as certain saints' days, when one is supposed to hear Mass – occur throughout the year, requiring attendance, before or after work. Belonging to various Catholic societies also brought with it such requirements as to say, daily, Morning and Evening Prayer, or prayers to the Virgin, as in the rosary and the *Angelus* devotions, and so on. It was a highly regulated, indeed (if taken seriously, as Eliot did) daily rule of prayer and observance, year in, year out. It appealed, in other words, to that 'intellectual and emotional impetus towards necessary order discoverable throughout Eliot's poetic and critical career'[97] and his life itself. 'Order' is one of those recurring terms in Eliot's writing, and the devout Anglo-Catholic's routine was indeed an ordered one. Repeatedly, in poetry and prose, he emphasises the need for discipline in the religious life. Regarding Baudelaire, for example, Eliot singles out for praise the French poet's proposal of a life of order and discipline, and indeed of austerity, in the practice of the faith. Eliot, quoting it, calls it a 'great passage':

> *Faire tous les matins ma prière à Dieu.... Faire, tous les*
> *soirs, une nouvelle prière, pour demander à Dieu la vie et*
> *la force pour ma mère et pour moi ... obéir aux principes de*
> *la plus stricte sobriété, dont le premier est la suppression de*
> *tous les excitants, quels qu'ils soient.*[98]

Such order, of course, is particularly appealing, psychologically, to those who are acutely aware of disorder – whether in the world at large, or perhaps even more disturbingly, in their own lives. Those who are tormented by disorderliness, in all its ramifications, personal and societal, are drawn to the precision of disciplined ritual and a detailed, authoritative spiritual regime. In this way, the Anglo-Catholicism of his day appealed to something very deeply-grounded in Eliot's temperament, but it is well to observe, acknowledging his wide-ranging interests within its various groupings, that we should resist confining him exclusively to one Anglo-Catholic tradition.

His reasons for becoming an Anglican and, specifically, affiliating himself with its Anglo-Catholic 'party', were obviously profoundly important to him, but the attraction of joining and belonging to a movement that appeared to have the promise of carrying the future of the Church in Britain with it (and wherever Anglicanism's influence had spread in the Empire's then-formidable global presence) and enlisting many of the brightest and best of the younger clergy and laity in its ranks, should not be underestimated. Between 1920 and 1933, 'the number of clergy and laity enrolled at the Anglo-Catholic congresses ... jumped from 13,000 in 1920 to some 70,000 in 1933'.[99] Probably precisely because Christianity, in general, was otherwise, at that time, in the early throes of its demise in Britain (from '1900 to 1934 ... church attendance in urban Britain had declined about 25 percent despite a 50 percent increase in population'[100]), this movement, inspired by the past, but looking confidently to the future, seemed to offer the best – perhaps, the only – hope of regenerating English Christianity. Eliot believed, like the majority of Anglo-Catholics, that if the burgeoning forces of secularisation were to be reversed and England were to return to the saving truth of the Catholic faith, it would only be through what Hugh Ross Williamson (whose Anglo-Catholicism was also nurtured between the wars) has called 'the instrumentality of the Church of England':

> It should be possible to preach the Faith within [that Church]
> and ultimately win from the Erastian element and the pseudo-

Nonconformists sufficient Catholic converts to make the Establishment itself seek reconciliation with the Holy See.[101]

Yet, in spite of its astonishing advances, Anglo-Catholicism was never
in any danger of becoming part of that establishment, always existing
'in an atmosphere of minor controversy',[102] its counter-cultural ethos
having just the whiff of a 'naughty underworld'.[103] We know that
Eliot's own politico-religious outlook had more in common with
the right-wing *Action Française* than with Fr Groser and Christian
Socialism. But the Anglo-Catholicism to which he was drawn, at the
time when his allegiance became well known, was certainly not dominated by politically conservative views. In any case, Eliot rejected
the identification of the Church with an 'oligarchy or class', which
was one of the dangers, he argued, of 'an established Church',[104] and
criticised the conception of the 'Community of Christians' as

> merely the nicest, most intelligent and public-spirited of the
> upper-middle-class[105]

– as in his own family's American Unitarian tradition with its air of
social and moral superiority.

Several 'wealthy and titled Anglo-Catholic laymen' were
crucial in the early days of the movement.[106] Charles Lindley
Viscount Halifax (1839-1934), 'the most prominent and saintly of
Anglo-Catholic laymen', was exceptional amongst the aristocracy,
not typical, in his leadership of the Anglo-Catholic movement as
president of the English Church Union and in his instigation of the
'Malines Conversations' with Cardinal Mercier, in the 1920s, which
seemed to offer the promise of reunion between the Churches of
England and Rome and which Eliot commended in *The Idea of a
Christian Society*.[107] As Colin Stephenson has argued, Halifax 'had
given up all his worldly prospects' as an aristocrat to follow his
religious vocation.[108] He was President of The League of Our Lady
which organised the first pilgrimage to the shrine of the Virgin
at Walsingham in the 1920s.[109] Because of activities such as this,
Halifax had had to leave the court of Edward VII, when Prince of
Wales, in case his ecclesiastical interests led to the future monarch
being accused of being pro-Catholic. Of the several aristocrats
who made their way into the Anglo-Catholic priesthood, Rose
Macaulay provides an hilarious caricature in the person of

> the Rev. the Hon. Father Hugh Chantry-Pigg, an ancient
> bigot, who had run a London church several feet higher than
> St. Mary's Bourne Street and some inches above even St.

Magnus the Martyr, and, being now just retired, devoted his
life to conducting very High retreats and hunting for relics
of saints, which he collected for the private oratory in his
Dorset manor house.[110]

To the extent that Anglo-Catholicism is an eccentric version of Anglicanism, it was identifiably British in a Britain that was still nominally
Christian and which has always been receptive to eccentricity – such
idiosyncrasy being tolerated, even encouraged, as a kind of satirical
reinforcement of the institutions and conventions it subverts and upon
whose enduring stability and vigour its *outré* character depends. The
very eccentricity of Anglo-Catholicism – doctrinally and aesthetically
– made it possible for such as Eliot to become and remain an 'Anglican',
which is always less important for an Anglo-Catholic than his or her
identity as a 'Catholic'. Anglo-Catholics – like Evangelicals in this, as
in some other matters – place little importance on the 'Church of England' brand (so to speak), even repudiating it: 'nowhere in our services
do we refer to or profess belief in the Church of England', Manning-
Foster pointedly indicates, arguing that members of the Church of
England repeatedly affirm that they belong to the Catholic Church.[111]
In a letter, Eliot refers to 'my catholicism'; nowhere, to my knowledge,
does he refer to 'my Anglicanism'.[112] Travelling in Turkey, Fr Chantry-
Pigg, hearing the phrase, 'Church of England' in conversation, is awa-
kened from his slumbers to correct the nomenclature referring to the
Church to which he belongs: 'the eternal Church of Christendom. The
only holy, Catholic and Apostolic Church' and notes 'one example of
our branch of it', an Anglican church in Istanbul.[113] The Englishness
of Anglicanism satisfied the significant cultural, historical and literary
components of Eliot's faith:

> it would have been strange if a man so much in love with
> English tradition, and so deeply read in Dryden, Johnson and
> Coleridge, had not felt himself drawn towards the living and
> visible Church of England.[114]

But Anglo-Catholicism fulfilled his intellectual, theological and spiritual requirements, making him a participant (as he gratefully reflected)
in Catholic Christendom:

> if Anglo-Catholicism has assisted a few persons to leave the
> Church of England [for Rome] who could never have rested
> in that uneasy bed anyway, on the other hand it has helped
> many more ... to remain within the Anglican Church.[115]

Like most Anglo-Catholics, Eliot was an opponent of parliamentary interference in the Church's worship, and at the very beginning
of his Anglo-Catholic life joined in the criticism of the proposals for
the revision of the Prayer Book which, in 1927, were set before a
Parliament 'elected by persons of every variety of religious belief or
disbelief'.[116]

Anglo-Catholicism's abiding tension with the establishment is indicated in the long-standing wariness of the bishops fully to embrace
the movement. In 1900, for example, the archbishops of Canterbury
and York agreed that 'the Church of England does not at present
allow Reservation in any form'.[117] This, of course, is one of the great
paradoxes of Anglo-Catholicism, where so much emphasis is placed
on the doctrine of Apostolic Succession, but in combination with
a usually dim view of the actual holders of episcopal office – principally, because they have been seen to be the main obstacles to the
advance of Catholic faith and practice in Anglicanism. Ronald Knox
observed that Anglo-Catholics spoke of bishops as if they were a
'secret band of criminals'.[118] In Anglo-Catholic lore, stories are told
of parish priests offering prayers for the bishop of their diocese 'and
all other aged incompetents'. Having attended the confirmation of
his godson, Adam Roberts, in Westminster Abbey in 1955, Eliot was
pleased to find, he told the boy's mother afterwards, that the bishop
in question (Launcelot Fleming of Portsmouth) was neither 'dull nor
feeble'.[119] Of course, there have been bishops who have been definite
Anglo-Catholics (Michael Furse of St Albans, enthroned in 1920, was
probably the first, followed by Walter Frere of Truro in 1923, and
several since), but even Catholic-minded prelates, having to placate
Protestant complainants in their dioceses, have tried to bring Anglo-
Catholics into conformity with more mainstream Anglican practice. It
is worth noting that in 1911 all the bishops of the Church of England
had agreed that they would sanction reservation of the sacrament for
the purposes of sick communion.[120] Yet it was not until the 1930s
that a bishop – Alfred Blunt of Bradford – actually had a tabernacle
with reservation in his private chapel.[121] The 1911 decision was not
all that Anglo-Catholics could have hoped (and they went forward,
regardless), but it was beyond anything that was even conceivable a
generation before.

The episcopacy had by no means become entirely Catholic-minded by the inter-war period. The notorious Bishop E.W. Barnes of
Birmingham (who went there in 1924), regarded much that Anglo-
Catholicism held dear to be mere superstition, and was an active per-
secutor of the movement in his diocese, refusing to institute priests

to parishes unless Catholic practices (often long established) were abandoned. It is to Bishop Barnes that Eliot refers for 'comic relief' in 'Thoughts after Lambeth'. He was a favourite target. Eliot had attacked him earlier (in 1928), both in 'A Dialogue on Dramatic Poetry' and in 'A note on Richard Crashaw', where Barnes is called 'religious' in the same sense in which Shelley's poetry might be so described.[122] Barnes rejected the Virgin Birth; the key Anglo-Catholic doctrine of the objective Real Presence in the Mass (which he regarded, contrariwise, as a subjective 'psychological process')[123] and, especially, reservation of the sacrament and devotions to it. At St Aidan's, Small Heath in Birmingham, the 'psychological process' was reserved and the controversy between Anglo-Catholics there and their bishop became national news.[124] As his rejection of the Virgin Birth indicates, Barnes was a Modernist, not an Evangelical, and Modernists were, in a sense, more formidable enemies of Anglo-Catholics than Evangelicals, who, although they might seem the natural opponents of Catholicising tendencies in the Church, held as strongly as Anglo-Catholics to key orthodox doctrines and shared much of their moral theology. Sheila Kaye-Smith has argued that the fiercest attacks, throughout the history of the Revival, came not from Evangelicalism, but from Latitudinarianism (an older term for Modernism). Ollard, in his history of the Revival, speaks of the 'fungus of Latitudinarianism'.[125] Predictably, Rose Macaulay has a satirical swipe at the Modern Churchmen's Union (the principal clerical organisation of Modernists) which, at a summer conference affirms the novel heresy of 'partial diluvianism', whereby the biblical Flood had not 'covered the whole earth'.[126] Eliot may have been the principal Modernist in poetry, but, like his co-religionists, he was definitely not a Modernist in theology.

4

The function of Anglo-Catholicism as the exponent of the Catholic character of the Church of England, recalling it to its true identity, united all Anglo-Catholics, whatever divisions there may have been amongst them with regard to liturgical arrangements and (for example) interpretations of their relationship with the papacy. They particularly rejected the idea that Anglo-Catholicism was just another movement or division within Anglicanism that could be tolerated along with Evangelicals and Modernists, with their tendencies, respectively, to Protestantism and Unitarianism. Anglo-Catholics 'vehemently resent being regarded as a party or school of thought within the Church of England', Manning-Foster wrote:

> The Church of England is either Catholic in the sense that she is fundamentally one with the Greek and Roman Churches or she is not. You cannot have it both ways.[127]

From this position, the Oxford Movement and the ensuing Catholic Revival are 'not the commencement of a new party or school of thought ... [but] a return to first principles' of Catholic belief and order.[128] Anglo-Catholics look back to the first thousand years of Christendom, 'when it was outwardly united in one universal Church'.[129] The purpose of the movement, Kaye-Smith notes arrestingly, is to 'bring itself to an end as quickly as possible'. So far from wanting to establish another permanent party in the Church of England, for Anglo-Catholics, the 'whole point' of the Revival

> is the conversion of England, the restoration of the Anglican Church to the fullness of Catholic faith and practice which are hers by right of her inherent catholicity.... [Anglo-Catholics] are unable to contemplate their continued existence as a party.[130]

The series of national Anglo-Catholic Congresses, in the interwar period, were the most obvious sign of the movement's unity, visibility and determination to bring the English Church into visible union with the Western Church. (There were regional ones, as well, as at Leeds in 1922.) The first Congress was held in 1920:

> On St. Peter's Day, 1920... [we] watched twelve hundred vested priests and a score of overseas bishops, headed by our own great silver crucifix and smoking censers, process along Holborn to High Mass at St Alban's Church; while similar scenes were being enacted by the laity at eight other London churches.[131]

16,000 membership tickets were sold to that Congress and, of London venues, only the Royal Albert Hall was big enough to accommodate the multitude.[132]

At that first Congress, there was only one English diocesan bishop present – Ridgeway of Salisbury – as the general suspicion in Anglicanism at large (and especially amongst the bishops) about Anglo-Catholicism continued, in spite of the fact that the Catholic Revival had been touching virtually all aspects of Church life, in one way or another, for generations and the Oxford Movement had begun with a defence of episcopacy and the doctrine of the Apostolic Succession.

In the cathedral church of the Bishop of London, St Paul's, the Dean and Chapter had refused the Anglo-Catholics permission to hold a concluding Thanksgiving service there, at the end of the 1920 Congress, even though it was only to be a *Te Deum* and they had promised not to use incense (always bound to get up an irritable Protestant's nose).[133] Undaunted, the Anglo-Catholics processed across the river to Southwark, and (as the organiser of the Congress recorded) a devout crowd moved over London Bridge, very different (and, symbolically, in the opposite direction) from that Dantesque mercantile multitude, famously envisaged by Eliot in these very years, in *The Waste Land*, flowing across the bridge into the inferno of the City ('I had not thought death had undone so many'):[134]

> by 7.30 on Friday evening the queue of people waiting to get into Southwark Cathedral stretched from the Cathedral gates right across London Bridge to the Monument. It is the first time, surely, at any rate since the Reformation, that London Bridge heard a great crowd singing to the honour of the Mother of our Lord, as the waiting multitude sang again and again, 'Hail Mary, Hail Mary, Hail Mary, full of grace'.[135]

Eliot could scarcely have been unaware of these great events, which were not only taking place around him in the City, but in a Church in which he had already displayed considerable interest, and, swiftly, they had their mollifying effect even on the Dean and Chapter at St Paul's: at the second Anglo-Catholic Congress, in 1923, the opening service was High Mass in the Cathedral and incense was used.[136] With good reason, as Nigel Yates has observed, Anglo-Catholicism at this time was 'both triumphant and triumphalist'.[137]

This Congress, at which the leading figure was Bishop Frank Weston of Zanzibar, is regarded as the most important, although several more were to follow, at regular intervals, in the inter-war period. To the alarm of the Archbishop of Canterbury, Randall Davidson, the second Congress sent a telegram to the Pope with 'the respectful greetings of 16,000 Anglo-Catholics'.[138] (It should be noted that a message of obedience was also sent to the Archbishop, as well as greetings to the King and the other patriarchs, but, of course, amongst these, it was the address to the Western patriarch that was controversial and distinctively Anglo-Catholic). In Weston's address to the assembled delegates, he focused on the Mass, Confession and fasting, concluding with a discourse on the Blessed Sacrament (the principal subject of the third Congress in 1927) in which he urged them to 'make your stand for the Tabernacle, not for your own sakes but for the sake of truth first':

> For the truth; because the one great thing that England needs to learn is that Christ is found in and amid matter – Spirit through matter – God in flesh, God in sacrament.

In other words, they were to fight for the truth of the doctrine of the Incarnation and its expression in the Eucharist and in reservation of that Blessed Sacrament in the tabernacle. In a series of ringing exhortations to the movement, which are still quoted today, Weston concluded by warning Anglo-Catholics that victories for the eucharistic reservation and for ritual at large needed to be accompanied by witness and service in the community:

> You cannot claim to worship Jesus in the tabernacle, if you do not pity Jesus in the slum. Mark that: that is the Gospel truth....
>
> If only you listen tonight your Movement is going to sweep England.... If you are Christians, then your Jesus is one and the same: Jesus on the throne of his glory, Jesus in the blessed sacrament, Jesus received into your hearts in communion, Jesus mystically with you as you pray, and Jesus enthroned in the hearts and bodies of his brothers and sisters up and down this country. And it is folly – it is madness – to suppose that you can worship Jesus in the sacrament and Jesus on the throne of glory, when you are sweating him in the bodies of his children.

For Weston, the social gospel was (and needed to be, if the movement were to be authentically Christian) bound up with the advances in doctrine and worship which the movement had now secured:

> You have got your Mass, you have got your Altar, you have begun to get your Tabernacle. Now go out into the highways and hedges. Go out and look for Jesus in the ragged, in the naked, in the oppressed and sweated, in those who have lost hope, in those who are struggling to make good. Look for Jesus. And when you see him, gird yourselves with his towel and try to wash their feet.[139]

If this heavenly faith were to be of earthly good, in other words, Christian action in society was imperative. Here, too, the doctrine of the Incarnation inspired Anglo-Catholic social and political movements in which Eliot, especially through his contribution to various conferences and journals, actively (but not unambiguously) participated and which we shall examine in detail in chapter 6.

This address by Weston in the Royal Albert Hall in July 1923 made a tremendous impact, part of which was due, undoubtedly, to the prelate's rousing vision of the movement sweeping the country. Anglo-Catholicism, he taught, must not be added to the traditional 'parties' of the Church of England – Low, Broad and High. In a circular letter to Congress delegates, he disregarded what he dismissively termed as the 'shibboleths' of those divisions: 'We stand or fall with Christ's Church, catholic and apostolic'.

> And we wait patiently till the Holy Father and the Orthodox Patriarchs recognize us as of their own stock. We are not a party: we are those in the Anglican Communion who refuse to be limited by party rules and party creeds. Our appeal is to the Catholic Creed, to Catholic worship, and to Catholic practice.[140]

5

Frank Weston's emphasis on the Mass in his addresses, and the celebration of many Masses during the course of the Congresses, demonstrated the centrality of eucharistic teaching and devotion in Anglo-Catholic theology and spirituality. Anglo-Catholics adhered to the 'Six Precepts of the Church':

1. To be present at Mass every Sunday, unless prevented by illness or urgent necessity; and also, if possible, on all holy days of obligation.
2. To keep the days of fasting and / or abstinence, unless dispensed therefrom.
3. To go to Confession at least once in the year.
4. To receive the Blessed Sacrament at least three times a year, and always at Easter if possible.
5. To contribute regularly, and according to means, to the support of the Church and the clergy.
6. Not to marry within the forbidden degrees of kinship, and to keep the other marriage laws of the Church.[141]

As the ordering of this list shows, for Anglo-Catholics, as for Catholics, at large, it is (as the clichéd saying goes) the Mass that matters. By using this very term, Anglo-Catholics indicated their unity with the Western Church, specifically with regard to what is known (among many titles) as the sacrament of unity: 'it signifies our oneness with Catholics throughout the world'.[142] In Protestant, Evangelical traditions, the emphasis falls on the Word of God, the preaching of it and the individual believer's discernment of its meaning in his or her life. In Catholic theology, while both word and sacrament are central to faith, in practice, the focus is strongly on communal participation in the 'Body of Christ' (the company of all faithful people, living and departed), mediated through the sacraments; and the most important sacrament (given such designations as 'the Blessed Sacrament', for this reason) is the sacrament of the altar, of the Body and Blood of Christ, taken in Holy Communion.

In Anglicanism, the two sacraments of the Gospel, Baptism and the Lord's Supper – the so-called 'dominical' sacraments, as having been instituted by Christ, the Master – are approved in the Thirty-Nine Articles. In Anglo-Catholicism, however, the seven traditional sacraments of the Catholic Church are affirmed: baptism and confirmation, eucharist, holy orders, matrimony, penance and extreme unction (anointing with oil, usually given when a person is '*in extremis*'). At the beginning of Eliot's Anglo-Catholicism, he received the two sacraments of initiation – baptism (from a priest) and confirmation (from a bishop) – and was, thereby, eligible for reception of Holy Communion. Further, in accord with Catholic teaching that the communicant should be in a state of grace (that is, absolved from sin) when receiving communion, he regularly availed himself of a fourth sacrament, that of confession and absolution. When he married Valerie Fletcher, in 1957, they celebrated the sacrament of matrimony (in which the man and the woman themselves are the ministers of the sacrament) and extreme unction, from a priest, would have been available to him in his last days. In 'Animula' (1929), he refers paradoxically to 'living first in the silence after the viaticum',[143] a reference to Holy Communion given to those in likelihood of immediate death (the Latin word used for 'provision for a journey' and, ecclesiastically and metaphorically, applied to provision for the passage from this world to the next). The only sacrament which Eliot did not seek was that of orders.

Like the religion of devout Catholics generally, his was a richly sacramental faith, but as he frequently had more than weekly recourse to Mass and because, by Anglican standards, his devotion to the sacrament of penance was especially conscientious, his Anglo-Catholicism may be said to have been conspicuously sacramental. This has its source in his profound appreciation of the centrality of the doctrine of the Incarnation in the Catholic faith: with Pascal, Eliot would have affirmed that *'l'Incarnation montre à l'homme la grandeur de sa misère, par la grandeur du remède qu'il a fallu'*.[144] Further, the philosophical idea of the intersection of the timeless with time (which appealed deeply to him) is seminally expressed in the event of the Incarnation, which is extended in sacramental religion and, therefore, in the Mass.

6

Anglo-Catholic teaching about the Mass is that it was instituted by Jesus, who commanded his apostles and their successors to consecrate bread and wine, as he had done, to be his flesh and blood, and to make a perpetual memorial of his death before the Father. As Vernon Staley puts it (in one of the classic manuals of Anglo-Catholic teaching), the Holy Eucharist is a feast upon a sacrifice.[145] The body and the blood of Christ are first offered to the eternal Father, and then partaken of by the communicants. Staley focuses particularly on the word translated as 'remembrance' (in Christ's charge, 'This do in remembrance of me'):

> The Greek word for 'remembrance' has a distinctly sacrificial meaning.... In each case [in Scripture] it is used of a remembrance before God, and not before man.... All that our Lord Jesus Christ did when He instituted the blessed Sacrament was sacrificial; it was all done in sacrificial terms, at a sacrificial time, and for a sacrificial end.

Hence, the Anglo-Catholic emphasis on the 'Holy Sacrifice' of the Mass. But this does not imply any repetition of the sacrifice of the cross, or any renewal of Christ's sufferings or death. These happened once for all and cannot be repeated. Neither is anything wanting in his sacrifice or sufferings which the Eucharistic Sacrifice supplies. But what is affirmed is that, in the Holy Eucharist, Catholics plead before God the One Sacrifice once offered upon the cross, even as Christ himself presents the same offering in heaven. Thus, the fathers of the Church spoke of the Holy Sacrifice of the altar as 'the unbloody sacrifice'. Understood in its ancient and Catholic sense, Staley continues, the Eucharistic sacrifice is 'the continual remembrance of the sacrifice of the death of Christ', and he argues that this is a teaching which 'the English Church has never disowned':

> In fact, she could not disown it, without forfeiting her claim
> to be a portion of the Holy Catholic Church of Christ.[146]

The doctrine had been affirmed by Anglican theologians, through the ages, including Lancelot Andrewes, Jeremy Taylor (who taught the doctrine of the Real Presence at the eucharist, but attacked Roman transubstantiation), William Laud and John Cosin – all in the seventeenth century – as well as the nineteenth-century Tractarians and their successors. This Real Presence of Christ in the eucharist is one of those points where Catholic teaching contrasts fundamentally with Protestant theology, which, in varying degrees (most radically, in the memorialism of the Swiss Reformer, Zwingli), denies any specific divine presence in the service of the Lord's Supper. The Caroline theologians, with the English Church being threatened by followers of such Reformers with their un-Catholic ideas about the sacrament, frequently refer to a 'substantial presence'. Transubstantiation (seen as developing later than Catholic ideas of the sacrament in the first Christian millennium – it was not defined until the thirteenth century) is usually not insisted upon by Anglo-Catholics. The change in the elements is real (they always affirm), but of a metaphysical and not a material kind.

For the Anglo-Catholic communicant, such as Eliot, the Incarnate Lord Himself is truly contained in, with and under the elements of bread and wine by virtue of the priest's consecration of those elements at the Mass, which are then received by the communicant, as Eliot writes in 'East Coker':

> The dripping blood our only drink,
> The bloody flesh our only food....[147]

'In spite of this', he continues, 'we like to think / That we are sound, substantial flesh and blood', whereas the true reality (he implies) is in the Real Presence of the Body and Blood of the Lord. The key word, there, is 'substantial', pointing to the issue of the transformation of the substances in the Mass, which is the true life, rather than our mortal bodies of flesh and blood.[148]

Their holy communion, for Anglo-Catholics, is the most solemn moment in their entire worshipping lives, as the wafer bread (or Host – from Latin *hostia*, or sacrificial victim) and the chalice, containing the Precious Blood, having been successively elevated for adoration, and the priest having communicated himself, are brought down to the altar rail for the people's communion. There, the sacrament is taken kneeling, and in both kinds (one of the few details of ritual in which Anglo-Catholics differ from Roman Catholics who usually communicate under the species of bread alone, although Anglo-Catholics, like Roman Catholics, usually take the wafer directly on the tongue, from the priest – differentiating themselves again from Anglicans, in general, who receive it in the hand, to put it in their mouths themselves).

Christ is always present when the Sacrament is offered according to His instructions, at the Last Supper, regardless of the faith or lack thereof of the participants – again, contradicting much Protestant teaching (in this case, of receptionism, where the efficacy of the sacrament depends upon the faith of the recipient). It is the difference between an objective Presence and a subjective experience. A worthy communion, effective, beneficial and salvific, depends (of course) on living faith, but not the validity of the Mass and the consecration at its climax and heart, which work and have effect because of Christ and not the worthiness of the recipient or, for that matter, of the celebrant.

While the Thirty-Nine Articles of Religion are thought of as presenting the more Protestant-leaning aspects of Anglicanism, the twenty-ninth indeed affirms the Catholic doctrine that all communicants receive the Body and Blood of Christ objectively – the outward Sign, Bread and Wine, and the Thing Signified, the Lord Himself – in Holy Communion. But only the faithful and properly disposed receive the spiritual nourishment of Christ in the Eucharist, which is the benefit.[149]

Because of the centrality of the Mass, and the devotion of Anglo-Catholics to the eucharistic Real Presence – the High Mass (sung, with chant and polyphony, with three sacred ministers and acolytes, and incense) is, inevitably, the climax of Anglo-Catholic worship – special attention and reverence are given to the places where the sacrifice of the altar is offered and to the episcopally-ordained priesthood which offers it. Thus there developed the great churches of the Catholic Revival (often described as shrines, emphasising their holiness), with their rich traditions of solemn liturgy and music, evangelical preaching of the truths of the Catholic faith, nurturing of the spiritual life and of the legendary reputations of the devoted priests and confessors who were rectors and vicars in them, throughout the worldwide Anglican Communion. Yet, for all the very strong personalities who have been such notable warriors in the history of the Anglo-Catholic cause (such as Hope Patten at Walsingham) and even less well-known, but still very gifted and eccentric figures, like Eric Cheetham at Eliot's St Stephen's, the priest at the altar and in his sacramental ministry at large, is utterly impersonal. In this conception of ministry, nothing could be further removed from the cult of the personality of such as the revivalist preacher. Eliot's celebration of impersonality, in the evolution of his literary criticism, found a powerful parallel, in his religious life, in the emphasis on objectivity and impersonality in the classical, sacramental understanding of the Catholic priesthood and the Eucharist itself, as expressed by Kaye-Smith:

> A religion whose central act of worship is the Mass will be delivered from the thraldom of the pulpit and dependence on the 'acceptable preacher'. One of the first rules of art is to merge the personality of the artist into the work that he is doing, and as priestcraft comes to be considered more and more as an art, and the saying of Mass is standardized by rules which are artistic as well as ecclesiastical, the intrusion of the personality of the priest into his work grows less and less.[150]

The minister in the pulpit faces his congregation, winning their attention and, it is hoped, their commitment, through the power of his oratory and the sincere emotion of his delivery; the priest in the sanctuary, in the eastward position (used universally in both Anglo-Catholicism and Roman Catholicism during Eliot's lifetime) has his back to the people for most of the liturgy and is substantially concealed in his vestments, his anonymity further ensured by his enclosure within the age-old ceremonies of the Mass. It is the contrast between personality and impersonality and all who know Eliot's writings know how deeply he yearned to embrace the latter dispensation:

> only those who have personality and emotions know what it means to want to escape from these things.[151]

7

In spite of the desire for the reunion of the Western Church, the attitude of Anglo-Catholics to the Roman Catholic Church, especially in England, was, at best, ambiguous, while much admiring and imitating what they saw of the Roman Church in Europe.[152] When they were not alluding to the Catholic Church in England as the 'Italian Mission' ('when Father Chantry-Pigg said "Italian Mission", a look of particular malevolence slightly distorted his finely arranged features'[153]), they more charitably argued (but in direct contradiction of Roman Catholic teaching) that there had in fact been an internal break within the Catholic Church in England, which led to the existence of two separate streams.[154]

In response, the attitude of English Catholics to Anglo-Catholicism was similarly unpromising. With the confidence that came with the restoration of the hierarchy and the steady stream of converts to the True Church, the antagonism of Roman Catholics towards Anglo-Catholics, in particular, started to appear in sharp relief. This is more intense than Roman Catholic negativity towards other branches of Protestantism far removed from any identifiably Catholic characteristics of theology, liturgy or spirituality or even towards easy-going, middle-of-the-road Anglicanism. English Roman Catholics would speak of Anglo-Catholics with unconcealed contempt, as

> so sad, so perverse, so self-torturing, so unworthy; so foolish even, and useless[155]

– language they would never use, for example, about Quakers or Unitarians.[156] The absurdity of the restoration of the second, but Roman Catholic shrine at tiny Walsingham, in the wake of the Anglo-Catholic restoration a few years before, is a sorry reflection of this situation of Catholics in competition with one another.[157] This dislike is no doubt bound up, in England, with an historically-based hostility or resentment towards the Established Church at large and its occupation of the cathedrals and ancient parish churches which, had the Reformation not occurred, would be in Roman hands; and as a result of the long history of persecution of Catholics in Britain. But possibly a more deep-seated distaste derives from Roman Catholic recognition that Anglo-Catholics are not only aping them without committing to the full panoply of Catholic doctrine which (in their view) can only be experienced in communion with their Church and obedience to and recognition by the papacy, but in the realisation that that imitation produces liturgical and musical performance of more finesse and solemnity than most English Roman Catholic parishes and cathedrals would have the expertise, resources or even the will to match. The expression on the face of the priest of the neighbouring Roman Catholic parish to Fr Chantry-Pigg's very elevated Anglo-Catholic St. Gregory's becomes distorted with bigotry when

> the St. Gregory's clergy and choir filed in chanting, incense-swinging, saint-bearing processions out of their church door and round the square which both churches served.[158]

Like most Anglo-Catholics, Eliot regretted what he regarded, even before his 'conversion', as the error of the 'divorce from Rome', with its detrimental effect on British 'religious history'.[159] He told Bonamy Dobrée that it seemed almost inevitable that Canterbury should eventually be superseded by Rome; but, in the meantime, the Church of England was the Catholic Church in England.[160] This was the typical Anglo-Catholic position in the inter-war years. Fr Hope Patten of Walsingham, for example,

> saw no future for the Church of England unless it returned to communion with Rome under the leadership of the Pope.

But this view was held in company with the belief in the validity of the orders and ministrations of the priests of the Church of England, such as himself:

> equally, until the very end, there was no sign that he was not a loyal Anglican, in that he had never expressed any doubt about the validity of his orders.... He had always affirmed that the Church of England was the real Ecclesia Anglicana and the Church of Rome was an intruder in this country.[161]

Undoubtedly, the most serious Roman Catholic assault on the Anglo-Catholic position came in the very years when the movement was approaching its zenith (and, for that very reason, may have provoked the assault). In 1896, Pope Leo XIII issued the encyclical, *Apostolicae Curae*, which declared that Anglican ordinations to the priesthood were null and void, being invalid through defect and intention (specifically, with regard to ordination for the offering of the holy sacrifice of the Mass).[162] That many parts of the Eastern Church hold that Anglican orders are as valid as those of the Roman Catholic Church did little to ameliorate the profound disappointment of this judgement by the Patriarch of the West, to whom Anglo-Catholics naturally looked as their ultimate ecclesiastical authority.

Anglo-Catholics (and especially, amongst them, Anglo-Papalists) continued to make their claims for their fidelity to the contemporary Western Church, although the leader of that Church had informed them, officially, that their deacons, priests and bishops were merely Protestant laymen. This is the most startling evidence of the ability of Anglo-Catholics to abide in a condition of ambiguity. Some, most notably, the Oxford theologian and Warden of Keble College, Austin Farrer, rejected the papacy outspokenly. In a sermon in 1960 in the chapel at Pusey House, in Oxford (like his college, another foundation dedicated to the ideals of Anglican Catholicism in the city of its nineteenth-century re-birth), 'On being an Anglican', Farrer would have startled his congregation (Jeremy Morris writes, in his essay on 'the travails of Anglo-Catholicism') when he declared:

> I dare not profess belief in the great Papal error. Christ did not found a Papacy.… Its infallibilist claim is a blasphemy, and never has been accepted by the oriental part of Christendom. Its authority has been employed to establish as dogmas of faith, propositions utterly lacking in historical foundation. Nor is this an old and faded scandal – the papal fact-factory has been going full blast in our own time, manufacturing sacred history after the event.

Farrer most likely had the definition of the doctrine of the bodily Assumption of the Virgin Mary, defined as an article of faith just ten years before, particularly in mind. Morris remarks that his statement is 'all the more surprising, considering Farrer's seemingly impeccable Anglo-Catholic credentials'. He points out that Farrer, having been involved in the discussions and report of *Catholicity* published in 1947 by a group convened by Dom Gregory Dix would not have objected 'to the concept of primacy' of the Pope; rather to 'the concept and declaration of infallibility itself, and of course the two Marian dogmas of the Immaculate Conception and the Assumption'.[163] What this demonstrates, again, is the complexity of Anglo-Catholicism and the way in which committed Anglo-Catholics can differ from one another in articles of belief. As we will see in the next chapter, Eliot had no reservations about the doctrine of the Assumption, nor its papal definition.

Even English converts to Roman Catholicism could have a low regard of its local manifestations. 'God's Architect', Augustus Pugin, thought that it was a good thing that Catholics had lost the English cathedrals and churches at the Reformation, as, instead of being merely neglected (as they had largely been by the Anglicans through the eighteenth century, for example), they would have been actively ruined. The nineteenth-century Anglo-Catholics could be counted on to preserve and renew the Gothic tradition. That Pugin's fears were well-founded was revealed as the twentieth century unfolded and reforming Roman Catholics did their destructive work, in their very own cathedrals, including Pugin's masterpieces. The Roman Catholic Bishop of Birmingham removed the rood screen at St Chad's in 1967, in an act described by Nikolaus Pevsner as 'vandalism unmitigated'. An Anglo-Catholic priest, Brian Brindley, saved it and installed it in his parish church of Holy Trinity, Reading.[164] Anglo-Catholics could be laughed at as 'A-Cs' (amateur Catholics), while Roman Catholics were 'R-Cs' (real Catholics), but in practical situations like these, away from the formulations of curial theologians, the recognition of where the genuine spirit of Catholicity was abiding in England seemed far from being self-evidently confined to the True Church.

The 'Malines Conversations' of the early 1920s in Belgium, between groups of Anglican and Roman Catholic theologians, initiated by Viscount Halifax and under the presidency of Cardinal Mercier, issued in agreement about the primacy of the Pope; the sacrifice of the Mass and the Real Presence, and the divine institution of the episcopacy. Halifax published the report of the conversations in 1928. There was 'no tangible result', but the meetings 'indirectly stimulated the movement for cooperation' between the two communions',[165] further stimulated, for a time, half a century later, by the ecumenical movement in the wake of Vatican II. Eliot was embracing Anglo-Catholicism in a period (so different from today) when the division with Rome appeared to have some chance of healing, in spite of the resentment of these continental advances, at home, by English Roman Catholics, on the one hand, and Anglican Protestants on the other.[166]

Such pronouncements by Eliot as 'the alternative to hell is purgatory' and his deference to the teachings of one to whom he referred as the 'Supreme Pontiff',[167] contradicting, explicitly, the Prayer Book's Article 22 ('Of Purgatory ... a fond thing vainly invented ... repugnant to the Word of God') and, implicitly, Article 37 (where it is announced that 'the Bishop of Rome [the pope] hath no jurisdiction in this Realm of England'), would still have been agitating John Bull and, indeed, most Anglican bishops of the 1920s (although many of them had, by then, embraced much of what the Catholic Revival was promoting and were adorning themselves with pectoral crosses, episcopal rings, and mitres).[168]

Indeed, Eliot may have been more 'Roman' in his Catholicism than many of his contemporary Anglo-Catholics and, indeed, than pre-Reformation Anglicans. That he was not English-born and was very much attuned to the history and artistry of Western European civilisation may have contributed to an openness to Rome which, culturally, restricted even definitely Catholic-minded English-born Anglicans. He described the encyclicals of the papacy, such as *Quadragesimo Anno* (1931) of Pius XI (reaffirming the social teaching of Leo XIII in his famous *Rerum Novarum*), as 'essential texts'[169] and called the 'Doctor Angelicus' of Catholicism, St Thomas Aquinas, 'the master'.[170] They expressed the teachings of 'the Universal Church' and Eliot believed that the only way the 'national Church' could 'safeguard ... the purity or the catholicity of its doctrine' would be by recognising that 'theology has no frontiers'.[171] In other words, the extent to which a Church was nationalistic impaired its validity, doctrinally. He rejected Middleton Murry's concept of a 'National Church' which 'degraded' Christianity to nationalism, rather than raising the nationalism to Christianity.[172] When the Oxford Movement started, Sheila Kaye-Smith observes, it was with the assertion of the authority of the Holy Catholic Church

> as against the limited conception of a self-determining, self-sufficing national church.[173]

His English friends perceived the un-English 'taint of Rome' in Eliot. In 'Stepping Heavenward' (1931), Richard Aldington, the novelist and biographer, referred to him satirically (and Roman-wise) as the 'recently beatified Father Cibber', recalling Alexander Pope's splenetic attack on Colley Cibber, appointed poet laureate in 1730, as hero of *The Dunciad*.[174] That the Catholic poet, Pope, was implicated in Aldington's jibe adds to its Roman satire. The Pope of Russell Square (where Faber and Faber had their offices), as Eliot was called, 'had an air', another friend, Russell Kirk, noted wryly, 'of writing *ex cathedra*'.[175]

The priests of the Society of Jesus in Ireland invited Eliot to Dublin to lecture them in 1936, decades before the post-conciliar ecumenical movement would have made such an event unremarkable. He gave the Jesuits a lecture on 'Tradition and The Practice of Poetry', where he argues the need for a powerful Catholic literature in a time of literary and cultural crisis.[176] Eliot expresses his regret, to his Irish audience, that W.B. Yeats 'came to poetry from a Protestant background', which led him to Orientalism, myths and legends. James Joyce, on the other hand,

> seems to me the most universal, the most Irish and the most Catholic writer in English of his generation.... What is most truly Irish ... is also most truly Catholic.[177]

Interestingly, when Eliot refers to the Jesuit poet, Gerard Manley Hopkins, he argues that while 'I cannot rate Gerard Hopkins so highly as most of my English friends do ... I like what he has to say much better than many of them'.[178]

Leaving Irish writers or writers who spent time in Ireland behind, Eliot then has recourse to his favourite Catholic poet:

> To have realised the Christian scheme in poetry is what makes
> the poetry of Dante so very great: but he had to have the
> background of theology and philosophy in order to do it.[179]

He affirms (in a statement that neatly combines the principles both
of Catholicism and cosmopolitan Modernism) that

> it is the endless task of men of letters to disturb the pro-
> vincialism of their particular place and time.[180]

Eliot's outlook was Catholic, both theologically and socio-culturally
and, thereby, the antithesis of Protestantism. In this respect, he found
himself entirely attuned to the mind of Catholic Europe.

Eliot went to Italy at the beginning of 1948, and in two letters to
Mary Trevelyan who was then travelling in Asia (dated, respectively:
St Gerlac. Vigil of the Epiphany and St. Honore du Faubourg – 5th
and 11th January), he mentions meeting the Pope (Pius XII) and the
favourable impression he had made. He found him less like a Headmaster than the current Archbishop of Canterbury, Geoffrey Fisher
(who had, indeed, been a Headmaster and was regularly charged with
behaving like one when he became a bishop). Further, Fisher had had
no time for Anglo-Catholics while Bishop of London (throughout
the war), and had attempted (unsuccessfully) to bring them to heel,
like troublesome sixth-formers.[181] The Pope gave Eliot two rosaries
and Eliot offers Mary the spare one, having already put the other one
into use.

As a publisher, Eliot was certainly ecumenical. At Faber and Faber,
he was mainly responsible for the 'very distinguished religious books
in our list', his long-time associate there, Peter du Sautoy, remembered, 'and they covered all denominations'.[182]

There was never any question, however, that Eliot would become a Roman Catholic, so long as he was an English citizen and a
naturalised Briton. Had the First World War never happened and he
had stayed in Europe, it is almost certain that he would have joined
the Church of Rome. But, in England, this was an impossible allegiance for him, not because of any doctrinal or liturgical reservations,
but because of the disconnection from the cultural life of the nation of
English Roman Catholics. So far from being part of the mainstream
of English life, A.L. Rowse has argued, English Roman Catholicism,
since the Reformation, has been a cultural curiosity:

> when children of these good Catholic families grew up [in the
> immediate post-Reformation period] they were sent abroad
> to Allen's foundations at Douai or in Rome, to Brussels or

St. Omer, Valladolid or Seville. One sees the formation of the English Catholic tradition, a self-contained minority with its affiliations abroad, with its own idiosyncrasy and peculiar place in the subsequent life of the country.[183]

Eliot certainly regretted this situation. For he acknowledged that

when we consider the western world, we must recognise that the main cultural tradition has been that corresponding to the Church of Rome ...

noting that, at the Reformation,

the separation of Northern Europe, and of England in part-icular, from communion with Rome represents a diversion from the main stream of culture.[184]

He also frankly admitted (in such works as *Reunion by Destruction* – see the following chapter) what was plainly obvious: that the Eng-lish Church fell short, in many ways, of the ideals of Catholic faith and practice. When Eliot was on the continent he would fulfil his religious obligations in Roman Catholic churches: in a letter to Mary Trevelyan (dated St Rigobert, 1950 – 4th January), he reports being driven to Mass at the Benedictine Abbey at Louvain by a Franciscan. But he was convinced that the Catholic Church in any nation must not only hold fast to orthodox doctrine, but be the religious expression of the culture of its people and, indeed, 'representative of the finest spirit' of its people.[185] This, he believed, the Church of England had achieved in what he regarded as its golden age, in the later sixteenth and earlier seventeenth century when Lancelot Andrewes, for example, became 'the first great preacher of the English Catholic Church'.[186] What Lockhart has said of Viscount Halifax, the lay leader of Anglo-Catholicism, can be applied to Eliot:

What restrained him [from Rome] was not any feeling *against* Rome but a feeling *for* the Church of England. He had a favourite phrase, *pietas Anglicana*, to describe a qual-ity possessing which a man would be securely anchored in Anglicanism, and without which he was in jeopardy every hour. It was a sense of the grandeur and continuity of the Church of St. Augustine, her lineage, her traditions, her in-alienable privilege as the Catholic Church in England. Her Orders were valid, her Sacraments – as none was better assured than Halifax – were effective.

*

In 1927, Eliot had stayed at Hickleton Hall with Halifax, by then 'the greatest living figure of the Catholic movement':[187]

> he accompanied his host each day to Hickleton Church, the little church close by the Hall, where they worshipped in a form which only an expert could have detected was other than the Roman Catholic mass, and where the building was exactly arranged with lights, lamps, pictures, images and the redolence of incense so as to have what one could only call a Catholic atmosphere.... But [Eliot] had not yet made the formal adherence to his new belief.[188]

On returning from Hickleton, Eliot wrote to the Reverend William Force Stead to ask if he could be 'confirmed in the Church of England'. As a Unitarian, he had not been baptised with the Trinitarian formula, so Stead advised him that he would need, first, to receive the sacrament of Baptism. Eliot's response, according to Robert Sencourt, their mutual friend, was to declare:

> William, I want to be baptized into the one true fold of Christ.[189]

Chapter Five

Anglo-Catholic in Religion (1927-1965)

It is commonplace to refer to Eliot's 'conversion' to Anglo-Catholicism. This is the customary term, in general Catholic discourse, to describe the process by which people from other Churches or none embrace the faith. So it is useful for marking Eliot's formal commitment of 1927 when he received the Christian sacraments of baptism and confirmation on 29th and 30th June, respectively.[1] And Eliot occasionally uses the word himself, of his own experience and more generally: 'scepticism', he wrote in 1932, 'is the preface to conversion'.[2] But he also noted that

> no one ever attempted to convert *me*; and, looking back on
> my pre-Christian state of mind, I do not think that such a
> campaign would have prospered.[3]

The sacramental ceremonies of his Christian initiation were administered in secrecy. The doors of Holy Trinity church at Finstock (near Witney, in Oxfordshire) were locked and a verger was posted on guard in the vestry as William Force Stead, chaplain of Worcester College, Oxford, administered adult baptism to Eliot at the font. The next day, he was driven to the private chapel of the Bishop of Oxford, Thomas Banks Strong, where the rite of confirmation was performed. Many years later, when Eliot was married to Valerie Fletcher, that sacrament was similarly secretly celebrated, early in the morning (6.15 a.m.) of 10th January, 1957, and not at their parish church, but at St Barnabas' Church, West Kensington (where Jules Laforgue, an important influence on Eliot's poetry, had married Leah Lee in 1886).[4]

While Eliot made no secret of his Christianity (and, of course, worshipped publicly), the sacramental sealing of his faith was, because of its solemnity, not for public advertisement. He was very critical of the mass-conversion rallies in the United Kingdom of the American evangelist, Dr Billy Graham, during the 1950s. Graham stirred up the mass hysteria, Eliot told Mary Trevelyan (after the crusade in

Glasgow in 1955), 'of people wanting to be made to believe while being past making the effort themselves'.[5]

Where 'conversion' is misleading, with regard to Eliot's faith, is in its suggestion of an instantaneous event, as a result of which the convert is changed utterly and a breach is made with his or her previous, unconverted, unregenerate life. He or she is 'born again'. Generally, in Christianity, this is much more likely to be experienced in the Evangelical tradition, in the moment of decision (which may occur, for example, at a revivalist meeting and which was cultivated at Billy Graham's crusades). This is where Anglo-Catholic tradition and Eliot's own spiritual experience part company from Protestant ideas of conversion, about which (especially the emotional element, which can play a powerful role) he was deeply suspicious, as were Anglo-Catholics in general: 'the Billy Graham mission ... spoke to the feelings and just said Come and surrender, then go back to your own churches and worship there, and do not think but feel'.[6] The Evangelical's sudden sanctification belonged to a different realm of experience from Eliot's. In this reserve, he owed something, for once, to Unitarian teaching, as expounded by his grandfather, the Reverend William Greenleaf Eliot:

> We do not believe in an instantaneous and miraculous change, by virtue of which he who is at one moment totally depraved can become in the next one of God's saints.... We have greater confidence in the change which comes through the quietness of thought.[7]

Accordingly, even when Eliot had become a prominent Anglo-Catholic layman and the best-known of Anglo-Catholic writers, he was at pains to point out that, as no-one ever attempted to convert him, so, in his Christian writings, he was not 'attempting to convert' his readers.[8] Yet, as his friend Martin Browne remembered, Eliot's faith, as a member of the Church of England (but only from middle age),

> meant passionately more to him than to most of those who had always had it.[9]

The term, 'conversion', in Eliot's case tends to diminish the importance of all the diverse elements that led up to his baptism and confirmation over so many years and, by implying certitude and finality, contradicts Eliot's conception of the individual Christian's experience – particularly that of 'every man who thinks and lives by thought'[10] – as a much more complex phenomenon, shot through with doubts and backslidings, throughout one's earthly pilgrimage. Eliot's was 'a profound doubting belief', Denis Donoghue writes, 'contiguous to Augustine, St. John of the Cross, and Pascal'.[11] The 'Catholic should have', Eliot wrote (after some six years as an Anglo-Catholic), '*absolute* ideals – and moderate expectations'.[12] The realisation of the ideals is the preserve of the saints; 'for us, there is only the trying'.[13] In what Russell Kirk describes as Eliot's fullest formal statement touching upon his conversion, we note the emphasis placed on the intellectual process which leads to belief:

> The Christian thinker – and I mean the man who is trying consciously and conscientiously to explain to himself the sequence which culminates in faith ... – proceeds by rejection and elimination. He finds the world to be so and so; he finds its character inexplicable by any non-religious theory: among religions he finds Christianity, and Catholic Christianity, to account most satisfactorily for the world and especially for the moral world within; and thus, by what Newman calls 'powerful and concurrent' reasons, he finds himself inexorably committed to the dogma of the Incarnation.[14]

What is notable here, as well, is that full Christian commitment is specifically understood by Eliot to be a grammar of assent culminating – in the Anglo-Catholic way – in the acceptance of that particular doctrine.

In relation to the reading and interpretation of Eliot's poetry and plays, 'conversion' is a term best avoided, having practically no relevance at all, for two reasons, to the understanding and appreciation of his verse. First, Eliot's poetry from his Christian period, beginning with 'Journey of the Magi' (1927) focuses, repeatedly and profoundly, on the difficulties of faith and the elusiveness of transcendental experience, while urging that it remains necessary, constantly, to strive towards these things. And, secondly, the word may foster the idea that the poetry (or any kind of literature) written by a convert is bound to have designs upon readers to lead them into the same experience; that it should be serving an evangelical purpose, culminating in a similar conversion and commitment from which the author's writing has derived. Eliot's poetry is no more attuned to this purpose than his Christian life was directed by the desire to convert others to the faith. To the Episcopalian priest who suggested to Eliot that *The Cocktail Party* was 'covertly all about the Mass', Eliot responded:

I really wanted to write a damn good play, and I hope I did.[15]

John Kwan-Terry calls *Ash-Wednesday* (written through the years 1927 to 1930) Eliot's 'conversion poem' while noting – correctly – that 'the very climax of the poem ... is fraught with ambiguity and uncertainty'. If this is conversion, in other words, it is not as the world understands the term.[16] Craig Raine writes tellingly that *Ash-Wednesday*

> is frequently misinterpreted as a poem of belief, when it is, in fact, a poem about the difficulty of religious belief.[17]

That Ronald Schuchard, in another recent study, concurs, indicates that the critical consensus is at last abandoning the notion of Eliot's conversion in the reading and appreciation of his poetry:

> It is ... unfortunate that *Ash-Wednesday* is so often presen-ted merely as Eliot's 'conversion poem', when it is in fact an extraordinary love poem of great personal intensity and spiritual discipline.... It is neither a devotional poem nor a poem of conversion; it represents the beginning of an exile's arduous lenten journey from a life of tormented love towards the prayerful hope of finding, like Dante, a *vita nuova* in di-vine Love.[18]

With reference to Eliot's politics, Kenneth Asher, in *T.S. Eliot and Ideology*, notes that while 'scholarly inquiry has for the most part agreed that a radical rupture took place in 1927, as Eliot's skepticism was overcome in one leap of faith',[19] there was, rather (Asher rightly argues), a gradual accumulation of reasons for his adoption of his ideological position. And David Moody reflects that the progress of Eliot's poetry, in the 'conversion' years, from *The Waste Land* (1922), through 'The Hollow Men' (1925) to *Ash-Wednesday* (1930), reveals 'a further development, not a new start', in the evolution of 'a consistent personality'.[20] Eliot himself reflected, some years after his formal commitment to Christianity, that

> what appears to another person to be a change of attitude and even a recantation of former views must often appear to the author himself rather as part of a continuous and more or less consistent development.[21]

His Anglo-Catholicism was the result of a logical progression. It was not a leap of faith.

1

In religion, of paramount importance, for Eliot, was 'the Love of God and a sound Catholic doctrine'.[22] The two were inextricable. The former (fulfilling the first Commandment) was insufficient, as, relying on our own perceptions, we may fail to determine matters correctly. A 'fixed point' is needed, to prevent 'our deflecting from the ideal course'. Catholic doctrine makes it possible that 'we may at any moment determine our position', by reference to it.[23] It is noteworthy that these comments were made not only in the early period of the Second World War, when people's minds and emotions required significant steadying, but also at the time of Eliot's work-in-progress on *Four Quartets*, where the metaphor of the 'still point' indicates the necessity of an external reference-guide for wandering humanity. This is symbolised, poetically, by the rocky outcrop, the Dry Salvages, off the Massachusetts coast in the midst of the turbulent Atlantic: a stable point of reference in the flux of human existence.

Catholics, Eliot insisted, should be convinced of the 'vast importance of adhering to, and developing, our dogmatic theology'.[24] Part of his attraction to thinkers and writers such as Lancelot Andrewes was the spirit and manner in which they explored theological ideas. 'The Incarnation was to him an essential dogma', Eliot writes of Andrewes,

> and we are able to compare seventeen developments of the same idea. Reading Andrewes on such a theme is like listening to a great Hellenist expounding a text of the 'Posterior Analytics'.... We find his examination of words terminating in the ecstasy of assent.[25]

For Eliot, the Word made flesh, the revelation of God in Christ, was the crucial doctrine of Catholic Christianity – as he wrote, ten years after his conversion:

> I take for granted that Christian revelation is the only full revelation; and that the fullness of Christian revelation resides in the essential fact of the Incarnation, in relation to which all Christian revelation is to be understood. The division between those who accept, and those who deny, Christian revelation I take to be the most profound division between human beings.[26]

Theology was, for Eliot, a 'science',[27] the discipline of faith which the Humanists and liberal Protestants had abrogated by divorcing themselves from this repository of impersonal wisdom to pin their hopes on spiritual whims and fancies – 'undisciplined emotions'.[28] He traced the decline in theology not merely from the Enlightenment or even the theological developments of the Reformation, but from the end of the Middle Ages (the epoch, for him, of Aquinas and Dante). Since then, there had been 'a progressive spiritual deterioration'.[29]

Not that Eliot regarded himself as a theologian. He was candid about his inadequacies in the field, reflecting in 1930, that he was a 'mere ignoramus'[30] and, in 1934, seven years after his baptism and confirmation, that

> I am painfully aware that I need a much more extensive and profound knowledge of theology.[31]

As late as 1947, he wrote to Mary Trevelyan remarking that he found it profitable to pass his time in complete idleness reading only theology.[32]

Eliot enjoyed discussing theological issues with informed interlocutors, writing to Paul Elmer More (a learned historian of Anglicanism) in 1931 that 'he was looking forward to long evenings enlivened by whiskey and tobacco and countercharges of heresy'.[33] *After Strange Gods: A Primer of Modern Heresy* was to be published a couple of years later, so aspects of orthodoxy and the challenges to it were particularly on Eliot's mind in these days. More (who was finding his own feet in the faith at this time) was looking forward to the occasions:

> Ah, theology is the only interesting topic after all, and to convict a devout Anglo-Catholic of heresy is something for which I would surrender ten good dinners.[34]

More never completely submitted to the Church – he refused to take Communion and declined confirmation on his death-bed. Eliot, for all his admiration for his friend, identified a 'cardinal error' in More's position on the sacrament of the Eucharist. More had announced: 'I do not accept the definition of sacrament as an *opus operatum* taken … absolutely'. And Eliot would also have rejected More's reluctance to submit to 'an *absolute* Church' (More's emphasis).[35] For Eliot, 'full Christian virtue cannot exist without full Christian belief',[36] and this meant for him an unqualified submission to the teachings of Catholic and Apostolic Christianity. Faith and its practice were inextricably linked; practice was the incarnation of belief, as Eliot reflected after more than twenty years as a devoted Anglo-

Catholic, touching, as he characteristically does, on the difficulties of living a life that is true to such principles:

> the reflection that what we believe is not merely what we formulate and subscribe to, but that behaviour is also belief, and that even the most conscious and developed of us live also at the level on which belief and behaviour cannot be distinguished, is one that may, once we allow our imagination to play upon it, be very disconcerting. It gives an importance to our most trivial pursuits, which we cannot contemplate long without the horror of nightmare.[37]

Eliot repeatedly rejected the idea that becoming a Christian provided a pat solution to (or an escape from) the world's problems, or made one's own personal life simpler and easier. Writing (in the early 1930s) of young people who were submitting themselves to Communist ideology ('the faith of the day') and were discovering, thereby, a 'godsend' in finding something in which to believe, he warned:

> Once they have committed themselves, they must find (if they are honest, and really growing) that they have let themselves in for all the troubles that beset those who believe in something.... They have joined that bitter fraternity which lives on a higher level of doubt; no longer the doubting which is just play with ideas ... but that which is a daily battle.[38]

2

It was in the autumn of 1933, the year of the centenary of the Oxford Movement, that (Eliot remembered) 'I first attended Mass at St Stephen's [Gloucester Road, South Kensington]'.[39] He had spent a year lecturing in America and was staying at a boarding house in West London run by W.E. Scott Hall, one of the bishops irregularly consecrated by Arnold Harris Mathew (as he called himself, when he wasn't the Revd Count Povoleri), the most extraordinary of the *episcopi vagantes* who lurked on the fringes of Anglo-Catholicism.[40] Eliot came to know his new vicar, the Revd Eric Cheetham,

> and not very long afterwards he offered me rooms, which had become available, in his presbytery in Grenville Place.

Eliot remained in the clergy house for seven years, first in Grenville Place, then in Emperor's Gate, where Fr Cheetham had rented the top part of the house. In 1940, with the war in its preliminary stages,

I retired to friends in the country and to my office in
Bloomsbury, and Father Cheetham found shelter in what
always seemed to me a characteristic choice of abode – the
basement of the Albert Hall.

Seven years in an Anglo-Catholic presbytery could not have failed,
in the first years of Eliot's commitment to the faith, both to have
made him very familiar with all its aspects but (as anyone who has
spent any time, let alone seven years, in any kind of clerical dwelling
will testify) to the less appealing and edifying elements of the Church
and of the priestly life. Yet Eliot emerged with his faith intact and,
for all we know, had it not been for the interruption of the war, may
well have stayed in the presbytery for many more years. For a parish
priest as flamboyant as Father Cheetham (Eliot noted his 'theatrical
gifts'), and as a vicar of a fashionable West End church and one of the
leading Anglo-Catholic shrines in England, it would not have been
unappealing, either, to have had as paying guest in the clergy-house
a literary figure who was increasingly distinguished and famous in
these years and on the way to becoming one of the best known of
Anglo-Catholic laymen in the twentieth century. Cheetham appointed
Eliot his warden just a year after the poet had come to the parish, in
1934, and Eliot remained in that position until the end of Cheetham's
incumbency in 1956 (and indeed beyond it, until April, 1959) and
continued worshipping at the church until his death six years later.

    He admired his vicar's 'liturgical sense of accuracy and precision',
his 'good taste and discretion' and his 'devotion to Catholic doctrine
and Catholic observance', combined with 'true evangelical zeal':

> He had a strong sense of pastoral responsibility, and I suspect
> that he often helped those who were in need of help, in ways
> which exceeded the bounds of ordinary pastoral activity.

Obviously, this was a parish priest for whom Eliot had the highest
regard, while noting his eccentricities: 'when we really love a person,
we love the weaknesses and foibles of that person. Eric Cheetham
was very lovable, and was also, at times, extremely irritating; and
one loved him the more for the irritation he caused'. Given the
importance placed by Anglo-Catholicism on the priesthood, it was
fortunate, indeed, for Eliot's faith in its formative years that he
came under the close, sustained influence of a parish priest he so
esteemed:

> We recognised in him qualities of integrity, generosity, and
> natural goodness developed by Christian discipline; we

recognised the strength and depth of his faith: but in the end the quality of which one is most aware in people one loves is simply – their lovableness.

The actor, Christopher Lee, was an altar server at St Stephen's, under Eric Cheetham, in the 1950s and, in his autobiography, provides some vivid recollections of his 'father in God' which resonate repeatedly with Eliot's appreciation from the same period:

He was a wonderfully jolly priest, the kind I always supp-osed G.K. Chesterton would have loved, who not only was a passionate theatre-goer, but had quite a theatrical flair him-self. He had a miniature motor-bike to make his rounds, and used to say wistfully that he only wished he might have ridden it up the aisle, only the Church would frown on him dispensing blessings from a Corgi.

Lee remembered Eliot as Cheetham's warden and how he would join the happy company at 'Father's flat in Clarehill Court' for lunch after Sunday High Mass:

I was very much influenced by the Father's capacity to come forward and mix with his flock on their own terms, admit the power of temptation and his own difficulties in resis-ting it. I loved his humour and the twinkling eyes when he admonished himself with a loud sibilant 'Sssshhhhh!' foll-owing some outrageous admission of his own failings. He had a marvellous loving kindness and took endless trouble and patience in explaining to me the ideals of discipline of the Church.

The details of this testimony indicate several reasons why Eliot himself was also drawn so compellingly, and over many years, to Fr Cheet-ham and why he remained at St Stephen's throughout the vicar's long incumbency when, had he not been satisfied, there were many Anglo-Catholic alternatives elsewhere in the West End and central London.

Lee observes of the parish priest in the confessional:

Nothing was ever dull with him. There was a pointed sub-tlety even in his drolleries, as when he'd say to me, 'I'm sure the Lord will forgive me if I say you really must be more precise when you come to confession'.

Such an emphasis on the necessity to be well prepared, especially with regard to the sacrament of penance, are notes that ring very true in our understanding of the priorities and characteristics of Eliot's practice of his own faith. But also important is the stress that Lee places on Cheetham's loving-kindness, his sense of humour and – particularly noteworthy – his affection for the theatre and theatre-people, and his own theatricality (a trait to which Eliot, too, was strongly drawn, especially in these years of his most active engagement with the stage):

> His own approach to his services had a theatrical flavour. In the vestry he'd be chatting with me and suddenly say, 'Must break off now and go and put my make-up on' or, 'I see we're just about sold out for the second house tonight'.[41]

From these affectionate reminiscences, of both Eliot and Lee, there emerges a decided 'camp' quality in the portraiture of Fr Cheetham. In this respect, it is an indication of the lack of consideration of Eliot's religious affiliation, in commentaries on his life, that the handful of biographers who have entertained the notion that Eliot had homosexual tendencies never pursue the idea that these might have resonated with Anglo-Catholicism, the homoeroticism of which we considered in the previous chapter. In this regard, it is worth noting that Eliot appears never to have been a server, nor was he ever a member of the *schola cantorum*, the two domains in which, for a layman, such an inclination might have found some fulfillment and, at least, association with the like-minded, by participation in the ornate ritual of the sanctuary and choir, and the haberdashery of the sacristy. For all his love of the Catholic ceremonies, like the majority of the laity (and, of course – in those days – all women), Eliot was an observer of the high ritual rather than a contributor to it. The only conspicuous and singular public ritual act which Eliot undertook, in addition to the various customary bodily gestures (genuflection, crossing oneself, and so on) which are performed in concert with everyone else at various points in the liturgy – such as at the *Incarnatus est*, in the Creed, when a genuflection was made, honouring the Incarnation – was to take the plate around for the collection during Mass. This, the job of a sidesman, was a normal act in any Anglican church, high or low.

George Every recalled for me that Eliot was concerned after Fr Cheetham's retirement that the liturgical tradition of St Stephen's might be upset by the new incumbent (a typical Anglo-Catholic anxiety). Eliot also approached Fr Geoffrey Curtis, of the Community of the Resurrection, about the matter, and he advised Eliot (so he told me) to transfer to nearby St Mary Abbots in Kensington High Street. There were no significant modifications (under Fr Wilfred Jennings), however, and Eliot continued to worship at St Stephen's for the remaining decade of his life, and his second wife does so to this day. There is a memorial stone to the poet on the south wall, requesting, in the Catholic way, that prayers be offered for the repose of his soul, and requiem Masses have been celebrated at St Stephen's on anniversaries of the poet's death.[42]

3

Mass and the liturgy

> After Eliot received the Eucharist and returned to his place, he seemed to fall 'flat on his face in the aisle, with his arms stretched out.... I realized that Eliot had just undergone a mystical experience'.[43]

At St Stephen's, Eliot was regular and frequent in attendance at Mass. This not only expressed the usual commitment of a devout Anglo-Catholic, but of someone who valued 'ritual and habit', which, he said, are 'essential to religion'.[44] It was a regime that had no purpose, so far as he was concerned, in terms of witness for others, let alone their conversion. Simply, he was obliged to do it. His faith entailed it:

> I do not go out to an early communion on a cold morning in order to convert my housekeeper, or to set a good example to the night porter of my block of flats before he goes off duty. If this was my motive, I had better not, for my own sake, go at all; and if the housekeeper and the porter suspected that this was my motive, they would – far from being softened – merely be justifiably irritated by my trying to interfere with their lives.[45]

Yet he was edified by the example of others, in their Catholic, sacramental observance, commenting of Simone Weil, for example, that she had an 'intense devotion to Our Lord in the Sacrament of the Altar'.[46]

Eliot participated in the annual Holy Week 'watch' before the tabernacle at St Stephen's, an ancient liturgical custom drawing attention both to Christ's Real Presence in the Eucharist and to his Passion ('Could ye not watch with me one hour?'[47]), taking place between the Maundy Thursday liturgy and the Good Friday liturgy of the Passion. Mary Trevelyan records in her diary for 1950 that Eliot had insisted on taking the 1 a.m. to 2 a.m. watch before the Sacrament that Easter (the custom being for women to watch during the day; men at night), and, the next day, looked particularly exhausted; while the poet wrote to her on 27th March, 1953, remarking that his only free evening for a visit would be Thursday, and on the following morning he would be beginning his watch at 9.30 until Mass began, as he had done the previous year. His reference is to the 'Mass of the pre-sanctified'.

Such liturgical devotion was noted by friends, from the beginning of his formal membership of the Church, even if Eliot had no intention of edifying them thereby. In either 1927 or 1928, Herbert Read, staying with the Eliots in their Belgravia home, recalled that one morning

> I lay still and saw first a hand and then an arm reach round the door and lift from a hook the bowler hat that was hanging there. It was a little before seven o'clock and Mr. Eliot was on his way to an early communion service. It was the first intimation I had had of his conversion to the Christian faith.[48]

This first intimation may have been more precise than Read noted; for such observance, if it were a weekday morning, marked Eliot out not only as a Christian but as an Anglo-Catholic.

In an unpersuasive distinction, Peter Ackroyd discriminates between Eliot's doctrinal allegiances and his Christian observances, noting that 'it may seem odd' to do so, but arguing that 'it is likely that his need for the latter came from a much deeper source'.[49] This is more than 'odd', for two reasons. First, for the Catholic, the discipline (and sacraments) of such as confession and the Mass are expressions of (and embody) the central doctrines of the faith; and, second, nothing came from a 'deeper source' in Eliot's being than his conviction of the truth of the dogma of Original Sin (and the concomitant Christian teaching of redemption from it). The sacraments – 'his Christian observances' – were the channels of grace of that redemption. Liturgy and doctrine were one, for Eliot.

As part of his rule of hearing Mass, Eliot was careful to note Holy Days of Obligation – days throughout the Church's year, in addition to Sundays, on which the faithful are supposed to attend Mass. These vary from country to country in the Roman Church, but usually include such feasts – dotted through the year – as Christmas Day, the Circumcision and Epiphany of the Lord, Ascension Day, Corpus Christi, Saints Peter and Paul, the Assumption of the Blessed Virgin Mary, and All Saints Day. Anglo-Catholicism followed the Roman lead in this matter (as in so many others), although Eliot was not always clear, noting that he was not sure, as a particular Tuesday (the feast of SS. Peter and Paul) approached, whether it was an obligation day, while remembering that it was for Roman Catholics.[50] Certainly, it mattered to him to get these rules of observance right.

They could lead to complications. In a letter to Trevelyan, dated 26th January, 1948, the Monday following Septuagesima (the third Sunday before Lent and the ninth before Easter), Eliot points out that the feast of the Conversion of St Paul (usually observed on the 25th January), had had to be transferred (a common practice) to the 27th, so that a full celebration of the apostle's feast (with First Evensong, Mattins and Second Evensong could be offered, the First Evensong of the feast not being displaced by the Second Evensong of Septuagesima). So, Eliot complains, he has to get up early again for another weekday Mass. He notes that Paul's conversion is an important event, and, on Friday of that week, there is the commemoration of Charles, King and Martyr (30th January) – a solemn day for a royalist. The devotion to St Charles is, in fact, an unusual feature of an Anglo-Catholic's regime (although others, such as Hope Patten of Walsingham, shared it) being, rather, a 'principle of High Church toryism'.[51] Charles is not, of course, a saint in the Roman calendar (usually rigorously observed by Western Use Anglo-Catholics like Eliot), and has never been formally canonised, but from 1662 to 1859 a special service was annexed to The Book of Common Prayer, for 30th January, by royal mandate, and the anniversary of the king's execution was to be kept 'as a day of national fasting and humiliation'.[52] John Henry Newman, in his Tractarian days,

> took up the traditional High Church cult of the Royal Martyr and … scrupulously observed January 30th as the day of the Martyrdom.[53]

In the twentieth century, and to this day, the Society of King Charles the Martyr organises commemorations which include, in Anglo-Catholic parishes sympathetic to the cult, solemn Masses beginning with the Introit:

> Let us rejoice in the Lord, celebrating the festival day in honour of blessed Charles the Martyr: at whose passion the Angels rejoice and praise the Son of God.

Several churches and chapels have been dedicated in the royal martyr's name.[54] Eliot's devotion to Charles is a royalist high church variation on the usual themes of his Anglo-Catholicism and indicates, again, not only the strength of his royalist convictions but his devotion to the Caroline Church. Yet he regarded the doctrine of the divine right of kings as 'noble but untenable'.[55] Charles, who visited Little Gidding after his defeat at the battle of Naseby in the Civil War, is remembered in Eliot's poem, coming under cover of darkness, as 'a broken king', in a sequence focusing on the way a spiritual place, 'where prayer has been valid', although obscure and unprepossessing in earthly terms, can redeem the mortal world's pains and defeats.[56]

On the feast of the Assumption in 1949, Eliot complained in a letter to Trevelyan about the discomfort his sense of religious obligation was causing him. Fr Cheetham celebrated such holy day Masses at 7.30 a.m. which meant that Eliot had to rise at 6.15, for there would be the time needed for formal dressing, as he dressed with particular formality in honour of certain saints, Trevelyan recalls, such as St Stephen, the patron of his church,[57] and then walk (he has the word in capitals) to Mass. The Assumption was an important feast for Eliot, as he always made his confession before it. Yet for all these complaints (which, of course, are tongue-in-cheek) he was prepared to go beyond the disciplines of the Western Church in observing certain self-imposed obligations. Such was Eliot's regard for the feast of the Transfiguration of the Lord (6th August) that he followed the practice of the Orthodox Church by observing it as an additional day of obligation.[58] He had wanted to venerate Saints Simon and Jude (28th October) in 1955, Eliot comments in a letter to Trevelyan, but he was concerned that the necessarily early morning attendance at Mass would aggravate his cold (Eliot was nearly 70 at this time) and, hence, prevent him from undertaking his secular duties. It was this sort of decision – he continues – that was always particularly difficult for him, as an Eliot: the decision between the duty to God and that to man. He would have preferred the former, but succumbed regretfully to the familial influence of those first twenty-one years and so acted on his family's precept that, in cases of doubt, it is one's duty to do the thing you least want to do.

Breakfast, however, would not have been part of that typical preparatory hour and a quarter prior to Mass. Like all pious Catholics (Anglican and Roman) of that era, Eliot rigorously kept the fast, from midnight, prior to receiving communion in the early morning, so that the Sacrament might be the first food to pass the communicant's lips that day. This practice had long been encouraged in the Church of England, Jeremy Taylor writing in the seventeenth century:

> Let us receive the Consecrated Elements with all devotion
> and humility of body and spirit; and do this honour to it, that
> it be the first food we eat ... that day.[59]

But, in Anglicanism, only Anglo-Catholics would rigorously keep the fast, regarding it as obligatory, in the Roman style. The relaxation of the fasting rules in the Roman Church (to just one hour before communion) has led to the possibility of the celebration of evening Masses, an early innovation of which (George Every told me in interview) Eliot strongly disapproved. The Friday fast, when Roman and Anglo-Catholics were used not to consume any meat, is now also redundant, but Anne Ridler recalled for me how Eliot would warn prospective Friday hostesses of the necessity (in his case) for fish. This would have been an exceptional, indeed almost unheard-of request, from an 'ordinary' Anglican. But Eliot was adamant that others should be aware of his position and the implications of his faith. Herbert Read, parodying Eliot by describing himself as an 'agnostic in religion', noted of his friend:

> a statement of differences he could respect; what he could not tolerate was any false interpretation of the position he himself held.[60]

On one occasion, Eliot did not communicate on the most important day of obligation – Easter Day – as he was unable, through illness, to receive the sacrament fasting. He wrote to the Episcopalian priest, William Levy, at Whitsun in 1954 (with a prayer for him, as Levy had undoubtedly celebrated Mass that morning), noting that the priest who had come to the clinic where Eliot had been hospitalised at this period arrived late and Eliot's breakfast and medication could not be delayed until after Mass.[61] Such scrupulosity may be almost impossible to credit today, although it would have been commonplace then. And the fasting rules, like other disciplines for the mortification of the flesh, would probably not have been as onerous for Eliot, with 'his natural asceticism',[62] as for those for whom such privations would have been temperamentally alien and extreme. A Puritan inheritance could prepare one very well for the disciplines of Catholicism.

Because of his strict attitude to the Mass and receiving communion, Eliot addressed the idea of reception of the eucharist by those who were not members of what he would have regarded as the Catholic Church, especially members of the dissenting or free Churches, whose ministers were not episcopally ordained. The matter came to a head in the debate over the Church of South India (which we will consider below), to which Eliot contributed the pamphlet, *Reunion by Destruction* (1943). But a decade earlier, he had broached the subject in 'Thoughts after Lambeth' – that is, after the once-a-decade meeting of the bishops of the worldwide Anglican Communion:[63]

> what is required is some theory of degrees of reception of the Blessed Sacrament, as well as the validity of the ministration

of a celebrant not episcopally ordained. My objection therefore is not to the admission of dissenters to the Altar – and
I do not wish to attack what has not yet been defended
– but to the propagation of this practice before theological
justification has been expounded. Possibly theology is what
Bradley said philosophy was: 'the finding of bad reasons for
what we believe upon instinct'; I think it may be the finding
of good reasons for what we believe upon instinct, but if
the Church of England cannot find these reasons, and make
them intelligible to the more philosophically trained among
the faithful, what can it do?[64]

Eliot's view, in relation to dissenters, was to harden as the years passed, but apart from the particular eucharistic issue here, the importance
of the passage is its expression of an Anglo-Catholic impatience,
on the part of someone devoted to the 'Blessed Sacrament', with the
Church's perceived prevarication on such crucial matters of Catholic
faith and order. We might also note the confidence with which Eliot
enters into debate and commentary on the hierarchy of the Church
which he had joined only a few years before.

Because of Anglo-Catholicism's appropriation of the full Catholic
teaching about the Mass, an important aspect of eucharistic life in
Anglo-Catholicism, and, therefore, in Eliot's practice of the faith, was
attendance at Masses of requiem, offered for the repose of the souls of
the faithful departed (and which take their title from the first word of
the Introit, at the beginning of the liturgy: '*Requiem aeternam dona eis,
Domine ...*', 'Rest eternal grant unto them, O Lord ...'). This, again, is
an aspect of Anglo-Catholic faith and practice which separates it from
all other varieties of Anglicanism. The offering of Masses in chantry
chapels, the chantry priests being paid to offer Masses in perpetuity
for the repose of the souls of the deceased founders of the chantries,
and which were flourishing in England on the eve of Reformation,
was one of those aspects of Catholic devotion which were rapidly
and utterly suppressed by the Protestant Reformers. The caricatured, insistently Anglo-Catholic priest in Rose Macaulay's *Towers of
Trebizond* is called Fr Chantry-Pigg.

The most important requiem Mass is celebrated on All Souls' Day,
2nd November, 'the Commemoration of all the Faithful Departed'. In
the course of the Mass, the famous sequence, '*Dies irae, dies illa ...*' –
'Day of wrath and doom impending ...' – is chanted, as Eliot directs it
should be, 'in Latin by a choir in the distance', as Thomas' martyrdom
approaches in *Murder in the Cathedral*. The women of Canterbury,

in English, simultaneously echo its rhythm (and vocabulary) in their verses beginning:

> Dead upon the tree, my Saviour,
> Let not be in vain Thy labour;
> Help me, Lord, in my last fear.[65]

Mary Trevelyan records in her diary for 1954 how Eliot, returning with her from the requiem Mass on All Souls' Day, was struck both by the repetition of the versicle, 'Rest eternal grant unto them, O Lord', and the mystery it foreshadowed:

> It's strange, this gift to human beings [he commented], that they are given of inventing words of which they don't know the full meaning.

Many years before, drawing attention in the *Criterion* to the death of the Austrian poet and dramatist, Hugo von Hofmannsthal (a convert whose journey of faith from despair to Catholicism has striking similarities to Eliot's),[66] Eliot requested simply of his readers, drawing on the standard Catholic formula:

> Of Your Charity Pray for the soul of Hugo von Hofmann-sthal.[67]

The same formula is used on Eliot's tombstone at St Michael's, East Coker. In his third essay on Baudelaire (1930), after conjecturing whether or not the Frenchman was walking amongst the lowest of the dead, Eliot reflected:

> we are not prevented from praying for his repose;[68]

while in *Notes towards the Definition of Culture* (1948), he introduces the theme of fostering devotion to the departed (which is linked to care for the unborn): 'a piety towards the dead, however obscure, and a solicitude for the unborn, however remote'. That piety, Eliot points out, has nothing to do with the 'vanities and pretensions of genealogy'.[69] It is, rather, a community of the living and the dead in the Body of Christ. In *Four Quartets*, it is an idea intimately linked to the more general theme of the celebration of the transcendence of time:

> And what the dead had no speech for, when living,
> They can tell you, being dead: the communication
> Of the dead is tongued with fire beyond the language
>   of the living.[70]

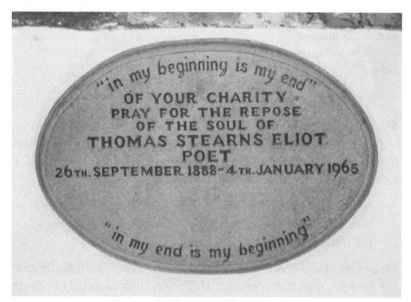

Eliot's tombstone, St Michael's, East Coker

'I am afraid of the life after death', Eliot had told Ezra Pound, as early as 1919.[71] The Catholic provision of prayers and Masses for the dead would have significantly alleviated that fear.

The climax of Eliot's worshipping week (which included daily private prayer and attendance at weekday Low Masses – said, not sung, by the celebrant, without any music or incense, usually without a sermon, and often at a side altar, with just two candles lit) was High Mass, late on Sunday morning, at St Stephen's. The six candles on the high altar would be ablaze, as the liturgy began with the *Asperges* – the sprinkling with holy water of the congregation by the coped celebrant, accompanied by the sacred ministers in dalmatic and tunicle, to the singing of the chant from Psalm 51, '*Asperges me, Domine, hyssopo…*' ('Thou shalt purge me, O Lord, with hyssop…').[72] All that followed, for the next 70 minutes or so, was celebrated with every adornment of ceremony and choral music and meticulous attention to the details of both, with much rehearsal beforehand.

The High Mass was the glory of triumphant Anglo-Catholicism. While more generally Anglican hymnody was used at various points (and, unlike Roman Catholic liturgy, enthusiastically, heartily sung by the congregation in a more typically Anglican way), much of the rite itself was sung by the sacred ministers and choir, with Gregorian chant and polyphony – therefore, much of it (apart from the three or four hymns) was in Latin. A server at St Stephen's in the early 1950s told me that Palestrina was one of the favoured composers at the church at that time.[73] For all of his praise of the Cranmerian language of the Prayer Book and that of the translators of the Authorized Version of Scripture, such as Lancelot Andrewes, Eliot believed that worship at its best was to be offered in the 'impersonal eloquence of the Latin language',[74] as, again, impersonality is celebrated and linked both to Catholic and Classical forms. Before his conversion, he had praised the poetic qualities of Latin hymnody as, once more, we see the importance of an initial aesthetic experience which was later to meld with his religious convictions:

> Apart from other justifications, the Latin hymns are a part of literature which ought to be studied by every person interested in the technique of verse.[75]

The 'Canon' of the Mass, its central, most solemn section, wherein the consecration of the bread and wine takes place, would be uttered '*in secreto*' – silently – the people being made aware at the point of consecration that it had occurred, by the priest's genuflection, followed by the elevation of the Host and then of the chalice of the Blood, both accompanied by the ringing of the consecration bell (a custom introduced in the twelfth century). Eliot and his fellow congregants would have looked up and adored (possibly silently uttering prayers prescribed in the devotional manuals), peering through the incense-clouded sanctuary, before crossing themselves and bowing their heads again in prayer as the Canon drew to its conclusion, lifting their eyes again when the priest, turning to the people, having made his communion, holding the paten aloft with the Host just above it, enunciated 'Behold the Lamb of God', to which they would have responded, three times, striking their breasts in rhythm with the words:

> Lord, I am not worthy that thou shouldst enter under my roof:
> but speak the word only, and my soul shall be healed ...

– remembered by Eliot in *Ash-Wednesday*, and rhythmically repeated (recalling its threefold liturgical repetition):

> Lord, I am not worthy
> Lord, I am not worthy
> but speak the word only.[76]

On the occasion of the visit of a bishop (usually chosen for his willingness to participate in the full pontifical liturgy), for such as the patronal festival on St Stephen's day, Solemn Pontifical High Mass would be offered, with additional ceremonies for the prelate and a processional hymn around the church, the mitred bishop conferring blessings on the genuflecting people as he passed, wrapped in swirls of incense and glorious music.

If Sunday High Mass was the weekly worshipping climax for Eliot, the Easter liturgy was the annual high-point. While his doctrinal attention was focused on the doctrine of the Incarnation, celebrated at the feast of Christmas (and especially at Midnight Mass), the culmination of the liturgical expression of Christian theology is the ceremonial of Holy Week, climaxing in the celebration of the Resurrection on Easter Day (which every Sunday in the Church's year commemorates and the centrality of which is affirmed by the placing of the order for the Mass immediately after Holy Saturday in the Missal). In the powerful but unfinished work, 'Coriolan', of 1931, one of Eliot's speakers says

> And Easter Day, we didn't get to the country,
> So we took young Cyril to church. And they rang a bell
> And he said right out loud, *crumpets*.[77]

It is a classic example, in his poetry, of how we need to be aware of Eliot's Anglo-Catholicism in order to understand what is being said. The 'bell' is the consecration (or sacring or Sanctus) bell to which we have referred. But for young Cyril – and possibly his cross-grained parents, too, wishing they were heading off to Maidenhead, rather being reduced to church-going to fill up the holiday – the sound of the bell and the sight of the Host, a doughy, dull-white circular disk in the distance, reminds him of the crumpet man, ringing his bell as he does his rounds and dispensing his wafer-like wares. Eliot's recorded reading of the lines is very amusing: the contemptuous utterance of 'church' by the thwarted and subsequently embarrassed parents and little Cyril's shrill exclamation.

The order for the Mass is located where it is in the Missal to incorporate it in the concluding events of Holy Week, during which the Lord's Supper was instituted, on Maundy Thursday, as the story of the Passion unfolds. This subject, commemorated at every Mass, was the most difficult for modern poetry, Eliot observed in a letter to Mary Trevelyan. In modern times, its *human* aspect was being over-emphasised and even Christians, considering that more terrible forms of torture were possible than crucifixion, appeared to be puzzled by the concept of the Lord's ultimate suffering. This was the terrible disease of contemporary speech, he continues. The idea of bearing 'the sins of the world' has been debased by equating it with the physical details of the Lord's death when, in Roman times, as before and since, even worse varieties of physical torture than crucifixion could be imagined and have been inflicted. He has in the back of his mind,

Eliot remarks, the idea for a meditation on the Passion in accordance with the sorrowful mysteries of the rosary. His plan was to point out (with reference to the Crucifixion) that different people, with their necessarily different nervous systems and degrees of consciousness, suffer in quite different degrees in the same situations. But human analogies for Christ's Passion were always dangerous, as were all attempts to do justice to it, verbally or visually.[78] He would no doubt have agreed with Mrs Alexander's simple but profound words:

> We may not know, we cannot tell,
> What pains he had to bear,
> But we believe it was for us
> He hung and suffered there.[79]

Like Milton, in this regard at least, having thought of the idea of a poetic work on the death of Christ, Eliot did not pursue it.

As I have noted, at St Stephen's, the liturgy was celebrated according to The English Missal, first published in 1933, supplemented by *Ritual Notes*. An altar server there in the time of Fr Cheetham and Eliot recalled Holy Week – the climax of the liturgical year – for me:

> I remember Holy Week well. It was very liturgical and ad-hered strictly to the *then* Roman rite according to the English Missal and *Ritual Notes*. Everything was very dramatic and to an extent theatrical as was Fr. Cheetham's wish with fading house lights, spotlights on the pulpit, tabernacle etc. I remember that only rattles *not* bells were used on Maundy Thursday.[80]

On Good Friday, Christ's reproaches were sung during the third part of the liturgy on that day, 'The Solemn Adoration of the Holy Cross':

> O my people, what have I done unto thee? or wherein have I wearied thee? Answer me!

Eliot punctuates the fifth section of *Ash-Wednesday* with the first reproach, but concludes it with the warmth of 'O my people', the reproachful phrase having been removed, as the spirituality of the poem moves towards a vision of redemption, as the poem at large has moved through Lent, from Ash Wednesday to Good Friday.[81]

Eliot expected, as he once observed, 'a body of priests who know what they are doing' and 'a body of worshippers who know what is being done'.[82] Such an expectation melds with the Anglo-Catholic commitment to professionalism in the performance of the liturgy and in all priestly functions and a laity knowledgeable of ritual and its meaning. If the liturgy, especially the Mass, was an extension of the Incarnation, nothing less than such an approach, by clergy and people, was acceptable. Eliot was not disappointed, in this regard, in Fr Cheetham. As he had suggested in the preface of 1926 to his edition of his mother's verse play, *Savonarola*, Eliot was to derive inspiration for life from liturgical worship:

> in genuine drama the form is determined by the point on the line at which a tension between liturgy and realism takes place.... The play, like a religious service, should be a stimulant to make life more tolerable and augment our ability to live.[83]

That Eliot derived such satisfaction, over a period of nearly forty years, from one of the most elaborate of the traditional forms of Christian worship, the Anglo-Catholic liturgy, in a church where its full celebration was offered, with beautiful music and Fr Cheetham's theatrical flair, suggests how important this element of his faith was for him in the matter of sustaining his soul and spirit. He was quick to repudiate the criticism that such preoccupations were with the trimmings of religion, rather than the faith itself:

> Pater undoubtedly had from childhood a religious bent, naturally to all that was liturgical and ceremonious. Certainly this is a real and important part of religion; and Pater cannot thereby be accused of insincerity and 'aestheticism'.[84]

And these sentiments are expressed more broadly by Eliot in 1948:

> the convert – and I think not only of conversion from one form of Christianity to another, but indeed primarily of conversion from indifference to Christian belief and practice – the convert of the intellectual or sensitive type is drawn towards the more Catholic type of worship and doctrine. This attraction ... may occur before the convert has begun to inform himself about Christianity at all.[85]

Clearly, as the evidence of Eliot's developing interest in Catholic worship, which we traced in chapter two, demonstrated, he is talking here about himself in the third person. Yet he was keen, as many Anglo-Catholics are, not to be seen as merely a 'ritualist'[86] and would have understood W.H. Auden's similar expression of disdain for such a categorisation, often leveled at Anglo-Catholics:

> Liturgically, I am Anglo-Catholic though not too spiky, I
> hope.[87]

Liturgical beauty was expressive of holiness. The Laudian Church, so admired by Eliot, had placed special emphasis on the aesthetic setting of worship. Even in the humble, rustic church at Little Gidding, the holiness of beauty was emphasised:

> The Communion Table was furnished with a Covering of
> blew Silk & gould; The pulpit & the Reading place were
> hung with Blew Cloath, & Silver Lace & fringe, with
> Cushions & Valence round about each, & both Silk Cov-
> erings on the Flower upon which the Communion Table
> Stood at ye End of the Chancell, with the Benches covered
> with Blew Taffety, & Cushions of fine Tapestry & blew
> Silk.[88]

Of Lancelot Andrewes, Eliot said that 'his bond was with the Church, with tradition. His intellect was satisfied by theology and his sensibility by prayer and liturgy'.[89] There is that key word, for Eliot, again: 'satisfied'; bland-sounding, but literally-meant. Nothing more is required. Once more, we sense that Eliot is talking, also, about himself or, at least, how he would like to be.

In liturgy, Eliot also held fast to the idea that cathedral churches should be the centre of diocesan worship and set a high standard in that regard for the local parishes. In June, 1951, he addressed the Friends of Chichester Cathedral (the cathedral church which had his closest friend amongst the episcopate, G.K.A. Bell, as its bishop for nearly thirty years; which had been Lancelot Andrewes' first see, and which was a well-known Anglo-Catholic centre) on the value and use of cathedrals. Eliot stressed, as their essential function, the main-tenance of high liturgical standards, recalling the origins of many of them as monasteries:

> The 'use' of the cathedral is for the performance of the
> complete liturgy of the Church for the Christian Year.... A
> cathedral is doing its proper work even when no one is pres-
> ent except celebrant, deacons and servers; and if it omitted
> a single service because no one attended it, then it would
> be failing in its proper work. This work is the continuity
> and completeness of the liturgy and the continuous prayer
> and worship by its clergy. A cathedral is a kind of monastic
> institution open to the public.[90]

In Eliot's reference to 'deacons', along with the celebrant, he is indicating the three sacred ministers of High Mass: celebrant, deacon and
sub-deacon, which should be the normative liturgical celebration in
a cathedral church, with its clerical and other resources, including
choristers. The Low Mass and other variants like the *Missa Cantata*
– sung, with incense, but with just one minister, the celebrating priest
– are merely substitutes. As in other places in his writings, Eliot
declares his preference for the solemn liturgy of High Mass, while
recognising that this is not to everyone's taste:

> I like a full liturgy myself, and what I call a full liturgy may
> be fuller than some people like.[91]

One can imagine the Anglo-Catholic Chichester Cathedral Friends,
who were to publish his address as a little book, smiling approvingly
at this candid confession.

4

The sacrament of penance

On 15th March, 1928, three weeks into the annual Lenten season
of penitence, Eliot told the priest who had baptised him, William
Force Stead, that he had made his first confession (one assumes, to
Fr Francis Underhill, who was then his spiritual director),

> and feel as if I had crossed a very wide and deep river:
> whether I get much further or not, I feel very certain that
> I shall not cross back, and *that* in itself gives one a very
> extraordinary sense of surrender and gain.[92]

He had made his confession on the day before Lent begins, Shrove
Tuesday (20th February, 1928).[93]

Eliot regarded Mary Magdalene, the penitent, as his particular saint
and a 'Very Proper Saint', he points out in a letter to Mary Trevelyan, with
an important position in the rosary, where she is usually meditated upon
in the first of the 'glorious mysteries' – that of the resurrection – when
the Lord's appearance to her at the tomb is recalled. In this letter, on the
feast of St Nathalie (27th July, 1953, five days after Mary Magdalene's
feast day), Eliot also points out to Trevelyan that the penitent is their
saint. The Gospel of the Mass for Mary Magdalene concludes with the
Lord's absolution: 'thy faith hath saved thee: go in peace'.

'Penitence and humility,' Eliot declared, 'are the foundation of
the Christian life'.[94] Certainly, they are intimately connected, as the
recognition of the need for penitence is contingent upon the humb-

ling process of facing-up to one's sins and shortcomings. Charles
Baudelaire, Eliot judged, possessed 'the greatest, the most difficult,
of the Christian virtues, the virtue of humility'.[95] Simone Weil had
'an almost superhuman humility'[96] and in 'East Coker' we are told
that 'the only wisdom we can hope to acquire / Is the wisdom of
humility: humility is endless'.[97] Of Blaise Pascal, Eliot exclaimed:
'How fast a hold he has of humility!'[98] Denis Donoghue reads 'The
Love Song of J. Alfred Prufrock', Eliot's first major poem, as 'a
transcript of someone's confession'.[99] John Crowe Ransom interprets 'Gerontion' as an old man's confession, addressed to Christ.[100]
The 'old man', we remember (and 'gerontion' is Greek for 'little
old man'), is the Pauline image of the unregenerate soul:

> I that was near your heart was removed therefrom
> To lose beauty in terror, terror in inquisition.[101]

The ascetic discipline was central to his rule of life, as Eliot revealed
in an unusually public expression (in *The Listener*) of the private persuasion of his faith:

> the Christian scheme seemed the only possible scheme which
> found a place for values which I must maintain or perish
> (and belief comes first and practice second), the belief, for
> instance, in holy living and holy dying, in sanctity, chastity,
> humility, austerity[102]

– an observation which incorporates the titles of the two best-known
devotional works of the seventeenth-century bishop, Jeremy Taylor:
The Rule and Exercise of Holy Living (1650) and ... *of holy Dying*
(1651). Taylor was a champion of sacramental confession, urging
the clergy on in its practice. A fortnight later – also in *The Listener*
– Eliot confesses to 'low appetites' and 'vulgar tastes' and how they
have been assuaged in his life:

> I have perceived their transience, their unsatisfactoriness, and
> the horror of satiety which is far beyond the famine of depri-
> vation.... Without the love of God there is no love at all.[103]

The life of sin is separation from the love of God. Recognition of
his sinfulness led Eliot, in humility, to the search for purification
which is the inspiration of the discipline of the confessional:

> for only in humility, charity and purity – and most perhaps
> humility – can we be prepared to receive the grace of God
> without which human operations are vain.[104]

In Eliot's devoted recourse to the sacrament of penance, he was again expressing the distinctively Anglo-Catholic cast of his Anglicanism. Such was the importance of auricular confession that Manning-Foster, in his study of Anglo-Catholicism, gives more space to the sacrament of penance than to that of the altar itself. Newman taught that, after Mass, confession was next in importance in the practice of the Catholic faith[105] and they are intimately linked – being in a 'state of grace' as a result of having confessed one's sins and being absolved was seen as a necessary prerequisite for reception of Holy Communion. The vast majority of Anglicans, in any age, never avail themselves of private confession at all (being satisfied with the General Confession, followed by the priest's absolution, in the public liturgy of the Eucharist), although the Order for the Visitation of the Sick, in The Book of Common Prayer and the First Exhortation at the Holy Communion there, do permit it.[106] The general Anglican position on penance is 'all may; some should; none must'. In practice, very few ever do. But Eliot was not merely nailing his colours to the ecclesiastical mast by frequenting the confessional. His regular use of the sacrament expressed the deep-seated sense of sin in his personality (not newly-discovered in Catholicism, but, much further back, deriving from his Calvinistic, Puritan ancestors' faith). Now, needing forgiveness, and expressing, at the beginning of his religious journey, a desire to submit himself to the most demanding of spiritual disciplines, he had found the sacramental means of assuaging sin. In this, he found a master in Pascal who meditated on '*nos impuissances:– orgueil et concupiscence*' and '*les remèdes:– humilité, mortification*'.[107]

Commitment to the sacrament of penance was one of those 'litmus tests' of genuine Anglo-Catholicism, marking it off even from the High Church tradition. More so than his devotion to the Mass, it provides conclusive evidence of Eliot's fidelity to that tradition of Christianity.

The standard objections of Protestants and probably of many Anglicans to this practice, once so zealously promoted by Anglo-Catholicism, are that, on the one hand, it cultivates an over-carefulness, morbidity and even an insincerity (in a persistent need to discover something to confess) and, on the other, an automatic idea of absolution from sin that fosters an attitude whereby sinning can repeatedly occur, as there is a ready solution to one's guilt. What is missed, in this assessment, is the situation which, indeed, the Prayer Book envisages and which is immediately pertinent to Eliot's case – namely, the Christian who has (as Geoffrey Faber wrote of John Henry Newman, in a book dedicated to Eliot 'with affection and respect') 'a deep and terrifying sense of sin'. Here, indeed, only auricular confession provides the necessary 'comfort or counsel'. It is a private, confidential forum in which the penitent can 'open his grief' and receive the grace of personal absolution. Faber could have been writing of his dedicatee and friend when he observed of Newman that 'the thickest root of [his] religious life lay in an unanalyzed, he would have said, unanalyzable, sentiment – a deep and terrifying sense of sin':

> The assurance [of God's love and mercy] is less real to him than the fear of condemnation and wrath. The fact of sin, its heinousness, its inconceivably ghastly consequences in the world to come – it is when he speaks of such topics as these that he speaks most obviously from the heart and with most effect.[108]

But, equally, sinning is part of ordinary human life and, as it is repetitive (in spite of all good intentions), so the remedy must be repeatedly used. For all the profundities of his sense of sin, Eliot also regarded the issue matter-of-factly (which, too, is a mark of the Catholic spirit; being febrile about man's corruption being an Evangelical characteristic):

> I shall no doubt do and say the wrong thing again and again; but the important thing is to be conscious of the error or weakness and of its nature, and then to be sorry for it.... We show our Christianity in the way in which we are aware of our faults and shortcomings, and the way in which we are sorry for them.[109]

Yet Eliot's use of the sacrament of confession was distinctively Anglo-Catholic (as opposed to that of devout Roman Catholics in his day) in that while he repeatedly affirmed its importance, he did not feel it was necessary to 'go to confession' every time he was intending to received Holy Communion or weekly (which, prior to Vatican II, was the usual Roman Catholic custom). Mary Trevelyan remembered that the poet claimed (in 1951) to attend the sacrament of penance only three times each year.[110] But even this was probably more often than most Anglo-Catholics for whom the general rule was that they should go to Confession at least once in a year, 'normally before receiving Holy Communion at Easter'.[111] Most Anglo-Catholics would not have a personal confessor distinct from their parish priest, for this reason. So, as Eliot had a regular confessor from the time of his conversion, we can assume that in those earlier and more troubled days, in his personal life, in the 1930s, and with something of the zeal of the convert he made his confession more frequently than in the 1950s. Yet, Eliot wrote to Mary Trevelyan (in January, 1950) commenting that prior to setting out for the unknown he likes as far as possible to be absolved from his sins and receive Communion (to be shriven and houselled, and relieved of his debts).

George Every recalled for me that Eliot preferred to have, as confessor, in that earlier formative period, a priest distinct from his vicar at St Stephen's, and that this remained his practice. The first of these was Francis Underhill, cousin of Evelyn Underhill, the famous author of *Mysticism*, who was successively Head of Liddon House, Dean of Rochester, and Bishop of Bath and Wells, becoming one of the earliest, definite Anglo-Catholic bishops in the Church of England. When Underhill went to Rochester in 1932, the priest and baronet, the Revd Sir Percy Maryon-Wilson, vicar of St Mary's, Somers Town, next to Euston Station (and who was made one of the guardians of the shrine of the Virgin at Walsingham in 1935) became Eliot's confessor.[112] He was followed by the Revds P.G. Bacon and F.L. Hillier (whom Eliot had met on retreat at St Simon's, Kentish Town).

Trevelyan records Eliot's account of his settled custom in the matter of the sacrament of penance, by 1953:

> I write to my Confessor [by this stage, Father Bacon] for an appointment. He always says 12.30 and invites me to lunch afterwards and I always accept as part of my penance. Sometimes I wonder if he remembers what I said last time and the time before and every time – always the same. When it is over, I say my penance.[113]

And this is the form of words which Eliot would have used, kneeling before the priest (either in a purpose-built confessional or in a secluded portion of the church where the priest was accustomed to hear confessions, wearing the purple stole of the penitential seasons, Advent and Lent):

> [Crossing himself, Eliot would say]
>   In the Name of the Father, and of the Son, and of the Holy Ghost. Amen.
>   Bless me, father, for I have sinned.
>   [The priest would then respond in this – or a similar manner – blessing Eliot, as he did so]
>   The Lord be in thy heart and on thy lips that thou mayest truly and humbly confess thy sins in the Name of the Father, and of the Son, and of the Holy Ghost.
>   [Then Eliot would say]

I confess to Almighty God, to Blessed Mary ever-virgin, to all the Saints, and to you, father, that I have sinned exceedingly in thought, word, deed, by my fault, my own fault, my own most grievous fault. Especially I have sinned since my last confession, which was...ago. [Here, Eliot would state how long ago it was, and would then confess all his sins.]

For these and all my other sins which I cannot now remember, I am very sorry, firmly resolve not to sin again, and humbly ask pardon of God, and of you, father, counsel, penance, and absolution.

[The priest would then respond to the sins mentioned, giving such counsel as was deemed necessary, and give a penance to be performed – usually including prayers, or a psalm or a hymn, less usually the 'Hail Mary'. Then he would pronounce absolution, making the sign of the cross, again, over Eliot]

I absolve thee from all thy sins, + in the Name of the Father, and of the Son, and of the Holy Ghost. Amen. Go in peace; the Lord hath put away thy sin.[114]

[Eliot would then go and say his penance, elsewhere in the church.]

The rite of sacramental confession is absolutely confidential – having the 'seal' upon it – so no confessor may reveal what is said, and as Eliot nowhere reveals the substance of his confession (apart from saying that what he confessed was always the same), this will never be known and speculation is both pointless and improper. What was important, of course – and this is the blessing of the sacrament for the penitent – is the opportunity to be completely honest about one's sins. Part of the tragedy of Baudelaire's life was, Eliot noted, that he was 'a confessor of sins who had never told the whole truth'.[115]

The phrase, 'Bless me father', explicitly recalling this rite, is found in the final section of Eliot's Lenten and most liturgical poem, *Ash-Wednesday, 1930*, as the speaker refers to the ongoing temptations of the sensual world which continue to bedevil him (and, it is implied, always will) in spite of all that he has accomplished, in the foregoing sections of the long poem, in the discipline of ascent. Such sins, of course, are typical of the kind which penitents confess, but no-one has expressed them so beautifully as in Eliot's lines which convey the allure of that bewitching world of temptation. Eliot observed Ash Wednesday, the first day of the penitential season of Lent, in traditional Anglo-Catholic style – as recalled by Mary Trevelyan in her diary for 1950:

> On Ash Wednesday we attended Matins and Ante-Communion and the Imposition of the Ashes at 11 a.m., then drove through St. James's Park to our respective offices.

With regard to the occasions on which he would confess his sins, Eliot had a rule of always attending before the feast of the Assumption (15th August), one of the days of obligation. In this, we have an explicit combination of two distinctively Anglo-Catholic convictions on Eliot's part – the use of auricular confession and the special importance given to that feast of the Virgin, unacknowledged (indeed, actively repudiated as unscriptural and unknown to the early Church) in Anglicanism outside specifically Anglo-Catholic circles. Only an Anglo-Catholic with a specific devotion to the Blessed Virgin would make such a rule for himself – to keep the feast and to go to confession before it. Making his confession at the Assumption (in August), as well as at Easter (in April) and at Christmas (in December) would have fitted well with Eliot's rule of three-times-per-year.

Related to Eliot's discipline of penance was his attitude towards the penitential seasons of the Church's year, Lent and Advent – especially the former. In his letters to Mary Trevelyan he refers to giving up gin (except on Wednesdays[116] – intruding the touch of the ridiculous into this self-imposed discipline in a very Anglo-Catholic way). 'He took Lent very seriously', Trevelyan writes, and had many rules and regulations,

> one of the oddest being that he didn't play patience *before* breakfast[117]

as, once again, the piety is agreeably touched with a sense of mischief. In Lent 1951, he was stricter, giving up smoking, also, before breakfast and not playing patience before lunch. He could note with satisfaction (she recalls in her Diary for 1953) that he had kept his Lent rule 'fairly well' and read 'the Propers' – that is, the readings for the Mass of each day – 'every morning'.

In 1955, Eliot had a 'substitute confessor' (his own being in hospital while Eliot, himself, was also not in good health). 'Rather useful', he commented to Mary Trevelyan:

> as I could confess the old sins without feeling embarrassed and I said – 'For these and all my other sins which were very limited owing to my illness' – which I thought rather neat![118]

The discipline of the confessional is referred to occasionally in Eliot's writings, in addition to the best-known reference in *Ash-*

Wednesday. In his preface of 1932 to *Bubu of Montparnasse*, for example – that tale of Parisian low-life by Charles-Louis Philippe, capturing the city's bohemian spirit which Eliot had discovered for himself in 1910 – he notes that

> this book has always been for me, not merely the best of Charles-Louis Philippe's books, but a symbol of the Paris of that time.... In a very much smaller way, Bubu stood for Paris as some of Dickens's novels stand for London.

Philippe dealt frankly (but without exploitation) in the morbid and the sinful, and Eliot – refusing to pronounce on the characters' immorality – praised *Bubu* as an inducement to humility and, in a sense, a moral tract. Drawing upon the customary formula of the penitent's confession to his priest, Eliot remarks:

> Even the most virtuous in reading it, may feel: I have sinned exceedingly in thought, word and deed.[119]

In 'Thoughts after Lambeth', Eliot calls for a clear statement on the matter of spiritual counsel. What is interesting in this passage is Eliot's implied recognition that the Anglo-Catholic position on the sacrament could not reasonably be expected to be adopted by the Church at large. This shows, early in Eliot's Anglo-Catholic life and even in the years of Anglo-Catholic triumphalism, that he could be restrained and appreciative of broader Anglican sensibilities (characteristics not usually associated with Anglo-Catholic apologists, especially in this period):

> I regret ... that the bishops have placed so much reliance upon the Individual Conscience.... I do not suggest that the full Sacrament of Confession and Penance should be imposed upon every communicant of the Church; but the Church ought to be able to enjoin upon all its communicants that they should take spiritual advice upon specified problems of life; and both clergy and parishioners should recognize the full seriousness and responsibility of such consultation.... Here, if anywhere, is definitely a matter upon which the Individual Conscience is no reliable guide; spiritual guidance should be imperative; and it should be clearly placed above medical advice.... In short, a general principle of the greatest importance ... might have been laid down; and its enunciation was evaded.[120]

In those final comments there is, nonetheless, a suggestion of the characteristic Anglo-Catholic impatience with the Anglican reluctance to take a clear stand on such issues, particularly, perhaps, those such as confession which carried the Roman taint, as well as frustration with bishops.

*

It is in Eliot's plays, however, that he most strongly urges the necessity for the formal confession of sin, implicitly within the Catholic sacramental system (portraying, that is to say, a figure as a type of father-confessor, and the penitent's rigorous preparatory searching of his conscience in his personal desire for absolution and atonement). In *Murder in the Cathedral* (1935), the references are most explicit – inevitably, given its mediaeval Catholic setting. Thomas rebukes the First Tempter who would stir up the too-human frailty of 'old Tom, gay Tom, Becket of London':

> Look to your behaviour....
> Think of penitence and follow your master.[121]

And in the presence of the Second Tempter, the Archbishop asserts his priestly authority, derived from the 'divine appointment' of Christ to Peter (and his successors), to absolve and, indeed, to excommunicate in the name of God:

> Shall I, who keep the keys
> Of heaven and hell, supreme alone in England,
> Who bind and loose, with power from the Pope,
> Descend to desire a punier power?[122]

The motif is played out finally when the unexpected Fourth Tempter (the most serious, since he is closest to Thomas and a proponent of the deadliest of sins) reminds him of his ghostly authority:

> You hold the keys of heaven and hell,
> Power to bind and loose: bind, Thomas, bind,
> King and bishop under your heel.[123]

At his martyrdom, in Thomas's last words, as he commends his soul to God, Eliot uses phrases from the confessional formula of the *Confiteor* ('I confess ...') from the priest's introductory prayers prior to Mass:

> Now to Almighty God, to the Blessed Mary ever Virgin,
> to the blessed John the Baptist, the holy apostles Peter and
> Paul....[124]

At the very core, however, of Eliot's next play, *The Family Reunion* (1939), we find, in its modern setting, a concentration of attention on the process of the recollection of sin and the desire for repentance: it is, to use Agatha's term, a theatrical 'pilgrimage of expiation' (pilgrimage itself, in Catholic tradition, customarily involving recourse to sacramental confession). Harry retreats to Wishwood for a contemplative experience of self-discovery (retreats, also, traditionally featuring confession of sin). He is haunted by the faces and circumstances of a traumatic past and he needs, if he is ever to be freed from the despair they are daily imposing on his spirit, to encounter them courageously and (in humility) to be purged from their influence. Agatha (the name of the virgin martyr, probably of the fifth century, who is listed in the Canon of the Mass and who is invoked against fire) promises that, at this moment of grace, all time will be gathered together and stand still:

> When the loop in time comes – and it does not come for
> every body –
> The hidden is revealed, and the spectres show themselves.[125]

Harry's situation is given dramatic force by his impatience for confession and, hence, liberation from his sinfulness. As in *The Cocktail Party* (1950), where the penitents turn to a psychologist as their 'confessor', so in *The Family Reunion*, Harry would bare his soul to Warburton, the family's G.P.:

> What I'm telling you
> Is very important. Very important.
> You must let me explain, and then you can talk.
> I don't know why, but just this evening
> I feel an overwhelming need for explanation.[126]

This is not merely a desire to discuss the experience of evil, but a determination that is driven by an unpredictable and inexplicable infusion of grace. Agatha discerns this mystery, in mystical and biblical terms, in dialogue with Harry:

> Accident is design
> And design is accident
> In a cloud of unknowing.
> O my child, my curse,
> You shall be fulfilled:
> The knot shall be unknotted
> And the crooked made straight.

Her references here to the 'cloud of unknowing' recall the concept of man's separation from God described in the famous fourteenth-century mystical treatise of that name (upon which Eliot draws

again in 'Little Gidding', V). The unknown author encourages
the contemplative to meekness, and insists, when referring to
counsel, on the necessity for the penitent to follow his confessor's
advice.[127]

The problem with *The Family Reunion*, Hugh Kenner has written, is the difficulty of discovering the apparently impressive
revelation which is supposed to have 'freed Harry' and sent him
off in penance to 'work out his salvation with diligence'.[128] What is
certain, as Agatha's closing speech affirms, is the importance, for
Eliot, of 'the pilgrimage / Of expiation', of intercession by those
who would be expiated, and, in a closing Anglo-Catholic touch,
by necessity to pray, also for the 'departed – May they rest in
peace', that they, too, may know 'redemption'.[129] 'What we have
written', Agatha reflects, 'is not a story of detection / Of crime and
punishment':

> but of sin and expiation....
> It is possible that sin may strain and struggle
> In its dark instinctive birth, to come to consciousness
> And so find expurgation.[130]

The Family Reunion concludes with a simulation of the ceremony
of *Tenebrae* – the special form of Matins and Lauds provided for the
last three days of Holy Week. The Latin name – meaning 'darkness'
– refers to the ceremony of extinguishing the lights in church, one
by one, during the service, in symbolic anticipation of the rising of
the Son of Righteousness on Easter Day. It is an ambiguous close to
the work – penitential, by virtue of its quasi-liturgical reminiscence
of Good Friday, but pregnant with hope.

Replying to Michael Redgrave's question about what Monchensey
would do after the play, Eliot replied that he thought the aristocratic
Harry and his servant 'would work in the East End of London' – an
Anglo-Catholic resolution indeed.[131]

In *The Cocktail Party*, the *via mystica* is celebrated again as a
mode of achieving the grace for repentance. The Unidentified Guest,
who is to emerge as confessor, rebukes an obtuse Edward:

> You are nothing but a set
> Of obsolete responses

and counsels him,

> The one thing to do
> Is to do nothing. Wait.[132]

Waiting upon God, in stillness, is a recurring theme in Eliot's writing, linked to the *via negativa* of the mystics and the spirituality of the admired Simone Weil, author of *L'attente de Dieu* (1950, translated as *Waiting on* [or *'for'*] *God*). This is a prelude to purgation, confession, 'sudden solitude in a crowded desert'[133] paralleled in *The Cocktail Party* by Julia's desire to travel in the lift unaccompanied: 'in a lift I can meditate'.[134] As in St John of the Cross's writings, the terrifying process of darkness and aloneness is the way of *askesis*, purgation; and Celia, who is possessed by a 'sense of sin',[135] brings the theme of redemption in *The Cocktail Party* to a climax when she informs Harcourt-Reilly, the now Identified Guest, that

I feel I must ... *atone* – is that the word?[136]

He, in the role of confessor, absolves Celia (as he absolved Edward) from her sins: 'Go in peace, my daughter. Work out your salvation with diligence'. This is the vocabulary of the confessional and Eliot does not allow to go unnoticed the theological point that the confessor is merely acting on behalf of God, administering a divine mystery; for Harcourt-Reilly remarks to Julia:

when I say to one like [Celia]
'Work out your salvation with diligence', I do not understand
What I myself am saying.[137]

He is acting in the name of the Lord (using a scriptural injunction[138]), not as the Lord.

Aloneness as the necessary prelude to atonement for sin is as urgently insisted upon in Eliot's last plays, *The Confidential Clerk* (1954) and *The Elder Statesman* (1959). Lady Elizabeth tells Colby (in the former work) that he needs, in order to encourage his interior life, the society of 'intellectual, well-bred people / Of spirituality'.[139] She admits that they are a rare breed, as the announcement of one of them, Sir Claude Mulhammer – 'All my life / I have been atoning'[140] – suggests. Colby recalls Mulhammer's reminiscence of an act of penance (the details of which, Mary Trevelyan contends, were connected with Eliot's childhood[141]):

I was struck by what you said, a little while ago,
When you spoke of never having understood your father
Until it was too late. And you spoke of atonement.
Even your failure to understand him, of which you spoke
  – that was a relationship

> Of father and son. It must often happen.
> And the reconcilement, after his death,
> That perfects the relation.[142]

Eliot's father died in 1919, disappointed (as was Eliot's mother) that his son had not returned to the United States, after completing his doctoral studies at Oxford, and to a career as a philosopher.[143]

Colby exclaims, in the wake of Mulhammer's reminiscence: 'I only wish / That I had something to atone for!'[144]

In *The Elder Statesman*, Claverton tells Monica that his difficulty has been that he has never been able to love; but where love is possible, some release from the burden of sin (both serious sin and what Eliot said elsewhere he most feared, the 'constant, daily, petty pusillanimity'[145]) is possible also. Confession to the beloved is redemptive:

> If a man has one person, just one in his life,
> To whom he is willing to confess everything –
> And that includes, mind you, not only things criminal,
> Not only turpitude, meanness and cowardice,
> But also situations which are simply ridiculous,
> When he has played the fool (as who has not?) –
> Then he loves that person, and his love will save him.[146]

The lack of love between Claverton and Monica's mother prevented him, he explains, from easing his conscience earlier in life:

> How open one's heart
> When one is sure of the wrong response?
> How make a confession with no hope of absolution?
> It was not her fault. We never understood each other.[147]

Claverton's subsequent desire to confess to his daughter – 'I've made my confession to you, Monica'[148] (and we remember that the mother of St. Augustine, the author of the most famous of Christian confessional/autobiographical works, was St. Monica) – is the act of purgation in this play which forms its dramatic climax. It is the willingness to confess that matters too – not so much the degree or type of sin:

> It's harder to confess the sin that no one believes in
> Than the crime that everyone can appreciate....
> What has made the difference in the last five minutes
> Is not the heinousness of my misdeeds
> But the fact of my confession.

Claverton expresses the very familiar emotion of relief and release to which many penitents customarily refer, especially after their first experience of sacramental confession:

> I feel at peace now.
> It is the peace that ensues upon contrition
> When contrition ensues upon knowledge of the truth....
> I've only just now had the illumination
> Of knowing what love is....
> I have been brushed by the wing of happiness[149]

– as Eliot had been, in his recent blissful marriage. *The Elder Statesman* is dedicated, indeed, 'To My Wife'.

Of course, these plays are not only (or, possibly, even importantly) autobiographical and it would be an exaggeration to suggest that they are, explicitly, explorations and celebrations of the sacrament of penance. Yet the language of the processes and spirituality associated particularly with that sacrament recurs remarkably often in these later and last works of Eliot's creative life. We can reasonably conclude from this that that particular and important aspect of Anglo-Catholic sacramental Christianity: the examination of conscience, the making of one's confession and the experience of the grace of God's love in absolution and after the penance has been completed, was not only a major and perpetual discipline in Eliot's own religious life (as we know it was), but something which he regarded as of central and essential moral significance for human beings.

5

The life of prayer

More so than any other aspect of religious routine and discipline, prayer and meditation were emphasised by Eliot, time and again, as the bedrock of faith, sustaining the Christian in daily life, especially in the secular world. There were 'only four ways of thinking', Eliot asserted in 1931 ('to talk to others, or to one another, or to talk to oneself, or to talk to God'),[150] and the greatest of these was the last – that is, prayer. Such discourse springs from meditation on the divine. 'The highest life is the life of contemplation', Eliot reflected.[151] 'Contemplation, we need to remind ourselves often, is the highest form of human activity'.[152] Vigilance, Craig Raine declares, is 'the Eliotean gift'.[153] But typically, for Eliot, even this activity had to be structured and part of a routine.

He was strongly drawn to the life of religious communities, where prayer could be pursued in a highly disciplined environment of communal as well as individual devotion. These religious orders made an important impact on Anglo-Catholic life in general. They were available for 'retreats', where individuals and groups from parishes would experience something of the monastic life, over several days, under the direction of a retreat-master (usually an ordained member of one of the religious communities). Eliot particularly valued this kind of availability of the enclosed life for those who found existence in the world trying and demoralising. Writing in the midst of the diurnal pressures of being in London during the Second World War, he reflected:

> It will become more and more a question whether something corresponding to the monastic seclusion, some form of complete or temporary withdrawal from the affairs of the world, will be one of the great remedies for the dehumanizing effect of a civilization of busybodies.[154]

In *The Idea of a Christian Society*, Eliot criticises Coleridge (in his elaboration of his theory of the 'clerisy') for failing to recognise 'the enormous value which monastic orders can and should have in the community', noting that he could not

> conceive a Christian society without religious orders, even purely contemplative orders, even enclosed orders.[155]

Eliot wanted his ideal community to have

> a *respect* for the religious life, for the life of prayer and contemplation, and for those who attempt to practise it.[156]

Referring in 1940 to a report by the Bishop of Winchester, Eliot regrets that nothing is said about 'the possible usefulness of religious communities in country districts'.[157] In a letter of 19th December, 1944 to Mary Trevelyan, he refers to Christmas as a season which, with its round of social engagements (which can obscure its religious significance as the feast of the Incarnation), he would prefer to spend always in a monastery; while five years later, after seeing the film, *Angelina*, in London and being pursued by a certain busybody who had a bone to pick with him, he wrote that he was looking forward to two days of seclusion (he emphasises the word) with no visitors.[158] The desire to withdraw from human community, at least to the extent that it was secularised, humanistic and determinedly irreligious (as it mostly is, in the modern age) was deep-seated in Eliot, deriving from his generally negative estimation of the human condition. He regarded this desire for detachment, indeed, as a sign of positive development in the religious life:

> there is a very profound kind of boredom which is an essential moment in the religious life, the boredom with all living in so far as it has no religious meaning.[159]

This, it has to be said, is antithetical to the communal characteristics of Catholicism and its emphasis on all believers as common members of the Body of Christ, and has something of the taint, as Eliot himself might have described it, of Protestant individualism. He recognised (he wrote to Paul Elmer More, in a letter dated 'Shrove Tuesday, 1928') 'the void that I find in the middle of all human happiness and all human relations and which there is only one thing to fill':

> I am one whom this sense of void tends to drive towards asceticism or sensuality, and only Christianity helps to reconcile me to life, which is otherwise disgusting.[160]

Nearly twenty years later, writing to Mary Trevelyan, he referred to his disgust with human nature.[161] Eliot was not temperamentally receptive to overtures of love, Christian or otherwise, communal or individual:

> When I was very young, I didn't like people because I was afraid they would be kind to me.... Now I suspect almost everyone of liking me because they want to get something out of me.[162]

Not surprisingly, he approved of the maxim of Old Foxey in *The Old Curiosity Shop*: 'Always suspect everybody', quoting it twice in letters (nearly three years apart) to Trevelyan.[163]

Eliot pondered the idea of a permanent arrangement with a religious community. In March, 1928, during Lent, he had taken a vow of celibacy (such as professed members of religious orders do, along with poverty and obedience).[164] Like Pascal, he was attracted to the life of the tertiary (the 'third order' which came into existence in the thirteenth century, offering opportunities for self-dedication in the religious life, in association with a religious order, for members living and working in 'the world'). Eliot opined that

> There will be [in 'every planned society'].... secular 'orders' into which the active politician and business man can withdraw for a while for contemplation, and so make contact with those who are less involved in the struggle for existence.[165]

In his sermon at Magdalene College, Cambridge, Eliot begins with an extended comparison between the collegiate hierarchy and that of a monastery, likening himself – as an Honorary Fellow – to a tertiary who 'retires there from time to time to participate in the life and share its rigours and austerities'.[166] Tertiaries customarily observe a rule of prayer and observance and while, as it turned out, Eliot did not formally enter upon such an arrangement with one of the Anglican religious communities, he certainly submitted to the kinds of disciplines of prayer in the midst of daily life characteristic of the devoted tertiary. 'I can get through a whole section [chaplet] of the Rosary in the Underground going home', he observed to Mary Trevelyan in 1952, 'especially if the train stops long at Leicester Square'.[167] The following year, he told her that he used the rosary as part of his evening prayers, and at a pre-Christmas sherry party in 1954, when he presented her with one, Trevelyan records Eliot showing her how to use it and remarking that he said the rosary prayers (the most repeated being the 'Hail Mary') every night.[168]

He observed rules in his prayerful intentions too: 'I shall pray for you daily', he told Trevelyan, before setting out for America in 1955, 'as I have always done for a long time'.[169] And frequently, elsewhere in her diary, she recalls Eliot remarking on the difficulty he experienced in prayer, and the length of time he was engaged in it. Silent prayer, in fact, was an aspect of their religious lives which they frequently shared:

> then off we bustled to St Stephen's [she notes] to our annual attendance at Tenebrae, that great, dark, magnificent service. We said our prayers in a gradually darkened church for one-and-a-half hours, then drove home in pouring rain.[170]

Discipline and regularity in the life of contemplation, as well as requiring conviction and devotion, also demanded (in Eliot's view) intelligent instruction.

It was part of the duty of any educational system in a Christian society, Eliot believed, to supplement its pursuit of knowledge of the material world with instruction in the art of keeping in touch with the realm of the spirit. He wrote, with considerable force, in 1932 – about the time, as we shall see, of his first visit to the monastic house at Kelham, Nottinghamshire – in this passage (from 'Modern Education and the Classics') which he chose to conclude *Selected Essays*:

the hierarchy of education should be a religious hierarchy. The universities are too far gone in secularization, they have too long lost any common fundamental assumption as to what education is for.... There are other reasons, and of the greatest weight, for desiring to see a revival of the monastic life in its variety, but the maintenance of Christian education is not the least.... As the world at large becomes more completely secularized, the need becomes more urgent that professedly Christian people should have a Christian education, which should be an education for this world and for the life of prayer in this world.[171]

Three well-known communities for male religious in the Church of England, fruits of the Catholic Revival, were of particular interest to Eliot: the Society of the Sacred Mission (SSM) at Kelham; the Society of St John the Evangelist (SSJE) at Cowley, near Oxford, and the Anglican Benedictine Community (OSB) at Nashdom in Buckinghamshire. Viscount Halifax, who was such an important influence on Eliot's early Anglo-Catholicism, had tried his own vocation at Cowley and made an annual retreat there.[172] In the academic year, 1932-3, when Eliot was at Harvard as Charles Eliot Norton professor, he attended Mass at the Cowley Fathers church of St John the Evangelist on Beacon Hill in Boston.[173] George Every, who was a lay brother at Kelham, first met Eliot there just prior to his profession in September, 1933 when, after the first of many visits (two or three times each year for several days[174]) during the years leading up to the Second World War, the poet presented to the community Paul Elmer More's five-volume work, *The Greek Tradition*. A year later, Eliot wrote in *The Harvard Advocate*, affirming again the connection between true education and the consecrated life of prayer:

I believe that if education is not rearranged by people with some definite social philosophy and some notion of the true vocation of man, the only education to be had will be in seminaries and colleges run by Jesuits.... The only two men I know who have had what seemed to me hopeful theories of education and put them into practice, are Father Herbert Kelly of the Society of the Sacred Mission in Nottinghamshire, and Canon Iddings Bell of Providence, Rhode Island.... I know of no other ventures in higher education of equal interest to these.[175]

The library at Nashdom Abbey

Kelham was a congenial spiritual home for Eliot (Every commented) during the writing of *The Rock*, *Murder in the Cathedral*, 'Burnt Norton' (the first of the *Four Quartets*) and *The Family Reunion*.[176] Once the war had interrupted the poet's visits, however, he did not renew them:

> I think as he grew more celebrated he grew afraid of crowds
> of admiring young. The students in those days made up the
> larger part of the community at Kelham. In 1933-4 he was
> just a friend. By 1939 he had become a celebrity.[177]

Yet Eliot's stays at Kelham (where much of the regime was carried out in silence), well in excess of the schedule of retirement an ordinarily devout Anglo-Catholic layman would sustain and which were originally encouraged by his first confessor, Francis Underhill,[178] did not, however, take the form of a planned retreat. For such organised excursions, Eliot preferred to go either to the Cowley Fathers at Oxford ('for whom', Fr William Levy has commented, 'he had a warm feeling'[179] and where his friend, Viscount Halifax, had made his annual retreat until his death in 1931) or to the Benedictines at Nashdom Abbey. The Cowley and Nashdom houses were probably the best-known retreat centres in the Anglican Communion. When Fr Levy was planning a holiday in England in 1952, Eliot remarked to him of Nashdom:

> I will take you with me to an abbey I stay at on occasion.... One day I will go there to stay permanently. It suits me. I would have no guests then, but you could come every year for a week or two, being a priest.[180]

Such was the profound appeal of the Anglo-Catholic monastic life to Eliot. We note the determination with which he makes his declaration – 'One day I will go there to stay permanently'. This is not the kind of comment that someone as scrupulous as Eliot, and in a letter to a priest, would make lightly. Had he not married Valerie Fletcher five years later, we can be fairly certain that this is how his life would have ended. And the perceptive Hans Meyerhoff, to whom we owe the *verbatim* report of 'Mr Eliot's Evening Service' at St Thomas's, Washington, D.C., in 1948, came away from the poet's address with this insight:

> Did he not belong more rightfully in a monastic order than in the Fellowship of the respectable, upper-class citizens gathered in the Parish House of St. Thomas's church? In a monastic order there would be no irreconcilable conflict between mystic, poetic ecstasy and the practical pursuits of life.... Nor would the cycle of his life have to deny its origin or stopping places on the way.[181]

That, at various times in his life, Eliot found Kelham and Cowley congenial (as well as the more exotic Nashdom) indicates (like his interest in Little Gidding) that he was not excessively – and certainly not exclusively – 'spiky' and could appreciate the more temperate Catholic tradition of the Church of England which foundations like Cowley represented.

While staying at Cowley, indeed, Eliot met Dom Gregory Dix, OSB (1902-52),[182] the Nashdom monk (from 1948, Prior), author of *The Shape of the Liturgy* (dedicated to the Cowley Fathers), and one of the most distinguished liturgical scholars the Church of England has produced.

Kelham, too, was a centre of liturgical study. In *The Liturgical Movement* (1954), J.H. Srawley refers to the lasting value of the Revd A.G. Hebert's 'well-known book, *Liturgy and Society* (1935)'.[183] In this work, Hebert (who was an SSM priest) indicates something of the impression Eliot's regular presence must have made among the brethren. He refers to *The Rock* (1934) on no less than three occasions, calling it a 'great' expression in poetry of a new interest in the liturgy (being fostered, of course, principally by Anglo-Catholics) and, indeed, concludes his book with this command of the Rock:

> I say to you: Make perfect your will.
> I say: take no thought of the harvest,
> But only of proper sowing.[184]

*

For Eliot, spiritual perfection could only be aspired to through submitting oneself to sustained authority and direction, in all kinds of matters of the faith. When he was asked to be a godfather, by Janet and Michael Roberts, for their third child Adam, in 1940, Eliot responded to the request in a letter, pointing out that he had been advised by his spiritual director that four godchildren were as many as a man should undertake. The Roberts' son would be number four, for him, and he added that any further bookings of this kind would require a special dispensation.[185] The letter is (to a degree) light-hearted, on a happy occasion, but it nonetheless resonates with the importance Eliot placed on authority in spiritual matters and, thereby, obedience, and the 'endless' humility that requires, as well as his recognition of the obligations which a conscientious godfather, such as he would be, must fulfil.

Eliot's long-standing colleague at Faber and Faber, Peter du Sautoy, reflected that

> it was impossible to be long associated with Eliot without being aware that he was a deeply religious man.[186]

This did not mean that Eliot ever came to a position where the demands of his Anglo-Catholicism had become less challenging – on the contrary, in fact (as he reflected in 1948, twenty-one years after his conversion):

The more conscious becomes the belief, so the more conscious becomes unbelief: indifference, doubt and scepticism
appear.... A higher religion imposes a conflict, a division,
torment and struggle within the individual.[187]

Much of that torment appears to have been happily resolved, in the
final years of Eliot's life, in his fulfilled marriage to a fellow Anglo-
Catholic. 'It was a deep and full marriage', du Sautoy remembered,
'of body, mind, heart and soul'.[188]

6

The Blessed Virgin Mary

> There *ought* to be a shrine of the BVM at the harbour mouth
> of a fishing port.
>
>   (Eliot, in 1947)[189]

By the 1920s, Sean Gill writes, 'Marian devotion had become one
of the hallmarks of advanced Anglo-Catholicism'.[190] The hymn, 'Ye
who own the faith of Jesus', with its rousing chorus, 'Hail Mary, full
of grace', had 'become something of an anthem for Anglo-Catholics
by the time of the first [*sic*, it was the second] Anglo-Catholic congress in 1923'.[191] Eliot's devotion to Mary places him, as surely as any
other aspect of his faith, securely in the Anglo-Catholic tradition.
As noted previously, he had a rule of always making his confession
before the feast of the Assumption (15th August).[192] Writing to Fr
William Levy on 21st August, 1954, a few days after the feast day,
Eliot commented:

> It is good to see how the Veneration of the B.V.M. [Blessed
> Virgin Mary – the standard Catholic abbreviation], for in-
> stance, *fits in* inevitably to Catholic doctrine: to see it as
> naturally growing out of the Faith, instead of something
> added on to it.[193]

Mary Trevelyan records her discussion of the dogma with Eliot in
1950, the year in which it was defined by Pius XII (although it had
been a matter of Catholic faith and observance for many centuries
and also in Orthodox Christianity as the 'Dormition'). While many
Protestants (and, indeed, Anglican theologians even of moderate
Catholic persuasion, like Austin Farrer, were outraged by the papal
definition of the dogma[194]), Eliot had no difficulty with it and was

content to explain this article of faith, Trevelyan records, as 'Our Lady by-passing Purgatory'[195] – the very allusion to Purgatory, of course, being another Anglo-Catholic element which would have stirred many Anglicans' and Protestants' criticism.

The veneration (as Eliot correctly calls it, not 'worship') of the Virgin Mary is another of those practices, like auricular confession and belief in the holy sacrifice of the Mass, which differentiates Anglo-Catholicism from High Church Anglicanism, not to mention Anglicanism in general. Veneration of the Virgin is accompanied, in Anglo-Catholicism, with acceptance of the papal dogmas about her, such as the Immaculate Conception and the Assumption; of the idea of Mary as Mediatrix, presenting the petitions of her faithful clients to the Trinity, and the observance of all the devotional customs associated with the age-old Marian cult in the Catholic Church. Shrines and statues of the Virgin are found in Anglo-Catholic churches worldwide, and probably the most famous Anglo-Catholic parish in England, at Walsingham in Norfolk (supported by Eliot), is a shrine to Mary. Prayers to the Virgin, such as the rosary petitions (which Eliot used daily), including the 'Ave Maria...', 'Hail Mary...' and the 'Salve Regina...', 'Hail, holy Queen...', make their way, in various forms, into his poetry: effortlessly, unaffectedly, inevitably.

The *Angelus* devotion, commemorating the Annunciation by the archangel Gabriel to the youthful Virgin and the subsequent Incarnation of Jesus, was said after High Mass each Sunday at St Stephen's, Gloucester Road, in typical Anglo-Catholic fashion.[196] Eliot, along with his fellow parishioners, would have replied to the priest's series of 'Hail Marys' with the response, requesting Mary's mediating prayers:

> Holy Mary, Mother of God, pray for us sinners, now and
> at the hour of our death.

Eliot includes part of this response in *Ash-Wednesday, 1930*. He dated a letter to Mary Trevelyan by the feast of the Assumption, in 1949, noting the day of obligation in block letters after.

Eliot's use of the rosary was central to his devotion to the Blessed Virgin. Writing to Mary Trevelyan on 11th January, 1948, and noting the feast of St Honore du Faubourg, Eliot offers her the choice of one of two rosaries blessed and given to him by Pius XII (of whom he had had an audience the previous week). As she made no response, in a letter of 26th January, 1948 (dated also Septuagesima), he repeats the offer of a good rosary (with the phrase in block letters this time) that he will not give to anyone who would not keep it in constant use. In her diary for 1950, Trevelyan notes how Eliot's papal rosary lost a bead and, not surprisingly, 'put him off his stride'.

*

Where the Virgin's presence and influence in Eliot's spirituality is most strikingly expressed, however, is in his poetry. In general, when references are made to women in his *oeuvre*, prior to *Ash-Wednesday*, *1930*, they are almost entirely negative, even if that negativity took different forms: from the alluring, but unobtainable femininity of Prufrock's mermaids at the end of his 'Love Song' (preceded, in the same poem, by the arch and equally unobtainable women 'talking of Michelangelo'), to the disappointed Romanticism of the female speaker in 'Portrait of a Lady', to the series of alarming women in *The Waste Land* (1922) – suicidal sybils, false prophetesses, and neurotic, promiscuous and hysterical female denizens of the debauched demi-monde of the Modernist metropolis. In 'The Hollow Men' (1925), we have (for the first time) a brief glimpse of hopefulness in the midst of the abject despair of these wastelanders, bereft of hope, consigned to Hell, in the form of 'the perpetual star / Multifoliate rose', a reference to Dante's vision of the Virgin in his *Paradiso* (23) where she is evoked in terms of the arrayed petals of the mystic rose in the empyrean. The allusion is oblique and, in the context of the despairing lives of the hollow men, it presents only a hopeless hope. Nonetheless, it is a significant moment in Eliot's poetry as the first sign of the possibility of redeemed life and, crucially, mediated through a vision of the Virgin: 'The hope only / Of empty men'.[197] Christopher Ricks points out that, originally, 'The Hollow Men' ended on this optimistic note[198] – very different from its ultimately despairing close with 'a whimper'.

In 'Journey of the Magi' (1927), where the marked change in Eliot's personal and poetic vision becomes substantial, we escape from the despairing landscape of the wasteland to a 'temperate valley', with the powerful sense, in Dantean phrase, of a *vita nuova*. Nonetheless, as in *The Waste Land*, if less threateningly, the female presences here, 'the silken girls bringing sherbert', represent the allure of the fallen world which can deflect even the wisest men from their pilgrimage.

Ash-Wednesday, 1930, I have argued elsewhere,[199] is the most important Marian poem, in English, of the twentieth century, so we should consider it in detail in chapter 7, which is devoted to the few works in Eliot's *corpus* which are obviously and substantially of explicitly Anglo-Catholic character.

In *Four Quartets*, on the other hand – beginning with 'Burnt Norton' in 1935 and completed during the Second World War – the Christian theological component, let alone Anglo-Catholicism, is seldom overt. Only in the fourth, lyrical section of each Quartet, rather like the brief scherzo in a sonata, do we encounter a sustained statement of Christian doctrine of Catholic persuasion, in a poetic guise, and it is noteworthy that this section is the shortest of each of the four poems (which are, essentially, philosophical works, meditating upon time and timelessness and on the processes of poetic creativity which mediate these concerns). In the sequence, Eliot refers to God the Father ('Burnt Norton'), the Son ('East Coker'), the Virgin Mary ('The Dry Salvages') and the Holy Spirit ('Little Gidding'). The poems, in turn, are devoted to each of the four classical elements of creation: air, earth, water and fire. 'The Dry Salvages', summoning memories of Eliot's childhood and youth beside the Mississippi and the Atlantic off the Massachusetts coast, where he sailed, recalls the particular association of the Virgin with the sea, as *Stella Maris*, Our Lady Star of the Sea.

The theological lyric in 'The Dry Salvages' is in the form of a prayer to Mary, for protection, and with the understanding that she is the one, archetypically, who, like so many fishermen's mothers and wives, saw her son setting forth on a journey, Jonah-like, to 'the dark throat' of death and who can no more be saved from this destiny by the prayers of this world than be preserved from danger by the warning bells of the ocean. We are reminded of the Psalmist's reference to those that 'go down to the sea in ships, that do their business in great waters' (107, 23) and, symbolically, of the Christian community, in Eliot's reference to 'fish' itself, an ancient symbol of Christ. To begin the poem, Eliot notes a 'shrine' to the Virgin:

> Lady, whose shrine stands on the promontory,
> Pray for all those who are in ships, those
> Whose business has to do with fish, and
> Those concerned with every lawful traffic
> And those who conduct them.
>
> Repeat a prayer also on behalf of
> Women who have seen their sons and husbands
> Setting forth, and not returning:
> Figlia del tuo figlio,
> Queen of Heaven.

> Also pray for those who were in ships, and
> Ended their voyage on the sand, in the sea's lips
> Or in the dark throat which will not reject them
> Or wherever cannot reach them the sound of the sea
>   bell's
> Perpetual angelus.[200]

The 'shrine' Eliot had in mind was the church of Notre Dame de la Garde, high up overlooking the Mediterranean at Marseilles but he also insisted, in a letter, that it could be any shrine to the Virgin,[201] which was true to the general thesis of the Quartets that the moment of perception of the eternal in the midst of temporality may occur at any time or any place. From his childhood, Eliot was familiar with the image of Mary atop the church of Our Lady of Good Voyage in Gloucester, Massachusetts, located on Prospect Street on a promontory overlooking the harbour, even if the Unitarian lad had never entered the Catholic building:

> Between the towers ... is a large statue of Mary, her left arm
> holding a fishing vessel and her right arm raised in a gesture
> of blessing or peace.[202]

The relationship of Mary with the ocean is emphasised by sanctuaries all along the shores of the Mediterranean and, thereby, with seafarers and fishermen. From the cathedral in Crotone, on the gulf of Taranto, a Black Madonna is taken to the headland church of Our Lady of Capo Colonna, on the second Sunday in May, then carried over the sea, by night, in a torchlight procession of fishing boats whose masters hope to secure the Virgin's protection. It is such ancient Catholic associations and traditions, and the prayers which accompany them, which Eliot evokes.

That the poet should devote this theological section of the third Quartet to the Virgin indicates his view of her enjoying a dignity and importance, if not comparable to, certainly approaching that of the Holy Trinity, whose Persons are the subjects of the other three theological lyrics. It is a clear expression of his Anglo-Catholicism. Also, within the context of this Quartet at large, which is a poem 'whose subject is the need for obedient submission before the great annunciations which impose costly demands upon men and women',[203] it is obviously apt that the Virgin should be at its heart.

As the essential philosophico-theological teaching of *Four Quartets* is the apprehension of the intersection of the timeless with time,

*Statue of the Virgin atop Our Lady of
Good Voyage in Gloucester, Massachusetts*

the necessity to be alive and alert to the intimations of spiritual in-sight which may be revealed in the midst of ordinary activity, the appropriateness of the Virgin, whose annunciation is the Christian archetype of such a 'still point' is evident. But in addition to the Virgin of the Annunciation, Eliot particularly embraces the idea of Mary as *Mater Dolorosa*, the Mother of Sorrows, in reference to the women who suffer while their menfolk undertake hazardous, life-threatening work at sea. But she is also there, crowned, as the 'Queen of Heaven'.

The paradoxical phrase in Italian which Eliot incorporates into his lyric, '*Figlia del tuo figlio*' ('Daughter of your son') is from the prayer (in the final canto of Dante's *Paradiso*) of St Bernard of Clairvaux to the Virgin on behalf of the seeker aspiring to attain ultimate salvation and who, therefore, has reached the point of maximum need and supplication:

> Vergine madre, figlia del tuo figlio
> Nel ventre tuo si raccese l'amore
>   per lo cui caldo nell' etterna pace
> *così è germinato questo fiore.*
>
> (*Paradiso*, XXXIII, 7-9)

(Within your womb the love was made to burn again, by whose warmth in the eternal peace this flower has thus bloomed.)[204]

This looks forward, in Eliot's sequence, to the fourth and final Quar-tet, 'Little Gidding', the poem of pentecostal fire, which closes in Dantean reference, again, to the burning fire of love, initiated at the Annunciation, in union with the mystical rose (another ancient image of Mary, the *rosa mystica*): when 'the fire and the rose are one'.

The closing reference, in the prayer to the Virgin in 'The Dry Sal-vages', to the 'perpetual angelus', referring to the thrice daily (early morning, noon and evening) repetition of '*Ave Maria*', three times, with versicles and a collect as a memorial of the Incarnation, is both appropriate to the Virgin in the general context of Catholic devotion, but specifically apt in the context of this poem and the thought of the Quartets at large, for it mimics the bells at sea, which are warn-ings to sailors in their hazardous progress. And, paradoxically, as a regularly-timed devotion, it figures the perpetual possibility of lib-eration from the time-bound world – of timelessness in the midst of time. For Eliot, the Virgin Mary, through the prayers and poetry associated with her, facilitated that essential transcendental quest.

7

Episcopacy and the Apostolic Succession

Typically, as an Anglo-Catholic, Eliot had (on the one hand) a high theory of the episcopate, in connection with the doctrine of apostolical succession, but (on the other) was inclined to a dim view of the contemporary occupants of episcopal thrones. He told Mary Trevelyan, in 1944, that the only bishops for whom he had any affection were G.K.A Bell of Chichester (1881-1958) and Cosmo Gordon Lang of Canterbury (1864-1945), both favourably inclined towards (if not firmly within) the Anglo-Catholic tradition.[205]

An event in East Africa, in 1913, brought the issue of Anglo-Catholic understanding of episcopacy into sharp focus, and was a foretaste of the dispute (also in the mission field) into which Eliot was drawn thirty years later in the debate over the Church of South India. Several Protestant missions were operating in East Africa, in addition to the Anglican (and Evangelical) Church Missionary Society. Two Anglican bishops, of Mombasa and Uganda, advocated, and on at least one occasion celebrated, joint communion services with Anglicans and the other non-Roman bodies (including even the Friends – or Quakers – who, rejecting any concept of a sacrament of the Lord's Supper, were placed in the peculiar position, considering the purpose of the service, of having to refuse communion). The bishops intended the event to initiate a scheme of wholesale reunion, to supersede the situation where the several Christian denominations appeared to be competing for the souls of the heathen. 'The prestige of the Christian religion in Africa', wrote Karen Blixen in her famous autobiography (about this period, and from first-hand experience), 'was weakened by the intolerance that one Christian Church showed towards the other'.[206]

The Anglo-Catholic hero, Frank Weston, bishop of Zanzibar, charged his episcopal brothers of Mombasa and Uganda (in a complaint to Archbishop Davidson of Canterbury) 'with the grievous faults of propagating heresy and schism'.[207] He argued that the episcopate was of divine institution and their action, by bringing Protestants who did not acknowledge that institution and the succession that flows from it, to an Anglican altar, amounted to an act that was 'hostile to Christ's Holy Church'. Those bishops, he continued, were the English branch of the 'universal College of Bishops':

> a Bishop sent from England to Africa goes out, not as a Bishop
> of the English Church, but simply as a Catholic Bishop, who

Frank Weston, Bishop of Zanzibar

owes his consecration to the universal Episcopate represented to him by prelates of the Church in England.[208]

Non-episcopal Churches, such as those represented at Kikuyu (where
the service was held) were not in full communion with the Catholic
Church, so for them to receive holy communion there was heretical
and schismatic.

The seriousness of the East African affair and its impact on English
religious life – the remarkable attention paid to it a matter of months
before the outbreak of the Great War – is recorded by Archbishop
Davidson's biographer, Bishop Bell:

A public controversy on an astonishing scale started in the English Press, and continued for a long while throughout the Churches. To some, the scheme ... seemed a magnificent move forward to Christian reunion. To others, it appeared to be 'a certain step to the disruption of the Anglican communion'.[209]

Writing to *The Times* on 19th December, 1913, Bishop Gore of Oxford, one of the minority of bishops of Catholic inclination, declared

I doubt if the cohesion of the Church of England was ever more seriously threatened than it is now.[210]

The Bishop of Zanzibar came to England to present his objections in person. Weston had many supporters – among them W.B. Trevelyan of Liddon House, who was the uncle and godfather of Mary Trevelyan, Eliot's Anglo-Catholic friend and correspondent.

Archbishop Davidson, finding himself once again between the Scylla and Charybdis of Catholic and Protestant Anglicanism, championed the *via media*, cleverly referring to the authority of the Caroline divines to whom Anglo-Catholics regularly deferred:

The words and acts of many leading High Churchmen in Caroline days, as well as the carefully chosen sentences and, it may perhaps be said, the significant silences in some of our formularies, throw a grave *onus probandi* upon those who contend for the rigid and uncompromising maintenance of the absolutely exclusive rule.[211]

With regard to the service at Kikuyu, he affirmed that it was acceptable for a Protestant communicant, desiring the Sacrament but unable to access the ministrations of his own Church (or an Anglican, in the same position, seeking communion in a Protestant service) to proceed to communicate. In the matter of a joint communion service, however, he would make no concession and agreed with Bishop Weston that the Kikuyu service was 'admittedly abnormal, admittedly irregular' and that 'we shall act rightly, in abstaining at present from such Services'. Later, in some private notes, Davidson was less diplomatic, noting that the service was 'rash' and conducted in ignorance of 'large principles which cannot be put out of sight'.[212] His successor at Canterbury, the more Catholic Cosmo Gordon Lang, described the service as a 'great mistake'.[213]

Like the Kikuyu controversy, the proposal, in the next generation, for a Church of South India brought the theology of episcopacy and the apostolic succession, as it was understood by the Church of England, into serious question – especially for Anglo-Catholics, like Eliot, who regarded these teachings as the non-negotiable bedrock of Catholic order and of the Catholic claims of the Church of England (with regard to the validity of ordinations and, thereby, the validity of the Church's sacraments administered by her episcopally-ordained priests). Viscount Halifax commented (in 1930) that if the Church of South India came into being 'I should have to leave the Church of England'.[214]

This, Michael Yelton has argued persuasively, would have been a much more significant controversy 'had it not been for the overwhelming impact of external events'[215] in the midst of the Second World War.

The idea of an ecumenical Church of South India, in which Anglicans would combine with non-episcopal Protestant Churches, for the purpose of unity and strength of mission, had, in fact, been raised as early as 1920, at the Sixth Lambeth Conference and surfaced again in 1930. The proposals remained before the Church, and, in response to them, in the 1940s, Eliot combined with a group of distinguished Anglican apologists to produce for the 'Council for the Defence of Church Principles' a number of pamphlets attuned to an ideal set out on the inside front cover of the one he wrote – the seventh in a series of nine, pointedly entitled *Reunion by Destruction*. Eliot and the writers sought

> the preservation of those fundamental principles of the Faith and Order of the Catholic Church which are clearly taught and enjoined in the Book of Common Prayer, in the belief that without these principles, which are now endangered by certain reunion proposals, the attainment of oecumenical reunion and the maintenance of the unity of the Anglican Communion are alike impossible.

The list of contributors to these tracts includes two Cowley Fathers and the Revd A.G. Hebert from the Society of the Sacred Mission at Kelham.

Some months prior to its composition and publication, on 26th January, 1943, Eliot had set out for Lambeth Palace with a deputation to confront Archbishop William Temple about the South India Scheme, which the Primate supported. In his biography of Temple, F.A. Iremonger records that Lord Quickswood (whom Eliot regarded as doctrinally sound but lacking in punch[216]) introduced the deputation and stated that the Scheme offered no security of orthodoxy ... it would introduce schism into the Anglican Communion.... Canon Demant criticized the Scheme as being an example of an indigenous local expression of Christianity, to which many equally dangerous parallels could be found in the history of the Church.[217]

In his subsequent pamphlet, Eliot addresses his polemic 'to the Laity' and while he begins with a lengthy profession of moderation and reasonableness, he soon makes his absolute opposition to the South Indian project clear:

> What is a matter of mere 'order' for one person – that is, a matter of efficient administration – may be a matter of faith for another; and equivocation on matters of faith and order ... is apparent in the South India Scheme.[218]

Referring negatively to the Protestant Churches involved as 'sects', 'dissenters' and 'nonconformists', Eliot isolates the 'vexed question of Episcopacy and the Apostolical Succession'. To overlook it produces merely a 'phantom unity' – a phrase he had used before in 'Thoughts after Lambeth' where he had similarly criticised the bishops for failing to demand from the Free Churches what, in *Reunion by Destruction*, he calls 'any particular theory or interpretation of the Episcopate as a condition of reunion', which was tantamount to asserting that 'we beg that Nonconformists should accept the Episcopate as a harmless formality' when, from an Anglo-Catholic's viewpoint, 'the issue turns on the meaning we attach to the solemn phrase *of divine appointment*'.[219] He rebukes the proponents of reunion for regarding such a matter as negotiable:

> Episcopacy may be of divine appointment, they say; but even if Our Lord divinely appointed it, He is indifferent whether any member of His Church believes that He did so. From the point of view of the Church of South India it is merely 'an additional interpretation ... not binding on the united church'.

And, of course, Eliot recognises that if vagueness is tolerated regarding episcopacy and apostolic succession, then the validity of orders and sacraments is called into question. The issue

> cannot be separated from that of the validity of orders and the validity of the Sacraments; it is part of a fatal crack which runs through the Constitution of the South India Church

from top to bottom. The priest may believe that the power to celebrate a valid Eucharist would not be his, unless he had been ordained by a bishop. But in the Church of South India he would not be justified in teaching his flock that this is so, because it is a 'debatable matter'.[220]

Eliot's position is not only an Anglo-Catholic extremist response. The Book of Common Prayer and the Canons Ecclesiastical both affirm the necessity of episcopal ordination. Leonard Hodgson, Regius Professor of Divinity at Oxford from 1944 (and, it should be noted, regarded as an active ecumenist) in his study of *The Doctrine of the Church as held and Taught in the Church of England*, published in 1946, asserts

> The Church of England believes itself to have been privileged to maintain a ministry united to that of the apostles by unbroken continuation of ordination....[221]

And he further writes in *Anglicanism & South India* (published in the same year as Eliot's pamphlet) that

> theological principle forbids us to equate episcopal and non-episcopal ministries.[222]

As Dom Gregory Dix reflected:

> You cannot by-pass the episcopate in the workings of an episcopal church.[223]

Eliot probes the reasons for the willingness to compromise these theological principles and finds the old bogey of relativism and liberalism, familiar to him from his Unitarian past:

> it is assumed that each body – Anglican, Methodist, Presbyterian and Congregationalist – is in possession of some part of excellence and truth, and that these parts only need to be combined. It is never suggested that any body may contribute anything in the way of falsehood. It is apparently an assumption of such a scheme, that everybody is right.... we must suppose that anything is reasonable which does not offend the majority in a synod of the new church – a synod in which the judgment of the bishops may be overruled by the opinion of the laity.[224]

In other words, from his viewpoint, everything was wrong about it – philosophically, as well as theologically.

Eliot acknowledges two formidable objections to his position: that the witness to Christianity in South India was difficult enough, as it contended with the other great religions of the sub-continent, without being further thwarted by internal divisions amongst Christians and that, as the present debate amply demonstrated, there were substantial theological divisions in the Church of England at home, yet Eliot and his co-complainants were demanding of the Church of South India the full theological consistency and agreement which were notoriously absent from the provinces of Canterbury and York. To the first, Eliot responded that allowing the ecumenical project in South India to go ahead would only encourage a view that was becoming widespread (he feared) among Christians – that the Churches should be 'united across all divisions', a position implying

> not only that they should aspire and strive towards reunion, but that the only essential doctrines are those which they *all* hold in common.[225]

It was particularly necessary in those places where the local circumstances were given highest priority to recognise the consequences of making theological truth (as he saw it) subservient to these. For the result would be a merging of all Churches into 'a national system of minimal Christianity'. Two years before, in the *Christian News-Letter*, Eliot had written:

> What we have to guard against [is] a kind of National Christianity, the vagaries of which would be free from the control of any theological authority.[226]

To the second objection – that theological disarray in Anglicanism elsewhere makes demands for its rigorous Catholicity in South India unreasonable – Eliot responds that the Church of England was not founded (as it appears the South India Church will be) either on the spurious principle 'let us unite, in the hope that in twenty years' time we shall agree' or upon an agreement to differ. There is a difference

> between an existing Church within which scandalous divergences of doctrine and practice have grown up, and a new Church to be erected *upon the foundation* of divergences.

To unite, in inter-communion, with Christians who protest against episcopacy means the Church of England

> is surrendering its claim to be a Church, and is accepting the status of a society.[227]

Eliot's impatience with the scheme is reflected in sarcastic notes: 'this happy result, in which nobody has anything of importance to surrender'; dismissive abuse: 'the Church of South India is a pre-fabricated church.... [the Draft Constitution] reads like the prospectus for a company flotation'; doom-laden prophecy (with Arnoldian echoes):

> the peace of death will descend. No liberty may be affected: and so long as men are free to do as they please, they tend to think that all is well...

and an exclamatory conclusion:

> twenty patient years to build what is only an elaborate arti-fice! Twenty years to construct a pantomime horse![228]

Such quotations demonstrate how unpleasant Christians can be to one another in controversy, but we need to remember that *Reunion by Destruction* (as its title suggests) is a polemical, occasional pamphlet (and Eliot's language is in that tradition) and, most importantly, that he believed profoundly in the principles that were at stake here and the danger to them which this proposal posed. Any means in the process of having it rejected were justified. More soberly, and in his more familiar reflective mode, he also writes:

> the way to perfection is not to be found through voluntary liquidation; by further and further relaxation of conditions of membership; by the abolition of theology in favour of a few formulae which anybody may interpret as he likes; by ceasing to be a church and becoming a benevolent associa-tion.... [The scheme prefigures] the gradual disappearance of Christian spiritual values, the substitution of words for realities, of humanism for faith.[229]

In that last phrase, Eliot recalls his entire spiritual journey – 'the way to perfection', indeed – in the opposite direction.

Early in 1943, Eliot asked Mary Trevelyan to visit Lord Lang, then just retired, to discuss the South India scheme, and she communicated to Eliot the former Archbishop's strong negative views of the subject. Eliot replied (in a letter of 8th March, 1943) that he was most interested to know Lang's mind and relieved to learn that his views were sound. There is no question that Eliot would have also endorsed Weston's judgement of Kikuyu and, like Anglo-Catholics in general, would have found Davidson's public response too ambiguous. Kikuyu, like South India a generation later, presented the ambiguous situation, for

Anglo-Catholics, of an Episcopal Church sitting lightly to episcopacy and, worst of all, some of her bishops approving it.

Suffering an attack of influenza at the very time his pamphlet was to be distributed by the Council for the Defence of Church Principles, Eliot wrote in apology to Mary Trevelyan (on 14th December, 1943) indicating that her delayed copy would be sent, with his inscription, in a week's time. In the following days, he became something of a spokesman for the opponents of the South India controversy and writing again to Trevelyan in a letter dated for the Holy Innocents, 1943 (28th December), Eliot notes how his recuperation has been ended by invitations to address various small groups of parish clergy on the matter in distant corners of remote dioceses. One of these priests, perhaps, was the vicar of the church in a particularly inaccessible part of England who became the subject of one of the amusing Anglo-Catholic anecdotes of the post-War years. He placed in the porch of his church the following notice: 'Members of the Church of South India may not communicate in this church'. The likelihood of such a member making his or her way from the sub-continent to this distant spot in England, for the purpose of receiving Holy Communion, would seem slight indeed, but he obviously felt (perhaps after reading Mr Eliot's pamphlet) that the theological point needed to be made.

In 1948, when the Lambeth Conference gave the Church qualified approval, the Whit Monday pilgrimage to Walsingham was made in reparation for the South India scheme.[230] In 1955, a state of limited inter-communion between the Church of South India and the Church of England was approved by the Convocations of Canterbury and York. 40,000 Anglicans in the Nanydal district of South India refused to join the Church, so the victory of Eliot's opponents was, at best, a qualified one.[231] Nonetheless, the Catholic principles he and many others had advocated had definitely been decisively compromised. People (including priests) left the Church of England for Rome over this issue. It is interesting that Eliot continued to abide in the theological ambiguity it indicated, suggesting that, on balance, for him, other elements of the Anglo-Catholic position outweighed this rather important point of theology.

Eliot's views on the matter inevitably remained unchanged. The report of his address to a gathering of Washington Episcopalians in 1948 notes:

> Mr Eliot did not set too high a store by the ecumenical movement as an instrument of Christian restoration. Those

who were least dogmatic on theological grounds were most extreme in embracing the ecumenical idea; thus the religious principles behind the idea did not measure up to the zeal of the protagonists for the idea. The purity of the 'Catholic' tradition and orientation of the Church of England was a matter of serious, general concern to Mr Eliot.

Eliot told his audience that he had been asked to write a report on the South India scheme and had devoted 'some years of private study' to it:

> He came to the conclusion that union of the Churches in South India could only be had at the unacceptable price of sacrifice of religious principles. Similarly, he expressed strong disapproval of the negotiations concerning the poss- ible merger of the Presbyterian and Episcopal Churches in the United States. These negotiations, he reported, were vie- wed by responsible circles in the Church of England with 'great apprehension' and as a 'most dangerous trend'.[232]

Inevitably, the scheme appears in Macaulay's *Towers of Trebizond* and Aunt Dot observes that Father Chantry-Pigg is strongly opposed to it, pointing out to Russian communists (who had some difficult coming to grips with the issue) that the Church's

> odd behaviour in South India was discrediting it and driving many people to the Roman obedience, and what a mistake it all was, South India, I mean, and the Roman obedience, he spoke very strongly against it, but one could see that they couldn't really take in about South India, though they quite understood about Rome, because of course they dislike it too.[233]

From today's perspective, of course, what is remarkable – as with the Prayer Book controversy of 1927-8 – is that the issue generated as much interest and controversy as it did.

*

In Eliot's last years, from 1958 to 1963 (two years before his death), he was a member of the Commission for the revision of the psalter in The Book of Common Prayer. The Commission's intentions were to replace those words and phrases in the Coverdale version of the psalms which had become obsolete or which plainly misrepresented the original text: 'the Commission ... never at any time intended to produce a new translation of the Hebrew'.[234] This restraint – ensured by the formidable representation of conservative Church musicians and literary figures on the Commission – coupled with Eliot's increasing infirmity, undoubtedly accounted for his small contribution to discussion, speaking only occasionally 'to plead for the retention of an old phrase'.[235] As in theology, so in liturgy, the Modernist in poetry was a conservative.

The Commission met at a religious house in the East End of London (the Royal Foundation of St. Katharine) which Eliot also visited independently in these years.[236] The venue could scarcely have been more congenial for the Anglo-Catholic poet, given its history and character. Since the granting of its charter by Queen Matilda in 1147 and its creation as a royal peculiar under the patronage of the queens of England by Queen Eleanor in 1261, it was secured against dispersal at the time of the monastic dissolution (the pious Catherine of Aragon was allowed by Henry VIII to continue as patroness throughout her unhappy life). For more than two centuries, until 1825 when the original St Katharine's was demolished to make way for the dock that bore its name, a continuous life in community of prayer and worship according to the rule of St. Augustine was pursued there:

> throughout its whole post-Reformation history the rule of daily recitation of Mattins and Evensong had been maintained at St. Katharine's.[237]

It was an even more impressive witness to the historic Catholic spirit and character of Anglicanism than Little Gidding itself.

A new church in Regent's Park immediately replaced the old foundation, but as it was not in possession of the facilities for community life – the original St Katharine's was designated a 'hospital', a place of spiritual hospitality not only for the brethren and tertiaries, but for any itinerant Christian in need of the refreshment of prayer – the former tradition of unbroken watching and service temporarily lapsed, being restored, eventually, after the Second World War by Queen Mary when St Katharine's returned to its original home in East London. Its first master was the Revd St John Groser (to whom we have referred before). He quickly re-established its witness as a religious community open to the world by encouraging retreats and, characteristically, by engaging St Katharine's in Christian social welfare activity amongst the poor in the neighbourhood. New buildings – quarters for priests and sisters, a retreat centre, and a small chapel (adorned with fine fourteenth-century stalls from the first St Katharine's, an exquisite

Jacobean pulpit and, in time, the crucifix used in the film of *Murder in the Cathedral*, as a memorial to Fr Groser who had played Thomas) – were constructed on the site of the church of St James, Ratcliffe, where Lancelot Andrewes had worshipped as a child and which had been destroyed by the 'dark dove' of the bombing raids during the Second World War. By the 1970s, the community was under the care of the fathers of the Community of the Resurrection.

It was to this place that Eliot was drawn in his last years, with its quiet rose-garden and its *Angelus* bell at noon, recalling the Annunciation and Incarnation, amidst the grime and bustle of Stepney, in that region of London where so much of the heroic work of the Catholic Revival had been accomplished since the nineteenth century. Its regular prayer life (the Divine Office was recited each day) centred on the daily offering of the sacrifice of the Mass, and its conspicuous links with the monarchy and with the unbroken tradition of Catholic Christianity in England, surviving the Reformation, and with its care passing into the hands of religious men under vows, made it a definitive expression of the ideals to which Eliot's Anglo-Catholicism had always aspired.

Chapter Six
A Christian State

[Anglo-Catholicism] has always obtained the adherence of individuals from various social groups, and so far as they came from the more dominant classes, these tended to be rebels, both in theology and in social gospel, from the groups to which they belonged. Anglo-Catholics, still more than Roman Catholics, among the prosperous classes, have usually been individuals or families engaged in a nexus of relationships with a society holding other views. In this peculiarity, I think, lies a great social potency of Anglican Catholicism in a changing and dissolving society; this (as against its sporadic tendency to a kind of parochialism) renders it the more adapted to win the community of the future.

(Eliot, 'The English Situation', Christendom,
June 1940, 103)

Anglo-Catholicism has been conspicuous, since the nineteenth century, in its active support of movements for social reform. It was closely allied with the Christian Socialist initiatives of such as the Guild of St Matthew, founded by Stewart Headlam in 1877, in which 'Maurician and Tractarian ideals were united in an alliance with principles avowedly socialist'.[1] A decade later, the Christian Social Union came into existence at the instigation of the prominent Anglo-Catholic, Scott Holland, and was an enterprise for which Eliot's friend, Maurice Reckitt, had great admiration.[2] As we have noted, the Incarnational teaching of Anglo-Catholicism led the advocates of the movement to extend

> the idea of the Church as a society so as to include the whole of humanity.... All aspects of human affairs were relevant to Christianity ...[3]

as was the whole spectrum of society. The movement (Nicholas Williams wrote in retrospect in 1976) was 'the only part of the Church of England to have had any real contact with the working class'.[4] The underprivileged, the marginalised and the eccentric have traditionally found a welcome in Anglo-Catholicism which was denied to them (or, they sensed, would be denied to them) in mainstream, 'respectable' Anglicanism.

1

From the early 1930s, Eliot began writing intermittently for a variety of periodicals, expressing his concern for the role which he believed the individual Christian, and the Church at large, ought to be playing in the area of social and economic reform. It is significant that in one of the earliest of these contributions, where he attributes his 'only reasonable notoriety' to the 'composition of verse and jingles',[5] he promotes, first, the idea (soon to become characteristic of his polemic) of directing problems of a societal nature to formulation in spiritual terms (for 'I believe that all our problems turn out ultimately to be a religious problem'[6]). Second, he champions the Church itself as the solution to the 'problem', for it guaranteed an orthodox response to what were, ultimately, spiritual problems. In a discourse on Christianity and Communism, he argued that the Church was the 'necessary' institution:

> I aim at orthodoxy. For heresy, which consists in emphasising one aspect of the mystery to the exclusion of the other, is a natural tendency of the mind; a complete living orthodoxy is (except through the infusion of exceptional grace) almost impossible to the frail human being at every moment of his life; which is the one reason why the Church is necessary.

Learning, in 1935, that the Church Assembly (forerunner of today's General Synod)[7] had been discussing the principles of Social Credit, Eliot warned them of the need, rather, to promulgate the Church's orthodox teachings:

> [They] should give their time to considering the fundamental moral laws founded on Christian theology, and content themselves with proclaiming positively any violation of these laws which they observe (as Churchmen) in the present order. If the voice of the Church spoke with authority on that point, the result would be disturbing enough, and

more hopeful, than anything that has been accomplished by
the present Church Assembly.[8]

A familiar note is sounded here, too (we hear it also in the better-
known, 'Thoughts after Lambeth', four years before), as Eliot
expresses his impatience with the Church of England's reluctance
to make clear dogmatic statements. This is a characteristic Anglo-
Catholic complaint and one of the reasons why Roman Catholicism
has attracted numerous Anglo-Catholics over the years, especially
at times of doctrinal crisis in the Church of England.

Also particularly characteristic of Eliot is the suspicion, here,
about ecclesiastical 'talkfests', as we would call them today, especially
when they were avid for new theories (like Social Credit) to solve old
problems. Collective social ideas were in general unappealing to Eliot
who preferred to concentrate his attention on the careful ordering of
the individual's spiritual state, with reference to priestly direction and
orthodox theology, rather than programmes for society's rehabilitation
at large. His praise of Simone Weil for her opposition to the concept of
Christianity as an effective force for redemption in the *Massenmensch*
indicates this preference:

> She was by nature a solitary and an individualist, with a pro-
> found horror of what she called the collectivity – the monster
> created by modern totalitarianism. What she cared about was
> human souls.[9]

Because Eliot rejected the idea of plans for converting the world to
Christianity, he addresses his argument to individuals:

> I have no expectation and no desire to enforce the non-
> Christian to obey rules of life in which he cannot believe; I
> should only wish to persuade him, by practical results, that
> that rule of life is better than his own, if he has any.[10]

Part of that persuasion, he argued soon after his rebuke of the Church
Assembly, in a second article in *The Listener*, 'The Search for Moral
Sanction', was to demonstrate – given that 'the mind really does abhor
disorder' – that 'men and women must seek for some sanction for their
behaviour'.[11] There is a dearth of coherent policy on a governmental and
national level, he observes: the contemporary 'lack of system, which
Christianity cannot possibly accept'. This elicits a challenge from him:

> We need a kind of economics which will ask the question:
> Why? What is it good to do?[12]

But it is not finally by addressing ourselves to economics or sociology that we will discover a durable principle of order (always such
an important concept for him: socially, aesthetically, spiritually),
but, rather,

> we must find out what is the meaning of 'Good'.[13]

Eliot affirmed, very early in his career as a commentator on social
affairs from an Anglo-Catholic perspective, that 'we can surely labour towards a social justice in this world', but the justification for
such labour, always for him, was in order to 'prepare souls to share
not only here but in the Resurrection'.[14] As he commented, in the last
number of the *Criterion*:

> for myself, a right political philosophy came more and more
> to imply a right theology.[15]

2

Anglo-Catholic priests with whom he was associated in these
matters, such as St John Groser and Canon V.A. Demant, were
Christian Socialists (a tradition continued in a later generation by
the controversial Mervyn Stockwood, Bishop of Southwark, and
others). Demant and Maurice Reckitt (Demant's and Eliot's mutual
friend) established the periodical *Christendom* in 1931. Reckitt was
also the editor of *The Church Socialist* and a member of the Research
Committee of the Christian Social Council and of the Committee
of the Anglo-Catholic Summer School of Sociology which Eliot
addressed in 1933. He wrote a number of books from a Christian
Socialist standpoint, including *Faith and Society* (1932), and had
been a contributor to an influential volume of essays, *The Return
of Christendom* (1922). Eliot's friendship with Reckitt, which
began in the early 1930s, extended over many years. There is, for
instance, a letter of the poet to Mary Trevelyan of 27th July, 1953,
where he reports his attendance with Reckitt at an open-air Mass
at St Anne's, Soho, where they huddled together in the rain under
Reckitt's umbrella.

The Return of Christendom was introduced by Charles Gore,
who had been bishop of Oxford until 1919, and who, in the spirit
of his collection *Lux Mundi* (1899), stressed in his Introduction the
doctrinal implications of Christian social activity. These anticipate
the social and cultural aspects of Anglo-Catholicism which Eliot
was to approve in the early years of his commitment:

> [We] see the visibly organized Church with its sacramental fellowship as belonging to the essence of the religion of the Incarnation. This organized Church is the Body of Christ. It is His organ and instrument for action in the world. It is commissioned not only to proclaim a truth but to live a social life.... In a word, these writers are both Christians and Catholics.[16]

Reckitt and Demant were also enthusiastic about the economic, social and political theory known as Social Credit. Ezra Pound was amongst those it had influenced. This had been founded by the Scottish engineer, Major Clifford Hugh Douglas in the 1920s, its theories being disseminated in a series of his books, including *Social Credit* (1924). Douglas was in close collaboration with Alfred Richard Orage, the leading 'guild socialist'. Essentially, Social Credit was opposed to the dominance of economics by finance; but the key to its appeal to individuals who also shared common ideals with Eliot would have been its emphasis on the individual, as opposed to the collective (which included its opposition to the degradation of farming to a commercial enterprise) and its celebration of cultural heritage. Yet Social Credit, like Douglas' work at large, 'reflects a wide diversity of ideas and ideals'[17] and we would be right to imagine Eliot's wariness of such small 'c' catholicity.

More congruent with Eliot's Christian social thought in those inter-war decades were the writings of the historian Christopher Dawson (1889-1970), a convert from Anglo-Catholicism to Rome in 1914. A student of history and sociology, Dawson was an ecumenist who wrote (for example) about the Oxford Movement and several books on the relationship of religion and culture in the modern state. His central argument, about which Eliot would have had no reservations, was that the Catholic Church, in mediaeval times, was the essential factor in the rise of European civilisation. As Eliot himself writes, approvingly, in his major essay on Dante: in that epoch, 'Europe was still more or less one'.[18] He would also have concurred with Dawson's celebration of the two orders of society in the pre-Reformation world: religious communities and the natural community of the peasant society, linked to the soil and part of, although subordinated to the Church through an hierarchy. Yet Roger Kojecký argues persuasively, in the standard study of Eliot's social criticism, that Eliot would not have endorsed the tendency to totalitarianism in Dawson's theories.[19] Writing in the years of the defeat of Hitler and the rise of Stalinism, Eliot equated totalitarianism with 'the desire to return to the womb'.[20]

Eliot's relationship with these individuals, activities and movements was, in various ways, ambiguous. In this area of his religious activity, he kept something of a distance from his co-religionists. George Every told me that Fr St John Groser, of Christ Church, Stepney, the charismatic East End reformer, and Eliot, were simply not on the same wavelength.[21] Historians commenting on Anglo-Catholic socio-political thought have observed, for example, that disestablishment was one of the goals of the movement,[22] yet Eliot was firmly opposed to it. When he appeared in Oxford to deliver the opening address to the Anglo-Catholic Summer School of Sociology in September, 1933 (such an invitation indicating, incidentally, how quickly his standing and authority in Anglo-Catholicism had been recognised), he began (in a paragraph that was to be later excised) by remarking that this was 'by no means the first occasion on which I have had to speak in public on a subject outside of my competence'.[23] He warned the gathering of self-confessed socialists that as Catholics, also, in their examination of the proposals for social rehabilitation set before them, their obligation was 'to criticise the moral assumptions' implicit in these schemes. Moreover, they were to be on their guard against 'two chief pitfalls' (totalitarianism and egalitarianism):

> The ideas of authority, of hierarchy, of discipline and order, applied inappropriately in the temporal sphere, may lead us into some error of absolutism or impossible theocracy. Or the ideas of humanity, brotherhood, equality before God, may lead us to affirm that the Christian can only be a socialist. Heresy is always possible.... true worldly wisdom leads up to, and is fulfilled in, and is incomplete without, *other-worldly* wisdom.[24]

Tellingly, Eliot's summary of Catholic orthodoxy, here, consists of these elements: authority, hierarchy, discipline and order.

Of the two potential errors he identifies, it was the second – that only egalitarian socialism, amongst political theories, was compatible with Christianity – which was, indeed, in the mind of Pius XI in his encyclical of 15th May, 1931, *Quadragesimo Anno* (published in England as *The Social Order*). This elaborated upon and confirmed the thesis of *Rerum Novarum* of 1891, Leo XIII's commentary on the conditions created by the Industrial Revolution. Pope Pius highlights the incompatibility of strict socialism with Catholicism and his encyclical was source-material for Eliot's *Idea of a Christian Society*, a few years later.

Eliot also takes the opportunity of the Anglo-Catholic Summer
School to pillory American liberal Protestantism in the person of
Woodrow Wilson, whose scheme for a League of Nations after the
First World War was vitiated, in Eliot's view, by his lack of the discipline of orthodoxy and the restraint of Catholicism, thus obscuring
from him what Eliot regarded as the correct Christian attitude to the
perfection of mankind: the absolute ideal tempered by a moderate
expectation.

> [Wilson was] a Professor ... of the science of government,
> and I believe a member of one of the dissenting sects in
> America. His whole conception seems to me ... to illustrate
> that exaggerated faith in human reason to which people of
> undisciplined emotions are prone.... The great weakness of
> Woodrow Wilson was a theological weakness.[25]

And, as history was to show, the League was a failure. Eliot's dismissive reference to Wilson's theological background refers to his
strict Presbyterianism, described by Patrick Devlin as puritan in its
morality, patriarchal in its approach to the ordering of family life,
and unwavering in its belief in God the avenger.[26] This, combined
with Wilson's prominence in higher education in the United States,
made him a very familiar type of the Protestant sages which Eliot
knew well, a generation earlier, from his own Calvinist (although,
eventually, Unitarian), American background. Hence the tartness of
the dismissive rebuttal.

It appears that Eliot entered the fray of debate about Christianity
and society, in this manner, largely because of his dissatisfaction with
the way in which the Church's position was being articulated by its
spokesmen (in those days, principally, bishops), rather than because
of a more positive enthusiasm for making such contributions. He
was irritated into print by woolly thinking, especially when it came
from the leaders of the Church to whom the faithful should be able
to turn with confidence for orthodox guidance in matters temporal
as well as spiritual. The Church Assembly was a repeated target
(and afforded the opportunity for some typical Anglo-Catholic
bishop-baiting):

> The one attempt [at the Church Assembly], and a lamentable
> failure it seems to have been, to say what is and is not
> the Church's business, came from the Bishop of Jarrow,
> who remarked neatly that 'it was not the business of the
> Church to make society fit for men, but to make men fit for

society'. To employ the Bishop's own turn of speech, we may suggest that if we are respectful enough to believe that this statement has meaning, then it is heretical; and that if we are respectful enough, not to question its orthodoxy, we must admit that it is meaningless.[27]

When a bishop makes a mistake, Eliot wrote to Mary Trevelyan on 8th March, 1943, paraphrasing Conan Doyle, he is in the first rank of criminals.

Eliot rebuked the Church for not challenging socio-political theories from a theological perspective and, thereby, giving guidance to its people:

It sometimes seems as if the Church was opposed to Communism, only because Communism is opposed to the Church. I have at hand a book containing statements by Sir Oswald Mosley, which anyone with the merest smattering of theology can recognise to be not only puerile but anathema. So far as I know, the Church has given no direction to the Faithful in response to these statements.[28]

Eliot's vocabulary is instructive here – particularly the capitalised reference to 'the Faithful' and the use of the Greek term, 'anathema' (from the Hebrew verb 'to curse'). This is not language one usually associates with Anglicanism (even Anglo-Catholicism), but with Roman Catholicism and ceremonies of pontifical malediction. Similarly, the idea of the Church giving decisive direction to its people about such as Mosley's book (which, we sense, Eliot would like to have put on the *Index Librorum Prohibitorum*) is also an un-Anglican conception. The passage expresses again Eliot's Anglo-Catholic impatience with mainstream Anglicanism's reluctance to pronounce decisively on theological matters.

In party-political terms, Eliot was naturally drawn to the Tories, but writing to George Every and admitting this, he points out that he is wary of becoming involved even with them and he closes the letter by reflecting that contemplating socio-political matters for longer than an hour leaves him completely puzzled.[29] Nonetheless, in 1939 he travelled to Cambridge to deliver a series of lectures on these very topics which were to become *The Idea of a Christian Society*, his major statement as an Anglo-Catholic political and social commentator.

3

Eliot delivered his lectures in March, 1939, at Corpus Christi, Cambridge, when the Revd Charles Smyth – a friend with whom he had stayed on previous visits to the university – was Dean of Chapel. The immediate genesis of the talks was a letter to *The Times* (5th October, 1938) by Dr Joseph Oldham (founder of the Moot and editor of the *Christian News-Letter* – see below), which posed the question:

> May our salvation lie in an attempt to recover our Christian heritage, not in the sense of going back to the past but of discovering in the central affirmations and insights of the Christian faith new spiritual energies to regenerate and vitalise our sick society?... nothing short of a really heroic effort will avail to save mankind from its present evils and the destruction which must follow in their train.[30]

And their 'immediate context', Denis Donoghue writes, 'was Eliot's sense of the intolerable position of those who try to lead a Christian life in a non-Christian world'.[31] The urgency of the contemporary international situation in 1939 was, of course, also behind Oldham's letter and Eliot's response. He had written in 'A Commentary' in the *Criterion* in October, 1938 that 'there seems no hope in contemporary politics at all'.[32] Twelve years later, Eliot confessed to Mary Trevelyan that he felt even worse in 1950 about the future of the world than he had in these years leading up to the Second World War:

> I have never in the whole of my life felt so deeply depressed – worse than in 1938 – not at the thought of war but of what lies behind it.[33]

This was the abiding principle of evil in humanity, deriving from Original Sin.

Corpus was a natural destination for Eliot, in those days, as Paul Elmer More's experience of dining there, a few years before, suggests:

> Last Sunday I dined in Hall with [Will] Spens the Master of Corpus Christi [from 1927].... The Master and some of the Fellows are also very High Church.... Among others I met a Fellow named Smyth, who had been at Harvard and in the West, and who showed something of the *élan* and free expansiveness one expects from the better men in America.... Smyth is... one of Eliot's contributors to *The Criterion*.[34]

More's assessment of the Master's churchmanship was correct,
as Spens' article 'The Eucharist' in *Essays Catholic & Critical*,
indicates:

> It is precisely because devout reception unites us to our Lord
> that the Reserved Sacrament is His body, that He is present
> in a special manner, and that He can be thus adored.[35]

Eliot was in definite Anglo-Catholic company in a college whose
name, indeed, recalled the Latin form of the Mass and devotions to
the Sacrament of the Altar on Corpus Christi day.

In his lectures there on the idea of a Christian state, Eliot takes as
a 'norm'

> the idea of a small and mostly self-contained group attach-
> ed to the soil and having its interests centred in a particular
> place, with a kind of unity which may be designed, but
> which also has to grow through generations.[36]

This looks forward to the communities referred to in two of the *Four
Quartets*, 'East Coker' and 'Little Gidding', which he was to complete in the next couple of years. Especially, as Eliot does not envisage
a religious community, *per se*, at East Coker, it is in the village life
there, where he refers to communal 'earth feet, loam feet, lifted in
country mirth / ... in their living in the living seasons',[37] that we see
the immediate link between his poetry and Christian-social theorising
(rather than the allusions to the regime of the Ferrars at Little Gidding
where its self-consciously quasi-monastic ordering is more important
than its rural setting):

> for the great mass of humanity whose attention is occupied
> mostly by their direct relation to the soil, or the sea, or the
> machine, and to a small number of persons, pleasures and
> duties.... [a]s their capacity for *thinking* about the objects
> of faith is small, their Christianity may be almost wholly
> realised in behaviour: both in their customary and periodic
> religious observances, and in a traditional code of behaviour
> towards their neighbours.[38]

For some years, Eliot had been celebrating the settled and cohesive
qualities of rural community, praising, in 1931,

> a primarily agricultural society, in which people have local
> attachments to their small domains and small communities,
> and remain, generation after generation, in the same place.[39]

In *Christendom*, in 1940, reflecting on 'The English Situation' with regard to nurturing religious life, he juxtaposes modern humanity 'cheerfully plodding the road from nowhere to nowhere' with community rooted in the soil:

> communal religion needs settled communities in which to flourish; and once communal religion goes, most individual religion goes. It is the exceptional man who can retire to the desert to pray – and the still more exceptional man who can maintain his devotional life in a railway waiting-room full of strangers.... The agricultural community is the most stable.[40]

In an essay (1941) on Rudyard Kipling, a favourite poet and storyteller, Eliot praises his celebration of 'the essential contact of the civilization with the soil', even though 'Kipling's vision of the people of the soil'

> is not a Christian vision, but it is at least a pagan vision – a contradiction of the materialistic view: it is the insight into a harmony with nature which must be re-established if the truly Christian imagination is to be recovered by Christians.[41]

Eliot's most sustained celebration of the soil comes in the essay 'Virgil and the Christian World' of 1951, where he defends his preference for the 'world' of the Roman poet to that of Homer. In the *Georgics*, Virgil exalted 'the fundamental duty of any people to cherish the land', while the Greeks were less 'civilised' because of their contempt for the 'banausic occupations'. Virgil's devotion to Rome which

> was founded on devotion to the land; to the particular region,
> the particular village, and to the family in the village

derived from a 'sensibility ... more nearly Christian than that of any other Roman or Greek poet'.[42]

This agricultural-cum-spiritual idealism, attempted during Eliot's lifetime, in the United States, by the so-called 'Southern Fugitives' (including Eliot's friend, Allen Tate, the Roman Catholic poet and critic), with their cultured agrarianism, sits very oddly – it has to be said – with Eliot's metropolitan, cosmopolitan High Modernism, and what we know of his own personality. Like Baudelaire, he was 'never at ease in the country'.[43] Yet the rural community, in *The Idea of a Christian Society*, is an ideal model, serving the purpose of demonstrating to 'the great mass of humanity ... how far their lives fall short of Christian ideals'.[44] And as Charles Taylor has shown, in his recent monumental philosophical study, *A Secular Age*, this religion of the soil (*religion du terroir*) not only has a formidable history, but a plausible social purpose:

> Collective rituals were important to everybody, because on them depended the general welfare, success of crops, health of animals, protection against cholera.... And, indeed, this range of practices was thought to hold 'depuis des temps immémoriaux'.[45]

Further to his explanation of his Christian community, Eliot repudiates Coleridge's notion of the 'clerisy' as guardians of right belief and action:

> In any Christian society which can be imagined for the future – in what M. Maritain calls a *pluralist* society – my 'Community of Christians' cannot be a body of the definite vocational outline of the 'clerisy' of Coleridge: which, viewed in a hundred years' perspective, appears to approximate to the rigidity of a caste. The Community of Christians is not an organisation, but a body of indefinite outline; composed of both clergy and laity.[46]

Moreover, he does not envisage 'a society consisting exclusively of devout Christians':

> It would be a society in which the natural end of man – virtue and well-being in community – is acknowledged for all, and the super-natural end – beatitude – for those who have the eyes to see it.[47]

He would not 'compel belief and would not impose the necessity for insincere profession of belief',[48] but advanced, rather, the guarantee which he believed to be provided by the existence of an Established Church in relation both to the State and to the cultural tradition of the nation and which aimed to inform the decisions of its legislators, and which would provide, at the same time, a reference point for the 'great mass of humanity' in matters of faith and morals. The existence of such an established body in the national life is, for Eliot, the essential emblem of the nation's desire for civilisation.

He had to concede, however, that if the Church were to make the impact he desired, then it needed to be evangelical. Yet his warning that 'it is not enthusiasm, but dogma, that differentiates a Christian from a pagan society'[49] suggests the spirit in which he hoped such

evangelism would be undertaken. It will basically be an appeal to the
intellect and the moral sense, rather than to the emotions; and to the
truths of revealed religion, rather than to the social expediency of the
Christian ethic:

> What is worst of all is to advocate Christianity, not because
> it is true, but because it might be beneficial....
>   To justify Christianity because it provides a foundation
> of morality, instead of showing the necessity of Christian
> morals from the truth of Christianity, is a very dangerous
> inversion.[50]

The authority of this theological teaching, he argues, would be weakened if various varieties of it were peddled by the different Christian
sects. So his idea of the Church's role in a Christian society implied
the 'existence of one Church which shall aim at comprehending the
whole nation'. It was necessary, in biblical metaphor, that the 'great
majority of the sheep belong to one fold'. That 'fold', in England, of
course, was the Church of England:

> If the idea of a Christian society be grasped and accepted,
> then it can only be realized, in England, through the Church
> of England.[51]

He was well aware of the besetting danger of ecclesiastical establishment, known as Erastianism (the ascendancy of the State over
the Church in ecclesiastical matters, named from the sixteenth-
century Swiss theologian, Thomas Erastus). In the fourth section
of 'The Aims of Education' – entitled 'The Issue of Religion' – he
notes that too close identification of Church and State 'can lead to
oppression from which there is no escape':

> we need a Church capable of conflict with the State as well
> as co-operation with it.... And, owing to human fallibility,
> we may sometimes need the State to protect us against the
> Church.[52]

But, as we have said, Eliot had no time for disestablishment. The
Church, he had observed as early as 1920, was a 'pillar of the social
and political system'.[53] As the 1920s progressed, there was much talk
about disestablishment, especially during the debate over the revision
of the Prayer Book, where Parliament could make legislation for
the Church's liturgy. Yet Eliot believed, at this very time, that if it
were disestablished, it would 'lose its whole reason for existence'.[54]
Many years later, he told the parishioners of St Thomas' Church,

Washington, D.C. – who would have been unlikely to approve the connection between Church and State at the heart of a nation's governance – that the English Church should do nothing to disestablish itself.[55] He had made it clear, however, at the Malvern Conference, a few years before, that 'the union of Church and State is one thing, their identification is another'.[56] 'Conflict' between 'Church and State', he was to argue later, is inevitable in a society where there is a 'higher religion'.[57] The following statement (from 'The English Tradition', published one year after *The Idea of a Christian Society*) is a definitive outline of Eliot's views:

> There was a good deal of what we should call Erastianism, certainly of nepotism, in the mediaeval Church. And for Erastianism itself there is something to be said.... At least, we must recognize a wide difference, for good and for bad, between the situation of Church and State in the later eighteenth century and that of a Church in a modern state controlled by an openly, or almost openly, infidel government. There was a great deal of corruption in the Church, but a church can be corrupt without being Erastian.... We must remember that the independence of the Church may be bought at too high a price too, if that independence relieves it of its contact with the mass of the nation.[58]

Without establishment, there are merely sects:

> I am convinced that you cannot have a national Christian society, a religious-social community, a society with a political philosophy founded upon the Christian faith, if it is constituted as a mere congeries of private and independent sects.[59]

*

The main argument of *The Idea of a Christian Society* is that the correct ordering of such an entity must be based on sound Catholic doctrine, unequivocally taught and applied to all social, economic and moral issues in the society by the Established Church. In an appendix to the work, Eliot insists that the Church must propagate its 'perpetual message' – 'to affirm, to teach and to apply, true theology'[60] – and 'true theology' for him was the Catholic faith. It was a matter of returning to essential principles:

> we need to know how to see the world as the Christian Fathers saw it; and the purpose of reascending to origins is that we

should be able to return, with greater spiritual knowledge, to our own situation. We need to recover the sense of religious fear, so that it may be overcome by religious hope.[61]

The Idea of a Christian Society is of interest now, when the ideals it proposes can no longer be imagined ever coming into existence, for the way Eliot's theory of the State reveals the essential Catholic theology and spirituality which inform it and these are most evident when he is expressing his reservations about (rather than his enthusiasm for) socio-political solutions to the world's problems, and affirming the abiding truths about the human condition to which he avers here and in his writings in general.

4

Eliot's social theorising has usually been presented in terms of his wholehearted sympathy with the notion of attempting, in a period of social upheaval, the reduction of the principles upon which the English state was constructed – provided that any principles could be found – to basic formulae; to examine these with reference to Christian precepts, and (if disagreement resulted) to propagate Christian solutions for society's reformation. Certainly, that challenging project is enunciated in his writing and Eliot participated in it, but insufficient account has been taken of his disillusionment and irritation (revealed in some unpublished correspondence) with the activities of such as the Moot and other kindred bodies of which it had been thought he was totally supportive and with which, indeed, he persisted in association over several years.

Eliot participated in the wartime Malvern Conference of 1941 on 'The Life of the Church and the Order of Society'. Other participants included his friend, Maurice Reckitt, Canon Demant and the writer, Dorothy Sayers. The prominent Anglo-Catholic theologian, E.L. Mascall, was also present and the conference itself was organised by William Temple (then Archbishop of York) with the intention of finding 'the right starting point and so to lay down sound principles' rather than 'to draw up anything resembling a political programme'.[62] Eliot's contribution was an address, 'The Christian Conception of Education', which concludes mischievously with a repudiation of the notion that solutions for the Christian rehabilitation of society might come out of large-scale congresses such as Malvern (attended by twenty bishops and more than one hundred and twenty priests). The necessary thought, on the contrary, he commented is not to be accomplished by conferences and manifestoes, but by the patient toil of various minds in the humble and submissive hope of the direction of the Holy Ghost.[63]

There, again, is the emphasis on the individual's submission and Eliot's abiding reservation about collective action.

Similarly ambiguous was Eliot's association with the 'centre of Christian discourse', established at St Anne's House, Soho, in 1943. Reckitt, again, was prominent here, as was Dorothy Sayers and her fellow-novelist and Anglo-Catholic, Rose Macaulay. Although drawn to it, Eliot expressed (in a letter to Mary Trevelyan of 17th May, 1943) a certain dissatisfaction with it. He had taken the chair there the evening before, he writes, but the lecture was wrong and so was the audience – the discussion was very strained and Eliot left, he concludes, feeling most dispirited. Some months later, in another letter (11th March, 1944), Sayers (Epiphanius to Eliot's Chrysostom) is satirised in a jingle for not saying her prayers; he records his offer to attend St Anne's once more in the spirit of a concession and, we may surmise, out of a sense of duty (viewing it as a 'queer menagerie'), and expresses a reluctance to have his involvement advertised in public. A broadcast, he indicates, was quite out of the question.

The same hesitancy emerges again, two years later, when Eliot shrank from the prospect of being associated in print with the *Christian News-Letter* and its proposed article on the church reunion plans in South India (although, as we have seen, in 1943 he had gladly submitted in this matter to the wishes of the overtly Catholic-minded Council for the Defence of Church Principles, and wrote *Reunion by Destruction* for them). He escaped (Eliot writes humorously to Trevelyan, on 16th September) just as the board of the *News-Letter* was on the brink of printing the item with his name on it. He was suspicious of their political tendencies: always to *gauche*, never to *droit*, reservations which he did not have about the explicitly Catholic-minded Council. This indicates what was at the heart of Eliot's recurring problems with several of these groups and individuals. He was at one with them, theologically, insofar as they could be seen to be Catholic; but he was generally dissociated from their political leanings. Once even their commitment to Catholic theology became questionable, then Eliot had to try and extricate himself (easier said than done when he had such an ingrained sense of the necessity to perform public duties for the common good).

In her diary for 1943, Trevelyan recalls Eliot's association with the St Anne's 'theologians' and notes that her friend 'found them an increasing burden and generally came back very depressed from their meetings'. Her recollections are supported by a letter of Eliot to her dated Whit Monday, 1944 (29th May) where he expresses both his affection for her brother John, whose opinions tended towards right reason so long as they were not contaminated by the *Christian News-Letter*, and his suspicions about the usefulness of meetings and conferences, in general, for constructive thought. Then follows not only a striking expression of Eliot's loss of sympathy with the Moot (described as 'Joe Oldham's old lot', in a letter to Trevelyan, 2nd July, 1948) and its programme – which was a focus of all the Christian social activity with which Eliot was at least tangentially involved during the war years – but also the revelation that his persistence with it, and such activity in general, was due to a sense of personal obligation to the people involved. Joseph Oldham (1874-1969), an ecumenist, had formed this discussion group in 1938. It met annually in a retreat setting for several long weekends until 1947. Its discussions, carefully organised by Oldham, revolved around the idea of ways in which order might be restored to British society and culture, a matter of abiding interest to Eliot. The problem, it appears, was the imprecision of the theological focus of the group. Did he *have* to go to a meeting of the Moot in June? Eliot asks Trevelyan. Certainly, his only reason for attending is that Dr Oldham would be hurt if he failed to appear. If only he could be in Africa, Eliot continues, where people would not always be pressing obligations upon him which they considered to be his duty, and – moreover – expected him to regard as an honour and a privilege.

In another complaint, four months later (in a letter of 30th October, 1944) when the Christian Frontier Council and the *Christian News-Letter* are viewed from a more theological standpoint, Eliot suspects Protestantism and – almost as bad – Oldham's prose style is found wanting. The Frontier appeared to Eliot as the Liberal Party at prayer, and the *News-Letter*, with Oldham's wearying articles, was amounting to nothing more than Panprotestantism rampant.[64] Another letter – dated St. Basile (2nd January), 1945 – bemoans again the theological shortcomings of both the Council and its organ. He finds various members of the group trying in various ways: Eleanora Iredale is very sound, he observes, but talks and talks, like Benedick, and nobody heeds her; Lord Hambleden is sound too, but meek and mild; and Philip Mairet is ineffectual, through humility and deafness, even though his views are also sound. The result is that the bias of the *News-Letter* is always Protestant.

Researching Eliot's involvement with these organisations, Dr Kojecký has been beguiled by the attendance figures from their meetings, and has too simply concluded, from Eliot's presence, that he supported what the bodies stood for and were doing and saying. Eliot's frank letters to Mary Trevelyan show that the situation was far less cut and dried and, indeed, that had it not been for his high sense of personal responsibility (which had its origins in his socially-conscious Unitarian upbringing and his characteristic courtesy) to various individuals involved in them, Eliot would almost certainly have severed his connection.

In a statement which, we sense, goes very deep, Eliot reveals (in *Notes towards the Definition of Culture*) his scepticism about collaborative projects, after many years' involvement in such enterprises:

> Men who meet only for definite serious purposes, and on official occasions, do not wholly meet. They may have some common concern very much at heart; they may, in the course of repeated contacts, come to share a vocabulary and an idiom which appear to communicate every shade of meaning necessary for their common purpose; but they will continue to retire from these encounters each to his private social world as well as to his solitary world.[65]

The theological problems Eliot discerned in the deliberations of the Frontier Council were similar to what he found, in these years, in the Church at large. William Temple succeeded Cosmo Gordon Lang, whom Eliot had esteemed, at Canterbury in 1942. Temple was closely associated with members of the Moot, and with the Frontier Council in the founding of the *Christian News-Letter*. Part of Temple's background had been his association with the 'Life and Liberty Movement', a largely clerical organisation devoted to disestablishment, which urged that the established character of the Church obscured its role in the spiritual life of the nation by involving it with unessential temporal matters. Eliot disagreed completely with this view. The Movement had as its aim 'to win for the Church the liberty essential to fullness of life'[66] – precisely the kind of almost meaningless, platitudinous language that would make Eliot bristle (especially emanating from Churchmen and, worst of all, bishops). In opposition to it were such as Dr Hensley Henson (a High Churchman who, nonetheless, eschewed party dogmatism) and Viscount Halifax, leader of the Anglo-Catholic laity.[67]

There was no question on whose side Eliot was to be found in this debate. Further, as Bishop of Manchester and Chairman of the

Doctrinal Commission, Temple was noted for his liberal views on
other matters – for instance, in his submission for the revision of the
Prayer Book in the 1920s, which was known as the 'Grey Book'[68]
(as distinct from the Green Book and the Orange Book prepared by
Anglo-Catholics and moderate High Churchmen, respectively – the
Evangelicals remaining aloof from the process). In conversation with
me, Anne Ridler remembered that Eliot found Temple 'too free thinking, too vague', while George Every told me that Eliot thought of
Temple, by the time he was Archbishop, as belonging to an 'Hegelian
generation', being 'too fond of synthesising and the pat solution'.
Temple had trained as a philosopher and 'the Neo-Hegelian position
from which he set out coloured all his later thinking'.[69]

The Archbishop was not long for Canterbury. He died in October,
1944. Writing to Mary Trevelyan on the 30th of that month, Eliot
added a charitable postscript recalling their criticism (and affirming
it here) of what they regarded as Temple's suspect theology, but regretting his early passing.

5

When Eliot began his engagement with Christian social teaching,
he would use such phrases as 'social justice' (in an article to *The
Listener* in 1932, to which we have referred) and it was, obviously,
an important goal of the Anglo-Catholic Christian Socialists. But
his views underwent a significant change over the next decade or
so. Writing to Trevelyan, near the end of the war, he claimed that
social justice is the business of politicians, not of Christians, and
he expressed his worry over the desire of Church people to prove
their interest in social reform. What does 'social justice' mean, after
all? he continues. It is what all governments promise but only partly
achieve – even granting that different people have different ideas of
its meaning. In any case, 'social justice' was a political concern and
he had arrived at the opinion that the Church should not commit itself
actively to any political scheme.[70]

Then, in one of Eliot's most amusing epistles to Trevelyan (dated
St. Francois de Sales – 29th January, 1945) he tells her that he had
been ignoring all the manuscripts at Faber and Faber claiming his
attention in order to devote his time to a small book (*Notes towards
the Definition of Culture*) with which he hoped to blow up the Moot.
Explosives are again in his thoughts, in a note of thanks – 16th September, 1946 – for Trevelyan's present to him of the works of Mme.
de Sévigné (with their reflections on the community at Port-Royal

so beloved of Eliot's admired Pascal), where he remarks that the gift has cleared his mind most satisfactorily of two evils: the *Christian News-Letter* and the atomic bomb. A postscript is added where Eliot regrets his inability to dodge the Dickensian wiles of Oldham, and he draws Trevelyan's attention to a *News-Letter* supplement by *Civis* (a high civil servant who reeks of such a position) out of which Eliot had hoped to make a resigning point, but 'Artful Joe' (Oldham) has managed to commit him to writing a reply which he has signed 'Metoikos'. Kojecký judges Eliot's response 'surprisingly critical',[71] but (as we have seen) Eliot had been critical of the journal and much that it stood for, and those associated with it, for years. *Civis* was John Maud (later Lord Redcliffe-Maud), then a politics don at University College, Oxford. Eliot came to the conclusion that the *Christian News-Letter* was simply irrelevant. Writing to Trevelyan, who was then travelling in Burma, he commented that the future of the Orient, like that of the world in general, is unlikely to have anything to do with the programme and ideals of the journal.[72]

6

Eliot's other substantial statement in prose of his theory of a Christian society is his modestly-entitled *Notes towards the Definition of Culture*, written as the Second World War was coming to an end but not published until 1948, the year of Eliot's Nobel Prize and his appointment to the Order of Merit. By this time his poetic career (although not his poetic-drama career) had reached its climax (and, virtually, its conclusion) in *Four Quartets*. In other words, *Notes* (unlike the pre-war *Idea of a Christian Society*) is the work of an internationally-acknowledged sage, addressed to the very different cultural environment of the post-war world and in the context of what Eliot now directly calls Britain's 'apostasy' from the Christian religion[73] – the very term used by John Keble in the Oxford assize sermon on 'national apostasy' which launched the Catholic movement in the Church of England in 1833. In these post-war years, there was, on the one hand, a yearning for a revival of the certainties and securities of life (which the religious resurgence and general social conservatism of the 1950s – although shortlived, as it turned out – expressed), in tension with what transpired to be a more enduring scepticism about all kinds of authority, social, political or religious, which had its revolutionary flourishing in the later 1960s. This continues to the present and is, indeed, one of the explanations for the eclipse of Eliot's reputation since his death in 1965.[74]

This 'essay' which 'aims at least at the merit of brevity'[75] is dedicated to Philip Mairet and Eliot expresses his debt to Demant, Dawson and Mannheim in the preface. So, the work comes out of Eliot's socio-politico-theological activities and associations during the previous decade, which we have discussed. The particular impulse behind it is his recognition 'that our own period is one of decline':

> that the standards of culture are lower than they were fifty
> years ago; and that the evidences of this decline are visible
> in every department of human activity ... [76]

– the most important of which would, of course, for Eliot, be religion. Indeed, he envisages a time approaching when there will be '*no* culture' (his emphasis), and, this implies, no religion too – in John Lennon's phrase – because of Eliot's theory of the interdependency of religion and culture. One cannot exist without the other. Or, possibly, religion would survive but be so marginalised and ineffectual as to have no formative role or influence in the society, 'religious thought and practice' becoming an isolated phenomenon cultivated by groups lacking any 'communion' with anybody else.[77] One of the reasons that Eliot, unlike many Anglo-Catholics of his generation, supported the perpetuation of the Established Church is that he saw it as a safeguard against such utter disconnection from the life of the nation.

He was by no means alone, amongst prominent Christians of Catholic persuasion, in being agitated by the post-war condition of Western Christendom. The very year of the publication of *Notes* saw mounting tension between the West and the Eastern bloc and Pope Pius XII characterised the 1948 Italian election, being fought between Christian democrats and the Popular Front of communists and socialists, as a battle for 'Christian civilization'. The April poll 'was conducted with maximum involvement of bishops, clergy, religious, and seminarians throughout Italy', the Christian Democrats being narrowly elected.[78]

Eliot insists at the outset of *Notes* on the necessity for a widespread religious consciousness for the sustaining of cultural life:

> No culture has appeared or developed except together with
> a religion.... The culture being, essentially, the incarnation
> (so to speak) of the religion of a people.... There is an aspect
> in which we can see a religion as the *whole way of life* of a
> people, from birth to the grave, from morning to night and
> even in sleep, and that way of life is also its culture.[79]

This connection of religion and culture (often 'unconscious'[80]) is the book's *leitmotif* and he acknowledges his 'temerity' in using such 'an exalted term' as 'incarnation' in the discussion;[81] but the nexus of culture and religion resonated deeply with him, his own commitment to the Church of England being determined, principally, by his recognition and appreciation of the fact that the cultural life of the country that had become his home was inextricably bound up with Anglicanism: 'what we call the culture, and what we call the religion, of a people are … different aspects of the same thing'.[82] Eliot catalogues something of that '*whole way of life* of a people, from birth to the grave', in a much-quoted, Betjemanesque passage:

> Derby Day, Henley Regatta, Cowes, the twelfth of August,
> a cup final, the dog races, the pin table, the dart board,
> Wensleydale cheese, boiled cabbage cut into sections, beet-
> root in vinegar, nineteenth-century Gothic churches.…[83]

This shows, he contends, that 'the actual religion of no European people has ever been purely Christian, or purely anything else', and he does not deny the spiritual impurity of such interaction:

> bishops are a part of English culture, and horses and dogs are
> a part of English religion.… It is inconvenient for Christians
> to find that as Christians they do not believe enough, and that
> on the other hand they, with everybody else, believe in too
> many things.[84]

Having such cultural roots and tolerating a theological and ritual diversity without parallel in any other Christian communion, Anglicanism was scarcely well placed to be always attuned to (or even aware of) the Catholic interpretation and expression of human life and civilisation. Eliot was prepared to admit the combination of 'unity and diversity in religion', but he insists that the essential teachings of the Catholic faith must be maintained. There may be,

> that is, universality of doctrine with particularity of cult and
> devotion …[85]

which will include 'many variations of order and ritual'.[86] Obviously, nowhere is this more the case than in the Church of England which 'has comprehended wider variations of belief and cult than a foreign observer would believe it possible for one institution to contain without bursting'.[87] Eliot's is scarcely the vocabulary of commendation here. The guarantee of the Catholic character of the Church of England depended upon its recognition of an authority transcending its national boundaries and traditions. What was needed, indeed, was a 'universal religion',

> higher than one which any race or nation claims exclusively
> for itself.[88]

That 'universal' Christian religion is, of course, by definition, the Catholic faith, hence, Eliot's allegiance to it, above any nationalistic bond with the Church of England, for all his cherishing of its local cultural significance and its established status.

He is writing the book, he points out, because he is concerned about 'Christian culture, with the Western World, with Europe, and with England'. We should read that catalogue, evaluatively, I would suggest, in a descending order. 'The culture of Europe', he writes, has 'deteriorated visibly within the memory of many who are by no means the oldest among us', and he allows himself 'an incidental flourish', in Arnoldian style, to 'relieve [his] feelings' and those of 'a few of his more sympathetic readers' – evoking the destruction of

> our ancient edifices to make ready the ground upon which
> the barbarian nomads of the future will encamp in their
> mechanised caravans.[89]

The tension in Eliot's argument (valuing the national cultural role of the Church of England while yearning for Catholic unity of faith, and with the added powerful ingredient of his profound appreciation of Europeanism) is clearly exposed when he considers the situation (always vexing for Anglo-Catholics) of English Roman Catholics:

> Roman Catholics in England are, of course, in a more cen-
> tral European tradition than are Anglicans; yet because the
> main tradition of England has been Anglican, they are in
> another aspect more outside the tradition than are Protestant
> dissenters.[90]

Yet Anglican England cannot be separate from European culture, even if it has defined itself in opposition to it (as Protestantism depends for its continuance, he argues, on the health of that against which it protests):

> The maintenance of English culture is contingent upon the
> health of the culture of Latin Europe, and upon continuing to
> draw sustenance from that Latin culture.[91]

In ecclesiastical terms, only Anglo-Catholicism, within the Church of England, actively witnesses to the appreciation of that broader Euro-pean and Latin culture. Much else in Anglicanism resists it – England is a 'Protestant country'.[92] But, Eliot is arguing, in that very resistance it is depending upon the Latin culture for its self-definition.

He rejects the promise of a solution to the decline of religion he has identified (and, concomitantly – on his theory – of culture in general) which the ecumenical movement, gathering strength at this time, purported to be offering. Obviously behind Eliot's rejection, in these years, is his recent conspicuous involvement in the protest against the ecumenical Church of South India: 'an ecclesiastical unity cannot be imposed in the hope that it will bring about unity of faith', he argues.[93] While he regretted the 'schisms of the sixteenth century' – that is, the Reformation – which led to 'the disintegration of European culture',[94] these could not be patched up by the diluted theology of modern ecumenicity. The reunion of Anglicans and Dissenters, he claims, would lead to the further disintegration of a disintegrating culture.[95]

The most telling perspective of *Notes*, however, is European, not narrowly English. Especially in its concluding sections, Eliot reveals his reverence for the culture of Europe, and indeed, repeatedly indicates its superiority to English culture, especially when he enters the field of his own cultural expertise: 'Dante is certainly greater than Milton', he writes; Goethe is a greater man than Wordsworth, and 'no English poet contemporary with Wordsworth can enter into comparison with Goethe at all'. In a rare personal reference, he points out that his own poetry would not have been possible were it not for the French poetic tradition, from Baudelaire to Valéry.[96] Such an appreciation of European culture had been repeatedly expressed in his prose:

> The English Church has no literary monument equal to that of Dante, no intellectual monument equal to that of St. Thomas, no devotional monument equal to that of St. John of the Cross, no building so beautiful as the Cathedral of Modena or the basilica of St. Zeno in Verona. But there are those for whom the City churches are as precious as any of the four hundred odd churches in Rome which are in no danger of demolition, and for whom St. Paul's, in comparison with St. Peter's, is not lacking in decency.[97]

The 'spiritual organism of Europe' is Christian: 'the common tradition of Christianity … has made Europe what it is' and

> I do not believe that the culture of Europe could survive the complete disappearance of the Christian Faith…. If Christianity goes, the whole of culture goes.[98]

Referring, twice, in the closing pages to the 'two thousand years of Christianity', Eliot implies a seamless, organic development. Protestantism is a deviation from this religious sequence and cultural advancement and enrichment, and does not figure in his conspectus of 'the legacy of Greece, Rome and Israel, and the legacy of Europe throughout the last 2,000 years', except as a diversion from the central tradition of Catholic Rome:

> When we consider the western world, we must recognise that the main cultural tradition has been that corresponding to the Church of Rome. Only within the last four hundred years has any other manifested itself; and anyone with a sense of centre and periphery must admit that the Western tradition has been Latin, and Latin means Rome. There are countless testimonies of art and thought and manners; and among these we must include the work of all men born and educated in a Catholic society, whatever their individual beliefs. From this point of view, the separation of Northern Europe, and of England in particular, from communion with Rome represents a diversion from the main stream of culture.[99]

And he closes with the warning voice of the poet of *The Waste Land*, but now, in 1948, after another, possibly even more culturally-cataclysmic war:

> In a world which has seen such material devastation as ours, these spiritual possessions are also in imminent peril.[100]

*

Like *The Idea of a Christian Society* – and, indeed, like most of Eliot's poetry (and for the same reason, as we shall argue in the next chapter) – *Notes towards the Definition of Culture* is only, very occasionally, identifiably and explicitly Anglo-Catholic in reference and emphasis. The broad audience that Eliot aspires to address would not be reached were these works to be narrowly confessional in that way. It is a case of occasional references revealing his churchmanship, as in his allusion to the 'exemplars of sanctity' (that is, the saints and the cult of them) whose examples should form part of our 'full cultivation of the spiritual life' so as we will not 'sink into despair'. The implication is that we should be seeking their assistance, through prayer, but it is not spelt out.[101] Then, if culture is to be cultivated at the highest level, Eliot argues, this will be the responsibility of the most cultivated, as, in the past, it depended upon those immersed in the traditions of monasticism, including its demand of celibacy. In this historical Catholic context, Eliot criticises Puritanism and Protestantism, in their political as well as their religious dimensions, for their exaltation of egalitarianism which led to the dissolution of what they regarded as the privileged life of the monasteries (in addition to their detestation of their religious traditions), a stance he sees as akin to modern socialistic ideas. Socialist progressives of the present argue that

> in the society of the future the culture which has been the possession of the few must be put at the disposal of everybody. This assumption and its consequences remind us of the Puritan antipathy to monasticism and the ascetic life: for just as culture which is only accessible to the few is now deprecated, so was the enclosed and contemplative life condemned by extreme Protestantism, and celibacy regarded with almost as much abhorrence as perversion.[102]

Elsewhere, he urges that 'the secular priest must not be wholly unpractised in meditation'.[103] Only an Anglo-Catholic would speak (in the Roman Catholic way) of a 'secular priest' (that is, as distinct from a priestly member of a religious order). But such touches are notable for their rarity in *Notes*, as in *The Idea of a Christian Society*.

The most important statement, however, is of the broadest Catholic kind. It is Eliot's declaration, which we have already noted, of the centrality of the Church of Rome and the Latin tradition in the European cultural (and, therefore, religious) heritage. On this, unquestionably, he placed the highest value. Quite simply, this explains his Anglo-Catholicism as an Englishman. The principles, aspirations and characteristics of Anglo-Catholicism came closest, in England, to that 'main cultural tradition', affirming explicitly the doctrines of the two thousand years of Catholic faith, while Anglo-Catholicism also belonged, very importantly, as part of the Church of England, to the local cultural world in which its bishops were part of the culture, and horses and dogs part of its religion.[104]

Eliot liked dogs, although cats more, and probably both species better than he did most members of the Anglican episcopate, but all of them were facts of English cultural life, as indeed was he, by 1948 – a member of the exclusive Order of Merit, in the reigning sovereign's gift, no less. He had become a fixture, almost an icon, of the very religio-cultural dispensation he was celebrating. Eliot, who in his American childhood saw himself as 'never anything anywhere',[105] a dispossessed northerner in the South, had found (on the threshold of middle age) a local habitation and, in time, a name. But even in this appropriation (of royalist Anglicanism) his essentially feline ambiguity persisted. Having taken his place at the centre of the establishment, Eliot – by the 1950s, the best-known Anglo-Catholic layman of his day – was (in the way typical of that eccentric allegiance) perpetually testing such boundaries, as intellectuals and poets always do.

The Englishness into which he was incorporated was, in his generation, still an identifiable cultural phenomenon. As an acute observer and chronicler of such *mores*, Jan Morris, has written:

> The national characteristics of the English had been universally recognized in the 1940s and 1950s. By the 1980s the English had no national characteristics. They had been obliged to think of themselves as multi-ethnic, multicultural, so that the very word 'English' had almost lost its meaning. They had been taught to be ashamed of their lost empire. They had been so bewildered by incessant legislation that they had almost forgotten the basic principle of their own law – that when the law is silent the citizen is free. One by one their most cherished institutions had been deliberately discredited, if not by politics, then by satire. They were almost comically subservient to American models: every youth craze, every semantic or artistic trend was copied, and from the passion for litigation to the style of television newsreading, in foreign policy as in social attitudes, slavishly the English tracked the footsteps of the Americans – whom, at the same time, in a grotesque echo of old supremacies, they all too often professed to despise.[106]

The importance of this analysis for our understanding of Eliot and his mind is that it reminds us that the Englishness he was defending (and explaining, thereby, his own fidelity to) was a different phenomenon from Englishness in our time, which, if Morris' thesis is accepted, no longer even exists. It had been culturally compelling in its distinctiveness and cohesion. As with Eliot's Anglo-Catholicism, to understand what Eliot found alluring in English culture we need to recover what it was like nearly a century ago. What both phenomena are like today gives us virtually no understanding of their appeal to him. It is futile (but irresistible) to speculate what Eliot would make of the cultural denouement Morris' account summarises, or (for that matter) of the role (if any) that the Church of England (let alone,

Anglo-Catholicism) has, now, in that broader multicultural context. But the Americanisation of English culture would certainly have struck him at least as ironic, with regard to his own biography. He, having journeyed so far from his provincial American childhood, would have found himself in old age, had he lived another twenty years, in a mere colony of its culture.

Anglo-Catholicism, the one part of Anglicanism that was attuned to the larger European Catholic 'centre', and was most actively seeking reunion with it, made it possible for Eliot to be a member of the Church of England (as he says).[107] He recognised that for others (as history has shown repeatedly, particularly at times when matters of Catholic doctrine and order were perceived to be under more than usual threat), it became, inevitably, the English station on the way to the Roman terminus. He does not see this as in any way surprising. Had he been a citizen of a European country (such as France or Germany, where, had it not been for the outbreak of the First World War, it is possible that he would have settled), it is unquestionable that Eliot, in embracing the Catholic faith, would have become a Roman Catholic. The extent to which one is separated from that European tradition – tending to the 'periphery' – one becomes (in the cultural term most dreaded by High Modernists like Eliot) provincial (or parochial), and provincialism in religion is Protestant sectarianism. 'Parochialism', as we see in the epigraph to this chapter, was recognised by Eliot as an abiding tendency of Anglicanism; even, indeed, of 'Anglican Catholicism'.

Crucial in informing Eliot's broader appreciation of Catholic religion and culture and their interdependency was his Modernist Europeanism (which needs always to be remembered, even – especially – as we recall his deep devotion to the golden age of the Church of England in the seventeenth century, and its expression in the works of such writers as Lancelot Andrewes, John Donne and George Herbert, which were 'something representative of the finest spirit of England of the time'[108]).

Yet it is not only the religious aspect of the Latin culture that is pertinent here. Eliot's pre-Christian classicism informs his cultural theory too. Learned in Latin and Greek, he delivered the Presidential Address to the Classical Association on 'The Classics and the Man of Letters' in 1942 and published three essays on Virgil. The best known, 'Virgil and the Christian World' (1951), belongs to these years when he was particularly pondering the European religio-cultural tradition and its accelerating disintegration, and, as we have seen, he links that classical poet (as many have done) to the new Christian dispensation. Eliot's deepest intellectual and artistic roots were in the European,

Latin and Catholic tradition. This was not a new revelation or a perspective acquired after years of practising the Catholic faith. Prior even to the sacramental beginning of his life as an Anglo-Catholic, in 1926, in his essay on Lancelot Andrewes, Eliot differentiates sharply between the sermons of Latimer, 'merely a Protestant' and 'the voice of Andrewes', with

> a formed visible Church behind him, who speaks with the old authority and the new culture. It is the difference of negative and positive; Andrewes is the first great preacher of the English Catholic Church.[109]

Eliot was a Western European, culturally-speaking, and his appropriation of this tradition, in all its rich history, dating from Israel, Greece and Rome, and through two millennia of Christianity, has, in fact, its seminal origins in his rejection of his natal Americanism and Unitarianism, the very embodiments of provinciality, parochialism and sectarianism. He was determined to travel (as he did, geographically, as well as intellectually and spiritually) as far as possible, culturally and in religion, from that negative, peripheral position to the true centre.

*

Au fond, Eliot's public participation in Anglo-Catholic activity for the achievement of a Christian state was unsatisfactory for him and increasingly disillusioning, because – probably inevitably, in a predominantly secular world – it could only proceed with various compromises, theological as well as socio-political. Apart from Eliot's temperamental aversion from collective action, he was prepared to give wholehearted support to such schemes, programmes and organisations only if it were clear that they were based upon and bore constant witness to the orthodox faith of the Catholic Church and a preoccupation (above all else) with the sanctification, in terms of that theology, of individual souls. His dissatisfaction and dissociation increased in proportion to his perception that these high ideals were not being aspired to, let alone achieved.

Chapter Seven
Anglo-Catholic in Literature

The extent to which Eliot was an Anglo-Catholic in literature, as well as in religion, has to take into account both his prose writings and his poetry (including his poetic drama). In prose, we note that his Anglo-Catholic life (1927-1965) began with the collection *For Lancelot Andrewes* (1928) and ended with *George Herbert*, his thirty-six page booklet for The British Council, published in 1962. In other words, he started and finished by writing in prose about two of the most famous priests in the Anglican Catholic tradition. Recent scholarship on Herbert has discerned a kind of High Church Calvinism in the poet's theology, as found in his masterpiece *The Temple*, but in Eliot's generation he and his poetry were consistently placed in the tradition of Laudian, Caroline divinity, with its emphasis on Scripture, classical and patristic learning, liturgical sacramentalism, profound individual piety, devotion to the English Church and the beauty of holiness and of language, and resistance to all that Puritanism stood for. Indeed, Muriel Bradbrook's essay of 1942, 'The Liturgical Tradition in English Verse: Herbert and Eliot', not only firmly sustains Herbert's place in this tradition but now links Eliot with him, in terms of it.[1] In Herbert's brief but celebrated ministry at Bemerton, near Salisbury, in the final years of his life, he was seen as the model of the English parish priest. Eliot's appreciation of the man, his spirituality and his poetry (to which we will turn below) provides a fitting conclusion to his Anglo-Catholic literary life.

1

The two great monuments to the literary genius of the English Church, both produced in what Eliot regarded as the golden age of English culture in the later sixteenth and early seventeenth centuries (before the 'dissociation of sensibility' which occurred during the Cromwellian revolution[2]), were The Book of Common Prayer (in evolution from

1549 to 1662, at the Restoration) and the Authorized ('King James') Version of the Bible (1611), on the committee for which sat Bishop Lancelot Andrewes. These, along with the great poets of the same period, were central to Eliot's appreciation of the literary heritage of Anglicanism. Just before his baptism, in May, 1927, at the time when revisions of the Prayer Book were being proposed, Eliot devoted one of the Commentaries in the *Criterion* to a criticism of such changes as were being urged, and indeed of change itself. As the literary critic, he focuses on some particular words:

> The Preface [to the proposed revision] reads like a rather embarrassed apology for change: everything is changing, so the Prayer Book must change.... But when fences are down the cattle will roam, including two vagrant beasts *infinite* and *eternal* [to replace, respectively, 'incomprehensible' and 'everlasting'], words which will wander so far, the fence of meaning being down, that they will cease to belong anywhere.[3]

And then, in December that year, recalling his earlier Commentary, he placed beauty and precision of language within the context of his own appreciation of the scholarly and literary tradition of the Church of England, under threat from the revisers:

> A few months ago, we had occasion to call attention to symptoms of decay in the wording of the Preface to the Revised Prayer Book. It is a pity when eminent ecclesiastics fail to think clearly, for if they cannot think clearly, they cannot write well.... To such men as Cranmer [principal author of the Prayer Book], and Hooker, and Andrewes (even without the translation of the Bible) our debt is almost incalculable.[4]

It was a debt both ecclesiastical and cultural:

> not the Church only, but the whole of English civilisation, is indebted to those men.[5]

The Prayer Book, Eliot maintained, could teach a man of genius or 'a man of first-rate ability short of genius, all that he needs in order to write English well'.[6] The prospect of the revision of this inspired language (which has now happened to the point where The Book of Common Prayer has virtually fallen out of use) appalled Eliot:

> Must we look forward to the day when the Collects [prayers] of Cranmer are revised for use in Anglican Churches, to make them conformable to 'contemporary English'?[7]

That day, of course, has come, although Eliot did not live to see it. The authorisation of the blandly-entitled 'Series One' in 1965, the year of Eliot's death, spelt the beginning of the end of the use of The Book of Common Prayer and, indeed, The English Missal in active worship in the Anglican Communion.[8]

We remember that in the earlier days of the Catholic Revival, in the nineteenth century, a priest's observance of all the liturgical provisions of The Book of Common Prayer was seen as a definite sign of his Catholic tendencies. For an Anglo-Catholic of Eliot's generation, however, neither the Prayer Book nor the King James Bible were held in particular esteem. The Bible was principally known, by Anglo-Catholics, from its use (albeit, very extensive) in the daily Divine Office and at Mass; and The English Missal, while drawing upon Prayer Book language and preserving Cranmer's collects, had superseded it in most Anglo-Catholic parishes (including Eliot's). So it was not for their theological or liturgical significance, so much as for their marks of linguistic genius and the richness of the culture of learning and devotion which they expressed, that Eliot (as the literary critic principally responsible, in the twentieth century, for restoring the appreciation of Elizabethan and Jacobean literature) esteemed them.

In this matter, therefore – although for literary rather than theological reasons – Eliot is more attuned to the spirit of Anglicanism, broadly understood, than we usually expect or encounter in Anglo-Catholicism. Accordingly, phrases from The Book of Common Prayer and the Authorized Version appear intermittently in his own poetry and prose, particularly in the period after his conversion. In the Prayer Book collect to be used when the Litany is not said, we find one of the most quoted of all phrases from that book:

> O God, the Creator and Preserver of all mankind, we humbly beseech thee for all sorts and conditions of men....

Eliot, recalling it in his essay on the subject, 'What is a Classic?', thereby enrols Cranmer's masterpiece amongst the other works to which this description may be applied:

> Among the people to which it belongs, [the classic] will find its response among all classes and conditions of men.[9]

In the Psalms, which Eliot knew principally from the daily offices of the Church, we find (for example) phrases from Psalm 130 and the Trinitarian '*Gloria Patri* ...' (customarily added to these Hebrew texts in Christian worship) –

My soul fleeth unto the Lord: before the morning watch, I
say, before the morning watch.... Glory be to the Father ... as
it was in the beginning, is now ...[10]

– in the first section of the third Quartet, 'The Dry Salvages':

Between midnight and dawn, when the past is all
    deception,
The future futureless, before the morning watch
When time stops and time is never ending;
And the ground swell, that is and was from the
    beginning....[11]

A Latinate use of English in the collect for Tuesday in the Easter
octave:

We humbly beseech thee, that, as by thy special grace
preventing us

(and which introduces this well-known occasional collect:

Prevent us, O Lord, in all our doings with thy most gracious
favour)

is recalled by Eliot in what is, by the twentieth century, an archaic use
of the verb, in the theological lyric in 'East Coker':

the absolute paternal care
That will not leave us, but prevents us everywhere.[12]

Eliot is using the verb in both the Cranmerian and modern senses
which are, of course, contradictory: 'prevent' as 'going before' (its
original Latin meaning) and 'stopping' something. God's solicitude
goes before us, but also stops us, Eliot is suggesting – presumably,
from sinning.

Well before his conversion, however, Eliot revealed his knowledge and appreciation of Prayer Book language. The final title for
the first section of *The Waste Land* was 'The Burial of the Dead', the
name of the funeral rite in The Book of Common Prayer, although, as
often in Eliot's earlier poetry, the use of a phrase from a classic text
is ironic here. The Prayer Book service is essentially and repeatedly
focused on the resurrection of the dead who are being buried. *The
Waste Land*, in spite of a desperate longing, insistently voiced, for
redemption to transcend the sin-laden suffering described there, expresses the disappointment and ultimate failure of this aspiration. In
an experimental lyric for the poem, written (Valerie Eliot comments)

'about 1914 or even earlier',[13] we also find the first sentence of the Order for the Burial of the Dead:

I am the Resurrection and the Life.

So, more than a decade before his familiarity with the language of the Prayer Book (as adapted to Catholic forms in The English Missal) in regular worship, Eliot was already not only familiar with it but drawn to the appropriation of this poetic prose for his poetry. It is another example of the importance of Eliot's aesthetic response to Christian culture prior, but leading to his submission to its doctrinal teachings.

Similarly, the impact of the nobility and precision of speech of the King James Bible on Eliot's poetry may be seen in numerous borrowings from it, of which the following from *Four Quartets* are representative of the ways in which he could incorporate that prose language and rhythm into his verse:

To every thing there is a season, and a time to every purpose under the heaven: A time to be born, and a time to die … a time to break down, and a time to build up; A time to weep, and a time to laugh.… (Ecclesiastes 3:1-4)

> … there is a time for building
> And a time for living and for generation
> And a time for the wind to break the loosened pane.…
> The time of the seasons and the constellations
> The time of milking and the time of harvest
> The time of the coupling of man and woman.[14]

(Much earlier, we also hear an echo of this biblical incantation on time in 'The Love Song of J. Alfred Prufrock': 'time to murder and create, / And time for all the works and days of hands … / Time for you and time for me, / And time …'.[15])

The following verse from Paul's first epistle to the Corinthians:

And now abideth faith, hope, charity, these three
(1 Corinthians 13:13)

is woven into these lines in the second Quartet:

> … there is yet faith
> But the faith and the love and the hope are all in the
> waiting.[16]

Then, a text from the Gospels:

And there shall be signs in the sun, and in the moon, and in the stars; and upon the earth distress of nations, with perplexity ...

(Luke 21:25)

re-emerges in 'The Dry Salvages':

> ... all these are usual
> Pastimes and drugs, and features of the press:
> And always will be, some of them especially
> When there is distress of nations and perplexity
> Whether on the shores of Asia, or in the Edgware
>   Road.[17]

Leonard Unger (in an essay, 'Intertextual Eliot') is right to observe that 'the Bible echoes and re-echoes in Eliot's poetry and frequently it is the device of rhythm which produces the echo',[18] but it is more likely that it was the liturgical use of the Bible (in the chanting of psalms, for example) which was Eliot's immediate inspiration for his borrowings. It is the Prayer Book and, more precisely, the Missal, with their spoken (or sung) use of scriptural texts in the liturgy, rather than the Bible itself, which was influential. This is the Anglo-Catholic aspect of the matter. Carol Muske rightly identifies the 'pattern of hesitancy', characteristic of the liturgical recitation of psalmody, with 'the great breathing caesuras' mid-verse, that is recalled in the opening lines (for example) of *Ash-Wednesday*.[19]

These great early modern texts of English divinity, which had inspired Eliot (and, of course, countless other poets writing in English through the centuries) were destined to be judged unworthy for the worship of the English Church by modern churchmen. As with the proposed revision of the language of The Book of Common Prayer, so with the disposal of the Authorized Version, Eliot was angered by what he saw as the Church's mindless commitment to change and the consequent elimination of this language of genius from public worship. Contributing an essay entitled 'New Translation of the Bible' to *Theology* in 1949, Eliot wrote:

> The prospect of a translation of the Bible to be made intelligible to persons of rudimentary education is somewhat disturbing.... To make a more intelligible translation should mean to make a translation which can be understood by those capable of understanding; it should not mean, but might easily slip into meaning, to make a translation which is *easy* to understand.

He warned:

> If the Church re-writes its Bible and its liturgies to conform
> with every successive stage of deterioration of the langu-
> age, the prospect is gloomy. For the speech of 'our people'
> is not only 'threadbare', but incapable of expressing exact
> and subtle thought.[20]

Eliot was writing when this movement, with regard both to Scripture and the liturgy, was just gathering momentum. Within twenty
years, the Roman Church would similarly have both a vernacular
and modernistic biblical and liturgical regime (disposing of the
Latin which, Eliot believed, was the best form of language to use
in worship), also plumbing the depths of banality of vocabulary and
rhythm of speech.[21] By 1961, when the *New English Bible* appeared,
Eliot's critique, in the face of this much more radical departure from
the classical tradition of scriptural and liturgical English prose, had
concomitantly intensified. He derided it as 'something which aston-
ishes in its combination of the vulgar, the trivial, and the pedantic':

> We ask in alarm: 'What is happening to the English lan-
> guage?'

He noted 'frequent errors of taste', 'monotonous inferiority of phras-
ing', 'Boeotian absurdities' and 'verbal infelicities', supported by
a host of examples, and he asks: given the principle on which this
translation is based – namely, that Scripture needs to be re-translated
in the current idiom of the declining English tongue – 'what is likely
to be the fate of the New English Bible eighty years hence?' It 'does
not seem to have occurred to the mind of the anonymous author of
this Introduction [to the translation]', he notes, tartly, 'that change
can sometimes be for the worse'.[22]

Eliot did not only read the Bible for its prose and its aesthetic
contribution to numinous liturgy, important as that was: 'the life
of a reading of Gospel and Epistle in the liturgy is in the music of
the spoken word'.[23] For in the second of two letters to the *Times
Literary Supplement* about the *New English Bible*, he challenged its
translators on a point of doctrine which often unites Evangelicals and
Anglo-Catholics in opposition to their modernist co-religionists:

> I am not a Hebrew scholar, nor am I versed in Biblical scho-
> larship. I have read that St. Luke was careful in his translation
> of Hebrew terms. But what I wanted to know was whether
> the learned committee believe that St. Luke believed in the

Virgin Birth? If so, what is the point of substituting *girl* for *virgin*, especially as the effect, besides raising the theological question, is to contribute to debasement of the noble prose of the Authorised Version?[24]

In his earlier letter, Eliot notes that 'both Liddell & Scott and Westcott & Hort give "virgin" as a correct translation.... What moved the learned committee to approve the change?'[25]

The *New English Bible* was intended for people who 'do not go to church' (in other words, its language was – as Eliot wrote elsewhere – a 'symptom of some very much deeper change in society and in the individual'[26]), so, not surprisingly, unlike the great Jacobean version that was appointed for use in divine worship, the issue of its liturgical function was not a priority for its translators and advocates. For an Anglo-Catholic like Eliot, it was both the effectiveness of the style of language in liturgical use and the orthodox doctrinal content of a translation, combined, which made a translation suitable for incorporation both in the Divine Office and Mass. The *New English Bible* failed those tests. In the coarseness of its language, its ignorance of the cadence of the spoken word and its theological imprecision, it reflected what Eliot described elsewhere as 'a death of the spirit'.[27]

2

That Eliot, in addition to the Prayer Book and the Bible, should focus particularly, in his recollection of Elizabethan, Jacobean and Caroline Anglicanism, on the life, spirituality and writings of Lancelot Andrewes indicates a more specifically Anglo-Catholic emphasis in his broadly Anglican conspectus of analysis, appreciation and appropriation of the literature of that period. Andrewes' sermons and his *Preces Privatae* were key works in the promotion of High Church values, stressing the sacramental and liturgical aspects of worship. He was 'an influential exponent' of the beauty of holiness which had been commended in the previous generation by Richard Hooker.[28] Moreover, his sermons were dedicated to King Charles, who commanded their publication, and much of their content drew its inspiration from the primitive Fathers of the Church and Andrewes' knowledge of the ancient languages. Here was a bishop who combined in his life and work the same notes of royalism, classicism and Catholicism which were central to Eliot's faith (and which, of course, Eliot had pointedly announced in the Preface to his collection *For Lancelot Andrewes*). Largely because

Vera Effigies Reuerendi in Christo
Patris Dñi: Lancełoti Andrewes
Epifcopi Wintoniensis,

Engraving of Lancelot Andrewes by Wenceslas Hollar (nd)

of Andrewes and his 'disciple', Archbishop Laud, there occurred in the 1620s and 1630s 'a transformation of the appearance of churches throughout the kingdom' and the re-enlistment of 'the arts to the service of the Church after many decades of austerity and icono-phobia'.[29] In other words, what Andrewes had successfully advocated was a foretaste of what Anglo-Catholicism was to achieve in the later nineteenth century.

Because Eliot was so palpably drawn to Andrewes, his life, wit-ness and works, he is a predictable but striking presence in Eliot's poetry – both before and after his conversion. Andrewes' 'Sermon 12 of the Nativitie: Christmas 1618' is drawn upon by Eliot in 'Geron-tion' (1920) – the poem with which he had intended to begin *The Waste Land*:

> Signs are taken for wonders. 'We would see a sign!'
> The word within a word, unable to speak a word.[30]

Andrewes had written (and preached):

> *Signes* are taken for wonders: (*Master we would faine see
> a Signe*, that is, a *miracle*).... *Verbum infans*, the *Word* with-
> out a *word*; the *aeternall Word* not hable [*sic*] to speake a
> *word.*[31]

So taken was Eliot by this worrying of the concept of the Word, that
he uses it again in the fifth section of *Ash-Wednesday*, extending and
elaborating Andrewes' conceit in the manner of a Metaphysical poet
from the same generation:

> Still is the unspoken word, the Word unheard
> The Word without a word, the Word within
> The world and for the world;
> And the light shone in darkness and
> Against the Word the unstilled world still whirled
> About the centre of the silent Word.[32]

And in his essay, 'Lancelot Andrewes', of 1926 (again, we note the
pre-conversion date) – which, Eliot remembered in 1961, was commissioned by Bruce Richmond of the *Times Literary Supplement*,
who picked up his chance remark that he admired the bishop[33] – Eliot
cites the passage from Andrewes' sermon which was such a rich resource for him as an example of prose 'which appears to retreat, to
stand still, but is nevertheless proceeding in the most deliberate and
orderly manner'. Eliot's use of Andrewes' language in his poetry
obeys that same discipline of style and order (the collection *For
Lancelot Andrewes* has 'essays on style and order' as its subtitle).

   Given his technique of pastiche (seen most extensively in *The
Waste Land*), Eliot was undoubtedly also drawn to the way Andrewes,
both in his sermons and the *Preces Privatae*, drew upon quotations
and echoes of Scripture, snatches from the liturgy and hymns of the
Church, excerpts from the Classics, proverbs and, indeed, idioms of
the common tongue. So, in his essay, the poet concentrates on the
studied linguistic attention that the bishop gave to his expression of
the Faith, quoting an example of Andrewes' customary exhaustion
of a word to extract from it every grain of meaning (from 'Sermon
5 of the Nativitie: Christmas 1610'), thus demonstrating the way
language can focus attention on a profound and complex spiritual
experience:

> Let us then make this so accepted a time in itself twice
> acceptable by our accepting, which He will acceptably take
> at our hands....[34]

Repetition and rhythm combine, in a manner of which Eliot was a master in his own incantatory poetry.

The most famous example of this indebtedness, of course, is at the beginning of Eliot's first Christian poem, 'Journey of the Magi', where he draws upon yet another of Andrewes' sermons on the Incarnation – 'of the Nativitie: Christmas 1622' – which Eliot also quotes verbatim in his essay on Andrewes (referring to 'this extraordinary prose ... flashing phrases which never desert the memory'[35]). They launch the poem rhythmically and syntactically:

> 'A cold coming we had of it,
> Just the worst time of the year
> For a journey, and such a long journey:
> The ways deep and the weather sharp,
> The very dead of winter.' ...

It is striking, indeed, that in Eliot's initial utterance as a Christian poet and that as one whose fame was founded on his revolutionary Modernist technique and subject matter, he should begin, not in his own voice, but in that of this scholarly man of prayer and bishop of Winchester from the seventeenth century. It is a testament to the importance for his conversion of his reading in the masterpieces of English divinity of the Caroline age, and particularly of the most Anglo-Catholic of those writers. Tellingly, when Eliot's own voice enters the poem it does so with a conjunction (indicating a link with that past and person and also echoing the familiar way in which verses begin in the Authorized Version, especially in narrative passages, like this, in which Andrewes had a hand). The supposedly dead words of time past are brought into living contact with time present:

> And the camels galled, sore-footed, refractory,
> Lying down in the melting snow.[36]

Here, in poetic utterance, is the presentness of the past, the communication of the quick and the dead, on which Eliot was to meditate much later in *Four Quartets*. Andrewes appears again at the end of 'Journey of the Magi' – although most commentators overlook it – in Eliot's appropriation of an unobtrusive phrase from the same sermon ('set down this'):

> but set down
> This set down
> This.[37]

Andrewes' imperative takes its place, effortlessly and inevitably, in the *vers libre* of the Anglo-Catholic Modernist.

3

In consideration of Eliot's poetry, both dramatic and non-dramatic, we have referred to various instances where his Anglo-Catholicism has informed his verse, or (as is more often the case) is subtly discernible in this or that allusion, or quotation. Eliot was, for the most part, a poet who was an Anglo-Catholic rather than an Anglo-Catholic poet. That is, for reasons which we have explained with regard to his ideas about conversion (and, particularly, about trying to convert others, through personal witness or writing), and because of his clearly-enunciated Modernist convictions about the 'impersonality' of poetry – and also because he would have realised that the specific, detailed emphases of Anglo-Catholicism were not usually susceptible to exposition and celebration in poetry addressed to men and women living in a secular age – he largely avoids writing what would be recognised as 'Anglo-Catholic poetry'. 'Journey of the Magi', a Christian poem, is not an Anglo-Catholic poem – although it was written in the year Eliot became an Anglo-Catholic. *Ash-Wednesday, 1930*, which he began writing in the same year, is an Anglo-Catholic poem (as we will see in detail below) not only because it contains, explicitly, several elements (devotion to the Blessed Virgin, references to the rite of Mass in The English Missal, part of the formula for auricular confession, a yearning for the intercession of the saints and so on) which are, obviously, precisely Anglo-Catholic (not only in their substance but in the language in which they are mediated) but because these are key reference-points in the meaning of the poem. Yet this is what makes it distinctive – indeed, almost unique – in Eliot's corpus of poetry. His 'A Song for Simeon' might be said to be an Anglican poem in the sense that it takes the canticle for Evening Prayer, the *Nunc dimittis*, as its frame (and The Book of Common Prayer translation of it for its source). But it is not an Anglo-Catholic poem in any definite way, unless one wanted to draw a very long bow and argue that its reference to Rome in the opening line: 'Lord, the Roman hyacinths...' is a coded indication of Anglo-Papalist tendencies![38]

Exterior of the church at Little Gidding

George Herbert, whose poetry Eliot increasingly admired, is the Anglican poet *par excellence*. His sequence, *The Temple*, is a veritable anatomy of Anglicanism (its doctrines, sacraments, ordinances, even its buildings – in poems about the church floor and windows, for example – and its liturgical seasons and calendar) and at the very centre (we may say, heart) of the sequence is, appropriately, the lyric 'The British Church'. This is undoubtedly Anglican poetry, and while Ronald Schuchard's contention that the 'spirit' of Herbert pervades Eliot's fourth Quartet, 'Little Gidding',[39] has some weight (and this is not surprising, as both poets were devoted to the place), *Four Quartets*, a philosophical meditation on time in a broadly Christian

Interior of the church at Little Gidding

spirit, with only occasionally explicitly confessional material, is in fact of very different poetic kind from *The Temple*.

The culmination and consummation of Eliot's poetic career, *Four Quartets* inevitably has some Anglo-Catholic (and, more generally, Catholic) elements: the lyrical prayer to the Virgin in 'The Dry Salvages'; the sequence closing with a poem on Little Gidding, thereby recalling and celebrating the Catholic-minded Caroline Church, dear to Anglo-Catholics; the reference, there, to prayer being 'valid' in a consecrated place (with the significant theological implications of that precise term, particularly with reference to the sacraments); allusions to mystical writers (like the Counter-Reformation Spaniard,

St John of the Cross) and to Catholic poetic literature, most notably, the *Divina Commedia*; and, of utmost importance, the major theme of the Incarnation (the doctrine which inspired Anglo-Catholicism from the beginning) which is affirmed at the heart of the sequence in its philosophical meditation upon the intersection of timelessness with time. 'The heart of Anglican theology is the doctrine of the *incarnation*'.[40]

Yet such is the range of philosophical, aesthetic and linguistic reflection in *Four Quartets* (and the relative scarcity of precisely Anglo-Catholic reference and even less that could be construed as directly revelatory of Eliot's own practice of Anglo-Catholicism) that it would narrow its catholicity of reference to call it an Anglo-Catholic poem or even a Catholic one, as such a description unavoidably brings the precise confessional implication with it. Vincent Buckley described it well as

> the most authentic example I know in modern poetry of a satisfying religio-poetic meditation.[41]

Russell Kirk is right in observing that, in the Quartets, Eliot 'had not demonstrated by his poems the truth of a creed; but he had shown, through imagery, how the believer comes to his belief'.[42] Others, it must be said, insist on the confessional reading. In a recent study, *Dove Descending: A Journey into T.S. Eliot 'Four Quartets'*, Thomas Howard concludes that 'anything but the blunt Catholic reading of the thing is mere whistling in the dark'. Reviewing the book and focusing on this statement, Daniel Varholy says that Howard is 'unwilling to allow the text to be deconstructed from the moorings of its Christian vision'.[43] But the moorings of a Christian vision – from which it would be perverse to want to release *Four Quartets* – are different from (and much less precise than) 'the blunt Catholic reading' Howard demands. Tennyson's *In Memoriam* has, intermittently, a Christian vision and possesses those moorings, but it is not a Catholic, Protestant or Anglican poem.

The matter is better clarified by looking, instead, at three works by Eliot which may be classified as 'Anglo-Catholic' rather than at those to which we are reluctant to assign the description. The first of them, chronologically, is one of Eliot's greatest achievements (demonstrating that it was possible to write a major poem within that context of faith and practice, even if Eliot chose, usually, not to do so); and if the second, *The Rock*, has not worn as well as other dramatic poetry by Eliot, it nonetheless includes some of his most powerful writing (and not only in the Choruses, which have remained in print); and the third, *Murder in the Cathedral*, is his most popular play. In these works, at least, if not elsewhere in his poetry (or only intermittently or elusively so), the Anglo-Catholic in religion was also an Anglo-Catholic in literature.

Ash-Wednesday, 1930

In *Ash-Wednesday,*[44] published in 1930 (and originally carrying a dedication to Vivien), Eliot explores most closely the feminine inspiration for faith in a Dantean celebration of a type of the Virgin as a figure of transcendental beauty. The portrait and characterisation of her, and the response of the speaker to her, together amount to an extraordinary reversal of the negative representation of women in Eliot's earlier poetry and the concomitant revulsion from or fear of them which his male speakers had repeatedly expressed. *Ash-Wednesday* is the finest Marian poem, in English, of the twentieth century and at least one critic has called it 'the greatest achievement of Eliot's poetry'.[45] It showed to his contemporaries, Russell Kirk has observed, that

> a man of genuine intellectual power and broad learning might believe in dogma... more important, he might experience something of the transcendent.... The intellectual public, or some part of that public, was moved.[46]

It is, in fact, a sequence of six poems, in the context of Eliot's favourite conceit of the journey or pilgrimage which informs so much of his verse (pre- and post-conversion). The first three sections were composed without the intention of the larger work, the second section ('Salutation' – with its obvious Marian allusion to the angelic greeting to Mary at the Annunciation) being the first of the three to be published, in 1927. By 1930, the whole design had evolved, with the addition of the final three sections. The title of the finished sequence, drawing these together, introduces two significant components of Eliot's Anglo-Catholicism – its penitential discipline and its liturgical expression (Ash Wednesday being the first day of Lent, the season of forty days of fasting and abstinence in preparation for Easter). In the Church's liturgy, from ancient times, ashes were imposed on the foreheads of penitents, in the form of a cross, to mark the beginning of this season of mourning and penance for wrong-doing and as a reminder of the dust whence humanity came and to which it shall return. As an Anglo-Catholic, Eliot attended this ceremony annually and (as we have seen) was rigorous in his rule of regular private confession of sin, beyond the usual practice even of devout Anglo-Catholics of his generation. So the poem has an unignorable autobiographical element, in terms of the poet's faith (which, like his view of life at large, tended to focus on a consciousness of human fallibility and the need to redeem the time), in addition to its more general meaning.

The idea of the *via negativa* informs the opening, incantatory lines which, in their rhythmic, repetitive character convey the idea of traditional liturgical language with its repetitions and rhythmical cadence. F.R. Leavis recognised, in the poem's rhythm, 'certain qualities of ritual'.[47] Referring to this 'ritual method' in *Ash-Wednesday*, Linda Leavell acknowledges sources in Anglo-Catholic liturgy but argues that the incantatory quality runs deeper than this, 'as deep as man's primal cry to his Maker'.[48]

Drawing upon a fourteenth-century poem by Guido Cavalcanti, *'Perch'io non spero'* ('Because I do not hope') and a versicle prior to Mass in the Ash Wednesday liturgy, *'Deus tu conversus vivificabis nos'* ('Lord, thou wilt turn again and quicken us'), as well as the Epistle for Ash Wednesday which urges a turning (and re-turning) to God, Eliot establishes a complex combination of an inability to turn ('Because I do not hope to turn again') with references to the necessity for turning, as the language of the poetry turns about these concepts, initiating, as it were, the very process that is being called into question. Further references in the opening strophe of its first section, to 'the agèd eagle', the 'power' and the 'reign', mediated negatively, nonetheless have positive implications. The eagle is that bird which, in old age, flies into the sun (or Son) to renew itself, and the power and the reign recall the power and the kingdom of the Lord's (or Son's) prayer (said repeatedly in Anglo-Catholic devotions, public and private – such as the rosary, to which Eliot was devoted).

From the beginning, the journey has been invested in ambiguity. How is it to be transmuted into transcendence? The first section gives some indication of the spiritual discipline which is required. It is another journey in reverse, as it were, like that of the Magi and again, much later, at the end of Eliot's poetic career, in the Quartets, when he tells us that old men need to be explorers, to return to their 'first world'. It is a version of the scriptural dictum that one must become like a little child in order to enter the kingdom of Heaven. In *Ash-Wednesday*, I, it is expressed in terms of the speaker's petition to be taught to 'sit still' (as children are). But *en attendant Dieu*, it transpires, the penitent is waiting for His revelation in female form. This is dimly anticipated in the closing lines of the first section, in quotation from the second part of the *Ave Maria*: 'pray for us sinners now and at the hour of our death'. Through poetry and liturgy – neither by theological nor explicit naming – the redemptive female influence is beginning to be summoned. Eliot had modified his earlier direct address to the Virgin in a draft of the poem: 'Holy Mary Mother of God...'.[49]

She comes before him, immediately, in the very opening word ('Lady') of the second section of the poem, originally published as 'Salutation'. Gabriel's 'salutation' to Mary is ironically recalled here for the difference, of course, is that it is the reluctant penitent, the poem's speaker, who salutes her and, in doing so, speaks not of life-bringing hope, but of the dire process of being devoured by death-dealing sin – represented by the three white leopards, symbolising the world, the flesh and the devil – who have all but consumed him. This method of ironic indirection is, generally-speaking, typically Modernist, but it is also specific to Eliot's religious apprehension – indicating the difficulty of belief and of submitting to its formulae and precise demands, even as he ultimately extols the necessity for both.

Yet the keynote, as it were, of that word, 'Lady', transfigures all that follows where Eliot continues the paradoxical idea of the *via negativa*, as denial is framed by affirmation. Bereft of hope and, now, of bodily strength too, he is in fact making himself available to new life by being stripped of all worldly attachments and aspirations (including spiritual ones). Eliot was strongly drawn to the writings of the Spanish mystic, St John of the Cross, the master of the negative way. It is in these circumstances that the advent of the Lady is of such significance. We note that she is not the Virgin, precisely, at this point, but one who 'honours the Virgin in meditation', as Anglo-Catholics were urged to do, and as Eliot did daily, in praying the rosary. But this is also typical of Eliot's tentative mode of spiritual advancement. Yet the celebratory tone is unmistakable and very striking, given all that has gone before in Eliot's poetry with regard to the representation of women. For this Lady is both good and lovely. Dressed in white, her attire matches his white bones, picked clean of flesh by the leopards as the various manifestations of whiteness tell of a rite of purification.

The aesthetic realisation of what is occurring, spiritually, remains important throughout the poem. It matters that the Lady is lovely and is dressed in a beautiful gown. Eliot repeatedly affirmed the incarnational teaching of Anglo-Catholicism that the divine was to be apprehended in the midst of created life and artistry and his poetry, here, enacts what he urges. It does so in the musical modulation of the verse, from the spare, though rhythmical, blank verse of self-emptying, to a lyrical, litany-like song of praise of the 'Lady of silences' who is now identified with Mary, not by explicit naming (Mary's name is heard only once in Eliot's poetry, in this poem) but in terms of her attributes: 'Torn and most whole', for example, in the virgin birth. Eliot dwells on the old idea of the mystical rose and of the garden, representative of virginity (but recalling, also, the Garden of Eden, where purity was sullied) and concludes this song with 'Grace to the Mother / For the Garden / Where all love ends'. The meaning is deliberately ambiguous: where all love has its fulfillment and where all loves are brought to completion and are transcended.

The carefully-evolved third section, originally published as 'Al som de l'escalina' (to the top of the stair) in 1929, describes the ascent of the penitent, in the spirit of St John of the Cross and his ascent of Mount Carmel, climbing a stairway of perfection. Eliot was to claim, in the Quartets, that 'Humility is endless'[50] and this is certainly a humbling experience, as the arduousness of the aspiration to perfection is detailed in terms of a slow progress from the 'first turning of the second stair', to eventually 'climbing the third stair'. The essence of the difficulty is the strong appeal of the sensual world, figured in a delicious pagan landscape, and in a favourite image of Eliot – the seductive power of female hair ('brown hair over the mouth blown'). Yet this vision, too, is instinct with ambiguity, for the landscape belongs to 'maytime', the Virgin's month, as well as the pagan time of fertility rites in celebration of the re-greening of the earth. And the pagan figure who is envisaged, playing on his flute, is dressed not only in green (the colour of nature) but in blue, 'Mary's colour' (as we are reminded later in the poem). These ambiguities indicate that the pilgrimage of ascent is not only progressing but is doing so under the influence, implicit and aestheticised as it may be, of the spirit of the Virgin.

The second half of the poem, its fourth, fifth and sixth sections, were written with the idea of a sequence and it is noteworthy that it is at the beginning of this part of the work that Mary is first mentioned by name, but in an aesthetic context, as the still unnamed female presence. The 'Lady' introduced in the second section is now seen to walk 'in white and blue, in Mary's colour'. Blue is 'the colour of space and light and eternity, of the sea and the sky':

From time immemorial blue has been the sacred colour, with magical properties, and in Constantinople, when the

Byzantine capital was the centre of Christian art, blue became the Virgin's colour, celestial blue, the colour of heaven.[51]

The woman remains here because, while possessing such attributes of Mary, she is still but a type of her, rather than the Virgin precisely. Yet her typicality is to bring her into unity. She is both ignorant, as a simple Hebrew girl might be, but also has 'knowledge of eternal dolour', explicitly recalling Our Lady of Dolours (or Sorrows) of the crucifixion – appropriately, in a Lenten poem. Within the large context of Eliot's thought and imagery, she has the power to revive the wasted land, to make strong the fountains and to make 'fresh the springs'. This is the antithesis of the parched, life-denying landscape of *The Waste Land*, where there was not even the sound of water. But she is a mystical figure, detached from the speaker, yet reviving his song, restoring 'the ancient rhyme' with 'a new verse'. Denis Donoghue reads the passage as corresponding to 'absolution'.[52]

This is Marianism discerned in the midst of the Modernist project of thematic and technical renewal. But for Eliot, that newness consisted in a knowledge of the tradition, not merely in novelty and iconoclasm. Renewing his faith, this unearthly, quasi-angelic being, with 'white light folded, sheathed about her, folded', restores his poetry. To close the section, the unnamed figure is described as 'the silent sister'. The reference is conventual. She is a figure of prayer, as Eliot pursues (as he does in the Quartets) the idea of the character of the language by which the Word may be mediated in words, to a sceptical twentieth-century readership, and in a reference to the disciplined life of monastic enclosure, to which he was strongly drawn. The phrase which rings through these lines is the imperative to 'redeem the time', from Paul's epistle to the Ephesians (5:16), 'for the times are evil'. Eliot never underestimates the difficulty of the process and conveys this tellingly at the end of *Ash-Wednesday*, IV, in this fragment: 'And after this our exile'. It is a quotation from the most loved of prayers to the Virgin, '*Salve Regina...*' ('Hail, holy Queen...'), of eleventh-century origins, customarily said at the end of the rosary meditation in which Eliot was well-practised. In addition to reinforcing the Marian and liturgical character of the poem and its spirituality – that is, its Anglo-Catholic character – what is telling about the phrase, in this negative reference to 'our' state of separation from God, is what is left out – the phrase which follows it in the prayer: 'show unto us the blessed fruit of thy womb, Jesus'. The Beatific Vision has yet to be achieved.

In the penultimate section, Eliot focuses on the issue of language and the burden it must bear if it is to communicate the Word, or Logos. Especially, this is difficult in an unbelieving generation and in a form of poetry, such as his and that of the Modernists in general, which eschews direct statement and which, also, is bound to reflect *les mots de la tribu* and speak of contemporary people's concerns. How can such an understanding of the modern world and of poetry in it be brought into conformity with Christian-Catholic teachings – particularly, here, with regard to the intercessory role of the Virgin? It is Eliot's double challenge – theologically and poetically, as the leading Modernist poet. Hence the tone of desperation (if not, precisely, despair) in the worrying of the concept of the search for the right word in a dispensation where 'the lost word is lost... the spent word is spent'.

Ironically, punctuating this anxiety about the silenced and silent Word, we have – for the first (and only) time in his poetry – the Word speaking, as Christ's reproach from the Cross, from the Good Friday liturgy 'of the Solemn Adoration of the Holy Cross' in The English Missal, is heard: 'O my people, what have I done unto thee'. Importantly, between these repeated reproachful utterances (but utterances, nonetheless) the silent sister is invoked, as Mediatrix with her Son and His Father. Although expressed in the tones of contingency, like the section as a whole, the speaker, in hoping that the sister will pray for the people who (in the biblical phrase) walk in darkness, who are the captives of sin and lust and worldliness, the mere entertaining of the hypothesis and the hope are, in the context of Eliot's poetry as a whole, nothing less than momentous. It is significant indeed that the wastelanders have been brought from their utter despair to a position where any kind of amelioration, let alone redemption, may be posited. The poetry gathers urgency through repetition of the insistent questioning: 'Will the veiled sister pray?' She is veiled as a religious sister, but also because her identity is not fully disclosed. The effect of her prayer will be stupendous: it will eradicate the inheritance of Original Sin, 'spitting from the mouth the withered apple-seed'. And its efficacy is instantiated in the fragment of the reproach which movingly closes the section: 'O my people'. The reproachful negativity of the dying Lord: 'what have I done unto thee' is eradicated and the redemptive embrace all but secured.

So typically of Eliot, the final section of *Ash-Wednesday* does not bring closure. The penitent has moved through Lent, from Ash Wednesday to Good Friday, as the quotations from the liturgical reproaches from the Cross indicate. We do not progress to the day of Resurrection, even as he beseeches the priest in the confessional – 'Bless me father' – without adding 'for I have sinned', suggesting that sin has been confessed and absolved in the course of the long penitential discipline. The seductions of this world, our human predicament of being caught between time and eternity, fleshliness and the life of the soul, are not transcended, and Eliot writes compellingly (and, indeed, beautifully) about the allure of these sexual and mortal influences. Such recognition adds immeasurably to the power of the poem: nothing could be less pietistically platitudinous or blissfully ignorant of the realities of the challenges involved. But the possibility of transcendence and resurrection has been glimpsed and, most importantly, the hope of a *vita nuova* has been invested in one who is now celebrated in a hymning catalogue of her various epiphanies in the course of the poem: 'Blessèd sister, holy mother, spirit of the fountain, spirit of the garden'. It is a Litany of the Virgin. As a mother, she will teach children – that is, those who are old in the ways of the world, but as infants in the life of the spirit – 'to sit still'. Only in stillness, as the Psalmist urges, can God be known. And the peace that this brings is conformity to the Father's purposes, as Eliot translates Dante in the *Paradiso*: 'Our peace in His will'. This, too, is a momentous development, for all the abiding contingency, as Eliot's earlier poems had abounded in references to the *Inferno* and *Purgatorio*. But most tellingly, as the poem closes, Eliot invokes the 'Sister, mother' again, as the 'spirit of the sea', *Stella maris*, drawing upon phrases from St Ignatius' prayer, *Anima Christi* (as the allusions to texts of Latin Christianity accumulate and are concentrated: 'Suffer me not to be separated'; '*Ne permittas me separari a te* ...') but applying them, now, to the Virgin: 'And let my cry come unto Thee'. To the very end, what is expressed is the hope that such an event may occur, rather than a celebration of its occurrence, and the fruits which that has brought to the life of the penitent. But the very proposal, in the wake of so much despair, is, in its own way, possibly an even more moving affirmation.

The combination and accumulation of allusions to prayers and liturgy, to spiritual exercises and, particularly, the sacrament of confession, but, most importantly, the slowly emerging central figure of the Virgin as 'the hope only / Of empty men' (in Eliot's phrase from 'The Hollow Men',[53] where she was briefly glimpsed as the *Rosa Mystica*), mark out this beautiful poem as Eliot's most accomplished Anglo-Catholic work.

The Rock (1934)

Commentators have disagreed about the importance of Eliot's contribution to *The Rock* – and, in particular, of the choruses (preserved in the *Collected Poems and Plays*) – in the assessment of his poetic development. The work was written to support Bishop Winnington-Ingram's ambitious Forty-Five Churches Fund to finance the building of new churches for the burgeoning suburbia of the Diocese of London in the inter-war years. Across the river, in Southwark, Bishop Garbett (also a High Churchman, but, like Winnington-Ingram, worried about Anglo-Catholic extremism) had a more modest and achievable campaign for twenty-five new churches.[54] Some churchmen were sceptical about Eliot's involvement, apprehensive that his poetry would be too modern and too difficult for a pageant for the masses. Of the 330 actors in *The Rock*, almost all, David Chinitz notes, were 'amateur volunteers'. Yet 20,000 people, mostly parishioners, came to see it during its two-week run in the cavernous Sadler's Wells theatre.[55]

Bernard Bergonzi judges only the choruses of *The Rock* as worthy of study, dismissing the play at large in a few sentences, because of its tendency to exhortation: 'harshly instructing the audience in Christian truth and haranguing them for their godless ways'.[56] His assessment draws a measure of support from Eliot's own comment in 'The Three Voices of Poetry' (1953) that he was relying on the second voice in these choruses and, thus, 'addressing – indeed haranguing' the audience.[57] We should be wary, nonetheless, of Eliot's characteristic self-depreciating assessments in such retrospective comments (he notoriously called *The Waste Land* 'the relief of a personal and wholly insignificant grouse against life; it is just a piece of rhythmical grumbling'[58]). Moreover, it is not necessarily the case that Eliot's use of the term 'haranguing' is as negative as Bergonzi's.

More positively, Robert Sencourt describes Eliot's analysis, in *The Rock*, of the relation of the Church of England to contemporary London as 'the believer's answer to the searchings and confusions of the agnostic, twelve years earlier in *The Waste Land*'.[59] But this is too simple as even the choruses (the play's best feature) do not embody Eliot's most articulate nor his most mature Christian response, in verse, to such issues. Yet the position of the choruses in the evolution of Eliot's poetic development, four years after his most explicitly Anglo-Catholic poetic work, *Ash-Wednesday*, and just one year before *Murder in the Cathedral* (where the Chorus plays a significant poetic and dramatic role), stirs our interest not only in his maturing choric technique, but in his ongoing concern (still occupying his attention in *Four Quartets*, composed through the ensuing decade) with the complex matter of expressing religious convictions in modern verse.

Eliot's involvement in the collaborative act of *The Rock* brought him into association with E. Martin Browne, its producer (the beginning of their twenty-five-years' partnership in poetic drama) as well as several Anglican priests, including the Revd Vincent Howson, whom Eliot describes in the prefatory note to the pageant as 'joint author'.[60] In the Preface, Eliot expresses his artistic debt to Browne:

> The scenario, incorporating some historical scenes, suggested by the Rev. R. Webb-Odell, is by Mr. E. Martin Browne, under whose direction I wrote the choruses and dialogues, and submissive to whose expert criticism I rewrote much of them.... For the sentiments expressed in the choruses I must assume the responsibility.[61]

There had been uncertainty over the title of the play – the suggestion of Lady Keeble – as, in Christian theology, the term can apply to Christ ('for they drank of that spiritual Rock that followed them: and that Rock was Christ', I Corinthians, 10:4) or Peter ('thou art Peter, and upon this rock I will build my church', Matthew 16:18). This second text (playing on Peter's name – *petrus* = a rock) is the scriptural authority on which the Petrine claims of the papacy are based, the two different identifications of the rock in the Bible being the focus of an important historic dispute between Catholic and Protestant Christianity about the source and exercise of spiritual authority. *The Rock* was not explicitly an Anglo-Catholic project, in spite of Eliot's prominent role in it, but he was aware of the problem which the title (and the character of The Rock, in the play) raised, as he wrote to Webb-Odell and Browne, in February, 1934, three months before it opened at Sadler's Wells:

> My only objection to *The Rock* is that the Rock himself, if he gives the title to the production, will be identified by most people as St. Peter pure and simple, which does directly conjure up to my mind the Petrine claims – which are hardly appropriate. Do you think this is a considerable objection or not? If not, then perhaps this is the best title.[62]

Browne himself had been worried about the ambiguity, having written to Eliot three months before:

Of whom is the Rock symbolical? I originally conceived
him as St. Peter – 'on this Rock will I build my Church ...'
But some have thought of 1 Cor. 10, 4: 'And that Rock was
Christ'. If you've got definite views, I shall be glad of them.
But you may not yet have considered the point.[63]

As it turns out, that Eliot and Browne kept the title was a wise decision, dramatically. The very uncertainty and ambiguity which surround
the Rock's identity is one of the work's few saving features as a form
of drama.

On his first appearance, the Rock announces that he has 'trodden
the winepress alone' and addresses two commandments to the awe-
struck chorus, who (in the stage direction) speak 'as the voice of the
Church of God':

I say to you: Make perfect your will.
I say: take no thought of the harvest,
But only of proper sowing.[64]

The quotations from Isaiah and Lamentations in this opening speech
are familiarly related to Christ's suffering – Lancelot Andrewes takes
the passage from Isaiah for the text of his seventeenth sermon 'Of the
Resurrection', insisting that the prophet is referring to Jesus: 'it can be
none but Christ'.[65] So, on his first appearance, we identify the Rock
with the Lord. And this idea is reinforced by the second chorus (including Eliot's quotation from the epistle to the Ephesians 2: 19-20):

Thus your fathers were made
Fellow citizens of the saints, of the household of GOD,
   being built upon the foundation
Of apostles and prophets, Christ Jesus Himself the chief
   cornerstone.[66]

Doubts about The Rock's identity arise, however, on his second
epiphany, at the midpoint of the action, when he declares that 'the
Gates of Hell shall not prevail' against the Church. Now, the Rock
appears as a guardian of souls, and this function, along with his use
of the words of Christ delegating temporal power in spiritual matters
to the apostles and their successors, align his characterisation with
St Peter. The gospel for St Peter's day, 29th June – when Eliot was
received into the Church in baptism – includes this very text.

The enigma of The Rock's identity is resolved towards the end of
the play where the legend of the founding of Westminster Abbey is
expounded by the Chorus Leaders:

> First you shall hear
> Of the Abbey Church of St. Peter, the abbey at West-
>   minster,
> How it was dedicated
> Not by the Bishop Mellitus, Bishop of London,
> Because one had been there before him
> One came, not with crowds and processions
> In view of the people, by day,
> But came alone in the night,
> Alone but for one of his trade:
> A fisherman served by a fisherman....

St. Peter (The Rock) and a Fisherman are seen returning to the Thames shore.

Fisherman: Who are you, Father? who have consecrated this church, as the Bishop was to have done to-morrow? You're one of the foreign clergy, I can see that, Father; but who are you, if you pardon me asking? Was all this by the Holy Pope's orders, Father?

Peter: By the order of one who came before him, my son. I am Peter, servant of God, once a fisherman like you.

Neatly, in these lines, Eliot has captured the essential teaching of the Apostolic Succession, in terms of a quaint tradition, while marginalising (if not overlooking) the papal Petrine claims. The preferred Anglo-Catholic idea of 'the Rock' referring to Peter is affirmed, but the origin of that idea in Christ's own words – 'of one who came before him' – is also noted. Also emphasising the Anglo-Catholic attention to episcopacy and its succession from the Apostles, was the closing of performances of the pageant with, as David Chinitz notes,

> a live Anglican bishop who, in full canonicals, as part of the final tableau, blessed the audience.[67]

Similarly expressive of Eliot's faith is the way *The Rock* is punctuated with references to the Incarnation. Ethelbert, the workmen's foreman in the play (which, as we might expect, is essentially about the building of new churches), expresses the germ of an idea involving the radical re-interpretation of the customary ordering of time to which, one year later, in 1935, Eliot is to give prominence in the opening lines of 'Burnt Norton' (which was to become the first of the Quartets, an extended meditation on time and timelessness).

Ethelbert's passage is cast in dialect; while the lines in 'Burnt Norton' give the philosophical hypothesis an incantatory pulse:

> There's some new notion about time, what says that the past
> – what's be'ind you – is what's goin' to 'appen in the future,
> bein' as the future 'as already 'appened....[68]

> Time present and time past
> Are both perhaps present in time future
> And time future contained in time past.[69]

In the play, a few lines later, a Saxon describes the Incarnation itself:

> Yet it is a beautiful faith, if it were true. That their god should
> have been born among men, of a humble man, and lived his
> life among folk like you and me, not kings and earls, and
> yet was truly god, and now is worshipped, they say, by very
> great kings: that is very wonderful.

The choric celebration of the doctrine (in Chorus VII) includes the Catholic emphasis on the community of Christians and the Body of Christ, the life of retreat from the world for prayer and mortification, and Eliot's characteristic critique of modern civilisation:

> What life have you if you have not life together?
> There is no life that is not in community,
> And no community not lived in praise of GOD.
> Even the anchorite who meditates alone,
> For whom the days and nights repeat the praise of GOD,
> Prays for the Church, the Body of Christ incarnate.
> And now you live dispersed on ribbon roads,
> And no one knows or cares who is his neighbour
> Unless his neighbour makes too much disturbance,
> But all dash to and fro in motor cars,
> Familiar with the roads and settled nowhere.
> Nor does the family even move together,
> But every son would have his motorcycle,
> And daughters ride away on casual pillions.[70]

The 'haranguing' element is decidedly there but, in the circumstances of a pageant play for church-people, that is not inappropriate. And when The Rock tells the Chorus that at 'every moment you live at a point of intersection',[71] of the opportunity of apprehending the eternal in the midst of time, he is anticipating what Eliot explores at much greater length and, it is true, in superior poetry in *Four Quartets*.

The dramatic scene of the fitting-out of the church is concentrated, as we would expect, on the sanctuary, and the vessels and other appurtenances for the Catholic celebration of the Mass:

> Curtains open, disclosing the apse completed, and an altar standing on the top of the hill. Craftsmen are shown in rhythmical movement: Painters frescoing the apse; Stone-carvers at work on the crucifix and the front of the altar; Wood-carvers making candlesticks and book-rest; Weavers and lacemaker producing curtains and linen cloth; Metal workers beating out chalice and paten; Illuminator decorating altar-book.[72]

The rhythmical movement of the workers is appropriately liturgical, anticipating the ritual which their craftsmanship will facilitate. The 'crucifix', to be differentiated from an altar cross, is a definite Anglo-Catholic touch.

The Crusade tableau in the pageant shows Eliot's attraction, again, to the Reproaches from the Good Friday liturgy (which, as we saw, he had used before in *Ash-Wednesday*). The versicle, *Sanctus Deus, Sanctus fortis, Sanctus immortalis* derives from this rite, and in the stage direction during the desecration of the church by the Protestant 'Preacher' and his mob, as the 'lights change to an angry glow', the 'reproaches' are sung in the background. This is a decisive creedal statement by Eliot, plainly recalling the Kensitite mobs who violently interrupted Anglo-Catholic liturgies and destroyed churches in his day.

The principal poetic interest of *The Rock*, which lies in the choruses, is also derived directly from Anglo-Catholic liturgy. The unnamed critic in *The Church Times* noted in review of the play:

> The great achievement of *The Rock* is the chorus. Mr. Eliot is greater as a poet than he is experienced as a dramatist, and he has put the best of his writing into the poetry of the choric comments on religion and life.[73]

Incantation, that recurring liturgical pulse in Eliot's poetry, is the most striking poetic device in the choric sections and, given the ecclesiastical theme, is very appropriate to the play. The *tedium vitae* is noted and the need for transcendence of it in communion with the Incarnate Word:

> O perpetual revolution of the configured stars,
> O perpetual recurrence of determined seasons,

> O world of spring and autumn, birth and dying!
> The endless cycle of idea and action,
> Endless invention, endless experiment,
> Brings knowledge of motion, but not of stillness;
> Knowledge of speech, but not of silence;
> Knowledge of words, and ignorance of the Word.[74]

Incantation is that technical element, in Eliot's poetry, which most directly derives from his Anglo-Catholicism, with its emphasis on chant, both in the endless repetitions of the Divine Office (especially in psalmody, the most musical of scriptural poetry) and of the rite of Mass, with its unchanging elements, in speech and music: in liturgical sequences, litanies, versicles and responses. The liturgy, whether in Latin or English, spoken or sung, is replete with incantation. Indeed, Eliot uses the word explicitly in Chorus IX, celebrating its mystical power, which can make perfect the imperfections of fallen discourse:

> Out of the sea of sound the life of music,
> Out of the slimy mud of words, out of the sleet and hail
>   of verbal imprecisions,
> Approximate thoughts and feelings, words that have
>   taken the place of thoughts and feelings,
> There spring the perfect order of speech, and the beauty
>   of incantation.[75]

Eliot gave special prominence to incantation in his poetic theory, acknowledging how primitive chanting is, writing of Edgar Allan Poe, for example, who had

> to an exceptional degree, the feeling for the incantatory element in poetry, of that which may, in the most literal sense, be called 'the magic of verse'.... this unchanging immediacy ... because of its very crudity, stirs the feelings at a deep and almost primitive level.[76]

In the same year, in verse, he names the device again, referring to its mystical qualities:

> The whispered incantation which allows
> Free passage to the phantoms of the mind.[77]

Such was the quality of this element, that its use by a poet in one language cannot be translated into another. Referring to Shakespeare, he asks:

> What can be translated? A story, a dramatic plot, the impress-
> ions of a living character in action, an image, a proposition.
> What cannot be translated is the incantation, the music of the
> words, and that part of the meaning which is in the music.[78]

This magical quality is based as much in repetition as rhythm, and
Eliot valued it as much in liturgy (where it is as old as liturgical
language itself), as in poetry. Mary Trevelyan recalled Eliot's 'annual
indignation' at the omission of the Sealing of the Tribes in the epistle
on All Saints' Day (as set down in The English Missal):

> Of the tribe of Juda were sealed twelve thousand
> Of the tribe of Reuben were sealed twelve thousand

... and so on, for the twelve tribes. Eliot commented (she notes),

> I remember the Vicar left them out last year. People are
> so afraid of repetition – they don't seem to realise it is the
> essence of poetry.[79]

Certainly, it is the essence of his poetry as it was of the liturgical
tradition he imbibed, as, for example, in the thrice-repeated 'Lord, I
am not worthy ...' at the Mass, accompanied by the rhythmical action
of breast-beating. In *The Rock*, some splendid incantatory writing,
in the choruses, is as powerful as much better-known passages elsewhere in Eliot's work:

> Some went from love of glory,
> Some went who were restless and curious,
> Some were rapacious and lustful.
> Many left their bodies to the kites of Syria
> Or sea-strewn along the routes;
> Many left their souls in Syria,
> Living on, sunken in moral corruption;
> Many came back well broken,
> Diseased and beggared, finding
> A stranger at the door in possession.[80]

And the incantation of light, in Chorus X, is as mesmeric in beauty
as the great hymn to light by Milton (another master of this device)
at the beginning of Book III of *Paradise Lost*:

> O Light Invisible, we praise Thee!
> Too bright for mortal vision.
> O Greater Light, we praise Thee for the less;
> The eastern light our spires touch at morning,

> The light that slants upon our eastern doors at evening,
> The twilight over stagnant pools at batflight,
> Moon light and star light, owl and moth light,
> Glow-worm glowlight on a grassblade.
> O Light Invisible, we worship Thee![81]

The sequence of Eliot's praise of Light Invisible: 'we praise Thee', 'we worship Thee' and so on is a direct borrowing from the great incantation to God in the liturgical hymn of praise, *Gloria in excelsis*, early in the Mass, after the penitential *Kyrie eleison*:

> We praise thee, we bless thee, we worship thee, we glorify thee, we give thanks to thee for thy great glory.

Where *The Rock* is richest, as poetry, in the use of incantatory language, especially in the choruses, it comes directly from (and speaks of) Eliot's Anglo-Catholic liturgical experience.

Further indication of *The Rock*'s Anglo-Catholic character is revealed when Rose Macaulay, in her last book, *The Towers of Trebizond* (1956), inevitably quoting from Eliot (always an expected presence in any later twentieth-century literary work of Anglo-Catholic provenance) has her narrator use lines not from his better-known poems nor from more recent works, like *Four Quartets*, where similar sentiments are enunciated, but from The Rock himself:

> ... for as T.S. Eliot points out:

> > The world turns and the world changes,
> > But one thing does not change.
> > In all of my years, one thing does not change.
> > However you disguise it, this thing does not change,
> > The perpetual struggle of good and evil.[82]

By 1956, *The Rock* had been mostly forgotten and was out of print, but the Anglo-Catholic Macaulay, who never puts a foot wrong in detailing that species of Christianity, knows that her Anglo-Catholic speaker would be drawn particularly to that play, with the further implication that, as a dutiful Anglo-Catholic, she had probably been to see it in performance in 1934.

Murder in the Cathedral (1935)

Like *The Rock*, *Murder in the Cathedral* belongs to the genre of 'liturgical drama' on which Eliot had lectured in his extension classes in London as early as 1918. Eliot refers, in his summary of this topic (which also included miracle and morality plays) to the 'peculiar charm' and the 'essential dramatic qualities' of plays of this ecclesiastical and Christian type.[83] Henzie Raeburn, E. Martin Browne's wife, astutely suggested that Eliot's original title for the play, *Fear in the Way* (the conflation of two phrases in Ecclesiastes 12:5) should be replaced by *Murder in the Cathedral*[84] – more direct, more concrete and with a *frisson* of the mixture of sin and sacrilege.

We can imagine that central to the appeal of this commission, for Eliot, was that he could write a poetic drama about sanctity, a concept to which he often refers (increasingly so, in succeeding years); and in choosing the subject of Thomas' twelfth-century martyrdom – obviously appropriate for the festival at Canterbury – he recalls not only that event but the formidable cult that was centred on the shrine at the cathedral, as a result of it. The same cathedral, of course, was to become the mother-church of worldwide Anglicanism after the mediaeval cult had been suppressed. So, at a twentieth-century festival at quintessentially Anglican Canterbury, to be celebrating the story of Catholic Beckett, is a way of affirming the Catholic origins of Anglicanism, especially (as we will see) as Eliot applies Anglo-Catholic liturgical language to the pre-Anglican story. Moreover, as this particular saint was also a bishop, in the Apostolic Succession – that central tenet of Catholic doctrine, much emphasised, as we have seen, in Anglo-Catholic polemic and in Eliot's most notable contribution to it in *Reunion by Destruction* – choosing an archiepiscopal saint for dramatic treatment, and with priests in attendance, at the mother-church of the Anglican Communion, affirms the importance of that principle of apostolic ministry for Anglicans who wanted to belong to Catholic Christendom at large.

The action of Becket's life and death, furthermore, took place in the high medievalism of the gothic setting of the cathedral – the ecclesiastical environment that was enthusiastically recovered by the Anglo-Catholic ritualists of the later nineteenth century as redolent of the Age of Faith – and during the liturgical observance of the 'octave', the eight days of the Christmas festival, as detailed by Eliot and which, in Anglicanism, is a liturgical arrangement only observed in the Anglo-Catholic tradition. The First Priest draws attention to this: 'Since the Holy Innocents a day: the fourth day from Christmas', to which the three Priests respond: 'Rejoice we all, keeping holy day' (from Psalm 42:4 as used in the introit, '*Gaudeamus*...' which came to be applied to the Mass for the feast day of St Thomas of Canterbury himself). The play's 'overall effect', David Chinitz has observed, 'is far more liturgical than melodramatic'.[85]

What is striking about this prominent liturgical element in *Murder in the Cathedral* is that Eliot does not draw substantially upon the Latin text from the Missal – which, historically, would have been used in the Christmas liturgy at Canterbury at the time of the martyrdom – but, with a conscious anachronism (emphasising, in reverse, the continuity which Protestantism had rejected), on the language of The Book of Common Prayer, embodying the reformed English liturgy in the vernacular by another Thomas (and Archbishop of Canterbury). Cranmer's liturgical language, composed under the pressure of reforming ideas from the continent, is used in celebration of the sanctity of his medieval predecessor in a play by a member of a catholicising movement bent on restoring the full Catholic character of the Church. To emphasise Catholic continuity rather than Protestant rupture, in *Murder in the Cathedral*, Thomas Becket himself uses Thomas Cranmer's words. Also, Eliot refers to The English Hymnal (like The English Missal, published in 1933 – the centenary of the Oxford Movement), the standard Anglo-Catholic musical compendium to that Missal.[86] The liturgical poetic language of *Murder in the Cathedral* conveys what Anglo-Catholic ecclesiology affirms.

More generally, this technique of anachronism subverts the order of time. Through a liturgically anachronistic language, Eliot not only binds Thomas Becket of the twelfth century to Thomas Cranmer of the sixteenth, but (to both of them) a third Thomas also – Eliot himself – of the twentieth century, who has used their language in this way. (A similar linguistic transcending of time, in time, occurs in 'East Coker' where Thomas Elyot of the sixteenth century is joined to Thomas Eliot of the twentieth; and, best-known of all, at the opening of 'Journey of the Magi', where Lancelot Andrewes' sermon of the Nativity melds seamlessly with Eliot's Modernist speech). These three apparently very different Thomases, 'too strange to each other for misunderstanding' are, through poetry, 'folded in a single party',[87] that of *Ecclesia Anglicana*.

The first appearance of the language of The Book of Common Prayer in *Murder in the Cathedral* is not, as it happens, in a liturgical prayer but in Thomas's sermon, which he delivers on Christmas morning, 1170, and which forms the 'interlude' between the play's two parts. Early in his homily, Becket declares:

> For whenever Mass is said, we re-enact the Passion and Death of Our Lord; and on this Christmas Day we do this in celebration of His Birth. So that at the same moment we

rejoice in His coming for the salvation of men, and offer again to God His Body and Blood in sacrifice, oblation and satisfaction for the sins of the whole world.

This is a striking conflation of the Catholic doctrine of the sacrifice of the Mass and the language of the Cranmerian prayer of consecration in the communion service of the Prayer Book which had been imposed upon the Church of England (as the thirty-first of the Thirty-Nine Articles printed therein states) to repudiate the very doctrine that Eliot uses its language, through Becket, to affirm:

Wherefore the sacrifices of Masses, in which it was commonly said, that the Priest did offer Christ for the quick and the dead, to have remission of pain and guilt, were blasphemous fables, and dangerous deceits.

As in Tract 90 (1841), John Henry Newman claimed (in an analysis much valued by Anglo-Catholics) that it was possible to show that even the Thirty-Nine Articles were patient of an orthodox Catholic interpretation, so, here, Eliot's Becket, at Mass and talking about Mass, uses several of these words of Cranmer from the consecration prayer of his supposedly reformed Lord's Supper in the course of presenting the Catholic doctrine of the eucharistic sacrifice:

... who made there (by his one oblation of himself once offered) a full, perfect, and sufficient sacrifice, oblation, and satisfaction, for the sins of the whole world....

The common phrase is 'sacrifice, oblation, and satisfaction'. What is omitted by Eliot is as important as what is included. The reformed doctrine of the sufficiency of the sacrifice of the Cross, insisted upon, in Cranmer's prayer, through repetition and the accumulation of synonyms: '*one* oblation of himself *once* offered ... a full, perfect, and sufficient sacrifice' (my italics), and asserted, again, in the thirty-first article –

the Offering of Christ once made is that perfect redemption, propitiation, and satisfaction, for all the sins of the whole world

– is pruned by Eliot to bring the language more firmly into conformity with the Catholic theology of the Mass.

This linguistic anachronism and selectivity implies and entails a defence of the Anglo-Catholicism which Eliot had recently embraced and which, to the audience of Anglicans of different degrees of churchmanship, at the Canterbury Festival, he would commend. The 1930s were confident, evangelistic years for Anglo-Catholicism and we note that it is in a sermon, precisely, that Thomas sets out the eucharistic doctrine which was a key article of faith for Anglo-Catholics of that generation. Virtually everybody in that original audience would have recognised the familiar Cranmerian phrases and cadence, from the communion service. Now they are being applied to the teaching of the Catholic sacrifice of the altar.

Eliot's composition of the sermon was influenced by Lancelot Andrewes (Eliot commenting, in 1961, that it was a 'faint reflection' of Andrewes' style[88]), another linguistic bridging of the division of Reformation, as Becket speaks in Andrewes' manner, focusing on the word, 'peace', and its multiple meanings:

> Now think for a moment about the meaning of this word 'peace'. Does it seem strange to you that the angels should have announced Peace, when ceaselessly the world has been stricken with War...? Reflect now, how Our Lord Himself spoke of Peace. He said to His disciples, 'Peace I leave with you, my peace I give unto you'. Did He mean peace as we think of it: the kingdom of England at peace with its neighbours, the barons at peace with the King, the householder counting over his peaceful gains...? If you ask that, remember then that He said also, 'Not as the world gives, give I unto you'. So then, He gave His disciples peace, but not peace as the world gives.... It is fitting on Christ's birth day, to remember what is that Peace which He brought.[89]

After Thomas's sermon, the cathedral priests ritually commemorate the three days which follow Christmas in the liturgical calendar: the feasts of St Stephen, St John and the Holy Innocents. The terminology that they use, 'the day of St. Stephen, First Martyr', 'the day of St. John the Apostle' and 'the day of the Holy Innocents', while close to that of the table of 'moveable and immoveable feasts' in the Prayer Book, is closer still to the description of the days in The English Missal. For example, in the Prayer Book, the 26th December is described as 'St. Stephen the Martyr' and the 27th as 'St. John the Evangelist'. In The English Missal, they are listed, respectively, as 'S. Stephen the First Martyr' and 'S. John, Apostle and Evangelist'. Moreover, Eliot's ceremonial directions – for example,

> Enter the Third Priest, with a banner of the Holy Innocents borne before him

– are immediately evocative of the Anglo-Catholic recovery of the ceremonial of pre-Reformation English Christianity and are elaborated (in the Anglo-Catholic way) as, previously, the two other Priests have brought in their processional banners and (the stage direction notes) 'The Priests stand together with the banners behind them'.[90]

In this section of *Murder in the Cathedral*, however, what is striking, again, is the linguistic anachronism of the language of the introits of these festival days, as sung by the priests, the introit being the first variable part of the Mass, composed from biblical sources, such as the psalms. These, of course, in the time of Thomas Becket, would have been in Latin, from the Missal.

Now, Eliot takes his texts, not even from The English Missal, but from The Book of Common Prayer (for example, from its version of the psalms by Miles Coverdale) and from that other great document of supposedly reformed English Christianity and of English language and literature, the Authorized Version of the Bible of 1611. Not only does Eliot use this Jacobean language anachronistically for the introits of the mediaeval Mass, but includes in that specifically Catholic setting one of the most contentious terms at the Protestant Reformation – the translation of '*ecclesia*' (by Catholicism, as 'Church'; by Protestantism, as 'congregation'). The introit for St John (taken from Ecclesiasticus 15:5) begins, in Latin, *'In medio Ecclesiae'* – 'in the midst of the Church' – which is, predictably, how it is translated in The English Missal. But Eliot prefers 'congregation'.

What may seem to be a confusion of tongues and theologies is deliberate: contradicting the order of time by applying a sixteenth-century reformed language to a medieval Catholic rite, Eliot heals the breach which Christian conflict over such words and meanings produced. The unity and continuity of the faith witnessed to at Canterbury in the twelfth century is thereby demonstrated to the Canterbury Festival-goers in the twentieth.

The Third Priest's introit for the Holy Innocents is richly biblical, expanding upon the spare liturgical material in The Book of Common Prayer, but retaining that diction as it appropriates the more generous provisions of the Missal. This is the introit in the Latin rite, from Psalm 8:3:

> Ex ore infantium, Deus, et lactentium perfectisi laudem, propter inimicos tuos.

Here is Coverdale's version of the verse, in the Psalms in The Book of Common Prayer:

> Out of the mouth of very babes and sucklings hast thou
> ordained strength, because of thine enemies ...

and this, The English Missal's:

> Out of the mouths of babes, O God, and of sucklings, hast
> thou perfected praise because of thine adversaries.

Eliot duplicates the Prayer Book's

> Out of the mouth of very babes ...

but goes on to include phrases not only from Cranmer's collect, epistle
and gospel for the day, but the richer liturgical material of the Missal,
as translated in The English Missal:

> As the voice of many waters, of thunder, of harps,
> They sung as it were a new song.
> The blood of thy saints have they shed like water,
> And there was no man to bury them. Avenge, O Lord,
> The blood of thy saints. In Rama, a voice heard, weeping.
> Out of the mouth of very babes, O God!

The third line here, 'The blood of thy saints ...', for example, is not in
the lections of The Book of Common Prayer for the Holy Innocents,
but is in the Latin Missal in the tract (the chant sung at Mass on penitential says instead of the 'alleluia') which appears, in this form, in
The English Missal:

> The blood of the Saints have they shed like water on every
> side of Jerusalem. V[ersicle]. And there was no man to bury
> them. V[ersicle]. Avenge, O Lord, the blood of thy Saints,
> that is shed upon the earth.

Nevill Coghill correctly notes the original biblical sources of these
various texts in his edition of *Murder in the Cathedral*,[91] but the more
immediate and relevant source was Eliot's encounter with this material in the Anglo-Catholic liturgy in the observance of the octave of
Christmas.

The last words of the play are in the language of The Book of
Common Prayer:

> Lord, have mercy upon us.
> Christ, have mercy upon us.
> Lord, have mercy upon us.
> Blessed Thomas, pray for us.

What Eliot has added, in the final line, to this incantatory formula, familiar to him from the daily offices of Morning and Evening Prayer, is the women's petition to their new saint to pray to God for them. Such prayers were explicitly excluded by Cranmer and the other reformers from their Protestantising liturgies to eradicate the practice of petitions to the saints which was based on the belief that they – principally, the Virgin Mary – would act as intermediaries between mankind and God. In combining the familiar language of such prayers, 'Blessed Thomas, pray for us', as found in the popular litanies of the saints, with the Cranmerian diction, Eliot, again, in the tradition of Anglo-Catholicism, would resolve the disagreement and restore what had been reformed, mutilated or simply suppressed into seamless accordance and unity with Catholic faith and order.

4

Eliot's last substantial published work was, as we have noted, neither a poem nor a play, but his essay on George Herbert. He had written about Herbert on several occasions, and, as Ronald Schuchard has demonstrated,[92] Eliot's estimation of the early-seventeenth-century poet-priest changed significantly (in a positive direction) during the 1930s. By 1938, in a little-known address to the Friends of Salisbury Cathedral (located near Bemerton, which had been Herbert's parish), at the invitation of the Dean, E.L. Henderson, Eliot ascribed to Herbert, as a religious poet, 'a pre-eminence among his contemporaries and followers'. He was 'the most intellectual of all our religious poets' and (now focusing on matters close to his own spirituality) a man 'for whom sin was very real, and the promises of death very terrible'. Revealing, also, of Eliot's own religious interests (and certainly surprising to those who read Herbert in terms of the temperate devotion of the *via media*), is Eliot's further assertion that

> the only poetry I can think of which belongs to quite the same class as Herbert – as expression of purity and intensity of religious feeling, and … for literary excellence – is St John of the Cross.

Unlike John Donne (for whom Eliot had had the highest regard), whose poetry yields 'clues to a peculiarly interesting personality' behind it, with Herbert

> we do not ask to know more of him than what is conveyed in his utterance of his meditations on the highest spiritual

mysteries. Within his limits, therefore, he achieves the greatest universality in his art; he remains as the human soul
contemplating the divine.[93]

Probably the key word in that high evaluation is 'universality'. We
know that it is a concept Eliot regarded as synonymous with the classical, Catholic temper.

Yet, in his major and final study of Herbert, in describing the poet's
Christianity, Eliot does concentrate on the particular, personal aspects
of Herbert's faith, which (he argues) inspired Herbert's verse:

> It was only in the faith, in hunger and thirst after godliness,
> in [Herbert's] self-questioning and his religious meditation,
> that he was inspired as a poet.

The Temple, Eliot continues, in the same vein and with the same
scriptural allusion, is

> the personal record of a man very conscious of weakness
> and failure, a man of intellect and sensibility who hungered
> and thirsted after righteousness.… [It is] a coherent sequence
> of poems setting down the fluctuations of emotion between
> despair and bliss, between agitation and serenity, and the dis-
> cipline of suffering which leads to peace of spirit.[94]

By this stage in Eliot's evolving appreciation of Herbert, we find that
Herbert sounds more like the Donnean personality from which Eliot
had differentiated him in the 1938 Salisbury Cathedral address – the
mixture of emotion and intellect, which he had always appreciated
in Donne: the association of sensibility, indeed, in which mind and
heart, the spiritual and the sensual self are united and find expression
in powerful and profound religious poetry.

In 'To Criticize the Critic', of 1961 (the year before), Eliot
affirms that Herbert was one of those who 'has best responded to my
need in middle and later age'.[95] His mature appreciation contradicts
the conventional idea of Herbert and of his verse as expressive of
the temperate, settled Christian life usually associated with the idea-
lisation of Herbert's biography in his last few priestly years and
the general notion of Anglican moderation between the extremes
of Protestantism and Rome, of which he has long been seen to be
one of the most noteworthy spokesmen (and which, indeed, he
celebrates in 'The British Church'). But Eliot divines, beneath the
polish and usually restrained expression of the lyrics (so apparently
different from Donne's anguished religious poetry, especially in the

Holy Sonnets) the intensity of Herbert's religious pilgrimage. For that reason, it speaks to Eliot as one who had known the ongoing struggle with scepticism and despair and who, from the beginning of his Anglo-Catholic life, had had a keen appreciation of the need for the most rigorous spiritual discipline. Eliot's repetition of the phrase from the fourth beatitude in Matthew's gospel, to 'hunger and thirst after righteousness', emphasises the character of this shared faith experience:

> these poems form a record of spiritual struggle which should touch the feeling, and enlarge the understanding of those readers also who hold no religious belief and find themselves unmoved by religious emotion.... *The Temple* is not to be regarded simply as a collection of poems, but (as I have said,) as a record of the spiritual struggles of a man of intellectual power and emotional intensity who gave much toil to perfecting his verses. As such, it should be a document of interest to all those who are curious to understand their fellow men.[96]

The key words here are as apt in the description of Eliot's own faith, as they are of Herbert's: especially the emphasis on 'struggle'; the portrait of Herbert as a man of 'intellectual power and emotional intensity'; the idea of him as a poet who 'gave much toil to perfecting his verses' of a religious kind (Helen Gardner's edition of the *Four Quartets* manuscripts shows Eliot in the same way); and noteworthy, too, is Eliot's commendation of *The Temple* as a work which should appeal to the non-Christian, as well as the person of faith – as has happened with his own poetry.

Where the booklet reveals its precisely Anglo-Catholic author is in Eliot's requirement of Herbert's reader that he or she should have an acquaintance with the 'liturgy of the Church' and 'the traditional imagery of the Church'. In referring to the second poem in the sequence, 'The Sacrifice', where Herbert uses the refrain 'Was ever grief like mine' (spoken by the Lord from the Cross on Good Friday – the 'sacrifice' which is the subject of the poem), Eliot stresses the liturgical influence in reference to The English Missal:

> We are ... better prepared if we recognise the Lamentations of Jeremiah, and the Reproaches in the Mass of the Pre-sanctified which is celebrated on Good Friday.
> Celebrant: I led thee forth out of Egypt....
> Deacon and Subdeacon: O my people....[97]

This was the liturgical source which Eliot himself had used poetically in *Ash-Wednesday*, his Lenten poem. Why 'better prepared'? Because, Eliot argues, Herbert had 'an ear trained by the music of liturgy'. That is, in the Anglo-Catholic way, Eliot is urging that it was from the liturgical Reproaches, rather than from the biblical account of the Passion, which was their source, that the incantatory device of the refrain in 'The Sacrifice' derives.

Similarly, in the account of Herbert's priestly ministry, the note of Eliot's Anglo-Catholicism emerges in the way he characterises and praises it:

> He was an exemplary parish priest, strict in his own obser-
> vances and a loving and generous shepherd of his flock....
> a little flock of rustics, to whom he laboured to explain the
> meaning of the rites of the Church, the significance of Holy
> Days, in language that they could understand.

We know that part of the fruit of that ministry was encouraging the parishioners to join their priest (as Izaak Walton wrote) 'dayly in the public celebration of Divine Service',[98] one of the ideals of the Catholic Movement. 'Seven whole days, not one in seven', Herbert wrote (in the poem that became the hymn that Eliot asked to be sung at his memorial service), 'I will praise thee'. And Herbert, like Eliot, was devoted to the sacrament of penance, one of the hallmarks of Anglo-Catholic spirituality. Eliot notes Herbert's zeal in fostering its use and his encouragement of other priests to make their people appreciate (what Herbert described and Eliot quotes as) 'the great good use of this antient and pious ordinance'.[99]

The restrained Anglican regime of Sunday worship and of general (non-sacramental) confession, in the course of that weekly public worship, belonged to another world from the Catholic-minded sacramental and liturgical spirituality to which both Herbert and Eliot were committed and which Eliot commended in his final literary work.

In Westminster Abbey, on 4th February, 1965, at Eliot's memorial service, choir and congregation, singing Herbert's 'King of glory, King of peace',[100] in fulfilment of Eliot's wishes, paid tribute, thereby, to both poets, and their witness to the Catholic tradition of the Church of England:

> King of glory, King of peace,
> I will love thee;
> And that love may never cease,
> I will move thee.

Thou hast granted my request,
Thou hast heard me;
Thou didst note my working breast,
Thou hast spared me.

Wherefore with my utmost art
I will sing thee,
And the cream of all my heart
I will bring thee.
Though my sins against me cried,
Thou didst clear me;
And alone, when they replied,
Thou didst hear me.

Seven whole days, not one in seven,
I will praise thee;
In my heart, though not in heaven,
I can raise thee.
Small it is, in this poor sort
To enrol thee:
E'en eternity's too short
To extol thee.

Conclusion

I don't believe that any religion can survive which is not a
religion of the supernatural and of life after death in some
form.... I think that the end of a purely materialistic civilization with all its technical achievements and its mass
amusement is ... simply boredom. A people without religion
will in the end find that it has nothing to live for.

(Eliot, BBC Radio interview, 1956)[1]

[No-one] has ever climbed to the higher stages of the
spiritual life, who has not been a believer in a particular
religion ... [with] his own religion of dogma and doctrine
in which he believes.

(Eliot, Preface to Thoughts for Meditation, 1951)[2]

Eliot lived to see the beginning of the decline of Anglo-Catholicism
and its influence in the Anglican Communion, after the Second World
War – a decline which was to be accelerated, in the years beyond Eliot's
death, in the wake of the so-called renewal of the Second Vatican
Council, when various ritual victories which had been hard-won by
Anglo-Catholics took on a pyrrhic quality when Rome herself began
to abandon her elaborate, age-old liturgies, and such as the Western
Use for High Mass was left virtually for Anglo-Catholics alone to
celebrate. Accompanying this (and of which the liturgical changes
were undoubtedly an expression) was a questioning of theological
certainties and authority – in such as Liberation Theology, politically,
and in an increasingly vocal scepticism, particularly amongst the laity
(now more educated than ever) about the Church's mandated moral
teachings – all of which amounted to powerful challenges to that Catholic orthodoxy to which Anglo-Catholics aspired. The rejection by
many Catholic laypeople of the papal condemnation of all forms of
birth control except the 'rhythm method' in the encyclical, *Humane*

Vitae (issued in 1968, the year of campus revolutions), is the most obvious example of this.

Moreover, the strength of the Anglo-Catholic movement, Michael Yelton has argued, had abided substantially in its strongholds in churches in the centres of large cities. Not only were many of these districts destroyed during the Second World War, but the dispersal of population from the inner cities to suburban areas took people to regions where Anglo-Catholicism, usually, had made much less impact.[3] Further afield, in the rural world, where there had been some significant Anglo-Catholic pockets, the increasing amalgamation of parishes usually had the effect of watering-down the extremities, both high and low, of once-separate churches and their individual traditions. The 'parish communion' movement, while emphasising an important principle of Anglo-Catholicism, namely the centrality of the Mass and the need for regular communion, made its celebration the normative rite of parish worship. This meant that (as with amalgamations) there was a broadening influence, in terms of ceremonial. So the need to emphasise sacramental, liturgical worship – by, for example, High Mass and outdoor processions – became less imperative as everyone, apart from extreme Evangelicals, was moving to the point where the Holy Communion service was their usual liturgy and where nearly all churches had at least some of the Catholic appurtenances of worship (candles, altar frontals, vestments, even weekday and holy day Masses) which could generally satisfy the Catholic-minded Anglican. Frequent communion (usually weekly, for the committed churchgoer) meant that special devotions to the Host in the Reserved Sacrament, in Benediction and other ceremonies – all once hallmarks of Anglo-Catholic parish life – had less purpose, further diminishing the distinctiveness of Anglo-Catholicism on which much of its missionary zeal and sense of identity depended. And, as in Rome, religious communities – concentrated centres of Anglo-Catholic faith, teaching and spirituality – suffered severely and many were dispersed or dissolved in the latter part of the twentieth century. In the same period, the very term 'Anglo-Catholic' started to fall out of fashion (probably because the phenomenon it described was ceasing to exist) and 'Anglican Catholic' started to replace it.

By remaining as a worshipper in the same parish church, St Stephen's, Gloucester Road, where Fr Cheetham's ongoing presence, at least through the first half of the 1950s, ensured continuity from the time of the heyday of the movement twenty years before, Eliot was preserved from immediate exposure to the burgeoning decline which did not really take its toll until the 1970s. Some Anglo-Catholic parishes resisted 'renewal', even then, but most, as Yelton puts it, have now lapsed into preserving

> some externals of Catholic worship with a wishy-washy theology overlaid with glutinous sentimentality.[4]

In other words, they have become like most contemporary, post-Conciliar Roman Catholic parishes, in theology and liturgy. As a result, there is virtually no parish today where the liturgy, theology and spirituality with which Eliot was familiar is wholeheartedly and popularly pursued, and Anglo-Catholicism as he knew it and was attracted to it, submitting himself to its rigorous disciplines of faith and practice, is no more. Little Gidding itself presents a telling example of this decline from Eliot's principles. In 1981, a community of 'Christ the Sower' was formally established there, with ecumenical worship, for members from the Roman Catholic, Anglican and Free Churches and the utterly non-sacramental Quaker tradition.[5]

This recognition of the extent to which Anglo-Catholicism has changed, declined and, virtually disappeared in our time, in terms of what Eliot would have identified as 'Anglo-Catholic' faith and practice, emphasises the importance of recovering what it was like in the years of his own practice of the faith, if we would understand his life, thought and work in that period and context. This has been the purpose of this book. Sheridan Gilley, a convert from Anglo- to Roman Catholicism, lamented (in 1996) that vanished world, 'the most culturally attractive form of Christianity that I have ever encountered', where he 'first learned of the doctrine of the Church':

> The decline of Anglo-Catholicism seems to me to be a serious impoverishment of Christianity. No one who has not known the High Church tradition from the inside can appreciate its seductive fascinations. It took all that is best and most beautiful in the Church of England, the King James Bible, the Book of Common Prayer, with its wonderful Cranmerian cadences, the ancient English cathedrals and parish churches, a tradition of literature and a tradition of learning, and the kindness, gentleness and tolerance of English life, and enriched them with judicious borrowings from the doctrine, devotion and scholarship of the wider Catholic world. It seemed the perfect meeting place between Catholicity and Englishness, without the harshness and philistinism of English Roman Catholicism, which has spent a generation destroying everything that

was most beautiful about itself. Now that whole Anglican gothic world has come to grief.[6]

In this succinct catalogue of the glories of Anglo-Catholicism, we have, indeed, the essence of what attracted Eliot to that theologically-profound, culturally-centred and numinously-beautiful English incarnation of the Christian, Catholic faith. And it was strongly attracted to him. His name and witness – usually in quotation from his poetry – became predictable presences in writings of an Anglo-Catholic kind (by Anglo-Catholics or about Anglo-Catholicism), from the 1930s. He became a much-admired expression of the tradition he had joined. For more than a generation, he was the unofficial representative (and the best-known contemporary example) of the Anglo-Catholic layman of the intellectual and cultured kind. So we find, for example, that the concluding chapter of one in the series of great twentieth-century archiepiscopal biographies, Charles Smyth's life of Cyril Garbett (1875-1955), Archbishop of York, has, as its epigraph, sixteen lines of quotation from 'East Coker' for which Smyth thanks 'Mr T.S. Eliot, O.M.'.[7] Garbett was a voracious reader. On his days off, the bishop 'used generally to carry in his pocket … a well-worn copy either of Wordsworth's *Prelude* or T.S. Eliot's *Four Quartets*'.[8] H.A. Wilson's *Received with Thanks*, published in 1940, is a collection of affectionate, celebratory biographical essays on several priestly heroes of the inter-war Anglo-Catholic movement. In the acknowledgements, Eliot is listed and a quotation from *Murder in the Cathedral* – 'O father, father gone from us, lost to us' (the First Priest's lament after Thomas' martyrdom)[9] – is applied to the account of the Solemn Mass of Requiem, of one of the priests, Harold Pollock, vicar of St Peter's, London Docks, a centre of the Catholic Revival.[10] And we have referred to Eliot's presence in the most famous of Anglo-Catholic novels, Rose Macaulay's *Towers of Trebizond*.

Yet, given the decline of Anglo-Catholicism, it was fortunate that (for the reasons we have considered, especially in Chapter 7) Eliot did not, for the most part, write poetry that was distinctively Anglo-Catholic in character and reference. In a Western world where even basic Christian references in literature now have to be spelt out even to otherwise well-read and intelligent people, a poetry of Anglo-Catholicism (if one could imagine such a phenomenon) would be as comprehensible and accessible to most readers today as the Rosetta Stone.

Eliot's poetry may be evasive, with regard to explicit evocation of what it meant to be, in his words, an 'Anglo-Catholic in religion', but the presence of that faith and practice is there, as we have suggested, in subtle and persisting ways. It was the central element, the still point, in the poet's world-picture, from the time of the composition of 'Journey of the Magi' in 1927, until his death in 1965, informing all that he did, in his creative work and, of course, his personal life. We cannot enter fully into the mind of the intelligence and spirit of those works of genius, in poetry, drama and literary criticism, nor into the life itself of the greatest poet of the twentieth century, until we have learnt of his faith, the ground of his being.

Appendix One

The Unpublished Letters and Diary of Mary Trevelyan

In the period 11th October, 1940 to 9th January, 1957, Eliot wrote regularly and often to Miss Mary Trevelyan, who preserved one hundred and twelve of his letters – seventy-four of them belonging to the most intensive period of this correspondence: the six years from 1943 to 1949.

Mary Trevelyan (1897-1983) was the daughter of the Revd G.P. Trevelyan and Eliot was inclined to introduce her (she notes in her diary for 1949) as the 'vicar's daughter'. She had trained, professionally, as an organist and choirmistress. Her musical ability was drawn upon by Eliot for the transcription of 'One-eyed Reilly', published at the conclusion of *The Cocktail Party* – the subject of a whimsical reminiscence in her diary (which she showed me) for 1948:

> We managed, with some difficulty, to transcribe 'One-eyed Reilly' – a song he had heard in his youth – for use in *The Cocktail Party*. Tom's singing was rather like an out-of-tune bassoon. However, I got it down on the back of an envelope and played it to him on the piano.

They had first met briefly (so her diary records) in July, 1938 at a Student Christian Movement conference held at Swanwick, Derbyshire, when Eliot gave a reading of *The Waste Land* and 'The Hollow Men', and Trevelyan – who was the director of music – had the responsibility of arranging his transport and accommodation. Later that year, she invited Eliot to another poetry reading at Student Movement House (of which she was the warden) in Russell Square, London. They did not meet again until 1940, at another reading for students, and the first letter to her from Eliot which Trevelyan preserved (dated 11th October, 1940) concerns arrangements for this third encounter. The correspondence concluded with a letter written by the poet on the eve of his second marriage in 1957.

Trevelyan retired from her work amongst overseas students in London in 1967 and received the CBE in 1968 in acknowledgement of her long contribution to their welfare. During her friendship with Eliot, they attended St Stephen's regularly, the basis of their friend-ship being their shared Anglo-Catholic faith. Eliot gave her a motor-car in which she drove him to Mass. Sometimes, Eliot would refer to Mary as 'Julia', and indeed, modeled that character in *The Cocktail Party* (written when their friendship was in mid-course) on her.

I arranged to meet Mary Trevelyan twice in 1975, in her flat on the London Embankment, at the suggestion of Helen Gardner who believed that, given Eliot's and Trevelyan's friendship, based on a shared Christianity, Trevelyan would be of invaluable assistance to me in my understanding of his Anglo-Catholicism. Miss Trevelyan allowed me to read her typed transcription of her selection of the letters, 'reproduced', she notes in her diary, to which she also gave me access, 'exactly as he typed or wrote them – spelling, punctuation and all'.

Trevelyan had prepared this material with the intention of pub-lication, but Valerie Eliot refused to give her permission for this. Eliot had urged Trevelyan, in a letter to her of 30th October, 1944, to preserve her letters to him and some of them were published (by Longmans in 1946), without indicating to whom they were address-ed, in her memoir, *I'll Walk Beside You*.

In addition to the poet's substantial correspondence with her (he had written her more than 200 letters in the course of their friend-ship)[1] and within her diary narrative (which he also admired, telling her, in a letter to her of 13th October, 1944, that he found it absorb-ing), Trevelyan recorded a number of her conversations with Eliot, which – she writes in a note at the beginning – she attempted to set down 'immediately after I had seen him'. These are not (therefore) *verbatim* records, of course – and I have used them sparingly – but the meticulousness of the diary (kept 'ever since my student days', Trevelyan also notes, on an 'almost daily' basis), its consistency throughout with the facts and opinions expressed in Eliot's letters, inspire more than a measure of confidence in their accuracy.

Eliot, as he emerges from his letters to Mary Trevelyan, and from her diary and accounts of their conversations, is an essentially private figure (in these years of his burgeoning international fame), anxious to communicate and share a variety of personal joys, disappointments and worries, mischievously exchanging gossip, often concerned about ecclesiastical controversies and matters of liturgy and theology (us-ually in connection with some mutual friend of his and Mary's), the penitent and communicant occasionally troubled about the quality of his devotional life: the churchwarden of St Stephen's, in other words, rather than the winner of the Nobel Prize and member of the Order of Merit. Trevelyan notes in her diary for 1948:

> In the Birthday Honours this year Tom received the ORDER OF MERIT – to him the greatest of all honours. In September he took the precaution [to avoid the public fuss of the event] of spending his sixtieth birthday at sea.... In November his painfully written *Notes Towards the Definition of Culture* [*sic* – '*towards*', as here, is usually, erroneously, given a capital 't'] was published after five years' hard work and had a mixed reception; there were complaints of its obscurity. My copy was inscribed 'in all simplicity'. In December came the Nobel Prize. The letters which followed me faithfully to Burma, Malaya, North Borneo and Thailand made little mention of these notable events.

I am grateful to Mary Trevelyan for giving me access to this important material, crucial to the understanding of Eliot's Anglo-Catholicism, for sharing her memories of Eliot with me and giving me permission to quote from her diary.

Appendix Two
The Unpublished Papers of George Every

In addition to six informative letters which he wrote to me and an interview in Oxford in which he responded to further queries, George Every (1909-2003) – whom Eliot knew from 1933 as a lay brother at the Society of the Sacred Mission, Kelham (a quasi-monastic Anglo-Catholic male religious community near Newark in Nottinghamshire) – kindly gave to me (on extended loan) two unpublished papers he had written since Eliot's death in 1965 about the poet's faith and its influence on his work: 'Living Tradition' and 'Eliot as a Friend and a Man of Prayer'. He also gave to me an unpublished transcription of a discussion in which Eliot took part in 1936 with the brethren at Kelham on the subject of religious drama, and – most interestingly – the draft of his unpublished verse play, *Stalemate*, dealing with King Charles's visit to Little Gidding (which Every had given to Eliot for comment in 1936). I have seen Eliot's unpublished letter of reply to Every concerning this work. *Stalemate* is most significant, of course, in relation to Eliot's own interest in Little Gidding in these years. He visited the church there soon after reading the play (in May, 1936) and that visit was to be commemorated in the poem devoted to Little Gidding, his last major poem and, so, in a sense, the climax of his *oeuvre*.

George Every eventually left Anglo-Catholicism for Roman Catholicism (in 1973, soon after Kelham closed), moving into St Mary's College, Oscott, the seminary of the archdiocese of Birmingham.

I was delighted to be able to inform Helen Gardner of the discovery of *Stalemate*, as she was working, at that very time, on editing the manuscripts of *Four Quartets*. In her edition, she opines that Eliot's reading of Every's play, where fire is linked with Little Gidding, inspired the poet's linkage of that element with the place in 'the discussion of victory and defeat in Part III' of the poem.[1]

Appendix Three
T.S. Eliot and C.S. Lewis

Eliot and Lewis were contemporaries and leading lay apologists, within Anglicanism, for the Christian faith in the modern secular age. The warming of their relationship, which took many years, is partly explained by Lewis' journey towards Catholic faith and practice within his Anglicanism. It is likely that his growing friendship with Eliot and increasing appreciation of his work influenced this marked change of churchmanship.

Lewis' Christianity began in the Ulster Protestantism of the Church of Ireland in which he was baptised, at birth, in 1898, with its conviction that the further removed was one's faith from Roman Catholicism, the nearer one approached to God. If anything, it was even more hostile to Anglo-Catholicism as representing the enemy within. Not surprisingly, with this background, Lewis retained an antipathy to Catholicism after his mature conversion to Christianity (around 1928, the same period as Eliot's baptism and confirmation), having been indifferent to his initial Church of Ireland affiliation. His friendship with the ultra-orthodox Roman Catholic J.R.R. Tolkien – the two of them were leading members of the group of 'Inklings' in Oxford – did not quell Lewis' deep-seated anti-Romanism, Tolkien always regretting that Lewis, in returning to Christianity, joined the Church of England, not Rome. Yet, as his Anglicanism developed, Lewis definitely became more Catholic in orientation, to the point where his observances and beliefs were accurately described (as John Wain, indeed, described them after his experience of the Inklings during the Second World War[1]) as Anglo-Catholic in character. This protracted journey in churchmanship paralleled Lewis's relationship with Eliot.

In literary terms, Lewis began in hostile repudiation of Modernism. 'I like lines that will scan', he affirmed, and he proposed a crusade against Eliot in 1926, initiating years of 'sniping at that poet'.[2] The sniping included ridicule of Eliot's newfound religious beliefs. He was characterised by Lewis as a 'Neo-Angular',

> trying to make of Christianity itself one more high-brow,
> Chelsea, bourgeois-baiting fad. T.S. Eliot is the single man
> who sums up the thing I'm fighting against.[3]

Eliot found himself being attacked not only by atheists and neo-
pagans for his reactionary *volte-face*, but, in Lewis' polemic, by a
fellow Christian (indeed, Anglican) convert.

Lewis even subjected the priest, William Force Stead, who had
baptised Eliot, to a prank. With some collaborators, he wrote a parody of Eliot's poetry and showed it to Stead who 'expressed a
serious enthusiasm for it. But this seemed to indicate not so much
that the poetry was good poetry as that Stead was a hopeless judge,
and shortly after this the prank petered out'.[4]

Lewis misconstrued Eliot's Anglicanism as 'High and Dry', 'not
merely sectarian', Humphrey Carpenter writes, but 'also emotion-
ally barren and counter-Romantic'.[5] Lewis had much to learn about
Anglo-Catholicism and Eliot. The catalyst in this process appears to
have been the poet and novelist, Charles Williams, a fellow Inkling,
whom Lewis revered and who, in turn, had a high regard for Eliot who
had commissioned and published several of Williams' idiosyncratic
mystical and quasi-historical works. Lewis would have understood
Eliot's judgement on Williams:

> He seemed to me to approximate, more nearly than any man
> I have known familiarly, to the saint ...[6]

such sanctity being demonstrated, for Eliot, by Williams' behaviour
in the unlikely setting of one of Ottoline Morrell's *soirées*:

> One retained the impression that he was pleased and grateful
> for the opportunity of meeting the company, and yet that it
> was he who had conferred a favour – more than a favour, a
> kind of benediction, by coming.[7]

By the time that Eliot and Lewis were introduced to each other by
Williams in Oxford in the last months of the Second World War, Lewis'
Anglicanism included associations with religious communities and
regular attendance at the Eucharist, on saints' days as well as Sundays, in the Anglo-Catholic way. The initial meeting, however, was
not a success:

> Eliot's opening remark scarcely delighted Lewis: 'Mr Lewis,
> you are a much older man than you appear in photographs'.
> The tea party progressed poorly, and was enjoyed by no one ex-
> cept Charles Williams, who seemed to be immensely amused.

Nonetheless, Lewis' essential conservatism, socially and religiously, which had grown on him over the years, made Eliot, in spite of his Modernist poetry, an increasingly sympathetic figure. Like Eliot, he abhorred liberalism in religious thought – satirised in the form of 'Mr Broad' in his *Pilgrim's Regress* (1933) – and by the end of the 1950s, he and Eliot had established a friendly rapport:

> One day in the summer of 1959 Lewis and Joy [Davidman, his wife of three years] had lunch with Eliot and his new wife Valerie. It was an event which the pre-war Lewis would have declared to be in every respect impossible.[8]

Earlier, however, both men would similarly have supposed that the happiness they both experienced in marriage – of being, in Lewis' phrase from Wordsworth, 'surprised by joy' – would also have been impossible. Their friendliness seemed to exemplify Eliot's theory in 'Little Gidding' about the resolution, under grace, of old antipathies.

Appendix Four
T.S. Eliot and Anti-Semitism

It is nonsense ... about Eliot being antisemitic. Of course
you can find what would now [1948] be called antisemitic
remarks in his early work, but who didn't say such things
at that time? ... [D]isliking Jews isn't intrinsically worse
than disliking Negroes or Americans or any other block of
people. In the early twenties, Eliot's antisemitic remarks
were about on a par with the automatic sneer one casts at
Anglo-Indian colonels in boarding houses.... Some people
go around smelling after antisemitism all the time.

(George Orwell, *Collected Essays*)[1]

One of the most serious and persistent charges to have been brought
against Eliot and his poetry and prose is that he was and they are
anti-Semitic. The seriousness of the allegation is intensified, in Eliot's
case, because of his publicly-professed Christianity.

To be anti-Semitic and Christian is a contradiction in terms. Founded by a Jew, Christianity developed out of Judaism: historically,
scripturally, theologically and liturgically. Yet the Church has traditionally taught the necessity of the conversion of the Jews to
the fullness of religious truth, and its cruel persecution of them at
various periods in history are amongst the most shameful episodes
of its chequered past. Although the immediate motivations of the
Holocaust, in the twentieth century, were nationalist and secular,
the phenomenon drew upon age-old prejudices against Judaism in
European Christian history. Even during the Nazi atrocities, it has
been alleged that Church authorities, in particular Pope Pius XII,
were negligent and tardy in coming to the defence of the Jews.[2]

To what extent, if at all, can Eliot be implicated in this ancient
prejudice? More specifically, can he be charged with having contributed to the persecution of the Jews under Nazism, through the
influence of his writings before the Second World War? If he was

an anti-Semite, how does this reflect upon his Christianity and our assessment of it?

Although allegations of Eliot's anti-Semitism have often been made and Christopher Ricks has devoted a chapter to the subject in *T.S. Eliot and Prejudice*,[3] the only complete study is Anthony Julius' *T.S. Eliot, anti-Semitism and literary form*,[4] where the title establishes the connection, embedding the allegation ('anti-Semitism') between the undeniable facts of Eliot's existence and his contribution to 'literary form'. Julius claims both that Eliot was thoroughly possessed of the prejudice and that he contributed to the persecution of the Jews, in the modern age, through his writings. 'Of the many different kinds of anti-Semite, Eliot was the rarest kind', he writes, 'one who was able to place his anti-Semitism at the service of his art' (p.11).

Jewish himself, Julius has dedicated the book 'In memory of my father', but it is a *cri de coeur* on behalf of the whole Jewish race and especially those murdered in the death camps.

Julius' intense personal engagement with his topic is revealed at the beginning of his study when he records that the lines in 'Gerontion' (1920),

> And the Jew squats on the window-sill, the owner,
> Spawned in some estaminet of Antwerp,
> Blistered in Brussels, patched and peeled in
>   London...

'sting like an insult' (p.1). Such references make his 'face flush' and cause him 'acute... indignation and pain'. He gives the line from 'Gerontion' in its original form, 'And the jew...', with the lower-case 'j', emphasising Eliot's alleged condescension.

From the outset, before Julius has assembled such evidence as he is able to bring to it, we confront the major problem with his argument. The author is aggrieved: he is Jewish and he has been gravely insulted by Eliot. These are facts which cannot be contradicted. But Julius deduces from that experience of outrage both the racist convictions and the anti-Semitic intentions of Eliot and their effect, on Jews and non-Jews alike, before the Holocaust and since. He demands a 'correct' response from all Eliot's readers (including those many distinguished Jewish critics who have not been similarly disquieted) to the half-a-dozen Jewish allusions in the entire body of Eliot's work, and to various other instances where Julius discerns an unspoken anti-Semitism.

Julius' technique is a species of intellectual and moral blackmail. To resile, in any degree, from his analysis (which proceeds from his personal pain) is to put oneself – at least, in his judgement – in the position of endorsing anti-Semitism and its malevolent consequences. His is (he tells us) a 'remonstrative exegesis'. Debate and disagreement are eliminated: Eliot's poems 'insult Jews: to ignore these insults is to misread the poems' (p.2). If you do not accept Julius' identification and evaluation of Eliot's alleged anti-Semitism and decline to be similarly outraged, you are not only mistaken, but you are part of the problem: you are an anti-Semite.

Such ideologically-driven analyses of literature have become familiar in the academy in recent decades, with the same intimidating pseudo-morality: failure to recognise that an author is promoting 'unacceptable' ideas and to concur that his work must be indicted for the beliefs and prejudices it allegedly proposes, is to align oneself with the oppressor. Objective truth is the last consideration in these enterprises, as texts have interpretations imposed upon them to fulfil pre-ordained prejudices of the 'School of Resentment'.[5] So Julius turns on the Jewish critic, Wolf Markowitz, for failing to denounce 'Gerontion',

> displaying a demeaning absence of resentment toward its author (p.49).

Proceeding from the assumption of guilt (in Ricks' phrase, 'that one knows rather than suspects'[6]) and looking for anti-Semitism everywhere in Eliot, Julius inevitably finds it even where it does not exist. As he admits:

> sometimes it is the absence of any reference to Jews in an essay, or the refusal to acknowledge the anti-Semitism of a favoured writer, which may be anti-Semitic (p.6).

Meeting the argument about the scarcity of anti-Semitic allusions, Julius protests that it is the 'centrality' not the 'quantity' that matters (p.8). But how 'central' to a writer's work or thought can a couple of dozen words in the context of hundreds of thousands be, particularly when some of these – as in 'Gerontion' – are spoken by a character created by the poet, not necessarily representative of the poet himself?

Gerontion's observation that

> the Jew squats on the window-sill...

is a negative portrayal, certainly, of a sub-human creature. But this is satirical poetry as much ridiculing the speaker, the 'little old man' synonymous with decaying European culture after the First World

War, as the subjects of his disdain, including Hakagawa, Madame de Tornquist and Fraulein von Kulp. Julius is not concerned with the 'prejudices' that these xenophobic caricatures might be said to reveal and chooses not to recall that the presentation of peoples in animalic and other sub-human forms has been the stuff of polemic and satire through the ages: it is not peculiar to anti-Semitism. In the Counter-Reformation, Lutherans and Calvinists were likened to the evil of the pestilence by their Catholic antagonists. Alexander Pope's indictments of his opponents were scathing, and he was repaid in kind, portrayed as a monkey (or 'A P-e', playing on his name) by his contemporaries.

Julius would argue that Jews are a special case, because of the particular persecution they have suffered. But can they be immune, thereby, from satirical portrayal, while they are part of the human race and share in the follies of humanity? Since the beginning of time, these have been exposed by the poets.

The genre of satire is no respecter of persons or of religions or races, and for Julius to argue that the passing reference to the Jew in 'Gerontion' (and, we should note, that it is one Jew, not necessarily the Jewish race) 'degrades' Jews (p.18), is as compelling as to argue that Milton's Paradise of Fools degrades Catholics or that Eliot's 'Sweeney' poems insult the Irish. The Irish critic, Denis Donoghue rejects the charge, commenting that to call Eliot anti-Irish is 'as specious' as to call him anti-Semitic. Julius, in turn, rebukes Donoghue, accusing him of not 'caring' about anti-Semitism (p.40). One suspects that what Donoghue cares about is the truth.

To demand sacrosanctity from critical literary presentation – 'there is never a good time to be unfair to Jews' (p.37) – may do more harm to the cause of arresting anti-Semitism than any negative allusions, because it proposes a superiority to criticism for a chosen race. Would Jews be prepared to extend to other races (such as the Palestinians) the same immunity that they require – or at least Julius, in their name, requires – for themselves?

Julius argues, as one of the reasons for his study, that 'we should "bother" about Eliot's anti-Semitism; we should also be "bothered" by it' (p.9). Two objections are to be made to this. First, it suggests – contrary to fact – that the matter has not already received adequate (some would say, more than adequate) treatment; secondly, the quantity of 'bother' that Julius brings to the subject is grotesquely out of proportion to its significance in Eliot's thought as revealed in his writing. 'Eliot's not anti-Semitic in any sense', observed Robert Lowell, too sweepingly, 'but there is a certain dislike of

Jews in those early poems'.[7] The second part of the comment puts the matter sanely.

A few glancing references to Jews and Judaism – already exposed and analysed on numerous occasions – do not make either an anti-Semite or a major theme to be 'bothered' about in a writer's work. Julius criticises A.D. Moody for treating Eliot's anti-Semitism in an 'endnote' (p.10). But that is to register its significance precisely and wisely. The most that Eliot could be charged with, the Jewish critic, Irving Howe has claimed, is 'a few incidental lines of bigotry'. Cynthia Ozick similarly fails to be 'bothered' by 'the handful of insults' (p.51). Not significantly bothered, either, is George Steiner, while he identifies some 'Jew-despising passages' in Eliot's 'very great poetry'. Julius finds it 'troubling' that yet another Jewish critic fails to be stung into 'resentment' (p.119).

As Julius fails to contextualise, within the corpus, so he fails to contextualise Eliot's remarks historically. This is the most serious intellectual flaw in his polemic. Eliot's offending passages represent Jews negatively and no-one would argue that that negativity is thereby excused by the facts of historical and cultural prejudice which made such statements (and not only about Jews) commonplace. But at least it is explained, and, more importantly, the degree of nastiness of his remarks may also be properly assessed (which cannot be so when they are taken out of context, which is Julius' procedure). From our modern perspective, we find it almost unbelievable that a writer of Coventry Patmore's intelligence and sensitivity, in his immensely popular Victorian poem, 'The Angel in the House', could write of Disraeli:

> In the year of the great crime
> When the English Nobles and their Jew
> By God demented...

and that the devout Catholic convert could later comment that, hating Disraeli as he did, ' "Jew" or any stone seemed good enough to throw at such a dog'.[8] In that period, religious and racial prejudice of all kinds was commonplace. Advertisements for domestic and farm staff in Australia regularly carried the statement: 'Catholics [sometimes, less impolitely, 'Irish', but meaning the same thing] need not apply'. Landlords of boarding-houses in New York, in the inter-war period, regularly posted the sign 'No Dogs or Irish' (we note the precedence) in their windows. In those days, Protestants made remarks about Catholics, and vice versa, which now would be unthinkable, even in Northern Ireland. Reviewing the 1935 New York premiere of Jewish

George Gershwin's African-American opera, *Porgy and Bess*, in the
restrained and respected *New York Times*, highly-regarded composer
and critic, Virgil Thomson, managed a triplicity of racial prejudice
in one phrase:

> At best it is a ... highly unsavory stirring-up of Israel, Africa
> and the Gaelic Isles.... Gershwin does not even know what
> an opera is.[9]

Eliot's comment, in *After Strange Gods* (1934), that in an ideal
society, 'reasons of race and religion combine to make any large
number of free-thinking Jews undesirable' – a very carefully qualified observation, where the emphasis is as much on 'free-thinking' as
it is on 'Jews' – is, in fact, bland in comparison with contemporary
remarks about Jews in (for example) Fascist polemic. As Christopher
Ricks has pointed out, Eliot's is a statement with which a rabbi might
'concur' and 'Eliot never spared free-thinking Christians' either.[10]
Moreover, it is Eliot's most negative comment. It causes Julius'
'indignation and pain' to 'become acute' (p.1). What language of
outrage, then, would Julius apply to the inter-war racial policies of
'White Australia', for example, when the condemnation of Jews as
'the scum of Europe' was officially endorsed?[11] He has sensationalis-
ed the small case against Eliot, isolated it from 'the larger ... question
of prejudice in general' in his work and failed to recognise historical
and cultural change and development: 'we wince now, with good
cause, from almost any use of the word "race" '.[12]

Commenting on D.H. Lawrence's remarks, just before the First
World War, on the 'fat fatherly Jews and their motor cars and their
bathing tents' which he encountered near Broadstairs in Kent, Brenda
Maddox points out that

> Lawrence spoke with the casual anti-Semitism common to
> his day. There is no disguising that his prejudice was gen-
> uine – he saw the Jews as very alien – but, ugly as some of
> his remarks appear to later generations, it was in no sense
> blind bigotry, as some of his enduring friendships prove.[13]

'I hate Jews', Lawrence wrote, in the 1920s, referring to his *avant-
garde* New York publisher, Thomas Seltzer, 'and I want to learn to
be more wary of them'.[14] Using bestial imagery, he spoke of 'money-
hogs in motorcars, mostly Jews'[15] and the priest of love also referred,
at the beginning of the 1930s, to 'those little Jew booksellers'.[16]
As Lawrence's biographer points out, none of this was exceptional
by the standards of the time. Yet it is at least as severe and more

sustained than the alleged egregious anti-Semitism of Eliot. Thomas
Edison (whom we would hope to credit with some enlightenment)
employed Paul Auster's father (a Polish Jew) in his laboratory, only
to take the job 'away from him the next day because Edison learned
he was a Jew'.[17] To suggest that Eliot's statements were exceptional,
in the circumstances and that period, is to fly in the face of history.
Indeed, a case could be made to show that his statements were mild
and few, compared to those of others of comparable educational and
artistic background.

Attempting to prove Eliot's guilt by association, Julius adduces
examples of Wyndham Lewis' and Ezra Pound's anti-Semitism, but
again, the context undermines rather than validates his argument.
Eliot's allegedly anti-Semitic remarks are pale in comparison with his
friends' virulence. Virginia Woolf (Eliot's friend and contemporary)
said of her marriage to Leonard:

> how I hated marrying a Jew – how I hated their nasal voices,
> and their oriental jewellery, and their noses.[18]

Yet she and her husband were mutually devoted. On the strength of
her phrases – and Julius' indictment of Eliot is based entirely on the
evidence of a few phrases – is Virginia Woolf, too, responsible for
the Holocaust?

In finding abundant examples of the prejudice, Julius does not
seem to realise that this further minimises the peculiarity and intensity (as he strives to present it) of Eliot's racism which, compared
to Henry Adams' or Sir Thomas Browne's (who referred to 'that
contemptible and degenerate issue of Jacob') is mild indeed. Eliot's
prejudice – such as it was – was part of the prejudiced world to which
he belonged. Again (as one must reiterate), this does not render it
excusable. But it was unexceptional. To single Eliot out for such a
savage indictment is a prejudice in itself, based (like so many prejudices) on historical ignorance.

Not to charge Eliot, an 'anti-Semitic demagogue' (p.124), with
anti-Semitism 'would be a failure in literary criticism', Julius alleges
(p.27) because Eliot is always and everywhere an anti-Semite. He
had an 'aesthetic commitment to anti-Semitism' (p.92) and wrote
'Jew-hating poems' (p.138). Whenever he is ambiguous or critical in
his assessment of human beings or of life, he is actually being anti-
Semitic, because his principal preoccupation was the persecution of
Jews through his poetry. Even though he may appear to be talking
about Yeats or Charles I or midwinter spring or rose gardens, these
are 'larger equivocations' which have their source and their true

meaning in his essential 'enterprise' – 'the exploitation of anti-Semitic discourse' (p.29).

Eliot's explicit denials of his alleged anti-Semitism are either ignored or perversely read as racist by virtue of their perceived flaccidity:

> I am not an anti-Semite [Eliot remarked in 1956] and never have been. It is a terrible slander on a man.... in the eyes of the Church, to be anti-Semitic is a sin.[19]

And Julius chooses not to refer to Eliot's article 'The Christian Education of France' (1941), where Eliot insists that there should be 'some organised protest against such injustice [to the Jews], by the French ecclesiastical hierarchy ... no French government ... would enforce such measures or keep them on its statutes'.[20] Rather, Eliot's denials of racism are 'so routine that this denial itself has become one of the incidents of anti-Semitic discourse' (p.32). In other words, if Eliot says he is not anti-Semitic, he is lying. And if he says nothing about anti-Semitism, he is anti-Semitic by his complicity in a conspiracy of silence; and if he talks about something entirely different, he is anti-Semitic anyhow because, somehow or other, everything he says is part of the anti-Semitism that dominated his thought. How this passage from *Notes towards the Definition of Culture* can be seen to be the work an anti-Semite is difficult to imagine:

> It seems to me highly desirable that there should be close culture-contact between devout and practising Christians and devout and practising Jews. Much culture-contact in the past has been within those neutral zones of culture in which religion can be ignored and between Jews and Gentiles both more or less emancipated from their religious traditions. The effect may have been to strengthen the illusion that there can be culture without religion. In this context I recommend to my readers two books by Professor Will Herberg published in New York: *Judaism and Modern Man* (Farrar, Straus and Cudahy) and *Protestant-Catholic-Jew* (Doubleday).[21]

The most disgraceful charge that Julius brings against Eliot is that his work, contributing to the 'anti-Semitism of his times' (p.33), is one of the causes of the Holocaust. '*After Strange Gods* coincided with the inauguration of the Hitlerian persecution', he writes (p.163), as if the coincidence were deliberately timely. And Eliot's 'poems ... are persecutory' (p.38), he asserts. By 'poems', of course, he does not simply mean the two or three out of dozens where Eliot makes specific references to Jewish characters (such as Bleistein), but all the poetry, which, in being almost entirely silent about Jews, is *ipso facto*, anti-Semitic.

Eliot admired the Marx Brothers' films and became a correspondent and, eventually, a close friend of Groucho. The Brothers' brand of humour was quintessential Jewish New York. Julius, no doubt, would contend that this was just another example of Eliot's anti-Semitism – an exploitative relationship in which the poet used the comedian for entertainment. If so, the accounts of the warm friendship by the witty and perceptive Groucho must be read as exercises in gross self-delusion. If Eliot was as rabidly and incorrigibly anti-Semitic as Julius contends, why would he enter into personal correspondence with and seek out the company of a Jew?

Indicting Eliot for prejudice, Julius reveals his own. He argues that 'the poetry up to and including *The Waste Land* resists paraphrase', 'while the poetry thereafter'

> is too pious to be capable of fostering anything other than virtue in its readers (p.76).

To dismiss Eliot's forty years of poetry after *The Waste Land* (1922) as a kind of Christian homily to pious good conduct (and how 'The Hollow Men' of 1925 would conform to this description is impossible to imagine) is both an extraordinary over-simplification (and, to use the methods of ideological discernment Julius employs in discovering anti-Semitism everywhere in Eliot) evidence of Julius' anti-Anglo-Catholicism. But some religious prejudices are more acceptable than others, as Julius berates Eliot for his Christian orthodoxy (see, for example, p.201).

In the selective prejudices of today it is not only possible but unremarkable for Gore Vidal to write, in the *New York Review of Books* in 1986, that 'Eliot ended a mere Christian'. Of this, Ricks asks:

> ought liberal readers of the *New York Review* to acquiesce so happily in a crass prejudice against Christianity such as they would never countenance against any other religion?[22]

A self-proclaimed 'liberal' (see, for example, p.116), Julius, like so many of that paradoxical breed, extends his liberality only so far as you are prepared to agree with him.

T.S. Eliot, anti-Semitism and literary form smacks of the totalitarianism it rebukes. As a guide to Eliot's poetry, prose and thought, it is so misleading as to be vicious.

Notes

Preface

1. Faber and Faber, London, 1970, p.11. Hereafter cited as '*FLA*'. A few years later, in 'Catholicism and International Order', in *Essays Ancient and Modern* (Harcourt Brace, New York, 1936), Eliot acknowledged that his announcement of affiliations had become 'too easily quotable' (p.135). The year before, in *After Strange Gods* (Harcourt Brace, New York, 1934), he had described it as a 'dramatic posture' (p.30). Hereafter cited as '*ASG*'. Sheila Kaye-Smith, although (at the time) an Anglo-Catholic herself and the author of the best short study of the movement, is severely critical of the term. It is 'an etymological atrocity', she argues, and suggests a 'limited universalism – which is absurd'. Further, if the Church of England is Catholic, all of it is, not a party or movement within it (*Anglo-Catholicism*, Chapman and Hall, London, 1925, pp.vi-vii. Hereafter cited as 'Kaye-Smith').

2. Maurras led the right-wing *Action Française*, which was condemned by Pope Pius XI in 1927. Eliot continued addressing Maurras as '*Cher Monsieur et Maître*' (in Peter Ackroyd, *T.S. Eliot*, Hamish Hamilton, London, 1984, p.76. Hereafter cited as 'Ackroyd'). By 1940, however, he had recognised that 'the Pope understood [the *Action*'s] tendencies better' ('The Diversity of French Opinion', *The Idea of a Christian Society*, 1939; Faber and Faber, London, 1982, p.134. Hereafter cited as '*ICS*'.)

3. In Ronald Schuchard, *Eliot's Dark Angel: Intersections of Life and Art* (Oxford University Press, Oxford, 1999), p.55. Hereafter cited as 'Schuchard'.

4. 'To Criticize the Critic' (1961), *To Criticize the Critic* (Faber and Faber, London, 1965), p.15. Hereafter cited as '*TCTC*'.

5. *TCTC*, pp.14-15.

6 Letter to Francis Birrell, 3rd September, 1933, in John Cooper, *T.S. Eliot and the Ideology of 'Four Quartets'* (Cambridge University Press, Cambridge, 1995), p.200 n.3.

   Stephen Spender recalled that 'Virginia Woolf needled Eliot about his religion. Did he go to church? Yes. Did he hand round the plate for the collection? Yes. Oh, really! Then what did he experience when he prayed? Eliot leaned forward, bowing his head in that attitude which was itself one of prayer... and described the attempt to concentrate, to forget self, to attain union with God' (in Russell Kirk, *Eliot and His Age: T.S. Eliot's Moral Imagination in the Twentieth Century*, 2nd edn, ISI Books, Wilmington, 2008, p.56. Hereafter cited as 'Kirk').

It was a discomfiting period for literary agnostics and atheists: 'a writer's going over to Rome in the early '30s was as expected as a writer's going over to Moscow after 1935' – Baron Alder (on Evelyn Waugh), 'Odd couple more equal than others', *The Australian Literary Review,* 1st October, 2008, 22. Hereafter cited as 'Alder'.

7. *TCTC*, p.15.

8. In *On Poetry and Poets* (Faber and Faber, London, 1957), p.209. Hereafter cited as '*OPP*'.

9. More, in a letter to his daughter, 30th November, 1928, in A.H. Dakin, *Paul Elmer More* (Princeton University Press, Princeton, 1960), p.267. Hereafter cited as 'Dakin'.

10. 3rd August, 1929. In J.D. Margolis, *T.S. Eliot's Intellectual Development 1922-1939* (The University of Chicago Press, Chicago and London, 1972), p.143. Hereafter cited as 'Margolis'.

11. 18th November, 1928. In Dakin, p.266. More's use of the word 'claptrap' comes from Eliot's statement of his beliefs in *For Lancelot Andrewes*.

12. 11th August, 1929. In Dakin, p.269 n.1.

13. Eric Sigg, *The American T.S. Eliot: A Study of the Early Writings* (Cambridge University Press, Cambridge, 1989), p.222. Hereafter cited as 'Sigg'.

14. In Kirk, p.232.

15. *Anglican Papalism: An Illustrated History 1900-1960* (Canterbury Press, Norwich, 2005), p.55. Hereafter cited as 'Yelton'.

16. Cleo McNelly Kearns, 'Religion, literature, and society in the work of T.S. Eliot', in A. David Moody, ed., *The Cambridge Companion to T.S. Eliot* (Cambridge University Press, Cambridge, 1994), p.89. Hereafter cited as '*Companion*'. Kearns also subjects Eliot's statement, in 'The Dry Salvages', about temporal existence and its inevitable separation from God – that 'the agony abides' – to an extraordinary interpretation which derives from ignorance of the subtleties of Christian allegiance: 'The use of the word *abide* in this line, so dark in its context, yet so deeply a part of Christian devotion and consolation (through the wide dissemination of the beloved hymn "Abide with Me") is characteristic of Eliot' (p.83). What is 'dark' about this plain phrase is what Kearns has done with it. 'Abide with Me', from Eliot's Anglo-Catholic perspective – apart from what he would have thought of it as poetry – expresses morbid, nineteenth-century Protestant sentimentality:

> Hold thou thy Cross before my closing eyes;
> Shine through the gloom, and point me to the skies.

It was to this very hymn that Eliot referred – 'the community singing of *Abide with me* at a torchlight tattoo' – as an example of 'humanistic religious sentiment' (*ICS*, p.96). To suggest that its mawkishness might be the inspiration of Eliot's use of the word 'abides' in *Four Quartets* is ludicrous: both as a reading of the phrase itself and in the context of the tension that Eliot is probing between this-worldliness (the agony that abides) and other-worldliness. In the hymn, 'abide' is an imperative calling upon God's presence at the hour of death, while 'abides' in the poem is a frank recognition of the 'agony' (with a pertinent recollection of the Greek *agon* or 'contest') of the persistent daily struggle of ordinary life without God.

17. *The Cambridge Companion to T.S. Eliot* purports to be 'a carefully coordinated and fully rounded introduction' to the poet by 'an international team of leading T.S. Eliot scholars' (*Companion*, blurb). One looks in vain, in its index, for

'Anglo-Catholicism' – or, indeed, for 'Anglicanism' – although 'Buddhism' is there, with several references.

18. A. David Moody, *Thomas Stearns Eliot: Poet* (Cambridge University Press, Cambridge, 1994), p.149. Hereafter cited as 'Moody'.

19. *The Complete Poems and Plays of T.S. Eliot* (Faber and Faber, London, 1969), p.92. All references to Eliot's poetry and plays are from this edition. Hereafter cited as '*CPP*'.

    Moody also writes that 'Eliot's book remained the Bible' (Moody, p.131). This, too, sounds a false note. It would be odd, indeed, if this were the case, for an Anglo-Catholic. His 'book', religiously speaking, was the Missal (in its English form), as well as The Book of Common Prayer, and devotional compilations such as *St Swithun's Prayer Book* (as Helen Gardner has suggested: *The Composition of 'Four Quartets'*, Faber and Faber, London, 1978, p.207). Of course, most of the material in these volumes was biblically-based, but it was through them that Holy Scripture was mediated to Anglo-Catholics. They, not the Bible, were Eliot's religious books.

20. Moody, p.149.

21. Moody, p.140.

22. It is interesting to reflect, generally, that the kinds of mistakes which one routinely encounters in the presentation of Eliot's Christianity are, today, by no means confined to studies of him and his works, or just to Anglo-Catholicism. One of the casualties of the cultural forgetting (and indifference) of this secular age is accuracy with regard to matters of religious doctrine and observance, deriving fundamentally, no doubt, from the view of scholars (who, in other matters, can be very precise) that these issues are no longer of any importance. Recently, I saw an advertisement for a performance of Handel's *Messiah*, by the distinguished Sydney Philharmonia Choir. The professionally-designed advertisement featured an image of Our Lady of the Sacred Heart. That this bore little or no relationship to the text or the spiritual/theological character of the oratorio or of what we can divine of Handel's Christianity was obviously of no account; that it was, generally speaking, a Christian/religious image was good enough.

23. Blurb for David Jones, *The Anathemata* (1952; Faber and Faber, London, 1972).

24. Kirk, p.225.

25. Letter to me, 7th February, 1994.

Chapter One

1. In Norman Foerster, *Humanism and America* (Farrar and Rinehart, New York, 1930), p.110.

2. Grover Smith, *T.S. Eliot's Poetry and Plays: A Study in Sources and Meaning* (2nd edn., The University of Chicago Press, Chicago and London, 1974), p.268. Hereafter cited as 'Smith'.

3. *CPP*, p.178.

4. *The Towers of Trebizond*, (1956; New York Review Books, New York, 2003), p.152. Hereafter cited as '*The Towers of Trebizond*'.

5. 'Thoughts after Lambeth', *Selected Essays* (1932; Faber and Faber, London, 1951), p.367. Hereafter cited as '*SE*'.

6. Alfred Hall, 'Introduction', *Aspects of Modern Unitarianism* (The Lindsey Press, London, 1922), p.14. Hereafter cited as 'Hall'.

7. 'Revelation', in *ICS*, p.191 n.9.

8. *ASG*, p.54. The italics are Eliot's.

9. 'Conclusion', *The Use of Poetry and the Use of Criticism* (1933; Faber and Faber, London, 1964), p.149. Hereafter cited as *'UPUC'*.

10. *Speculations* (1924; Routledge and Kegan Paul, London, 1960), p.33.

11. Letter to Paul Elmer More, 1936, in Margolis, p.145.

12. Sigg, p.vii.

13. *Notes towards the Definition of Culture* (1948; Faber and Faber, London, 1962), p.43. Hereafter cited as *'NTDC'*.

14. 'A Survivor's Tribute to T.S. Eliot', in James Olney and Lewis P. Simpson, eds, 'An Anniversary Issue: T.S. Eliot' *The Southern Review* (vol. 21, number 4, October, 1985), 1117: 'Eliot excels when he does not try to transcend his natural asceticism and his natural literary fastidiousness'. Hereafter cited as *'Southern Review'*.

15. 'In Adam's fall we sinned all'. Kirk, p.223.

16. Sigg, p.3.

17. Kirk, p.19.

18. David Edwards, 'Introduction', *ICS*, p.17.

19. Letter to Mary Trevelyan, 16th November, 1942. See Appendix 1 for an account of Eliot's letters to Mary Trevelyan (of which I have a photocopy of the typescript) and of her diary (also a photocopied typescript, in my possession).

20. Hall, p.9.

21. 15th April, 1915. *The Letters of T.S. Eliot*, Volume 1 1898-1922, ed. Valerie Eliot (Faber and Faber, London, 1988), p.96. Hereafter cited as *'Letters'*.

22. 4th May, 1919. *Letters*, p.290.

23. *The Education of Henry Adams: An Autobiography* (Houghton Mifflin, Boston, 1961), p.34. Eliot reviewed Adams' book in *The Athenaeum* (23rd May, 1919). 'The crux of Eliot's Christianity', on the other hand, writes Sigg, 'what made it unusual, interesting and so distant from Unitarianism was that it incorporated so much doubt' (p.30).

24. *ICS*, p.97. Eliot was referring to the writings of the German Nazi theologian, Wilhelm Hauer – 'the end product of German Liberal Protestantism, a nationalistic Unitarian'.

25. L.A. Garrard, in K. Twinn, ed., *Essays in Unitarian Theology* (The Lindsey Press, London, 1959), p.91; Adrian Desmond and James Moore, *Darwin* (Penguin, Harmondsworth, 1992), p.268. Hereafter cited as 'Twinn' and 'Desmond/Moore'.

26. In his 23rd May, 1919 review (in *The Athenaeum*) of *The Education of Henry Adams*, in Jewel Spears Brooker, 'Substitutes for Christianity in the Poetry of T.S. Eliot', in *Southern Review*, 904.

27. In *Letters*, p.3 n.1. In some notes, Eliot recorded that his father 'did not want to be a minister ... he wanted to be a painter'. He became, instead, President and Chairman of the Hydraulic-Press Brick Co. Inc. which owned brickworks in various parts of the United States (in Moody, p.371 n.14).

28. Sigg, p.6.

29. In Sigg, p.17.

30. Desmond/Moore, p.591.

31. In Manju Jain, *T.S. Eliot and American Philosophy: The Harvard Years* (Cambridge University Press, Cambridge, 1992), p.26. Hereafter cited as 'Jain'.

32. 'What is Christianity? A Linguistic Inquiry', in Twinn, p.99.
33. *Reunion by Destruction: Reflections on a Scheme for Church Union in South India: Addressed to the Laity* (Council for the Defence of Church Principles on the proposed Church of South India, London, 1943), p.19. Hereafter cited as '*RD*'.
34. Preface to Simone Weil, *The Need For Roots* (Routledge and Kegan Paul, London, 1952), p.ix.
35. 'The Problem of Education', *Harvard Advocate*, Freshman Number, 1934, 12.
36. 'Introduction', *ICS*, p.12.
37. 'The Christian Conception of Education', *Malvern, 1941: The Life of the Church and the Order of Society* (Longmans Green, London, 1941), pp.203-4. Hereafter cited as '*Malvern*'.
38. In Alder, 22.
39. In Alder, 22. Waugh took the title of his novel, *A Handful of Dust* (1934) from *The Waste Land*. Alder writes that its title was a 'warning against the naïve optimism of the romantic attitude' (Alder, 22).
40. Schuchard, p.55.
41. In E.J.H. Greene, *T.S. Eliot et la France* (Boivin, Paris, 1951), p.80.
42. 'Mon Coeur Mis à Nu', *Journaux Intimes*, in Y.-G. Le Dantec, ed., *Oeuvres Complètes* (Librairie Gallimard, Paris, 1954), p.1224.
43. 'What Dante Means to Me', *TCTC*, p.126.
44. Hall, pp.11, 15.
45. Hall, p.16.
46. In Desmond/Moore, p.378.
47. Charlotte Eliot, in Christopher Ricks, ed., *T.S. Eliot: Inventions of the March Hare* (Faber and Faber, London, 1996), p.125. Hereafter cited as 'Ricks'.
48. 'A Commentary', January, 1933, 248.
49. In Dakin, p.287.
50. Syllabus of second of six lectures in the 'Oxford University Extension lectures' series, given by Eliot in 1926 (in Moody, p.44).
51. 'Literature and the Modern World', *American Prefaces*, I.2 (Iowa City, November, 1935), 206.
52. *ICS*, p.60.
53. *ASG*, p.53.
54. In Kirk, p.xxi.
55. 'The "Pensées" of Pascal', *SE*, p.411.
56. *Ibid.*
57. In William Turner Levy and Victor Scherle, *Affectionately, T.S. Eliot: The Story of a Friendship 1947-1965* (Dent, London, 1968), p.121. Hereafter cited as 'Levy/Scherle'.
58. 'Eliot as a Friend and a Man of Prayer', unpublished paper (see Appendix 2).
59. Letter of 29th August, 1925, in Margolis, p.62 n.56.
60. In Herbert Read, *T.S.E. – A Memoir*, Monday Evening Papers, No. 5, Center for Advanced Studies, Wesleyan University, 26th April, 1965, pp.12-13. Hereafter cited as '*A Memoir*'.
61. Garrard, in Twinn, p.112.
62. Garrard, in Twinn, p.99.
63. Sigg, pp.6-7.
64. Hall in Hall, p.14.
65. *A Sermon preached in Magdalene College Chapel* (Cambridge University Press, Cambridge, 7th March, 1948), p.5. Hereafter cited as '*A Sermon*'.

66. *The Confident Years: 1885-1915* (Futton, New York, 1952), p.598.
67. T.S. Matthews, *Notes towards the definition of T.S. Eliot* (Weidenfeld and Nicholson, London, 1974), p.15. Hereafter cited as 'Matthews'.
68. 'Why Mr. Russell is a Christian', *Criterion*, August, 1927, 179.
69. In Janet Adam Smith, 'Tom Possum and the Roberts Family', *Southern Review*, 1060.
70. Ackroyd, p.21.
71. Quoted by Bernard Bergonzi, *T.S. Eliot* (Macmillan, London, 1972), p.2. Hereafter cited as 'Bergonzi'.
72. Conclusion to *UPUC*, p.148.
73. 'Building up the Christian World', *The Listener*, 6th April, 1932, 502.
74. *The City of London Churches* (Pitkin, London, 1973), p.22.
75. *CPP*, p.69.
76. *Savonarola – A Dramatic Poem* (R. Cobden-Sanderson, London, 1926), p.58.
77. K. Smidt, *Poetry and Belief in the Work of T.S. Eliot* (Routledge and Kegan Paul, London, 1961), p.3; H. Howarth, *Notes on Some Figures Behind T.S. Eliot* (Chatto and Windus, London, 1965), p.23. Hereafter cited as 'Smidt' and 'Howarth'.
78. Howarth, p.17.
79. In Sigg, p.154.
80. Diary for 1955.
81. S.T. Coleridge, *On the Constitution of the Church and State* (J.M. Dent, London, 1972), pp.39-40.
82. *ICS*, p.63. But Eliot also judged Coleridge's clerisy negatively: it approximated 'the rigidity of a caste' (*ICS*, p.68).
83. 'American Literature and the American Language', in *TCTC*, p.44.
84. Dated, in the Anglo-Catholic way, by reference to the liturgical calendar, St Peter and St Paul [29th June], 1942.
85. 'Popular Theologians: Mr. Wells, Mr. Belloc and Mr. Murry', *Criterion*, May 1927, 256.
86. Letter to Mary Trevelyan, 21st February, 1942.
87. 'American Literature and the American Language', *TCTC*, p.52.
88. Letter to Henry Eliot, 15th February, 1920. *Letters*, p.365.
89. 27th January. *Letters*, p.82.
90. Letter to Eleanor Hinkley, 27th November, 1914. *Letters*, p.73.
91. Austin Warren maintained that Eliot always retained the 'conscience-ridden' mentality of a New England Puritan. 'A Survivor's Tribute to T.S. Eliot', *Southern Review*, 1114.
92. 'Commentary', *Criterion*, April, 1931, in Kirk, p.157.
93. Sigg, p.5.
94. *Letters*, pp.58, 92.
95. 5th September, 1916. *Letters*, p.148.
96. See Levy/Scherle, where it is documented.
97. Letter to Conrad Aiken, 25th February, 1915. *Letters*, p.88.
98. 'Lancelot Andrewes', *FLA*, p.15.
99. In Howarth, p.17.
100. Jain, pp.xii, 63.
101. Jain, pp.96, 95.
102. Jain, p.114.
103. Jain, pp.134-7.
104. In Dakin, p.386.

105. 'The Literature of Politics', *TCTC*, p.141.
106. 'The Humanism of Irving Babbitt', *FLA*, p.104.
107. 'A Commentary', October, 1933, 118.
108. 'The Christian Conception of Education', *Malvern*, pp.204, 206.
109. 'The Humanism of Irving Babbitt', *FLA*, p.110.
110. In Dakin, p.339 n.81.
111. 'Second Thoughts about Humanism', *SE*, p.481.
112. 'The Humanism of Irving Babbitt', *FLA*, p.110.
113. The 'Preludes', she also contends, are a critique of Bergson's teaching. His idea that the *élan vital* was drawing life 'to ever higher levels of organisation' is opposed by Eliot's cosmos, which 'revolves ceaselessly, devoid of meaning and depleted of vitality' (pp.56-7).
114. *A Sermon*, p.5.
115. *SE*, p.48.
116. Jewel Spears Brooker, 'Substitutes for Christianity in the Poetry of T.S. Eliot', *Southern Review*, 905-6.
117. *SE*, pp.47-8.
118. In Howarth, p.308.
119. Letter of mid-July, 1911. *Letters*, p.23.
120. 'A Contemporary Thomist', *New Statesman*, 29th December, 1917, 312.
121. See Appendix 2 for an account of my meetings, correspondence with and access to the unpublished papers of George Every.
122. *Lord of Misrule: The Autobiography of Christopher Lee* (Orion, London, 2004), p.186. Hereafter cited as 'Lee'.
123. In Ricks, p.249.
124. Smith, p.282.
125. *Men and Women in T.S. Eliot's Early Poetry* (Lund University Press, Lund, 1996), p.66. Hereafter cited as 'Palmer'.
126. Jain, pp.111, 110.
127. *ICS*, p.153.
128. This was a concept which Eliot took, by his own admission, from Charles Williams' Fool in *The Greater Trumps* (1932). See Humphrey Carpenter, *The Inklings* (HarperCollins, London, 1997), p.98. Hereafter cited as 'Carpenter'.
129. In Ricks, p.124.
130. In Ricks, p.53.
131. Ricks, p.126.
132. Jain, pp.220, 143.
133. Jain, p.205.
134. Jain, p.207.
135. *Knowledge and Experience in the Philosophy of F.H. Bradley* (Faber and Faber, London, 1964), pp.167-8.
136. Jain, p.239.
137. In Ricks, p.105.
138. Jain, p.166. Writing of James, in the *New Statesman* in 1917, Eliot nonetheless asserted: 'James has an exceptional quality of always leaving his reader with the feeling that the world is full of possibilities – in a philosopher, a rare and valuable quality' (in Ricks, p.112).
139. Jain, p.167.
140. Jain, p.170.
141. Michael Yelton, *Alfred Hope Patten and the Shrine of Our Lady of Walsingham* (Canterbury Press, Norwich, 2006), p.16. Hereafter cited as 'Yelton, *Patten*'.

142. '*The Waste Land* in the Light of the "Cross-Correspondence" Scripts of the Society for Psychical Research', *Yeats Eliot Review*, Summer, 1995, 8.
143. In Ricks, p.142.
144. In Ricks, p.152.
145. Austen Warren, 'A Survivor's Tribute to T.S. Eliot', *Southern Review*, 1111. Eliot organised the lunch at Warren's request. The American graduate student was visiting London, researching Richard Crashaw; he met Eliot, and when Eliot asked him if there was anyone he would like to meet, Warren mentioned Evelyn Underhill whose *Mysticism* had been 'one of my favorite spiritual guides'. The lunch was a disappointment for Warren: 'I had expected the table talk to be mystical or theological: it was neither. Evelyn Underhill and Eliot politely talked personalities; asked each other in a gingerly, tactful way I have never forgotten, "Is he a nice person?" – a question to be answered by delicate characterization'.

     In 1936, Underhill published *Worship*, a comprehensive account of the Judeo-Christian history of liturgy. Like *Mysticism*, this was a standard volume in the libraries of Anglo-Catholic clergy and laity of Eliot's generation. The Rt Revd Francis Underhill was a prominent Anglo-Catholic, who had given an address in the series of talks on 'Our Position' at the first Anglo-Catholic Congress, held in London in 1920. He finished his career and life as Bishop of Bath and Wells.
146. Jain, pp.194-5.
147. In Jain, p.191. By 'Ignatian', Eliot is referring to the regime of extreme mortification of the sixteenth-century Spanish mystic, St Ignatius Loyola, author of the *Spiritual Exercises* and founder of the Society of Jesus (Jesuits).
148. Letter to J.H. Woods, 23rd March, 1917. *Letters*, p.171.
149. Letter to Eleanor Hinkley, 23rd March, 1917. *Letters*, p.169.
150. 'Revelation', in *ICS*, pp.181-2.
151. *CPP*, p.189.
152. 'Religion Without Humanism', in Norman Foerster, ed., *Humanism and America, op. cit.*, p.110. Eliot's emphasis. The forest sages were ascetics in the Eastern religions; the desert sages were Christian hermits, ascetics and monks who were mainly found in the Scetes deserts of the middle east, in the early Christian centuries. There were reputed to be thousands of them. The Victorines were of the School of St Victor, founded in the twelfth century, based at the Augustinian abbey of St Victor at the University of Paris. St John of the Cross and St Ignatius were sixteenth-century Spanish mystics on whose works Eliot draws in his poetry.

     Askesis is the Greek word for 'practice, training, exercise' from which 'asceticism' is derived – a way of life characterised by abstinence from worldly pleasures, especially sexual activity and the consumption of alcohol, with the aim of religious purification and including the practice of religious exercises rooted in the philosophical tradition of antiquity.
153. The standard collections of Eliot's essays from this period – *Selected Essays* and *The Sacred Wood* – being confined substantially to literary matters, give a distorted and limited view of Eliot's intellectual interests in this period. For example, he was reviewing 'philosophy, theology, biology and anthropology' for *The Monist* in 1917 (letter to his mother; 21st March, 1917; *Letters*, p.164). He could be sharply critical, too, at this time, of the 'philosophical Christian' who 'apologizes for the religion in which he would like to believe' – in *The Monist* in 1918, in Ricks, p.121.

154. 'Oh little voices of the throats of men', in Ricks, p.75.

155. In Ricks, p.105.

156. First essay (untitled), in J. Baillie and H. Martin, eds *Revelation* (Faber and Faber, London, 1937), p.12. Hereafter cited as '*Revelation*'.

157. 'The Modern Dilemma', *The Listener*, 16th March, 1932, 383.

158. Eliot to Paul Elmer More in August, 1929, in Jain, p.250.

159. This is quoted by the Anglo-Catholic Aunt Dot in Rose Macaulay, *The Towers of Trebizond*, p.274. This novel is one of the most important sources of mid-twentieth-century Anglo-Catholic ideas and practices.

160. 'Building up the Christian World', *The Listener*, 6th April, 1932, 501-2.

161. In Kirk, p.106.

162. 'A Note on Poetry and Belief', *The Enemy*, January, 1927, 16-17. Eliot's emphasis. By 'modernism', here, Eliot is referring to liberal theology. It was the usual term, then, for a growing body of theologians in the Church of England who were calling for the updating of various Christian beliefs and for relevance to modern thought and *mores*. Denial of such doctrines as the Virgin Birth was characteristic of modernists, the notorious Bishop Barnes of Birmingham being their most outspoken representative in the period between the World Wars.

163. In *Revelation*, p.34.

164. *NTDC*, p.32.

165. Jain, p.4.

166. Letter of 1945, in Ricks, p.411.

167. Letter to J.H. Woods, 28th January, 1915. *Letters*, p.84.

168. Letter to Conrad Aiken, 25th February, 1915. *Letters*, p.88. At the beginning of Eliot's stay, he was more positive, writing (on 14th October, 1914) to a Harvard friend, William C. Greene, who had been a Rhodes Scholar two years before: 'Oxford is a quiet and deserted place now, but, I expect, a better place to work in. At any rate, I find it exceedingly comfortable and delightful – and very "foreign"' (in 'Pilgrim Poets', *Oxford Today*, II, 2, Hilary Term, 1999, 26).

169. *Eliot's Early Years* (Oxford University Press, Oxford, 1977), p.58.

170. 'How Eliot Became Eliot', *The New York Review*, 15th May, 1997, 26.

171. See Richard Kaye, *Voluptuous Immobility: St. Sebastian and the Decadent Imagination* (Columbia University Press, forthcoming).

172. Jain, p.5.

173. 3rd April, 1910. *Letters*, p.13.

174. *Eliot's Early Years, op. cit.*, p.[15].

175. Jain, pp.20-1.

176. 'The possessors of the inner voice ride ten in a compartment to a football match in Swansea, listening to the inner voice, which breathes the eternal message of vanity, fear, and lust' ('The Function of Criticism', 1923, *SE*, p.27).

177. 'Thoughts after Lambeth', *SE*, p.375.

178. *ASG*, pp.58-9.

179. Eliot, 'Introduction', *Savonarola: A Dramatic Poem, op. cit.*, pp.ix-x.

180. 'The Function of Criticism', *SE*, p.29.

181. 'The Function of Criticism', *SE*, p.27.

182. *The Mask of Merlin: A Critical Study of David Lloyd George* (MacDonald, London, 1963), p.31.

183. 'Why Mr. Russell is a Christian', *Criterion*, August, 1927, 179.

184. [15th?] March, 1917. *Letters*, p.163.

185. T.C. and E.C. Jack, London, 1913, p.9 (author's italics). Hereafter cited as 'Manning-Foster'.

186. Jain, pp.x, 10.
187. 'Revelation', in *ICS*, p.175.
188. *A Sermon*, p.5.
189. Letter to Sydney Schiff, 6ᵗʰ December, 1920. *Letters*, p.425.
190. Kaye-Smith, pp.v-vi.
191. Kaye-Smith, p.40. Tract 80 was written by Isaac Williams.
192. 'The Dry Salvages', V, *Four Quartets*, *CPP*, p.190.
193. 'Revelation', in *ICS*, p.168.
194. *CPP*, pp.189-90.
195. *ICS*, p.79.
196. Jain, pp.82-3.
197. Jewel Spears Brooker, 'Substitutes for Christianity in the Poetry of T.S. Eliot', *Southern Review*, 913.
198. Eliot, in *Humanism and America*, described by David Edwards as 'a few sentences pregnant with self-revelation', quoted by him in 'Introduction', *ICS*, p.33.

Chapter Two

1. 26ᵗʰ April, 1911. *Letters*, p.19.
2. St Helen's Bishopsgate (thirteenth century), St Stephen Walbrook (built by Sir Christopher Wren, 1672-9), St Bartholomew the Great, West Smithfield (founded in 1123, one of London's oldest churches), and St Sepulchre-without-Newgate (founded around 1450, the City's largest parish church) are the others.
3. *CPP*, p.191.
4. *The Waste Land*, IV. *CPP*, p.71.
5. *ICS*, p.82.
6. Kaye-Smith, p.113.
7. *The City of London Churches, op.cit.*, p.26.
8. 'London Letter', *The Dial*, May 1921, 690-1.
9. *CPP*, p.192.
10. 'Eliot as a Friend and a Man of Prayer' (see Appendix 2).
11. *CPP*, p.62.
12. *London: Everyman Guide* (David Campbell, London, 1993), p.149.
13. *The City of London Churches, op.cit.*, p.26. Nancy Hargrove posits a contrast between St Mary Woolnoth and St Magnus the Martyr, claiming the former is identified with the criticised 'commercial' life of the City, whereas St Magnus, by the river, is associated with that life-giving (and purifying and baptismal) element (*Landscape as Symbol in the Poetry of T.S. Eliot* [University Press of Mississippi, Jackson, 1978, p.77]). This argument cannot be sustained, for two reasons. Firstly, Eliot admired the City churches, *toutes ensemble* – as his 'London Letter' reveals – and would hardly have been so disparaging of St Mary Woolnoth, generally accepted as one of the most beautiful, as to regard it as 'commercial'. Secondly, Hargrove has misread the reference, in *The Waste Land*, to St Mary Woolnoth. What she sees as complicity in the commercial business of the City – beginning its work at 9 a.m. – is, in fact (as one would suppose it to be, from a church), a critique of that time-bound and mercantile domain. The striking of the ninth hour, at St Mary Woolnoth, should remind those passing by of the traditional time of executions in British prisons and, also, of the archetypal execution – at the ninth hour – of Christ: a 'dead sound', indeed. The reminder fails, because the waste-landers are deaf to its spiritual

significance: they only hear the time of the commercial day's beginning, by which their lives are circumscribed. That they listen to the church clock and derive only this information from it, is the irony of Eliot's reference. If anything, St Mary Woolnoth is closer to the heart of his critique, geographically and spiritually, than St Magnus, which is on the edge of the City and next to the river and the life of its fishermen, rather than in the midst of the City's bankers.

14. *CPP*, p.77.
15. 'Notes on the Waste Land', *CPP*, p.78.
16. *CPP*, p.69.
17. Anglo-Papalism goes beyond the Anglo-Catholic in-principle acceptance of the papacy, the teachings about it and its infallibility, combined with the recognition that there has been an historic rupture between Rome and Canterbury which has impaired that relationship (while longing for it to be restored). Anglo-Papalists, rejecting this breach and the resulting ambiguity, maintain that Anglo-Catholics are under the authority of whichever pope is currently in office and that the Church of England has no existence independent of the Holy See. They would not accept Eliot's and other Anglo-Catholics' idea of the Roman Catholic Church in England as having the status of a sect. Anglo-Papalism expressed itself in such circumstances as the laying of the foundation stone, in 1931, at the Anglican shrine of Our Lady of Walsingham, by the Anglo-Papalist vicar, Hope Patten, on which he had inscribed (in Latin, naturally) that the restoration of the shrine had taken place in the pontificate of Pius XI, Bertram (Pollock, the Anglican bishop) being bishop of Norwich and Hope Patten *parochus* of Walsingham. Bishop Pollock (uncomfortable, in any case, with the neo-Lourdes that was blossoming in his diocese) was not best pleased, and demanded that his name be removed. The stone became known as the 'rock of offence' and was one of the reasons that 'more moderate Catholic parishes... felt that Walsingham was out of their sphere', with its papalist tendencies (Colin Stephenson, *Walsingham Way*, Darton, Longman & Todd, London, 1970, pp.160-1). Typically, in Anglo-Papalist parishes, such as St Magnus the Martyr, the liturgy was in Latin (in the days when only Latin was used in the Catholic Mass and the idea of a vernacular liturgy was unthinkable) and indistinguishable, in every ceremonial way, from the Roman liturgy of the time (whereas most Anglo-Catholics celebrated in the vernacular and used rites which, in varying degrees, showed some fidelity to The Book of Common Prayer and aspects of more mainstream Anglican worshipping and ceremonial customs). For a recent, full study of this most exotic extension of Anglo-Catholic faith and practice, see Michael Yelton, *Anglican Papalism, op. cit.*). To my knowledge, Eliot nowhere makes any reference to the phenomenon of Anglo-Papalism.
18. Yelton, pp.27, 33.
19. 3rd [?] October. *Letters*, p.474.
20. Kirk, p.125.
21. In Margolis, p.145.
22. Sigg, pp.221-2.
23. Helen Gardner (whose own background was High Church but not explicitly Anglo-Catholic) once commented to me that the crucial, defining characteristic of Anglo-Catholicism was the reservation of the sacrament of the eucharist. This, indeed, was one of the most controversial innovations of the ritualist movement and a distinctively Anglo-Catholic practice. Michael Yelton concurs: 'The

crucial point… was Reservation of the Blessed Sacrament' (Yelton, p.69). An example of the contentious character of this practice is an article in *The Church Times*, 6th January, 1933, 24 entitled: 'Reservation in Winchester Cathedral. The Dean Answers His Critics', although it is noteworthy that reservation had, by this stage, taken its place in cathedral churches, not only 'extreme' Anglo-Catholic parish churches and religious communities.

24. Chorus X, *The Rock*, *CPP*, p.166.
25. Jewel Spears Brooker rightly observes that Eliot's interest in Christianity did not 'appear suddenly' in his thirty-ninth year ('Substitutes for Christianity in the Poetry of T.S. Eliot', *Southern Review*, 899).
26. In Keith Crook, 'A Lost T.S. Eliot Review Recovered', *Yeats Eliot Review*, Fall, 1995, 91.
27. Nevill Coghill, *Murder in the Cathedral with an Introduction and Notes* (Faber and Faber, London, 1965), p.13.
28. 19th and 25th July. *Letters*, pp.41, 44.
29. Ricks, p.268.
30. Ricks, p.5.
31. Ricks, p.5.
32. 26th August. *Letters*, p.404.
33. '*Lune de Miel*', *CPP*, p.48.
34. George Every, 'Eliot as a Friend and a Man of Prayer', unpublished paper; and see Matthews, p.88.
35. Reported by Valerie Eliot, in Stephen Spender, *Eliot* (Fontana/Collins, Glasgow, 1975), p.51.
36. '"England and nowhere"', *Companion*, p.104.
37. *ICS*, p.76.
38. *ICS*, p.93.
39. *ICS*, p.74. But he held that the advantages for Christianity of establishment outweighed the disadvantages of Erastianism, providing 'an official recognition by the State, as well as an accepted status in the community and a basis of conviction in the heart of the individual'. Without an established Church, the Christian faith would be represented by 'a mere congeries of private and independent sects' (*ICS*, p.74). Eliot's views on this matter would not have been shared by most Anglo-Catholics who regarded the establishment as an inhibitor of the Catholic character and development of the Church of England, as in the parliamentary debates over the revised Prayer Book in 1927-8.
40. *ICS*, p.80.
41. 'The early poems', *Companion*, p.118.
42. Princess Margaret's High Church tendencies, especially during the 1950s, were widely regarded as another expression of her rebellious nature and her refusal to toe the royal line. In the nineteenth century, Queen Victoria was steadfastly opposed to the Catholicising movement in the Church of England during her reign. She was probably most at home, religiously, in the Presbyterian Kirk.
43. 'Thoughts after Lambeth', *SE*, p.381.
44. Routledge, London, 1989.
45. 'Catholicism and International Order', *Christendom*, September, 1933, 173.
46. '"Ulysses", Order, and Myth', *Dial*, November, 1923, 483.
47. In Moody, pp.43-4.
48. *CPP*, p.40.
49. Moody, p.62.
50. *International Journal of Ethics*, 27, no.1 (October, 1916), 111-12.

51. 1st June. *Letters*, p.299.
52. 'Baudelaire In Our Time', *FLA*, pp.70-1.
53. 6th October, 1920. *Letters*, p.412.
54. 3rd April, 1921. *Letters*, p.443.

Chapter Three

1. I have subsequently used the shorter spelling of 'Vivienne' – 'Vivien' – as she used this form herself (for example, in signing letters), as does Eliot in written references to her.
2. 'Eliot at Oxford', *Southern Review*, 898.
3. 13th May. *Letters*, p.180.
4. 28th June, 1917. *Letters*, p.186.
5. *SE*, p.109. Eliot used the phrase again, twenty years later, when he refers to withdrawing for contemplation to restore oneself for re-engagement with 'the struggle for existence' ('Planning and Religion', *Theology*, May, 1943, 104).
6. 'Tradition and the Individual Talent' (1919), *SE*, p.18.
7. 'Dante' (1929), *SE*, p.262.
8. T. Kelly, 'We sing the praise of him who died…', *Hymns Ancient & Modern Revised*, no.215.
9. 16th September, 1916. *Letters*, p.151. This disproves (as do other letters) Marja Palmer's contention that the 'unhappiness of his marriage to Vivien was hidden even to his own family for several years; it only became apparent in 1925' (Palmer, p.12).
10. 5th November, 1916. *Letters*, p.158.
11. 6th November, 1921. *Letters*, p.486. The nineteenth-century French psychiatrist, Pierre Janet, whose work Eliot had studied in his graduate seminar on psychology at Harvard in 1912-13, designated 'a malady of the will', deriving from 'lowered physical vitality' and 'which is characterised by ennui, hesitation, the diminution of the will, powerlessness to act, indecision', as '*abulia*' (see Jain, p.169). Marja Palmer, referring to Prufrock's 'erotic shortcomings', prompts us to speculate whether *aboulie* may have been similarly influential in suppressing Eliot's sexual potency at the time of his marriage and in its early stages (Palmer, p.35).
12. 'Baudelaire In Our Time', *FLA*, p.77.
13. *CPP*, p.16.
14. *CPP*, p.44.
15. 20th May, 1917. *Letters*, p.182.
16. 28th June, 1917. *Letters*, pp.185-6.
17. 'Morning at the Window' (1916), *CPP*, p.27.
18. 'A Cooking Egg' (1919), *CPP*, p.45.
19. *CPP*, p.65.
20. Bertrand Russell, *Autobiography* (Unwin, London, 1978), p.220. Hereafter cited as '*Autobiography*'.
21. *Autobiography*, p.242.
22. Ackroyd, p.66.
23. July, 1915. *Autobiography*, p.278.
24. Postmarked 10th November, 1915. *Autobiography*, p.280.
25. 11th January. *Letters*, p.127.
26. *Autobiography*, p.301.
27. Miranda Seymour, *Ottoline Morrell: Life on the Grand Scale* (Sceptre, London, 1992), p.332.

28. *CPP*, p.31.
29. 22nd November, 1917. *Letters*, p.210.
30. 4th June [?], 1919. *Letters*, p.301.
31. Ackroyd, p.84.
32. 'T.S. Eliot: The Savage Comedian and the Sweeney Myth', in Jewel Spears Brooker, ed. *The Placing of T.S. Eliot* (University of Missouri Press, Columbia, 1991), p.32.
33. Smith, pp.32-3.
34. Palmer, p.147.
35. *Letters*, p.232.
36. 2nd June, 1918. *Letters*, p.233.
37. 27th October, 1918. *Letters*, p.245.
38. *CPP*, p.22.
39. 29th October, 1919. *Letters*, p.342.
40. '*Ara Vos Prec*: Eliot's negotiation of Satire and Suffering', in Ronald Bush, ed. *T.S. Eliot: The Modernist in History* (Cambridge University Press, Cambridge, 1991), p.41. Hereafter cited as 'Bush'. '*Vus*' was a misprint for '*Vos*'.
41. Moody, p.37.
42. 21st March, 1920. *Letters*, p.374.
43. 17th March, 1921. *Letters*, p.440.
44. Letter to Richard Aldington, 16th September, 1921. *Letters*, p.469.
45. In a letter of 21st September, 1922. *Letters*, pp.573-4.
46. Palmer, p.13.
47. 'Lines for Cuscuscaraway ...', *CPP*, p.136.
48. 'T.S. Eliot', *Life*, 15th January, 1965, 92.
49. *SE*, p.21.
50. 20th July, 1921. *Letters*, p.462.
51. *Letters*, p.112 n.1.
52. *Letters*, p.xvii.
53. 23rd August, 1921. *Letters*, p.466.
54. At 'the Sitwell dinner', 28th June 1921, in Michael Holroyd, *Lytton Strachey: A Biography* (Penguin, Harmondsworth, 1979), p.823.
55. Russell, *Autobiography*, p.409.
56. 21st April, *Autobiography*, p.409.
57. 7th May, 1925. *Autobiography*, p.409.
58. Robert Sencourt, *T.S. Eliot – A Memoir* (Garnstone Press, London, 1971), p.121. Hereafter cited as 'Sencourt'.
59. In Ackroyd, p.206.
60. Sencourt, p.51.
61. Vivien's medication, indeed, could have contributed to their illnesses. See Anthony E. Fathman, M.D., 'Viv and Tom: The Eliots as Ether Addict and Co-Dependent', *Yeats Eliot Review*, Fall, 1991, 33-6. But that 'Vivienne was an ether-drinker.... is emphatically disputed by her brother Maurice' (Sencourt, p.59 n.22).
62. 30th September. *Letters*, p.58.
63. 'Beyle and Balzac', 23rd May, 393.
64. 'An Anglican Platonist: the Conversion of Paul Elmer More', *The Times Literary Supplement*, 30th October, 1937, 792.
65. *CPP*, p.38.
66. Eliot: 'The hatred of life is an important phase – even, if you like, a mystical experience – in life itself' ('Cyril Tourneur', 1930, *SE*, p.190).

67. *Revelation*, pp.31-2.
68. *Words Alone: The Poet T.S. Eliot* (Yale University Press, New Haven, 2000), p.275. Hereafter cited as 'Donoghue'.
69. Smith, p.x.
70. Sencourt, pp.112, 120. Russell Kirk records that Vivien attended a christening with Eliot 'as late as August 1932' (they were to part, for ever, the following year) – Kirk, p.152. This is the only instance I have encountered of Vivien attending a liturgical service with Eliot and her attendance may have been principally to fulfil the social obligation of this particular ceremony.
71. Ackroyd, p.162.

Chapter Four

1. *Reunion by Destruction: Reflections on a Scheme for Church Union in South India: Addressed to the Laity* (The Council for the Defence of Church Principles Pamphlet 7, London, 1943), p.13. Hereafter cited as '*RD*'. Evelyn Waugh summarised Ronald Knox's Anglo-Catholic view of the Church of England, before Knox's conversion to Rome in 1917: 'She was a true branch of the Latin Church of the West, which through an accident of history had been partly severed from the trunk. She was feloniously held in bondage by the state. She was justly entitled to all the privileges that had been hers in 1500 and to all the developments of the Council of Trent. It was her manifest destiny in God's own good time to return rejoicing to her proper obedience' (*The Life of Ronald Knox*, Chapman & Hall, London, 1959, p.109). Knox's convictions are representative of the general Anglo-Catholic view in the earlier twentieth century. The metaphor of being 'partly severed from the trunk' probably alludes to the 'branch theory', discussed below. Waugh was another convert of the same kind as Knox (from Anglo-Catholicism to Rome, in 1930).
2. That is, 'between the two wars'. 'East Coker', V. *CPP*, p.182.
3. Manning-Foster, p.29. John Calvin (1509-64) was the French reformer and theologian. Thomas Cranmer (1489-1556) was Archbishop of Canterbury from 1532.
4. Manning-Foster, p.29. 'The Book of Common Prayer is Catholic because it belongs to the Catholic Church, and, in using it, the Church clothes it, where it is bare, with the prayers and ceremonies of the past. Our loyalty is to Christ's Church, and to the Book of Common Prayer only as it belongs to this Church. It does not stand alone, apart from the Church from which it derives. What it asserts is Catholic; what it is silent about is supplied from Catholic tradition' (L.E.W. Renfrey, ed., *Catholic Prayers for members of the Church of England in Australia* (privately printed; 2nd edn., Adelaide, 1982, p.6. Hereafter cited as 'Renfrey').
5. The Prayer Book retained the calendar and prayers and readings for festivals, feasts and fasts; provided that priests in cathedrals and collegiate churches should receive the communion at least weekly, and, in the rubric prior to the prayers and readings for the First Sunday in Advent, directs that 'the Collect, Epistle, and Gospel, appointed for the Sunday shall serve all the week after' – envisaging celebrations not only on Sundays but daily. The daily Mass was a hallmark of an Anglo-Catholic parish.
6. Kaye-Smith, p.212. Kaye-Smith (1887-1956) was a prolific novelist, known as 'the Sussex writer' because of the setting of her novels in rural East Sussex. She

had married Theodore Penrose Fry, an Anglican priest, in 1924. By 1929, both she and her husband had converted to Roman Catholicism. These were the years (1927-8) of the bitter controversy over the revisions to The Book of Common Prayer. Anglo-Catholics objected to the rule of worship being determined by Parliament and it is likely that this was at least one of the negative reasons for Kaye-Smith's conversion. Her book on Anglo-Catholicism is the best short account of the movement and indispensable for an understanding of the mind of lay Anglo-Catholics at the time of Eliot's conversion.

7. In Charles Smyth, *Cyril Forster Garbett: Archbishop of York* (Hodder and Stoughton, London, 1959), p.377. Hereafter cited as 'Smyth'.
8. Professor Edward Freeman, Regius Professor of Modern History, University of Oxford; quoted in Manning-Foster, p.31.
9. Freeman, in Manning-Foster, pp.30-31.
10. In Manning-Foster, p.20.
11. Manning-Foster, p.78. Author's italics.
12. 'Foreword', in Paul Vaiss, ed., *From Oxford to the People: Reconsidering Newman & the Oxford Movement* (Gracewing, Leominster, 1996), p.viii. Hereafter cited as 'Vaiss'.
13. Peter Anson, *Abbot Extraordinary: A Memoir of Aelred Carlyle Monk and Missionary 1874-1955* (The Faith Press, London, 1958), p.54. Hereafter cited as 'Anson'. Not all Anglo-Catholics were enamoured of this theory. Manning-Foster describes it as 'very dangerous' because it induces complacency, when what is needed is reunion of the Western Church (Manning-Foster, pp.17-18).
14. Sheridan Gilley, 'The Ecclesiology of the Oxford Movement: a Reconsideration', in Vaiss, p.62.
15. Manning-Foster, p.20.
16. *A Dissuasive from Popery*, Part II, in P.E. More and F.L. Cross, *Anglicanism* (SPCK, London, 1935), p.162.
17. S.L. Ollard, *The Anglo-Catholic Revival: Some Persons and Principles* (A.R. Mowbray, Oxford, 1925), p.4. This book began as a series of lectures delivered at All Saints' Church, Margaret Street, one of the most important centres of Anglo-Catholicism in London. Hereafter cited as 'Ollard'.
18. Ollard, p.9. He quotes Johnson's expressed preference for Roman Catholics to Presbyterians.
19. Kaye-Smith, pp.15-16.
20. Ollard, p.82.
21. The worship at Little Gidding was richly, demandingly scriptural. Matins was said daily at 6 am. Every hour, there was a short fifteen-minute Office, with Psalms, a Gospel reading and prayers. The Psalter was read completely each day and the whole of the Gospels each month. At 10 am, daily, the Prayer Book Litany was recited and, at 4 pm, Evening Prayer was said, with a final evening service at 8 pm. Holy Communion, however, was only celebrated monthly. The sense of retirement from the world (given the isolation of the place and its smallness) and the devotion to a version of the Divine Office are reminiscent of Catholic monastic life, but the sacerdotal and sacramental arrangements, the absence of vows and, of course, the mixed sex, familial situation (in which children played an important part) are hardly prophetic of the later Anglo-Catholic religious communities in the Church of England. Nicholas Ferrar had only deacon's orders from Archbishop Laud, so he was not able to celebrate the Eucharist.

Graham Parry points out that the worship of the Ferrars (and, indeed, of their friend, George Herbert) required decency and fidelity to the Prayer Book, but it was not Laudian in elaboration of ceremonial or decoration. *Glory, Laud and Honour: The Arts of the Anglican Counter-Reformation* (The Boydell Press, Woodbridge, 2006), p.23.

George Tolley gives an informative account of the spirituality of Little Gidding in 'Nicholas Ferrar, Little Gidding and the Use of the Prayer Book', in *Church and King* (the magazine of the Society of King Charles the Martyr), Christmas, 2004, 8-12.

22. Preface to the fifth edition (Church Association, London, 1899), p.ix.
23. This dissatisfaction with the liturgy of the Church reached a crisis during the terrible suffering of the First World War. Catholic ministrations, both on the Front and at home, supplied what was sorely needed: 'During the war the custom of reserving the Blessed Sacrament, which had been the exception rather than the rule even in churches of the Movement, now became general, and before the Reserved Sacrament thousands learned the art of private prayer as they had never learnt it before in empty churches or in solitude at home. The devotional revival, which was the legitimate successor of the ceremonial revival, gathered its first strength during the dreadful years of the war' (Kaye-Smith, p.101).
24. 'Unenglish and Unmanly: Anglo-Catholicism and Homosexuality', *Victorian Studies*, 25 (2), 1982, 206.
25. A.L. Rowse, *Homosexuals in History* (Barnes & Noble, New York, 1977), p.218.
26. (1945; William Heinemann and Martin Secker & Warburg, London, 1977), p.681.
27. Rene Kollar, *Abbot Aelred Carlyle, Caldey Island, and the Anglo-Catholic Revival in England* (Peter Lang, New York, 1995), p.117. Hereafter cited as 'Kollar'.
28. Nigel Yates, 'Walsingham and Inter-War Anglo-Catholicism' [unpublished conference paper, 2008]. Not paginated. Hereafter cited as 'Yates'.
29. Pickering, p.202.
30. 'Eliot in the Theatre', *Southern Review*, 986.
31. Darton, Longman & Todd, London, 1972. Two years before, Stephenson had published *Walsingham Way*, his account of the ancient shrine which is also a biography of Father Hope Patten, its twentieth-century restorer. That book, too, is a fund of amusing stories and colourful characters, clerical and lay.
32. Alder, p.22.
33. H.A. Wilson, *Received with Thanks* (Mowbrays, London, 1940), p.106. Hereafter cited as 'Wilson'.
34. Kaye-Smith, p.34.
35. Kaye-Smith, p.24.
36. Wilson, pp.20-2.
37. Kaye-Smith, p.118. In 1882, only 9 churches used incense. By 1902, just twenty years later, 393 were using it (Yates).
38. Kollar, p.5.
39. 'Introduction', in Colin Buchanan, ed., *Anglo-Catholic Worship: An Evangelical Appreciation after 150 years* (Grove Liturgical Study 33; Grove Books, Bramcote, 1983), p.3. Hereafter cited as 'Buchanan'.
40. Kaye-Smith, p. 115.
41. Sheridan Gilley, 'The Ecclesiology of the Oxford Movement: a Reconsideration', in Vaiss, p.68.
42. Buchanan, p.6, n.2. That not all of these parishes were Anglo-Catholic indicates

the extent and success of Anglo-Catholic influence in the broader Church of England in that period. The last Archbishop of Canterbury to prefer to celebrate the Communion at the north side of the holy table (symbolically contradicting the idea of the sacrifice of the Mass) was Archbishop Frederick Temple who died in 1902 (Buchanan, p.6 n.2).

43. N.P. Williams, 'The Theology of the Catholic Revival', in N.P. Williams and C. Harris, eds, *Northern Catholicism* (SPCK, London, 1933), p.135.

44. 'On the Mysticism Attributed to the Early Fathers of the Church', *Tracts for the Times* (6 vols) (J.G. & F. Rivington, London, 1839-1841), vol. VI, p.185.

45. *CPP*, pp.160-1.

46. In Smith, p.256. *CPP*, pp.172, 38.

47. *The Towers of Trebizond*, p.226.

48. ' "Church Principles" and "Protestant Kempism" ', in Vaiss, p.31.

49. Kaye-Smith, p.66.

50. Kaye-Smith, p.80.

51. Kenneth Macnab, 'Mackonochie and the controversies over confession and ritual', in William Davage, SSC, ed., *In This Sign Conquer: A History of the Society of the Holy Cross (1855-2005)* (Continuum, London, 2006), p.88. Hereafter cited as '*ITSC*'.

52. Kaye-Smith, p.80.

53. 'Whose sins you forgive, they are forgiven', in Buchanan, p.33.

54. Kaye-Smith, p.62.

55. Kaye-Smith, p.73.

56. Michael Yelton and John Salmon, *Anglican Church-Building in London 1915-1945* (Spire Books, Reading, 2007), describing St Francis of Assisi, Petts Wood (near Bromley, in south-east London), constructed in 1934, comment that it is 'an example of how Anglo-Catholicism did in some cases migrate successfully to the suburbs and flourish' (p.59). That the point is worth making indicates that this was exceptional. Other examples in their book show how suburban congregations resisted the Catholicising of their parishes in the inter-war period (see pp.125-6). Hereafter cited as 'Yelton/Salmon'.

57. Yates.

58. Michael Yelton, *Alfred Hope Patten and the Shrine of Our Lady of Walsingham* (Canterbury Press, Norwich, 2006), p.216. Hereafter cited as 'Yelton, *Patten*'.

59. Yates.

60. In Yelton, p.13.

61. Yelton, *Patten*, p.45.

62. *Collected Poems* (John Murray, London, 2003), p.162.

63. Anson, p.55 n.11.

64. Kaye-Smith, p.123.

65. From his hymn, 'New every morning is the love'.

66. Yelton, p.100.

67. He was an influential advocate of the Parish Communion movement which carried church-people of most persuasions, apart from extreme Evangelicals, with it. His books, *Liturgy and Society* (1935) and *The Parish Communion* (1937), while generally Catholic in disposition are definitely not Anglo-Catholic, let alone Anglo-Papalist (as their mild titles, indeed, suggest). He did not hold, Michael Yelton writes, 'to the sacerdotal and hierarchical view of the Church' (Yelton, pp.101, 234).

68. *The Towers of Trebizond*, p.47.

69. *The Towers of Trebizond*, p.48.

70. Wilson, p.42.
71. In Kenneth Brill, *John Groser: East London Priest* (Mowbrays, London, 1971), blurb, p.17.
72. The extremism of the place was not complete in all details, as Lord Victor was not only married but had several children. Most Anglo-Catholic priests were celibate. Fr Cheetham, Lord Victor's successor, never married.
73. Yelton, pp.80-1. In Southwark, Bishop Garbett was more successful, at his diocesan Synod in 1925 in bringing about 'a unity which any other diocese might have envied' in relation to Reservation (Smyth, p.195).
74. Fr Chantry-Pigg declares that Corpus Christi is 'a great Christian festival and holy day, always kept in the Church of England' (*The Towers of Trebizond*, p.78). This shows the element of fantasy or wishful thinking which sometimes accompanied Anglo-Catholic polemic.
75. Yelton, p.82.
76. Recalled by Bishop Cyril Garbett of Southwark (later Archbishop of York), in Yates.
77. Yates.
78. 'These Holy Mysteries', in Buchanan, p.10.
79. P.J. Jagger, in Buchanan, p.13.
80. Frances Knight, 'The Influence of the Oxford Movement in the Parishes c.1833-1860: A Reassessment', in Vaiss, p.127.
81. Yates.
82. Yelton, pp.19, 107.
83. 'Poetry', in C.B. Cox and A.E. Dyson, eds, *The Twentieth-Century Mind* (Oxford University Press, London, 1972), p.307.
84. Kaye-Smith, p.133.
85. Kaye-Smith, pp.133, 123.
86. I am grateful to Mr Adrian Brink for this observation.
87. The familiar term, 'the Caroline divines', is somewhat misleading as it refers to clergy of High Church principles during the reigns of *both* James I and Charles I (not only the latter, as the adjective suggests). Andrewes, for example, died the year after Charles ascended the throne and William Laud's career and Catholicising influence were well advanced by this time, although he did not become Archbishop of Canterbury until 1633.
88. Parry, p.19.
89. Yates.
90. Yelton, p.155. Yelton gives a detailed account of the advances made at St Saviour's during Kilburn's incumbency, as the English Use was replaced by the Western Use (Yelton, pp.[152]-9). It is a study, in one parish, of the ways in which, slowly but surely, usually over several years, determined Anglo-Catholic incumbents could bring an established parish round to their ways of thinking and behaving, theologically and ceremonially. That Fr Kilburn, like so many of them, had a rare pastoral gift and was loved by his people (in this poor area of London) counted for much in achieving their compliance in ritual and devotional matters.

    When Fr Chantry-Pigg, Aunt Dot and the narrator visit the graves at Gallipoli, 'Father Chantry-Pigg said "*Requiem aeternam dona ei, Domine*", and Aunt Dot and I said "*Et lux perpetua luceat ei*" '. These would seem to be Anglo-Catholics of Anglo-Papalist tendencies (*The Towers of Trebizond*, p.39).
91. *Ritual Notes on the Order of Divine Service: A Guide to the Ceremonial of the Church*, 6th edn (William Walker, London, 1913), pp.v-vi. Hereafter cited as *'Ritual Notes'*.

92. 'One day I will go there to stay permanently'. Letter (1952) to the Revd William Turner Levy, in Levy/Scherle, p.43.

93. Yelton/Salmon, p.111. That this church today is mostly used by a Pentecostal group and has been completely stripped of its Catholic adornments is an extreme example, in one parish, of the general decline of Anglo-Catholicism which began after the Second World War.

94. *The Towers of Trebizond*, p.259.

95. The chasuble is the outermost vestment, uniquely worn for the celebration of Mass, by the priest. Decorated in the liturgical colour of the feast day or season during which Mass is being celebrated, it – more than any other vestment (being uniquely reserved for the Mass) – represented the doctrine of the eucharistic sacrifice. Many ritual battles were fought over it. To this day, in the extreme Low Church, Evangelical Diocese of Sydney, Australia, priests must sign an undertaking that they will not wear it before they can be inducted into their parishes. The baroque 'fiddle-back' chasuble (favoured by advanced Western Use Anglo-Catholics, but now virtually out of favour with everyone, except some Tridentine rite traditionalist Roman Catholics) was so-called because it was cut away as to look, from the back, like one of the instruments of the musical fiddle (or string) family – particularly the 'cello. In 'mid-Lent pink', Betjeman is referring to 'Laetare Sunday', the fourth Sunday in Lent – in the middle of those 40 days. On that day of rejoicing, instead of the usual penitential purple vestments of the season, priests wear rose-pink chasubles. 'Laetare' comes from the opening Latin word of the Introit of the Mass: 'Rejoice ye with Jerusalem...'). This little detail in Betjeman's poem is a characteristic Anglo-Catholic touch, scandalous indeed to Roman Catholics (who resent their traditions being appropriated by 'heretics', even though they have now abandoned many of those traditions themselves) and to Protestants, who would disapprove of them no matter who used them.

96. *Summoned by Bells: A Verse Autobiography* (John Murray, London, 2001), p.95.

97. James Olney, 'Editorial Note', *The Southern Review*, p.[870].

98. 'Baudelaire In Our Time', *FLA*, p.78.

99. Jeremy Morris, 'The Regional Growth of Tractarianism: Some Reflections', in Vaiss, p.142.

100. Kirk, p.183.

101. In Yelton, pp.52-3.

102. Kaye-Smith, p.166.

103. Kollar, p.[xi].

104. *ICS*, p.74. But the advantages for Christianity of establishment outweighed the disadvantages of Erastianism, providing 'an official recognition by the State, as well as an accepted status in the community and a basis of conviction in the heart of the individual'. Without an established Church, the Christian faith would be represented by 'a mere congeries of private and independent sects' (*ICS*, p.74).

105. *ICS*, p.80.

106. Sean Gill, 'Marian Revivalism in Modern English Christianity: The Example of Walsingham', in R.N. Swanson, ed. *The Church and Mary* (The Boydell Press for the Ecclesiastical History Society, Woodbridge, 2004), p.350. Hereafter cited as 'Gill' and 'Swanson'.

107. *ICS*, p.75.

108. *Walsingham Way* (Darton, Longman & Todd: London, 1970), p.158. A number

of aristocrats entered the priesthood, as Anglo-Catholics, including Lord Victor Seymour, who was vicar of St Stephen's Gloucester Road just before Eliot began worshipping there. By doing so, they were deviating, religiously, from the expectations of their class, not affirming them.

109. Gill, p.352.
110. *The Towers of Trebizond*, p.12.
111. Manning-Foster, p.13. 'One often hears people say that they have been baptized into the Church of England, which is impossible.... By Baptism we are made members of the holy Catholic Church, received, as the Prayer-book puts it, "into the ark of Christ's Church" ' (p.13).
112. 3rd August, 1929. To Paul Elmer More, in Schuchard, p.139.
113. *The Towers of Trebizond*, p.59.
114. Kirk, p.115.
115. 'Thoughts after Lambeth', *SE*, p.385.
116. In a review of several books, *Criterion*, July, 1927, 69.
117. In Lockhart, p.128. 'at present' may be seen as an indication, however, that the Primates were foreseeing a different situation in the future.
118. Kollar, p.118.
119. Janet Adam Smith, 'Tom Possum and the Roberts Family', *Southern Review*, 1068.
120. Yates.
121. Yelton, *Patten*, p.111.
122. 'Thoughts after Lambeth', *SE*, p.386; 'A Dialogue on Dramatic Poetry', *SE*, p.51; 'A Note on Richard Crashaw', *FLA*, p.97.
123. In Alec Vidler, *Scenes from a Clerical Life* (Collins, London, 1977), p.63.
124. A full account is given by Vidler (*op. cit.*). See Chapter V, 'Birmingham and Bishop Barnes'.
125. Ollard, p.9.
126. *The Towers of Trebizond*, p.82.
127. Manning-Foster, p.33.
128. Manning-Foster, p.34.
129. Kaye-Smith, p.172.
130. Kaye-Smith, p.142.
131. Wilson, p.43.
132. Wilson, p.79.
133. Wilson, p.82.
134. *CPP*, p.62.
135. Wilson, pp.88-9.
136. Wilson, p.110.
137. Yates.
138. G.K.A. Bell, *Randall Davidson: Archbishop of Canterbury* (Oxford University Press, London, 1952), p.1276. Hereafter cited as 'Bell'.
139. In Wilson, pp.119-121.
140. In Wilson, p.109.
141. Renfrey, p.11.
142. Manning-Foster, p.68.
143. *CPP*, p.107.
144. *Pensées*, 2 vols., ed. Z. Tourneur (Editions de Cluny, Paris, 1942), no.284. Hereafter cited as '*Pensées*'.
145. *The Catholic Religion: A manual of instruction for members of the Anglican Communion* (1893; Morehouse Publishing, Ridgefield, 1983), p.156. All that

follows in this paragraph is a summary from Staley's chapter on 'The Holy Eucharist'.

146. *Ibid.*, p.159.

147. *CPP*, p.182.

148. There is a parody of the Mass in Eliot's pre-conversion poem, 'Gerontion', of 1920, where the devouring 'Christ the tiger' comes in 'depraved May', 'To be eaten, to be divided, to be drunk / Among whispers'. *CPP*, p.37.

149. Material in these paragraphs summarises a fuller account of Eucharistic doctrine on the American Anglo-Catholic 'philorthodox' website: http://philorthodox. blogspot.com, September, 2008. The website, introduced in these terms, is a surviving remnant of Anglo-Catholicism: 'This site is dedicated to the traditional Anglican expression of the One, Holy, Catholic and Apostolic Church of Our Lord Jesus Christ. We profess the orthodox Christian Faith enshrined in the three great Creeds and the Seven Ecumenical Councils of the ancient undivided Church. We celebrate the Seven Sacraments of the historic Church. We cherish and continue the Catholic Revival inaugurated by the Tractarian or Oxford Movement. Definitely not "tepid centrist Anglicanism!"'

150. Kaye-Smith, p.148.

151. 'Tradition and the Individual Talent', *SE*, p.21.

152. Yelton, *Patten*, p.4.

153. *The Towers of Trebizond*, p.16. For all the extremity of his Anglo-Catholicism, Fr Chantry-Pigg will not accept the doctrines of the Immaculate Conception of the Virgin Mary or of her Assumption (important in Eliot's spirituality). They 'had been pronounced *de fide* too late to be part of pure Catholic heritage, by the rival branch of the Church, which he liked to thwart', Rose Macaulay's narrator observes (*The Towers of Trebizond*, p.49). This is part of the caricature of his finical principles, but it also reflects the tensions which could exist between Anglo-Catholicism and modern Roman Catholicism (the Assumption, for example only being defined as *de fide* in 1950).

154. Yelton, *Patten*, p.98. Anglo-Catholics could satirise the complaints of Old Catholic recusants in England, pointing out that they, too, had suffered for their maintenance of the Faith since the Reformation:

'We belong to an old Anglican family, which suffered under the penal laws of Henry VIII, Mary I, and Oliver P. Under Henry VIII we did indeed acquire and domesticate a dissolved abbey in Sussex, but were burned, some of us, for refusing to accept the Six Points [of Henry VIII, imposed in June 1539]; under Mary we were again burned, naturally, for heresy; under Elizabeth we dug ourselves firmly into Anglican life, compelling our Puritan tenants to dance round maypoles and revel at Christmas, and informing the magistrates that Jesuit priests had concealed themselves in the chimney-pieces of our Popish neighbours. Under Charles I we looked with disapprobation on the damn crop-eared Puritans whom Archbishop Laud so rightly stood in the pillory, and, until the great Interregnum, approved the Laudian embellishments of churches and services, the altar crosses, candles and pictures.... During the suppression, we privately kept outed vicars as chaplains and attended secret Anglican services.... [and so on, through the centuries, until the great dawn of the Oxford Movement, paralleling, in the Old Catholic history it parodies, the contemporary restoration of the Roman hierarchy in England]'. *The Towers of Trebizond*, pp.4-5.

155. Kollar, p.245.

156. I encountered this phenomenon, personally, many years ago, in the unpleasant

form of a fanatical Roman Catholic, the Oxford English Literature don, A.O.J. Cockshut. Waving The Book of Common Prayer at me, he demanded that I explain how Eliot could maintain that he was a Catholic while belonging to a Church which endorsed the un-Catholic, nay, anti-Catholic Thirty-Nine Articles of Religion. The response that, as 'the wideness in God's mercy' is 'like the wideness of the sea' (in Frederick Faber's words), so the house of Anglicanism has many mansions, including one in which a Catholic Christian can humbly, even happily find a home, did nothing to placate this frowning, pharisaical ultra-montanist. Dame Helen Gardner told me that she had been similarly confronted, on the same matter, by the febrile Mr Cockshut.

157. Sean Gill gives the details and dates in Gill, p.349.

158. *The Towers of Trebizond*, pp.16-17. Fr Chantry-Pigg is assailed by Catholic Commandos, on the one hand, and Protestant Storm Troopers on the other; his signs advertising 'Mass' defaced by 'You have no Mass' (by the Commandos) and crossed out and 'Lord's Supper' written over them by the Storm Troopers. 'Father Chantry-Pigg did not know which of these two bands of warriors he disliked most' (*The Towers of Trebizond*, p.17).

159. 'Blake', *The Sacred Wood* (Methuen, London, 1920), p.157. Hereafter cited as '*SW*'. Manning-Foster, typically of Anglo-Catholic apologists, writes of 'the deplorable division that took place in the Western Church at the time of the Reformation' (Manning-Foster, p.15).

160. 15th August, 1926. In Jain, p.230. Statistically, the prediction has come true in Britain where more Roman Catholics attend Mass today than Anglicans attend divine service. The same is true in Australia, where Anglicanism was also once dominant.

161. Yelton, *Patten*, p.233.

162. 'Catholic Commandos' break into Fr Chantry-Pigg's St Gregory's and leave a placard on the high altar: 'This is not an altar, for you have no Mass and no Sacrament and no priests to offer the Holy Sacrifice' (*The Towers of Trebizond*, p.18).
It was also argued, with regard to the matter of the Apostolic Succession, that Anglican orders were also invalid because of the breach in this Succession at the Reformation, so the bishops who ordained Anglican priests were not themselves validly consecrated, the historical continuity of the laying-on of hands having been broken. The Archbishops of Canterbury and York replied to the Pope in an encyclical letter (29th March, 1897) arguing that 'the Anglican Church makes it clear that she intends to confer the Office instituted by Christ and all that it contains'. They contended that the Church of England 'teaches the doctrine of the Eucharistic Sacrifice in terms at least as explicit as those of the Canon of the Roman Mass', and finally they pointed out 'that the words and acts required by the Pope are not found in the earliest Roman Ordinals, so that if their omission renders an Ordination invalid, the Orders of the Church of Rome are on no surer footing' ('Anglican Ordinations', in F.L. Cross, ed., *The Oxford Dictionary of the Christian Church* (2nd edn., Oxford University Press, Oxford, 1974, p.57).

163. Morris, in Swanson, p.358.

164. Rosemary Hill, *God's Architect: Pugin and the Building of Romantic Britain* (Allen Lane, London, 2007), pp.248, 555 n.54.

165. 'Malines Conversations', *The Oxford Dictionary of the Christian Church, op. cit.*, p.862.

166. Lockhart, p.340.

167. *ICS*, pp.55, 59.

168. Article 37, which sounds so Protestant, in fact reflects the situation that had obtained in England for centuries before the Reformation, in the view of certain Anglo-Catholic apologists. Statutes of the fourteenth century 'enacted that the Pope should not ... appoint to any bishoprics or benefices in England, and forbade any person to bring Papal bulls into England without the king's leave'. While remaining in full communion with Rome, the Church of England 'was yet an independent and self-governing organisation which claimed full powers of managing her own affairs'. She held the same doctrines as Rome, but she was not 'Roman Catholic' in the modern sense of the term at all. The distance of England from Rome, and the time that communications took, was a significant element in this ancient degree of independence, which included the development of English 'uses' in the liturgy, such as Sarum, Bangor and Hereford, recovered (as we have seen) by one faction of the Anglo-Catholic movement. (Manning-Foster, pp.27-8). Of course, these matters have been the subject of debate for centuries.

169. *ICS*, pp.85, 120.

170. *ICS*, p.112. Eliot's appreciation of St Thomas was mediated through the writings of Jacques Maritain, 'the most popular and influential exponent of neo-Thomism', Eliot declared, in 1928, in a review of Maritain's work in the *Times Literary Supplement*. 'We must recognize in his prose a poetic quality ... Maritain is the lyrist of Thomism' (8th November, 1928, 818).

171. *ICS*, p.76.

172. *ICS*, p.93.

173. Kaye-Smith, p.166.

174. In *Soft Answers* (Southern Illinois University Press, Carbondale, 1967), p.167. Hazlitt, in *English Comic Writers*, gives a very different assessment of Cibber from Pope's ridicule: 'Cibber, in short, though his name has been handed down to us as a bye-word of impudent pretension and impenetrable dullness by the classical pen of his accomplished rival [Pope], was a gentleman and a scholar of the old school; a man of wit and pleasantry in conversation, a diverting mimic, an excellent actor, an admirable dramatic critic, and one of the best comic writers of his age' (Taylor and Hessey, London, 1819, p.204).

175. That is, 'from the throne' (a reference to papal pronouncements made with the formal weight of the office of Pope, and hence infallible). Kirk, p.165.

176. Introduction by A. Walton Litz. Litz points out that the address was untitled, but he gives it this working title 'based on Eliot's opening paragraph'. *Southern Review*, 873.

177. *Southern Review*, 873-4.

178. *Southern Review*, 882.

179. *Southern Review*, 883.

180. *Southern Review*, 882.

181. 'He had no wish to go to London, nor had ever expected to do so.... And the idea of being involved in the ecclesiastical controversies for which, by that time, the vast diocese with its six hundred parishes was famous, or notorious, according to viewpoint, really horrified him'. His predecessor, Winnington-Ingram (who, unlike 'Fisher, was not unsympathetic to Anglo-Catholicism) had left a legacy of 'liturgical chaos which he thought an ordered and happy liberty'. In this, Anglo-Catholic priests could more or less do as they liked. William Purcell, *Fisher of Lambeth* (Hodder and Stoughton, London, 1969), pp.79, 81.

Fisher was succeeded in London by Bishop Wand in October, 1945. Wand had Winnington-Ingram's blessing and had an Anglo-Catholic past. Protestants demonstrated at his enthronement, having campaigned against him in his previous See of Bath and Wells, circulating photographs linking him with High Masses, statues, tabernacles and monstrances (John Peart-Binns, *Wand of London*, Mowbray, London, 1987, 129-130). Here was a bishop for London with a much more congenial churchmanship for Anglo-Catholics like Eliot than Geoffrey Fisher's!

182. 'T.S. Eliot: Personal Reminscences', *Southern Review*, 954.

183. *The England of Elizabeth* (Macmillan, London, 1951), pp.450-1.

184. *NTDC*, p.73.

185. 'Lancelot Andrewes', *FLA*, p.12.

186. *Ibid.*, p.15.

187. Lockhart, p.368.

188. Sencourt, p.104.

189. Sencourt, p.109. Eliot had first met Stead in 1923. A fellow American, he had been born in Washington in 1885 and had studied at the University of Virginia. Married, he came to London as an American consul but 'hardly had he done so than he found that literature and religion were his real bent in life'. He studied for the Anglican priesthood and served as chaplain at Worcester College, Oxford, and at the Anglican church in Florence. Richard Cobden-Sanderson, also a friend of Eliot, published Stead's religious reflections, *The Shadow of Mount Carmel*, in 1926. Writing to Sencourt, Eliot praised the work as one of the best examples of contemporary prose. Later, Stead wrote poetry in the style of Coleridge and a study of Christopher Smart. In 1939, he returned to America to become a professor at Trinity College, Washington (Sencourt, pp.104-5).

Chapter Five

1. It is sometimes said of Eliot (as, indeed, of others) that he was 'baptised in [or 'into'] the Church of England'. There is no such thing as Anglican baptism (see Manning-Foster, p.13). The baptised are made members of the Holy Catholic Church, received, as The Book of Common Prayer puts it, 'into the ark of Christ's Church'.

2. 'The Modern Dilemma', *The Listener*, 16th March, 1932, 383.

3. *A Sermon*, p.5.

4. Ackroyd, pp.162, 319.

5. Diary for 1955. In some notes for an address to the Ecumenical Club, also in 1955 (which Mary Trevelyan transcribed), Eliot links Dr Graham with the Moral Re-armament movement, which was also making some headway at the time, finding the evangelist's doctrines so vague and heavenly-minded as to gloss over true theology and its application in this world (meaning by that reference, no doubt, Incarnational theology in particular). 'Moral Re-armament' was an 'abuse of Christianity and of English' (*ICS*, p.82). The movement's concentration on social ills led (with similar theological imprecision) to gathering together all religious people (Christian, Jewish, Muslim) to fight this battle, regardless of doctrinal differences.

    When Fr Chantry Pigg, in Macaulay's *The Towers of Trebizond*, published the year later, 'mentioned this Dr. Graham, he looked scornful and disagreeable' (*The Towers of Trebizond*, p.49).

6. Dr Halide, who utters these words in *The Towers of Trebizond*, finds this commendable, as the lack of doctrine would stand a chance (she imagines) of appealing to 'Moslemism'. Rose Macaulay's contempt for such an un-intellectual, non-dogmatic religion is evident between the lines (*The Towers of Trebizond*, p.101). That Macaulay and Eliot nonetheless thought Dr Graham worthy of some discussion indicates the threat they saw to doctrinal Anglo-Catholicism which Evangelical religion was posing in the 1950s. As subsequent developments have shown, in the following decades, their fears were well-founded, as the Evangelical party gradually took over as the leading force in the Church of England and Anglo-Catholicism itself lost its doctrinal edge and appeal as it subsided into liberalism.

7. *Discourses on the Doctrines of Christianity* (American Unitarian Association, Boston, 1881), pp.128-9.

8. *ICS*, p.53. Earlier in the book, Eliot rejects the idea of a 'religious revival', in the usual sense of the phrase, and the use of a 'revivalistic vocabulary' (pp.42, 45).

9. *The Making of T.S. Eliot's Plays* (Cambridge University Press, Cambridge, 1969), p.6. Hereafter cited as 'Browne'.

10. 'The "Pensées" of Pascal', *SE*, p.411.

11. Donoghue, p.205.

12. 'Catholicism and International Order', *Christendom*, September, 1933, 176.

13. 'East Coker', V. *CPP*, p.182.

14. Kirk, p.127; 'The "Pensées" of Pascal', *SE*, p.408.

15. In David Chinitz, *T.S. Eliot and the Cultural Divide* (The University of Chicago Press, Chicago, 2003), p.130. Hereafter cited as 'Chinitz'.

16. '*Ash-Wednesday*: a poetry of verification', *Companion*, p.134.

17. *In Defence of T.S. Eliot* (Picador, London, 2000), p.318.

18. Schuchard, p.150.

19. (Cambridge University Press, Cambridge, 1995). Foreword. Hereafter cited as 'Asher'.

20. Moody, pp.115, 117.

21. Letter to Paul Elmer More, 27th March, 1936, in Asher, p.9.

22. 'The English Situation', *Christendom*, June, 1940, 108.

23. *Ibid.*

24. *Ibid.*, 102.

25. 'Lancelot Andrewes', *FLA*, pp.19-20.

26. *Revelation*, pp.1-2.

27. *Ibid.*, 103.

28. 'Catholicism and International Order', *Christendom*, September, 1933, 175.

29. 'Religion and Science', *The Listener*, 23rd March, 1932, 429.

30. Letter to Paul Elmer More, 28th October, 1930, in Christopher Ricks, *The Panizzi Lectures 2002: Decisions and Revisions in T.S. Eliot* (The British Library, London, 2003), p.85.

31. In Roger Kojecký, *T.S. Eliot's Social Criticism* (Faber and Faber, London, 1971), p.78. Hereafter cited as 'Kojecký'.

32. 14th August, 1947.

33. In Dakin, p.299.

34. *Ibid.*

35. Letter to Robert Shafer, 1st April, 1930. In Dakin, p.284.

36. *Christian News-Letter*, 3rd September, 1941.

37. *NTDC*, p.32.

38. 'Commentary', *Criterion*, April, 1933. In Kirk, p.181.
39. 'A Panegyric by Mr. T.S. Eliot', written for *S. Stephen's Magazine*, May, 1959. The details in the following paragraphs about the vicar of St Stephen's, Fr Eric Cheetham, are also from Eliot's address, as reprinted in the parish magazine.
40. Yelton, pp.198, 194-5. He was born Arnold Harris Matthews and had originally been ordained into the Roman priesthood in 1877.
41. Lee, pp.186-7, 189. 'Father Cheetham had a little rhyme about a greedy lad who "Of buns and tarts ate his fill, and made himself extremely ill", and adapted it to my case' (p.187).
42. For example, on the tenth anniversary on the evening of Wednesday, 15th January, 1975.
43. An eye-witness account from Wallace Fowlie of Eliot at the Cowley Fathers' church of St John the Evangelist on Beacon Hill in Boston, in 1932-3 when Eliot was Charles Eliot Norton professor at Harvard. In Kenneth Paul Kramer, *Redeeming Time: T.S. Eliot's 'Four Quartets'* (Cowley Publications, Lanham, 2007), p.10. Hereafter cited as 'Kramer'. This was a Mass at which there were only Eliot, Fowlie and one other congregant present, in addition to the priest. Needless to say – whether in such a relatively private situation or at a more public liturgy – such behaviour is far removed from what one would expect to encounter in mainstream Anglicanism.
44. 'The Humanism of Irving Babbitt', *FLA*, p.105.
45. *A Sermon*, pp.6-7.
46. Preface to *The Need For Roots*, *op. cit.*, p.vii.
47. Matthew 26:40.
48. *A Memoir*, p.14.
49. Ackroyd, p.163.
50. 25th June, 1954. Eliot dates the letter by St. Prosper and it is, indeed, the day of his death, yet it is not listed for observance in either the Roman or English Missal. One wonders what arcane calendar Eliot was using.
51. Paul Vaiss, 'Introduction', in Vaiss, p.8.
52. 'Charles I', *The Oxford Dictionary of the Christian Church*, *op. cit.*, p.269.
53. Peter Nockles, 'Church and King: Tractarian Politics Reappraised', in Vaiss, p.103.
54. There is a list at this website: http://www.skcm.org/SCharles/Cult/cult.html #ChurchesAndChapels – accessed 1/5/09.
55. 'Archbishop Bramhall', *Theology*, July, 1927, 16.
56. 'Little Gidding', *CPP*, pp.191-2.
57. Diary for 1942.
58. Letter of Eliot to W.T. Levy, 21st August, 1954. In Levy/Scherle, p.49.
59. In *Anglicanism*, eds P.E. More, F.C. Cross, *op. cit.*, p.506.
60. *A Memoir*, p,19.
61. The original of this letter is reproduced in part in Levy/Scherle, pp.51-2.
62. Austin Warren, 'A Survivor's Tribute to T.S. Eliot', *Southern Review*, 1117.
63. Beginning in 1867, convened by the Archbishop of Canterbury and named after his London residence, Lambeth Palace, where they were originally held. The huge growth in the number of bishops of the Anglican Communion during the twentieth century (462 attended in 1968, for example) has taken them to larger venues. The resolutions of the conferences are not binding, but are significant expressions of the mind of the Anglican episcopacy ('Lambeth Conferences', *Oxford Dictionary of the Christian Church*, *op. cit.*, p.795).

64. *SE*, pp.377-8.
65. *CPP*, p.273.
66. Hugo von Hofmannsthal (1874-1929), like Pascal, Maritain and Eliot, was drawn to the discipline of the monastic rule. On his death it was found that he had requested that he should be buried in the habit of a Franciscan friar. Brian Coghlan has written: 'there is a good deal of material for a constructive comparison of the courses taken by Hofmannsthal and Eliot from their original positions as prophets of despair (albeit in differing ways) to their later activities as artists of cultural-political significance, based on a decidedly Catholic viewpoint' (*Hofmannsthal's Festival Dramas*, Cambridge University Press, London, 1964, p.322).
67. 'A Commentary', October, 1929, 5.
68. 'Baudelaire', *SE*, p.429.
69. *NTDC*, p.44.
70. 'Little Gidding', I. *CPP*, p.192.
71. In Schuchard, p.119.
72. In Paschaltide, this chant is replaced, at the principal Sunday Mass where this introductory rite is performed, with the chant '*Vidi Aquam...*' ('I beheld water...'). Such details of ceremonial variation were familiar to all Anglo-Catholics, clergy and laity alike.
73. Mr Delian Bower. Letter to me, 22th October, 1975.
74. 'Johnson as Critic and Poet', *OPP*, p.177.
75. Noting J.S. Phillimore's *The Hundred Best Latin Hymns*, in *Criterion*, January, 1927, 156.
76. *CPP*, p.93.
77. *CPP*, p.128.
78. 27th February, 1944.
79. Mrs C.F. Alexander, 'There is a green hill far away...'.
80. Mr Delian Bower, letter to me, 22nd October, 1975. The Roman rite for Holy Week was extensively revised in the 1950s by Pope Pius XII. Mr Bower's allusion to 'the *then* Roman rite' refers to the liturgy as it was to be found in the Roman and English Missals before the innovations.
81. *CPP*, pp.96-7.
82. *NTDC*, p.24.
83. *Savonarola, op, cit.*, pp.x-xii.
84. 'Arnold and Pater', *SE*, p.440.
85. *NTDC*, p.80.
86. *The Value and Use of Cathedrals in England Today* (Friends of Chichester Cathedral, Chichester, 1952), p.6.
87. Recorded by Ursula Niebuhr, 'Memories of the 1940s', in Stephen Spender, ed., *W.H. Auden* (Weidenfeld and Nicolson, London, 1974), p.106.
88. John Ferrar, 'A Life of Nicholas Ferrar', in B.Blackstone, ed., *The Ferrar Papers* (Cambridge University Press, Cambridge, 1938), pp.27-8.
89. 'Lancelot Andrewes', *FLA*, p.25.
90. *The Value and Use of Cathedrals in England Today, op. cit.*, pp.5-6.
91. *Ibid.*, p.6.
92. Schuchard, pp.152, 169.
93. *Ibid.*, p.152.
94. *A Sermon*, p.[8].
95. 'Baudelaire In Our Time', *FLA*, p.78.
96. Preface to *The Need For Roots, op. cit.*, p.vi.

97. *CPP*, p.179.
98. 'The "Pensées" of Pascal', *SE*, p.414.
99. Donoghue, p.4. Donoghue also interprets *The Waste Land* (which he sees not as expressing universal despair, but personal *angst*) as moving towards 'an act of penance', a 'prologomena to penance' (pp.110-11, 118).
100. In Donoghue, p.80.
101. *CPP*, p.38.
102. 'The Modern Mind', *The Listener*, 16th March, 1932, 383.
103. 'The Search for Moral Sanction', *The Listener*, 30th March, 1932, 446, 480.
104. *ICS*, p.96.
105. In Manning-Foster, p.76.
106. '... if there be any of you, who by this means [the General Confession at the Holy Communion] cannot quiet his own conscience herein, but requireth further comfort or counsel, let him come to me, or to some other discreet and learned Minister of God's Word, and open his grief; that by the ministry of God's holy Word he may receive the benefit of absolution, together with ghostly counsel and advice, to the quieting of his conscience'. The wording, of course, is very careful, to avoid any suggestion that private, as opposed to public, general confession, should be mandated or usual. Such terms as 'Minister' and 'ministry' avoid the sacramental connotations of 'priest' (nonetheless used throughout the Communion Service, which was undeniably sacramental) and, going with this, is the repeated emphasis on the 'Word', rather than sacrament. Nonetheless, with little else to encourage them in the official formularies of the Church of England, Anglo-Catholics traditionally made much of this provision in order to support their promotion of auricular confession.
107. *Pensées*, no.198.
108. *Oxford Apostles: A Character Study of the Oxford Movement* (Faber and Faber, London, 1933), p.171.
109. *A Sermon*, pp.[8], 6.
110. Diary, 1951.
111. Renfrey, p.49.
112. Yelton, *Patten*, pp.117, 151.
113. Diary, 1953. The element of whimsy here, in what is a most serious matter, is a typical Anglo-Catholic touch.
114. There are variations in the form of auricular confession used in Anglicanism. Here, I have drawn upon two famous Anglo-Catholic manuals of the mid-twentieth century: *Saint Swithun's Prayer Book* and *The Cuddesdon Office Book* which can be regarded as representative of usual practice in England during Eliot's lifetime. Helen Gardner has suggested, indeed, that the former book was probably used by Eliot.
115. 'Baudelaire In Our Time', *FLA*, p.70.
116. 28th March, 1946.
117. Diary for 1950.
118. Diary for 1955.
119. Quoted in Matthews, p.33.
120. *SE*, pp.373, 374-5.
121. *CPP*, p.247.
122. *CPP*, pp.249-50.
123. *CPP*, p.253.
124. *CPP*, p.275.

125. *CPP*, p.289.
126. *CPP*, p.318.
127. Dom Justin McCann, ed., *The Cloud of Unknowing* (Burns, Oates and Washbourne, London, 1924), p.9 n.
128. *The Invisible Poet: T.S. Eliot* (Methuen, London, 1965), p.186. Hereafter cited as 'Kenner'.
129. *CPP*, p.350.
130. *CPP*, p.333.
131. In Kirk, p.222.
132. *CPP*, p.363.
133. *CPP*, p.294.
134. *CPP*, p.366.
135. *CPP*, p.414.
136. *CPP*, p.416.
137. *CPP*, p.421.
138. Philippians, 2: 12.
139. *CPP*, p.483.
140. *CPP*, p.465.
141. Diary for 1954.
142. *CPP*, pp.466-7.
143. See Sencourt, p.52.
144. *CPP*, p.467.
145. *A Sermon*, p.[8].
146. *CPP*, p.568
147. *CPP*, p.570.
148. *CPP*, p.572.
149. *CPP*, p.581.
150. 'Charles Whibley', *SE*, p.501.
151. 'Virgil and the Christian World', *The Listener*, 13th September, 1951, 412.
152. *The Value and Use of Cathedrals, op. cit.*, p.16.
153. *In Defence of T.S. Eliot, op. cit.*, p.444.
154. 'Planning and Religion', *Theology*, May, 1943, 104.
155. *ICS*, pp.35, 60.
156. *ICS*, p.60. Eliot's emphasis.
157. *Christian News-Letter*, 28th August, 1940.
158. Dated for Lady Day, 1949 – that is, the feast of the Annunciation of the Blessed Virgin Mary, 25th March.
159. *Religious Drama: Mediaeval and Modern* (House of Books, New York, 1954), p.[16].
160. In Margolis, p.142. It should be noted, of course, that this negative appraisal of human life and relations was written in the dying days of Eliot's troubled marriage to Vivien.
161. 19th February, 1944.
162. In conversation with Mary Trevelyan (her diary for 1955).
163. 21st February, 1942; 19th December, 1944.
164. Schuchard, p.157.
165. 'Planning and Religion', *Theology*, May, 1943, 104.
166. *A Sermon*, p.3.
167. Trevelyan diary for 1952.
168. Trevelyan diaries for 1953 and 1954.
169. Diary for 1955.

170. Diary for 1953.

171. *SE*, pp.515-16.

172. Lockhart, p.[203].

173. Kramer, p.10.

174. Kramer, p.10.

175. 'The Problem of Education', Freshman Number, 1934, 11. Bernard Iddings Bell was a priest of the Episcopal Church with whom Eliot was acquainted (information from the Revd W.T. Levy, letter to me, 14th March, 1976). He is mentioned also in a letter of Eliot to Mary Trevelyan, dated St Victor, 1949 (21st July), when he visited the poet in London, and in two letters of Eliot to her from the Hotel Windermere in Chicago, in 1950. Canon Bell, Eliot writes in the first of these (dated 16th October), was providing him with ecclesiastical society, and the same comment is made in the second letter (28th October). Eliot takes as a starting point for his series of lectures on 'The Aims of Education' in 1950 (in *TCTC*, p.61 n.2) Bell's *Crisis in Education* of 1949. And in 'The Literature of Politics' of 1955, 'Canon B.I. Bell' is described as a conservative whose views should be 'more widely diffused and translated, modified, adapted, even adulterated, into action' (*TCTC*, 141).

176. 'Living Tradition' – unpublished paper.

177. George Every, 'Eliot as a Friend and a Man of Prayer' – unpublished paper.

178. See Sencourt, p.112.

179. Levy/Scherle, p.69.

180. Levy/Scherle, p.43.

181. *Partisan Review*, Vol.XV, I, 1948, 137-8.

182. Levy/Scherle, p.69.

183. (Mowbrays, London), p.7.

184. (Faber and Faber, London, 1935), p.206.

185. Janet Adam Smith, 'Tom Possum and the Roberts Family', *Southern Review*, 1058.

186. 'T.S. Eliot: Personal Reminiscences', *Southern Review*, 953.

187. *NTDC*, p.67.

188. 'T.S. Eliot: Personal Reminiscences', *Southern Review*, 955.

189. A typescript note, attached to a postcard, signed by Eliot and dated '14.8.47', in Moody, p.233.

190. Gill, p.352.

191. Jeremy Morris, '"An Infallible Fact-Factory Going Full Blast": Austin Farrer, Marian Doctrine and the Travails of Anglo-Catholicism', in Swanson, p.362.

192. Mary Trevelyan, Diary, 1956.

193. Levy/Scherle, pp.49-50. Eliot's emphasis.

194. The papacy's 'infallibilist claim is a blasphemy.... Its authority has been employed to establish as dogmas of faith, propositions utterly lacking in historical foundation. Nor is this an old or faded scandal – the papal fact-factory has been going full blast in our own time, manufacturing sacred history after the event' (Austin Farrer in Richard Harries, ed., *The One Genius: Readings through the year with Austin Farrer* (SPCK, London, 1987, p.148)).

195. Diary, 1956.

196. Information given to me by Mr Delian Bower, a contemporary parishioner of Eliot at St Stephen's.

197. *CPP*, p.85.

198. *The Panizzi Lectures, op. cit.*, p.96.

199. Barry Spurr, *See the Virgin Blest: The Virgin Mary in English Poetry* (Palgrave

Macmillan, New York, 2007), p.177.

200. *CPP*, p.189.

201. In Helen Gardner, *The Composition of Four Quartets, op. cit.*, p.141.

202. Nancy Hargrove, *Landscape as Symbol in the Poetry of T.S. Eliot, op. cit.*, p.165.

203. Harry Blamires, *Word Unheard: A Guide through Eliot's 'Four Quartets'* (Methuen, London, 1969), p.109.

204. *Ibid.*, p.112.

205. Letter of 30th October, 1944. Bell, for example, was a definite ecumenist, supporting the Church of South India scheme and Anglican-Methodist reunion, neither of which was approved by Anglo-Catholics of Eliot's stamp (see 'Bell, George Kennedy Allen', *The Oxford Dictionary of the Christian Church, op. cit.*, p.152).

206. *Out of Africa* (1937; Penguin, London, 1954), p.54.

207. In Bell, p.694.

208. *Ibid.*, p.701.

209. Bell, p.694.

210. In Bell, p.694.

211. Bell, p.706.

212. Bell, p.796.

213. In J.G. Lockhart, *Cosmo Gordon Lang* (Hodder and Stoughton, London, 1949), p.242.

214. In J.G. Lockhart, *Charles Lindley – Viscount Halifax* (Part II: 1885-1934) (Geoffrey Bles, London, 1936), p.363.

215. Yelton, p.54.

216. Letter to Mary Trevelyan, 20th March, 1943.

217. (Oxford University Press, London, 1948), p.590.

218. *RD*, p.11.

219. *RD*, pp.14, 18; *SE*, pp.378-9.

220. *RD*, p.15.

221. (Basil Blackwell, Oxford), p.30.

222. (Cambridge University Press, Cambridge, 1943), pp.14-15.

223. *The Shape of the Liturgy* (Adam and Charles Black, London, 1945), p.729.

224. *RD*, pp.7,9.

225. *RD*, p.9.

226. 3rd September, 1941.

227. *RD*, pp.17, 13.

228. *RD*, pp.8, 12, 19, 21.

229. *RD*, p.20.

230. Yelton, *Patten*, p.177.

231. 'Church of South India', *The Oxford Dictionary of the Christian Church, op. cit.*, p.1294.

232. Reporter Hans Meyerhoff, *Partisan Review*, XV, 1, 1948, [135-6].

233. *The Towers of Trebizond*, pp.255-6.

234. Sencourt, p.171.

235. Sencourt, p.172.

236. Information from Fr Geoffrey Curtis, CR (1902-81), whom I visited at St Katharine's in 1975.

237. Catherine Jamison, *The History of the Royal Hospital of St. Katharine by the Tower of London* (Oxford University Press, London, 1952), p.52.

Chapter Six

1. Bernard Reardon, *From Coleridge to Gore: A Century of Religious Thought in Britain* (Longmans, London, 1971), p.212. Hereafter cited as 'Reardon'. 'Maurician' refers to the Anglican priest, F.D. Maurice (1805-72), who applied Christian principles to social reform. Theologically, he was a liberal rather than an Anglo-Catholic and his orthodoxy was constantly questioned.
2. *Ibid.*, pp.470-1.
3. L.E. Elliott-Binns, *English Thought 1860-1900* (Longmans, Green and Co., London, 1956), pp.281-2.
4. *The Catholic Standard*, Spring, 1976, 6.
5. 'The Modern Dilemma: Christianity and Communism', *The Listener*, 16th March, 1932, 382.
6. *Ibid.*
7. Officially, 'National Assembly of the Church of England', established in 1919 'to deliberate on all matters concerning the Church of England and to make provision in respect thereof'. The General Synod superseded it in 1970. The Assembly exercised great influence on the financial affairs of the Church of England, through the Central Board of Finance. (*The Oxford Dictionary of the Christian Church, op. cit.*, pp.288-9).
8. 'Douglas in the Church Assembly', *New English Weekly*, 14th February, 1935, 383.
9. Preface to *The Need For Roots, op. cit.*, p.xi. Eliot praised Rudyard Kipling for the same bias against humanity *en masse*: 'no one was farther than he from interest in man in the mass, or the manipulation of men in the mass: his symbol was always a particular individual' ('Rudyard Kipling', *OPP*, p.245).
10. 'Christianity and Communism', *The Listener*, 16th March, 1932, 383.
11. 30th March, 1932, 446.
12. *Ibid.*, 480.
13. *Ibid.*
14. 'Building up the Christian World', *The Listener*, 6th April, 1932, 502.
15. In Kirk, p.81.
16. *The Return of Christendom*, 'by a Group of Churchmen' (George Allen and Unwin, London, 1922), p.11.
17. 'Douglas Social Credit Secretariat' website, http://douglassocialcredit.com/origins (accessed 20th October, 2008).
18. 'Dante', *SE*, p.242.
19. Kojecký, p.164.
20. *NTDC*, p.68.
21. They may not have been on the same wavelength liturgically, either. Groser was a supporter of the 'English Use' in his parish – the only church in the East End, at the time, which followed it. Eliot's preference was for the Western Use (see Yelton, p.13).
22. Kenneth Mcnab, 'Mackonochie and Controversies', in *ITSC*, p.86.
23. In Christopher Ricks, *The Panizzi Lectures, op. cit.*, p.17.
24. Reprinted in *Christendom*, September, 1933, 174-5.
25. *Christendom*, September, 1933, 175-6.
26. *Too Proud to Fight* (Oxford University Press, London, 1974), pp.10-12.
27. 'Douglas in the Church Assembly', *New English Weekly*, 14th February, 1935, 382-3.
28. 'The Church and Society', *New English Weekly*, 21st March, 1935, 482.

29. 13th March, 1936. Unpublished.
30. In *ICS*, pp.85-7.
31. Donoghue, p.210.
32. 60.
33. Diary for 1950.
34. In Dakin, pp.265-6.
35. *Essays Catholic & Critical*, ed. E.G. Selwyn (SPCK, London, 1931), p.445.
36. *ICS*, p.31.
37. 'East Coker', I, *CPP*, p.178.
38. *ICS*, pp.28-9.
39. 'Commentary', *Criterion*, October, 1931, 72.
40. June, 1940, 105.
41. 'Rudyard Kipling', *OPP*, pp.245, 250.
42. *The Listener*, 13th September, 1951, p.412.
43. Herbert Read, *A Memoir*, p.21. See Kerry Weinberg, *T.S. Eliot and Charles Baudelaire* (Mouton, The Hague, 1969), p.41: 'the lifeblood of both Baudelaire's and Eliot's imagery is the setting of the modern city.... Baudelaire confessed that he hated open landscapes'.
44. *ICS*, p.29.
45. (The Belknap Press of Harvard University Press, Cambridge, MA, 2007), p.463.
46. *ICS*, p.42.
47. *ICS*, p.34.
48. *ICS*, p.28.
49. *ICS*, p.59.
50. *ICS*, pp.58-9.
51. *ICS*, p.51. This had been Eliot's consistent argument, for several years. In 'Thoughts after Lambeth', he wrote: 'If England is ever to be in any appreciable degree converted to Christianity, it can only be through the Church of England' (*SE*, p.383).
52. *TCTC*, p.113.
53. 'Euripides and Professor Murray', *SE*, p.60.
54. Letter to Bonamy Dobrée in 1926, quoted by George Every in 'Eliot as a Friend and a Man of Prayer' – unpublished.
55. 'Mr Eliot's Evening Service', *Partisan Review*, XV, I, 1948, p.[133].
56. 'The Christian Conception of Education', *Malvern*, p.211.
57. *NTDC*, p.68.
58. *Christendom*, December, 1940, 229-230.
59. *ICS*, p.50. The alliance between Church and State, Sheila Kaye-Smith points out, 'now often regarded as a Protestant innovation, is in reality both Catholic and ancient, but it presupposes a Christian and Catholic State' (Kaye-Smith, p.95).
60. *ICS*, pp.88-9.
61. *ICS*, p.62.
62. *Malvern*, p.vii.
63. *Malvern*, p.213.
64. A leaflet was distributed with the *News-Letter* issue of 6th March, 1940, explaining the purpose of the periodical:
    'The C.N.L. is a weekly letter with supplement, edited by Dr. J.H. Oldham. It was started in October, 1939, under the auspices of the Council on the Christian Faith and the Common Life, as part of a concerted Christian effort to understand the meaning of contemporary events so that the way to right action may be found.

It provides a means whereby individuals and groups all over the country may be united in this common enterprise'. The names of the Archbishop of York (William Temple), the Revd. V.A. Demant, Viscount Hambleden, Professor Karl Mannheim, J. Middleton Murry and Eliot are given in a list of collaborators.

65. *NTDC*, p.85.
66. In Bell, p.961.
67. *Ibid.*, p.968. Herbert Hensley Henson (1863-1947) was Bishop of Durham from 1920 to 1939. After the House of Commons rejected the revised Prayer Book in 1927-8, he became a fervent proponent of disestablishment. In this matter, he and Eliot would not have agreed.
68. *Ibid.*, p.1329.
69. 'William Temple', *The Oxford Dictionary of the Christian Church, op. cit.*, p.1347.
70. 21st January, 1945.
71. Kojecký, *op. cit.*, p.186.
72. 23rd February, 1948.
73. *NTDC*, p.34.
74. See my 'Introduction' in Barry Spurr, ed. *The Legacy of T.S. Eliot (Literature and Aesthetics*, Volume 18 Number 1, June 2008).
75. *NTDC*, p.57.
76. *NTDC*, p.19.
77. *NTDC*, p.26.
78. John Cornwell, *Hitler's Pope: The Secret History of Pius XII* (Penguin, London, 2000), pp.329-30.
79. *NTDC*, pp.15, 18. 31. (Eliot's emphasis).
80. *NTDC*, p.68.
81. *NTDC*, p.33.
82. *NTDC*, p.28. He repeats the point, for emphasis, on the following page.
83. *NTDC*, pp.31-2.
84. *NTDC*, p.32.
85. *NTDC*, p.15.
86. *NTDC*, p.29.
87. *NTDC*, p.73.
88. *NTDC*, p.31.
89. *NTDC*, p.108.
90. *NTDC*, p.74.
91. *NTDC*, p.75.
92. *NTDC*, p.72.
93. *NTDC*, p.19.
94. *NTDC*, p.29.
95. *NTDC*, p.79.
96. *NTDC*, p.112.
97. 'Lancelot Andrewes', *FLA*, p.13.
98. *NTDC*, p.122.
99. *NTDC*, p.73.
100. *NTDC*, p.124.
101. *NTDC*, p.32.
102. *NTDC*, p.33.
103. *NTDC*, p.84.
104. With typical Anglo-Catholic eccentric variation of the familiar theme, the occasional more exotic creature appeared: ' "Take my camel, dear", said my aunt

Dot, as she climbed down from this animal on her return from High Mass' – the once-famous opening sentence of the best-known Anglo-Catholic novel *The Towers of Trebizond*, p.3. Jan Morris, in her introduction (to the 1984 edition of the 1956 book) writes: 'There was a time when the opening line of this book entered the common parlance of educated English and American people. Nearly everyone I knew could quote it, and... [it] became a commonplace of badinage or social pleasantry' (p.v). Its disappearance from such cultivated discourse parallels the disappearance of the Anglo-Catholic world it represents.

105. Letter to Herbert Read, dated – tellingly – 'St George's Day, 1928', St George being the patron saint of England. In Herbert Read, *A Memoir*, pp.5-6.

106. *Europe: An Intimate Journey* (Faber and Faber, London, 2006), pp.218-19. Morris also notes the rise of Islam in British culture: 'The London Mosque towers grandly over Regent's Park.... And one of the most surprising experiences of European travel is to drive out of the Yorkshire hills, out of the country of Harry's Challenge and the Ripon Wakeman, into the old wool town of Bradford, and to find it full of Muslims – respectable Muslin families, disenchanted Muslin youths, militant mullahs and rich entrepreneurs. It is an Islamic sphere of influence' (p.315). Eliot's upstart 'Bradford millionaire' in *The Waste Land* (CPP, p.68) would, today, probably be Muslim.

107. 'Thoughts after Lambeth', *SE*, p.385.

108. 'Lancelot Andrewes', FLA, p.12.

109. *FLA*, p.15.

Chapter Seven

1. In *Theology* 44, February, 1942.
2. 'The Metaphysical Poets', *SE*, p.288.
3. 'A Commentary', *Criterion*, May, 1927, 190.
4. 'A Commentary', *Criterion*, December, 1927, 482.
5. 'The Prose of the Preacher', *The Listener*, 3rd July, 1929, 23.
6. 'The Classics and the Man of Letters', *TCTC*, p.148.
7. 'T.S. Eliot on the Language of the New English Bible', *The Sunday Telegraph*, 16th December, 1962, 7. Most ordinands today would not know what a Cranmerian collect was.
8. 'The history of the Anglican *liturgy* has continued since 1965, but the history of the Prayer Book ended with the authorization of Series One'. G.J. Cuming, *A History of Anglican Liturgy*, 2nd edn. (Macmillan, London, 1982), p.230 (Cuming's emphasis).
9. *OPP*, p.67.
10. Psalm 130, verse 6 and *Gloria*.
11. *CPP*, p.185.
12. 'East Coker', IV. *CPP*, p.181.
13. *The Waste Land: A Facsimile and Transcript, op. cit.*, p.130.
14. 'East Coker', I. *CPP*, p.177.
15. *CPP*, p.14.
16. 'East Coker', III. *CPP*, p.180.
17. 'The Dry Salvages', V. *CPP*, p.189.
18. *Southern Review*, 1100.
19. 'Something Upon Which to Rejoice: the First Section of *Ash-Wednesday*', *Southern Review*, 1153.
20. September, 1949, 337.

21. I have described and assessed this movement in my book, *The Word in the Desert: Anglican and Roman Catholic Reactions to Liturgical Reform* (Lutterworth, Cambridge, 1995).

22. 'T.S. Eliot on the Language of the New English Bible', *The Sunday Telegraph*, 16th December, 1962, 7.

23. *Ibid.*

24. 'New English Bible', *TLS*, 12th May, 1961, 293.

25. 'New English Bible', *TLS*, 28th April, 1961, 263.

26. 'Wordsworth and Coleridge', *UPUC*, p.75.

27. 'The Age of Dryden', *UPUC*, p.62.

28. Parry, pp.20, 18.

29. Parry, p.6.

30. *CPP*, p.37.

31. G.M. Story, ed., *Lancelot Andrewes: Sermons* (Clarendon Press, Oxford, 1967) p.85. Hereafter cited as 'Story'.

32. *CPP*, p.96.

33. 'Bruce Lyttleton Richmond', *Times Literary Supplement*, 13th January, 1961, 17.

34. Story, p.48. In a later sermon ('Sermon 10 of the Holy Ghost: Whit Sunday 1617') Andrewes extends even further his exegesis of 'acceptable': the Hebrew, Greek and Latin meanings are examined in turn, and the finer shades of meaning in its application in several of the canonical books are exhaustively recorded (Story, pp.286-8).

35. 'Lancelot Andrewes', *FLA*, p.22.

36. *CPP*, p.103.

37. *CPP*, p.104.

38. The kind of discrimination I am suggesting is familiar in the writings of many poets who, in their lives, espoused the various confessions of Christian faith. Gerard Manley Hopkins' poem, 'God's Grandeur', for example, is a Christian poem, but not an explicitly Catholic one. But we would be inclined to call 'Felix Randal', wherein Hopkins refers both to the 'sweet reprieve and ransom' of the confession, *viaticum* and extreme unction of the dying, and (autobiographically, as a priest) to ministering these consolations on Felix' death-bed, a Catholic poem. Even more so is John Betjeman's 'A Lincolnshire Church', celebrating (at greater length than Hopkins' sacramental references) the Real Presence in the tabernacle (lines which we quoted in chapter 4) and focusing on the rite of communion. These two poems could not have been written, in the way they are written, by a Calvinist, for example; whereas Hopkins' 'Hurrahing in Harvest', doctrinally-speaking, could have been. His 'May Magnificat' (with its celebration of the Virgin and the reference to the Latin canticle) would hardly have been a Presbyterian's subject, either, yet an Anglican (and not necessarily an Anglo-Catholic) could have written it (as it contains no references to controversial Marian doctrines like the Immaculate Conception or the Assumption).

39. Schuchard, p.185.

40. Douglas Hedley, 'Participation in the divine life: Coleridge, the vision of God and the thought of John Henry Newman', in Vaiss, p.239.

41. In Kirk, p.241.

42. Kirk, p.264.

43. Both the reference to Howard's study and the quotation from Varholy's review are in the review, in *StAR* [*sic*], July/August 2006, 43. I am grateful to Dr Stephen McInerney for drawing my attention to this review.

44. *CPP*, pp.89-99.

45. Linda Leavell, 'Eliot's Ritual Method: *Ash-Wednesday*', *Southern Review*, 1003. Other critics have been less complimentary (while being favourably disposed to Eliot generally). Austin Warren called *Ash-Wednesday* 'a convert's rather boring experiment but not much more.... The real triumph...comes in 1943 with the *Four Quartets*'. 'A Survivor's Tribute to T.S. Eliot', *Southern Review*, 1112-13.

46. Kirk, p.149.

47. *New Bearings in English Poetry* (1932; Penguin, Harmondsworth, 1963), p.98.

48. 'Eliot's Ritual Method: *Ash-Wednesday*', *Southern Review*, 1007.

49. Schuchard, p.153.

50. 'East Coker', II. *CPP*, p.179.

51. Marina Warner, *Alone of All Her Sex: The Myth and Cult of the Virgin Mary* (Vintage, New York, 1983), p.266.

52. Donoghue, p.155.

53. *CPP*, p.85.

54. See Yelton/Salmon, pp.10-11. They judge Winnington-Ingram's campaign to be ill-conceived: in many cases, the new churches 'were filled, if at all, for a relatively short time.... It is now clear that the Church overreached itself, and very soon regretted the increase in building which had taken place' (p.11). That there should have been the confidence in the future to inspire this campaign is further evidence of the optimism in the Church of England, largely generated by the growth of Anglo-Catholicism in the 1930s, but which was destined to last only for a generation.

55. Chinitz, pp.131-2.

56. *T.S. Eliot, op. cit.*, p.143.

57. *OPP*, p.91.

58. Ironically quoted at the beginning of Valerie Eliot's detailed edition of the manuscript, *op. cit.*, p.[1].

59. Sencourt, p.131.

60. *The Rock* (Faber and Faber, London, 1934, p.[5]. Hereafter cited as '*TR*'. References to the Choruses will be made to *CPP*. The play itself has been out of print since 1938.

61. *TR*, p.[5].

62. Bodleian Library, Oxford, MS Don.d.44 leaf 14; and Browne, p.27. There is some interesting material in these Bodleian papers (Don.d.44 and Don.d.43), including Eliot's pencilled draft of some choruses, dialogue, and arrangement of scenes, and a typewritten draft of the play. There is evidence of Eliot's difficulty with the dialogue (44 leaf 112).

63. Browne, p.26.

64. *TR*, p.9.

65. Story, p.220.

66. *CPP*, p.151.

67. Chinitz, p.132.

68. *TR*, pp.15-16.

69. *CPP*, p.171.

70. *CPP*, pp.152-3.

71. *TR*, p.52.

72. *TR*, p.76.

73. 1st June, 1934 (quoted in Browne, p.83).

74. *CPP*, p.147.

75. *CPP*, p.164.

76. 'From Poe to Valéry', *TCTC*, p.31.
77. 'To Walter de la Mare', *CPP*, p.205.
78. 'Goethe as the Sage', *OPP*, p.216.
79. Diary for 1955.
80. *CPP*, p.162.
81. *CPP*, p.166.
82. *The Towers of Trebizond*, p.151. *TR*, p.9. We can assume that Macaulay had a copy of the play to hand as the quotation is word perfect. She had probably attended it herself. Her book, *Some Religious Elements in English Literature* had appeared in 1931.
83. In Schuchard, p.45.
84. Browne, pp.54-5.
85. Chinitz, p.135.
86. Alan Smithies, 'A Layman Looks at the Liturgy', *The Catholic Standard*, November, 1975, 3.
87. 'Little Gidding', II. *CPP*, p.192; 'Little Gidding', III. *CPP*, p.196.
88. 'To Criticize the Critic', *TCTC*, p.20.
89. *CPP*, pp.260-1.
90. *CPP*, p.264.
91. *Murder in the Cathedral with an Introduction and Notes* (London: Faber, 1965), *passim*.
92. Schuchard, chapter 10, *passim*.
93. In Schuchard, pp.183-4.
94. *GH*, pp.19, 21, 23.
95. In *TCTC*, p.13.
96. *GH*, p.22.
97. *GH*, p.22
98. 'George Herbert', *Lives*, The World's Classics edn (Oxford University Press, Oxford, 1927), p.299.
99. *GH*, p.13.
100. Schuchard, p.197.

Conclusion

1. In Kirk, p.330.
2. Nagendranath Gangulee, ed. *Thoughts for Meditation: A Way to Recovery from Within* (Faber & Faber, London, 1951), p.13.
3. Yelton, p.56.
4. Yelton, p.63. Yelton argues that Anglo-Catholicism is 'rudderless' after Vatican II.
5. Kramer, p.258, n.5. An early sign of the post-war decline of the influence of Catholic principles in the Church of England was the inauguration in 1947 of the Church of South India, against which Anglo-Catholics and (as we have seen) Eliot himself had campaigned so vigorously, on the grounds that it was an offence against the idea of the Apostolic Succession and the role and necessity of the episcopacy. Then, the Church of England officially recognised the body in 1955. After this controversy was over (and, from a Catholic point of view, the cause was lost), Anglo-Catholicism, Michael Yelton observes, 'was constantly on the back foot' (Yelton, p.58). I attended the celebration of the sesqui-centenary of the Oxford Movement, a Mass offered by the

Archbishop of Canterbury, in the University Parks, in Oxford, in 1983. There were, perhaps, several hundred people there. It was a far cry from the tens of thousands who had attended the Pontifical High Mass for the centenary of the Oxford Movement, in London, in 1933, at the high watermark of the Anglo-Catholic revival.

6. 'The Ecclesiology of the Oxford Movement', in Vaiss, p.75.
7. Smyth, pp.[483], 21.
8. Smyth, p.400.
9. *CPP*, p.280.
10. Wilson, p.188.

Appendix One

1. The letters are now held in the Houghton Library at Harvard, together with other material, such as two unpublished poems written to Trevelyan by Eliot.

Appendix Two

1. *The Composition of 'Four Quartets'*, p.63.

Appendix Three

1. In Carpenter, p.206.
2. Carpenter, p.158.
3. In Carpenter, p.49.
4. Carpenter, p.21.
5. Carpenter, p.49.
6. In Carpenter, p.107.
7. In Carpenter, p.148.
8. Carpenter, p.246.

Appendix Four

1. In Kirk, p.176.
2. The literature on Christian anti-Semitism is vast. Some recent studies I have encountered include James Shapiro's *Shakespeare and the Jews* (Columbia University Press, New York, 1996) dealing with English attitudes towards Jews from Shakespeare's time until the eighteenth century and including such information about anti-Semitism as a law prohibiting sex between Christians and Jews, likening it to bestiality. Then Zdenek V. David, in 'Hajek, Dubravius, and the Jews: A Contrast in Sixteenth-Century Czech Historiography', *Sixteenth Century Journal*, XXVII/4, 1996, details the persecution of the Jews of Prague. Nonetheless, David notes that 'Pope Paul III (1534-1549) was moved to issue a bull in 1540 for the protection of the Jews, addressed to the bishops of Poland, Hungary, and the Bohemian lands' (1012, n.69). John Cornwell calls Pius 'Hitler's Pope' (in his book of that title: Penguin, Harmondworth, 1999), while Margherita Marchione calls him the 'Man of Peace' (in her book of that title: Paulist Press, Mahwah, 2003). Pius XII's attitude to the Jews during the Second World War remains a much-debated issue.

3. (Faber and Faber, London, 1988). Hereafter cited as *'Prejudice'*. Ricks argues that 'the question of anti-Semitism in Eliot is important exactly because it cannot be isolated for discussion; it entails the larger, though admittedly not more intense, question of prejudice in general' (p.28).

4. Cambridge University Press, Cambridge, 1995. All page references are in the text.

5. The phrase is Harold Bloom's, in *The Western Canon* (Harcourt Brace, New York, 1994): 'to read in the service of any ideology is not … to read at all' (p.29). Peter Washington has similarly exposed the misreadings endorsed by 'political correctness' in *Fraud: Literary Theory and the End of English* (Fontana, London, 1989): 'Colleges are not the place for inculcating doctrines but for examining and criticizing them' (p.11).

6. *Prejudice*, p.29.

7. In George Plimpton, ed., *Writers at Work* (Penguin, Harmondsworth, 1977), p.353.

8. In Norman White, *Hopkins: A Literary Biography* (Clarendon Press, Oxford, 1995), p.353.

9. In Ruth Leon, *Gershwin* (Haus, London, 2004), p.130.

10. *Prejudice*, p.43.

11. George King, 'Our recent past', *The Sydney Morning Herald* 'Good Weekend' magazine, 5th April, 1997, 6.

12. *Prejudice*, pp.28, 41.

13. *The Married Man: A Life of D.H. Lawrence* (Minerva, London, 1995), p.163.

14. *Ibid.*, p.289.

15. *Ibid.*, p.291.

16. *Ibid.*, p.505

17. Paul Auster, *The Invention of Solitude* (1982; Penguin Books, New York, 2007), p.52.

18. In Julia Briggs, *Virginia Woolf: An Inner Life* (Penguin, London, 2005), p.309.

19. In Levy/Scherle, p.81.

20. In *ICS,* p.138.

21. *NTDC*, p.70 n.1.

22. *Prejudice*, pp.59-60.

Bibliography

Primary sources

Bibliographical details of all works by T.S. Eliot referred to in this book are to be found in Donald Gallup, *T.S. Eliot: A Bibliography* (Faber and Faber, London, 1969).

Secondary sources

(In the following list, the place of publication is London, unless otherwise stated.)

Ackroyd, Peter, *T.S. Eliot* (Hamish Hamilton, 1984)

Acton, J.E. (Lord), *Essays on Church and State*, ed. D. Woodruff (Hollis and Carter, 1952)

Adams, Henry, *The Education of Henry Adams: An Autobiography* (Houghton Mifflin, Boston, 1961)

Addleshaw, G.W.O., *The High Church Tradition* (Faber and Faber, 1941)

Alder, Baron, 'Odd couple more equal than others', *The Australian Literary Review*, 1st October, 2008

Aldington, Richard, *Soft Answers* (Southern Illinois University Press, Carbondale, IL, 1967)

Andrewes, Lancelot, *Sermons*, ed. G.M. Story (Clarendon Press, Oxford, 1967)

Anson, Peter, *Abbot Extraordinary: A Memoir of Aelred Carlyle Monk and Missionary 1874-1955* (The Faith Press, 1958)

Asher, Kenneth, *T.S. Eliot and Ideology* (Cambridge University Press, Cambridge, 1995)

Auster, Paul, *The Invention of Solitude* (1982; Penguin Books, New York, 2007)

Baillie, J. and Martin, H. eds, *Revelation* (Faber and Faber, 1937)

Baker, E.A., *William Temple and His Message* (Penguin, 1946)

Baudelaire, Charles, *Oeuvres Complètes*, ed. Y.-G. Le Dantec (Librairie Gallimard, Paris, 1954)

Bell, G.K.A., *Randall Davidson: Archbishop of Canterbury* (Oxford University Press, 1952)

Bergonzi, Bernard, *T.S. Eliot* (Macmillan, 1972)

Betjeman, John, *Collected Poems* (John Murray, 2003)

Betjeman, John, *Summoned by Bells: A Verse Autobiography* (John Murray, 2001)

Betjeman, John, *The City of London Churches* (Pitkin, 1973)

Blackstone, B. ed., *The Ferrar Papers* (Cambridge University Press, Cambridge, 1938)

Blamires, Harry, *Word Unheard: A Guide through Eliot's 'Four Quartets'* (Methuen, 1969)

Blixen, Karen, *Out of Africa* (1937; Penguin,1954)

Bloom, Harold, *The Western Canon* (Harcourt Brace, New York, 1994)

Bradbrook, Muriel, *English Dramatic Form* (Chatto and Windus, 1965)

Brenan, Gerald, *St John of the Cross: His Life and Poetry* (Cambridge University Press, Cambridge, 1973)

Briggs, Julia, *Virginia Woolf: An Inner Life* (Penguin, 2005)

Brill, Kenneth, *John Groser: East London Priest* (Mowbrays, 1971)

Brilioth, Y., *The Anglican Revival: Studies in the Oxford Movement* (Longmans, Green and Co., 1925)

Brilioth, Y., *Eucharistic Faith and Practice Evangelical and Catholic* (SPCK, 1930)

Brooker, Jewel Spears, ed. *The Placing of T.S. Eliot* (University of Missouri Press, Columbia, MO, 1991)

Brooks, Van Wyck, *The Confident Years: 1885-1915* (Futton, New York, 1952)

Browne, E. Martin, *The Making of T.S. Eliot's Plays* (Cambridge University Press, Cambridge, 1969)

Buchanan, Colin, ed., *Anglo-Catholic Worship: An Evangelical Appreciation after 150 years* (Grove Liturgical Study 33; Grove Books, Bramcote, 1983)

Bush, Ronald, *T.S. Eliot: A Study in Character and Style* (Oxford University Press, New York, 1984)

Bush, Ronald, ed. *T.S. Eliot: The Modernist in History* (Cambridge University Press, Cambridge, 1991)

Carpenter, Humphrey, *The Inklings* (HarperCollins, 1997)

Carpenter, J., *Gore: A Study in Liberal Catholic Thought* (The Faith Press, 1960)

Chace, W.M., *The Political Identities of Ezra Pound & T.S. Eliot* (Stanford University Press, Stanford, CA, 1973)

Chapman, R., *Faith and Revolt: Studies in the literary influence of the Oxford Movement* (Weidenfeld and Nicholson, 1970)

Chevalier, J., *Pascal*, trans. Lilian A. Clare (Sheed and Ward, 1933)

Chinitz, David, *T.S. Eliot and the Cultural Divide* (The University of Chicago Press, Chicago, IL, 2003)

Church, R.W., *The Oxford Movement* (Macmillan, 1892)

Clarke, W.K.L., *Liturgy and Worship* (SPCK, 1932)

Coghill, Nevill, *Murder in the Cathedral with an Introduction and Notes* (Faber and Faber, 1965)

Coghlan, Brian, *Hofmannsthal's Festival Dramas* (Cambridge University Press, 1964)

Coleridge, S.T., *On the Constitution of the Church and State* (J.M. Dent, 1972)

Cooper, John, *T.S. Eliot and the Ideology of 'Four Quartets'* (Cambridge University Press, Cambridge, 1995)

Cornwell, John, *Hitler's Pope: The Secret History of Pius XII* (Penguin, 2000)

Cox, C.B. and Dyson, A.E., eds, *The Twentieth-Century Mind* (Oxford University Press, 1972)

Crook, Keith, 'A Lost T.S. Eliot Review Recovered', *Yeats Eliot Review*, Fall, 1995

Cross, F.L. ed., *The Oxford Dictionary of the Christian Church*, 2nd edn. (Oxford University Press, Oxford, 1974)

Cuming, G.J., *A History of Anglican Liturgy*, 2nd edn. (Macmillan, 1982)

Dakin, A.H., *Paul Elmer More* (Princeton University Press, Princeton, NJ, 1960)

Davage, William, ed., *In This Sign Conquer: A History of the Society of the Holy Cross (1855-2005)* (Continuum, 2006)

David, Zdenek V., 'Hajek, Dubravius, and the Jews: A Contrast in Sixteenth-Century Czech Historiography', *Sixteenth Century Journal*, XXVII/4, 1996

Demant, V.A., *God, Man and Society* (SCM Press, 1934)

Desmond, A. and Moore, J., *Darwin* (Penguin, Harmondsworth, 1992)

Devlin, Patrick, *Too Proud to Fight* (Oxford University Press, 1974)

Dix, Dom Gregory, *The Shape of the Liturgy* (Adam and Charles Black, 1945)

Donoghue, Denis, *Words Alone: The Poet T.S. Eliot* (Yale University Press, New Haven, CT, 2000)

Dugmore, C.W., *Eucharistic Doctrine in England from Hooker to Waterland* (SPCK, 1942)

Edwards, David L., *Leaders of the Church of England 1828-1978* (Hodder and Stoughton, 1978)

Eliot, Charlotte, *Savonarola – A Dramatic Poem* (R. Cobden-Sanderson, [1926])

Eliot, Valerie, ed., *The Letters of T.S. Eliot*, Volume 1 1898-1922 (Faber and Faber, 1988)

Eliot, Valerie, ed., *The Waste Land: A Facsimile and Transcript* (Faber and Faber, 1971)

Eliot, William Greenleaf, *Discourses on the Doctrines of Christianity* (American Unitarian Association, Boston, 1881)

Elliott-Binns, L.E., *English Thought 1860-1900: The Theological Aspect* (Longmans, Green and Co., 1956)

Faber, Geoffrey, *Oxford Apostles: A Character Study of the Oxford Movement* (Faber and Faber, 1933)

Fathman, Anthony E., M.D., 'Viv and Tom: The Eliots as Ether Addict and Co-Dependent', *Yeats Eliot Review*, Fall, 1991

Foerster, Norman, *Humanism and America* (Farrar and Rinehart, New York, 1930)

Gangulee, Nagendranath, ed., *Thoughts for Meditation: A Way to Recovery from Within* (Faber & Faber, 1951)

Gardner, Helen, *Religion and Literature* (Faber and Faber, 1971)

Gardner, Helen, *The Art of T.S. Eliot* (1949; Faber and Faber, 1968)

Gardner, Helen, *The Composition of 'Four Quartets'* (Faber and Faber, 1978)

Gibbons, Thomas, '*The Waste Land* in the Light of the "Cross-Correspondence" Scripts of the Society for Psychical Research', *Yeats Eliot Review*, Summer, 1995

Gordon, Lyndall, *Eliot's Early Years* (Oxford University Press, Oxford, 1977)

Gore, Charles, *The Body of Christ* (John Murray, 1901)

Greene, E.J.H., *T.S. Eliot et la France* (Boivin, Paris, 1951)

Hall, Alfred, ed., *Aspects of Modern Unitarianism* (The Lindsey Press, 1922)

Hargrove, Nancy, *Landscape as Symbol in the Poetry of T.S. Eliot* (University Press of Mississippi, Jackson, MS, 1978)

Harries, Richard, ed., *The One Genius: Readings through the year with Austin Farrer* (SPCK, 1987)

Hazlitt, William, *English Comic Writers* (Taylor and Hessey, 1819)

Hebert, A.G., *Liturgy and Society* (Faber and Faber, 1935)

Henson, H.H., *Retrospect of an Unimportant Life*, 3 vols. (Oxford University Press, 1942-50)

Herbert, George, *The Works*, ed. F.E. Hutchinson (Clarendon Press, Oxford, 1941)

Hill, Rosemary, *God's Architect: Pugin and the Building of Romantic Britain* (Allen Lane, 2007)

Hilliard, David, 'Unenglish and Unmanly: Anglo-Catholicism and Homosexuality', *Victorian Studies*, 25 (2), 1982

Hodgson, Leonard, *Anglicanism & South India* (Cambridge University Press, Cambridge, 1943)

Hodgson, Leonard, *The Doctrine of the Church as Held and Taught in the Church of England* (Basil Blackwell, Oxford, 1946)

Holroyd, Michael, *Lytton Strachey: A Biography* (Penguin, Harmondsworth, 1979)

Howarth, H., *Notes on Some Figures Behind T.S. Eliot* (Chatto and Windus, 1965)

Hulme, T.E., *Speculations* (1924; Routledge and Kegan Paul, 1960)

Hutton, W.H., *The English Church from the Accession of Charles I. to the Death of Anne* (Macmillan, 1913)

Iremonger, F.A., *William Temple Archbishop of Canterbury* (Oxford University Press, 1948)

Jain, Manju, *T.S. Eliot and American Philosophy: The Harvard Years* (Cambridge University Press, Cambridge, 1992)

Jamison, Catherine, *The History of the Royal Hospital of St. Katharine by the Tower of London* (Oxford University Press, 1952)

John of the Cross, St., *The Complete Works*, trans. and ed. E.A. Peers (1934; Anthony Clarke, Wheathampstead, 1974)

Johnston, W., *The Still Point* (Harper and Row, New York, 1970)

Jones, D.E., *The Plays of T.S. Eliot* (Routledge and Kegan Paul, 1960)

Jones, David, *The Anathemata* (1952; Faber and Faber, 1972)

Julian of Norwich, *Revelations of Divine Love*, ed. Dom Roger Huddleston (Burns, Oates and Washbourne, 1927)

Julius, Anthony, *T.S. Eliot, anti-Semitism and literary form* (Cambridge University Press, Cambridge, 1995)

Kaye-Smith, Sheila, *Anglo-Catholicism* (Chapman and Hall, 1925)

Kelly, H., *No Pious Person: Autobiographical Recollections*, ed. George Every (The Faith Press, 1960)

Kenner, Hugh, *The Invisible Poet: T.S. Eliot* (Methuen, 1965)

King, George, 'Our recent past', *The Sydney Morning Herald* 'Good Weekend' magazine, 5th April, 1997

Kirk, K.E., ed., *The Apostolic Ministry* (Hodder and Stoughton, 1946)

Kirk, Russell, *Eliot and His Age: T.S. Eliot's Moral Imagination in the Twentieth Century*, 2nd edn. (ISI Books, Wilmington, DE, 2008)

Kojecký, Roger, *T.S. Eliot's Social Criticism* (Faber and Faber, 1971)

Kollar, Rene, *Abbot Aelred Carlyle, Caldey Island, and the Anglo-Catholic Revival in England* (Peter Lang, New York, 1995)

Kramer, Kenneth Paul, *Redeeming Time: T.S. Eliot's 'Four Quartets'* (Cowley Publications, Lanham, 2007)

Lacey, T.A., *The Anglo-Catholic Faith* (Methuen, 1926)

Leavis, F.R., *New Bearings in English Poetry* (1932; Penguin, Harmondsworth, 1963)

Leavis, F.R., *Nor Shall My Sword* (Chatto and Windus, 1972)

Lee, Christopher, *Lord of Misrule: The Autobiography of Christopher Lee* (Orion, 2004)

Leon, Ruth, *Gershwin* (Haus, 2004)

Levi, P., *The English Bible 1534-1859* (Constable, 1974)

Levy, William Turner and Scherle, Victor, *Affectionately, T.S. Eliot: The Story of a Friendship 1947-1965* (Dent, 1968)

Lockhart, J.G., *Charles Lindley – Viscount Halifax*, Part II: 1885-1934 (Geoffrey Bles, 1936)

Lockhart, J.G., *Cosmo Gordon Lang* (Hodder and Stoughton, 1949)

Macaulay, Rose, *The Towers of Trebizond* (1956; New York Review Books, New York, 2003)

Maddox, Brenda, *The Married Man: A Life of D.H. Lawrence* (Minerva, 1995)

Manning-Foster, A.E., *Anglo-Catholicism* (T.C. and E.C. Jack, 1913)

Marchione, Margherita, *Man of Peace: Pope Pius XII* (Paulist Press, Mahwah, NJ, 2003)

Margolis, J.D., *T.S. Eliot's Intellectual Development 1922-1939* (The University of Chicago Press, Chicago, IL, 1972)

Matthews, T.S., *Notes towards the definition of T.S. Eliot* (Weidenfeld and Nicolson, 1974)

Matthiessen, F.O., *The Achievement of T.S. Eliot* (Oxford University Press, 1958)

Maycock, A.L., *Nicholas Ferrar of Little Gidding* (SPCK, 1938)

McCann, Dom Justin, ed., *The Cloud of Unknowing* (Burns, Oates and Washbourne, 1924)

McCormick, Donald, *The Mask of Merlin: A Critical Study of David Lloyd George* (MacDonald, 1963)

Menand, Louis, 'How Eliot Became Eliot', *The New York Review*, 15th May, 1997

Meyerhoff, Hans, 'Mr Eliot's Evening Service', *Partisan Review*, XV, 1, 1948

Moody, A. David, ed., *The Cambridge Companion to T.S. Eliot* (Cambridge University Press, Cambridge, 1994)

Moody, A. David, *Thomas Stearns Eliot: Poet* (Cambridge University Press, Cambridge, 1994)

More, P.E. and Cross, F.L., *Anglicanism* (SPCK, 1935, reprinted with new foreword, James Clarke, Cambridge, 2009)

More, P.E., *The Catholic Faith* (Princeton University Press, Princeton, NJ, 1931)

More, P.E., *The Sceptical Approach to Religion* (Princeton University Press, Princeton, NJ, 1934)

Morris, Jan, *Europe: An Intimate Journey* (Faber and Faber, 2006)

Newman, J.H., *A Grammar of Assent* (Longmans, Green and Co., 1895)

Newman, J.H., *Apologia Pro Vita Sua*, ed. M.J. Svaglic (Clarendon Press, Oxford, 1967)

Ollard, S.L., *The Anglo-Catholic Revival: Some Persons and Principles* (A.R. Mowbray, 1925)

Olney, James and Simpson, Lewis P., eds., 'An Anniversary Issue: T.S. Eliot' *The Southern Review* (vol. 21, number 4, October, 1985)

Palmer, Marja, *Men and Women in T.S. Eliot's Early Poetry* (Lund University Press, Lund, 1996)

Parry, Graham, *Glory, Laud and Honour: The Arts of the Anglican Counter-Reformation* (The Boydell Press, Woodbridge, 2006)

Pascal, B., *Pensées*, 2 vols., ed. Z. Tourneur (Editions de Cluny, Paris, 1942)

Peart-Binns, John, *Wand of London* (Mowbray, 1987)

Pearse, St-John, *Anabasis*, trans. T.S. Eliot (Faber and Faber, 1930)

Philippe, C.-L., *Bubu of Montparnasse*, trans. L. Vail (Weidenfeld and Nicolson, 1952)

Pickering, W.H.S., *Anglo-Catholicism: A Study in Religious Ambiguity* (Routledge, 1989, new edition, James Clarke, Cambridge, 2008)

Plimpton, George, ed., *Writers at Work* (Penguin, Harmondsworth, 1977)

Purcell, William, *Fisher of Lambeth* (Hodder and Stoughton, 1969)

Raine, Craig, *In Defence of T.S. Eliot* (Picador, 2000)

Rajan, B., ed., *T.S. Eliot: A Study of His Writings by Several Hands* (Dennis Dobson, 1947)

Ramsey, A.M., *From Gore to Temple* (Longmans, 1960)

Read, Herbert, *T.S.E. – A Memoir* (Monday Evening Papers, No. 5, Center for Advanced Studies, Wesleyan University, 26th April, 1965)

Reardon, Bernard, *From Coleridge to Gore: A Century of Religious Thought in Britain* (Longmans, 1971)

Reed, John Shelton, *Glorious Battle: The Cultural Politics of Victorian Anglo-Catholicism* (Vanderbilt University Press, Nashville, TN, 1996)

Renfrey, L.E.W., ed., *Catholic Prayers for members of the Church of England in Australia* (privately printed; 2nd edn., Adelaide, 1982)

Ricks, Christopher, ed., *T.S. Eliot: Inventions of the March Hare* (Faber and Faber, 1996)

Ricks, Christopher, *The Panizzi Lectures 2002: Decisions and Revisions in T.S. Eliot* (The British Library, 2003)

Ricks, Christopher, *T.S. Eliot and Prejudice* (Faber and Faber, 1988)

Rowell, Geoffrey, *The Vision Glorious: Themes and Personalities of the Catholic Revival in Anglicanism* (Oxford University Press, Oxford, 1983)

Rowse, A.L., *Homosexuals in History* (Barnes & Noble, New York, 1977)

Rowse, A.L., *The England of Elizabeth* (Macmillan, 1951)

Russell, Bertrand, *Autobiography* (Unwin, 1978)

Sayers, Dorothy, *The Poetry of Search and the Poetry of Statement* (Gollancz, 1963)

Schuchard, Ronald, *Eliot's Dark Angel: Intersections of Life and Art* (Oxford University Press, Oxford, 1999)

Selwyn, E.G., *Essays Catholic & Critical* (SPCK, 1931)

Sencourt, Robert, *T.S. Eliot: A Memoir* (Garnstone Press, 1971)

Seymour, Miranda, *Ottoline Morrell: Life on the Grand Scale* (Sceptre, 1992)

Shapiro, James, *Shakespeare and the Jews* (Columbia University Press, New York, 1996)

Shorthouse, J.H., *John Inglesant: A Romance* (Macmillan, 1902)

Sigg, Eric, *The American T.S. Eliot: A Study of the Early Writings* (Cambridge University Press, Cambridge, 1989)

Smidt, K., *Poetry and Belief in the Work of T.S. Eliot* (Routledge and Kegan Paul, 1961)

Smith, Grover, *T.S. Eliot's Poetry and Plays: A Study in Sources and Meaning*, 2nd edn. (The University of Chicago Press, Chicago, IL, 1974)

Smithies, Alan, 'A Layman Looks at the Liturgy', *The Catholic Standard*, November, 1975

Smyth, Charles, *Cyril Forster Garbett: Archbishop of York* (Hodder and Stoughton, 1959)

Spender, Stephen, *Eliot* (Fontana/Collins, Glasgow, 1975)

Spender, Stephen, ed., *W.H. Auden* (Weidenfeld and Nicolson, 1974)

Spurr, Barry, ed., *The Legacy of T.S. Eliot* (*Literature and Aesthetics*, Volume 18 Number 1, June 2008)

Spurr, Barry, *See the Virgin Blest: The Virgin Mary in English Poetry* (Palgrave Macmillan, New York, 2007)

Spurr, Barry, *The Word in the Desert: Anglican and Roman Catholic Reactions to Liturgical Reform* (Lutterworth, Cambridge, 1995)

Srawley, J.H., *The Liturgical Movement* (Mowbrays, 1954)

Staley, Vernon, *The Catholic Religion: A Manual of instruction for members of the Anglican Communion* (1893; Morehouse Publishing, Ridgefield, CT, 1983)

Staley, Vernon, *The Ceremonial of the English Church*, 2nd edn. (Mowbray, Oxford, 1900)

Stephenson, Colin, *Merrily on High* (Darton, Longman & Todd, 1972)

Stephenson, Colin, *Walsingham Way* (Darton, Longman & Todd, 1970)

Swanson, R.N. ed., *The Church and Mary* (The Boydell Press for the Ecclesiastical History Society, Woodbridge, 2004)

Tate, A., ed., *T.S. Eliot: The Man and His Work* (Chatto and Windus, 1967)

Taylor, Charles, *A Secular Age* (The Belknap Press of Harvard University Press, Cambridge, MA, 2007)

Tolley, George, 'Nicholas Ferrar, Little Gidding and the Use of the Prayer Book', *Church and King*, Christmas, 2004

Trevelyan, Mary, *From the Ends of the Earth* (Faber and Faber, 1942)

Trevelyan, Mary, *I'll Walk Beside You* (Longmans, Green and Co., 1946)

Twinn, K., ed., *Essays in Unitarian Theology* (The Lindsey Press, 1959)

Vaiss, Paul, ed., *From Oxford to the People: Reconsidering Newman & the Oxford Movement* (Gracewing, Leominster, 1996)

Varholy, Daniel, review of Thomas Howard, *Dove Descending: A Journey into T.S. Eliot's 'Four Quartets'*, *StAR* [*sic*], July/August 2006

Vidler, Alec, *Scenes from a Clerical Life* (Collins, 1977)

Walsh, Walter, *Secret History of the Oxford Movement*, 5th edn. (Church Association, 1899)

Walton, Izaak, *Lives*, The World's Classics edn. (Oxford University Press, Oxford, 1927)

Warner, Marina, *Alone of All Her Sex: The Myth and Cult of the Virgin Mary* (Vintage, New York, 1983)

Washington, Peter, *Fraud: Literary Theory and the End of English* (Fontana, 1989)

Waugh, Evelyn, *Brideshead Revisited* (1945; William Heinemann and Martin Secker & Warburg, 1977)

Waugh, Evelyn, *The Life of Ronald Knox* (Chapman & Hall, 1959)

Weil, Simone, *The Need For Roots* (Routledge and Kegan Paul, 1952)

Weinberg, Kerry, *T.S. Eliot and Charles Baudelaire* (Mouton, The Hague, 1969)

White, Norman, *Hopkins: A Literary Biography* (Clarendon Press, Oxford, 1995)

Williams, A.T.P., *Church Union in South Africa* (SCM Press, 1944)

Williams, Charles, 'The Recovery of Spiritual Initiative', *Christendom*, December, 1940

Williams, N.P. and Harris, C., eds, *Northern Catholicism* (SPCK, 1933)

Wilson, H.A., *Received with Thanks* (Mowbrays, 1940)

Yates, Nigel, 'Walsingham and Inter-War Anglo-Catholicism' [unpublished conference paper, 2008]

Yelton, Michael, *Alfred Hope Patten and the Shrine of Our Lady of Walsingham* (Canterbury Press, Norwich, 2006)

Yelton, Michael and Salmon, John, *Anglican Church-Building in London 1915-1945* (Spire Books, Reading, 2007)

Yelton, Michael, *Anglican Papalism: An Illustrated History 1900-1960* (Canterbury Press, Norwich, 2005)

Young, E. and W., *Old London Churches* (Faber and Faber, 1956)

Anonymous and other works

Hymns Ancient & Modern Revised (William Clowes and Sons [undated])
London: Everyman Guide (David Campbell, 1993)
Malvern, 1941: The Life of the Church and the Order of Society (Longmans, Green and Co., [1942])
Ritual Notes on the Order of Divine Service: A Guide to the Ceremonial of the Church, 6th edn. (William Walker, 1913)
St Swithun's Prayer Book (Darton, Longman & Todd [undated])
The Book of Common Prayer (Oxford University Press, Oxford [undated])
The Canon Law of the Church of England (SPCK, 1947)
The Cuddesdon Office Book (1940; Oxford University Press, 1961)
The English Hymnal with Tunes (Oxford University Press, 1933)
The English Missal for the Laity (W. Knott and Son, 1958)
The Holy Bible Appointed to be Read in Churches (Oxford University Press, Oxford [undated])
The Lambeth Conference 1930 (SPCK, [1930])
The People's Rosary Book, 10th edition (The Church Literature Association [undated])
The Return of Christendom, 'by a Group of Churchmen' (George Allen and Unwin, 1922)
The Tractarian Doctrine of the Mass (The Faith Press, 1928)
Tracts for the Times (6 vols) (J.G. & F. Rivington, 1839-1841)

Websites

http://douglassocialcredit.com/origins
http://www.skcm.org/SCharles/Cult/cult.html#ChurchesAndChapels

Index

BV - #0037 - 250222 - C0 - 234/156/18 - PB - 9780718830731 - Gloss Lamination